# THE LAW OF CONTRACT IN ENGLAND & WALES

Gregory J. Durston

Published 2023 by Abramis academic publishing

www.abramis.co.uk

ISBN 978 1 84549 814 6



Abramis is an imprint of arima publishing

arima publishing

ASK House, Northgate Avenue

Bury St Edmunds, Suffolk IP32 6BB

t: (+44) 01284 717884

www.arimapublishing.com

# Acknowledgments

I would like to thank the libraries of Kingston University, Lincoln's Inn, and the University of Law in Bloomsbury for their assistance in writing this book. On a personal basis, I would also like to thank Bertilla Chow, Robert Bellin, James Saunders, Rhoda Koenig, Victor Temple KC, and His Honour Nicholas Philpot for their very helpful comments on the manuscript.

# Foreword

The aim of this book is to provide a clear and readable exposition of the law of contract in England and Wales, albeit that, for reasons of succinctness, the inclusion of the Principality must usually be assumed. In doing so, it is hoped that it will fill the middle ground between the many brief introductions now available and the major works on the subject, such as *Treitel on the Law of Contract* and *Anson's Law of Contract*, or the almost canonical two-volume *Chitty on Contracts*.[1] Inevitably, this means that certain aspects of what is a vast field have had to be dealt with quite briefly or even ignored altogether, especially where they might be found in specialist works on, for example, the sale of goods or commercial law, or where they are now moribund or largely irrelevant in practice.

The book follows a traditional structure. It deals first with preliminary matters, such as sources of contract law and contractual interpretation, and then considers the essential requirements that must be present to form a binding agreement. Vitiating factors, which prevent a contract coming into existence or (more commonly) render it voidable after it has done so are then examined, as are terms, performance, and the discharge of contracts. The book finishes with the remedies, both common law and equitable, that are available for a breach of contract. Nevertheless, dividing the subject into coherent chapters can be very difficult, with some topics having strong claims for being discussed in more than one place, or in a different order. In these situations, and to avoid repetition, there is some cross-referencing in the text.

Historic, but still significant, contract cases are combined with very recent decisions, even if the latter are merely illustrative, to ensure a contemporary legal focus. A huge number of decided cases have been considered, if only briefly, in the book. For this reason, and to save space, the 'Table of Cases' below has been limited to a selection chosen for their historic importance or illustrative value. All other cases mentioned are referenced in full at one or more places in the main text. It should be noted that "claimant" is used for "plaintiff" for the same party to civil litigation, even where the case precedes the Woolf Reforms, unless found in direct quotation.

*Gregory Durston*
Northeastern University
London,
Easter, 2023

---

1 J. Beatson et al., *Anson's Law of Contract*, 31st edn. (Oxford: Oxford University Press, 2020); Edwin Peel, *Treitel on the Law of Contract*, 15th edn. (London: Sweet & Maxwell, 2020); Hugh Beale (ed.), *Chitty on Contracts*, 34th edn. (London: Sweet and Maxwell, 2022).

# Contents

# Select Table of Cases

| | |
|---|---|
| *Dickinson v Dodds* (1876) 2 Ch D 463 | 28 |
| *Dunlop Pneumatic Tyre Co Ltd v Selfridge Ltd* [1915] AC 847 | 109 |
| *Dunlop Pneumatic Tyre Company v New Garage & Motor co* [1915] AC 79 | 301 |
| *East v Maurer* [1991] 2 All ER 733 | 146 |
| *Eastwood v Kenyon* (1840) 113 ER 482 | 52 |
| *Ecay v Godfrey* [1947] 80 Lloyds Rep 286 | 125 |
| *Edgington v Fitzmaurice* (1885) 29 Ch D 459 | 132, 133 |
| *Edwards v Skyways* [1964] 1 WLR 349 | 79 |
| *Entores v Miles Far East Corporation* [1955] 2 QB 327 | 32, 34, 37, 39 |
| *Errington v Errington & Woods* [1952] 1 KB 290 | 43, 45 |
| *Felthouse v Bindley* (1862) 142 ER 1037 | 33 |
| *Fibrosa Spolka v Fairbairn* [1943] AC 32 | 200, 202 |
| *Fisher v Bell* [1961] 1 QB 394 | 24 |
| *Foakes v Beer* (1883-84) LR 9 App Cas 605 | 60 |
| *G Scammell and Nephew Ltd v HC & JG Ouston* [1941] 1 AC 251 | 83 |
| *Galloway v Galloway* (1914) 30 TLR 531 | 152 |
| *Geoffrey Alan Salt v Stratstone Specialist Ltd* [2015] EWCA Civ 745 | 140, 142, 144, 148 |
| *Gibson v Manchester City Council* [1979] 1 WLR 294 | 23 |
| *Glasbrook Bros v Glamorgan County Council* [1925] AC 270 | 54 |
| *Hadley v Baxendale* [1854] EWHC Exch J70 | 273 |
| *Hartog v Colin & Shields* [1939] 3 All ER 566 | 159 |
| *Heywood v Wellers* [1976] 2 WLR 101 | 284 |
| *Hirachand Punamchand v Temple* [1911] 2 KB 330 | 61 |
| *Hollier v Rambler Motors* [1972] 2 WLR 401 | 245, 250 |
| *Holwell Securities v Hughes* [1974] 1 WLR 155 | 35 |
| *Hong Kong Fir Shipping Co Ltd v Kawasaki Kisen Kaisha Ltd* [1962] 2 QB 26 | 226 |
| *Houghton v Trafalgar Insurance Co. Ltd* [1954] 1 QB 247 | 247 |
| *Household Fire Insurance v Grant* [1879] 4 Ex D 216 | 35, 36 |
| *Howard Marine v Ogden* [1978] QB 574 | 140 |
| *Hyde v Wrench* (1840) 49 ER 132 | 30 |

# Table of Statutes and Statutory Instruments

# Introduction

## Setting the Scene

The English law of contract regulates legally binding agreements in England and Wales, whether they involve the purchase of a cup of coffee, a train-ticket, or a super-tanker, and so facilitates the free alienation of goods and services in the market economy of this part of the United Kingdom. By doing this, it encourages effective interpersonal cooperation in a very large, highly complex, increasingly fragmented, and ever more mobile society. Its presence alone encourages many disputes to be settled amicably.

Even so, it should also be noted that the legal rules that make up the law of contract do not necessarily reflect the way in which contracting parties behave when faced by a violation of those rules. People are often more flexible in practice than the substantive law might suggest, only going to law as a final option, not least because it is usually an expensive, slow, and stressful process. Furthermore, some potential defendants are not worth suing, because they are impecunious and uninsured, however strong a possible contractual action against them might appear to be. Furthermore, as Salmon LJ noted in *Jones v Padavatton* [1969] 2 All ER 616, "Even today sometimes people forbear from mercy to enforce their undoubted [contractual] legal rights".

English contract law has been highly influential around the common law world and has even had some influence on the law of contract in Roman (or "civil") law countries. As a result of "choice of law" clauses, it is frequently chosen by foreign parties as the applicable law to govern their commercial contracts, even when neither has any connection to England. Thus, the parties to an agreement might stipulate that it will be "governed in accordance with the laws of England and Wales, and the Parties agree to submit to the exclusive jurisdiction of the English courts in respect of any claims arising under this contract". Such clauses will be firmly enforced, as was the case with a recent anti-suit injunction granted to insurers restraining proceedings from being brought in Canada in breach of an exclusive English jurisdiction clause: *AIG Europe SA & Others v John Wood Group Plc & Others* [2022] EWCA Civ 781. Frequently, these cases will be dealt with by the Commercial Court in London. It is also important to note that general contract law is the bedrock for several more specialist and highly regulated types of agreement which are now themselves academic subjects, such as employment law and the law governing landlord and tenant.

Like all common law subjects, English contract law is made up of case law (based on precedent), statutes, and statutory instruments. Of course, these are often combined, with statutes being interpreted by case law. However, some important contractual areas are governed purely by previously decided cases, while in many others the role of statute is relatively modest. For those from Roman law jurisdictions this can sometimes be confusing. A valuable recent contribution to the writing in this regard has been provided by a *Restatement of the English Law of Contract* (henceforth *Restatement*) drawn up by the distinguished Supreme Court judge and legal academic Lord Burrows, assisted by an advisory group of senior judges, lawyers, and law professors. (The first US *Restatement of Contracts*, on which it was modelled, was published by the American Law Institute as far back as 1933.) This provides, in less than 40 pages, a succinct statement of the main principles of English contract law, especially those based on common (or case) law, allowing readers to see how its elements fit together. It will sometimes be cited in this work as it provides a carefully considered summary of many contractual issues, although, of course, it is of purely advisory significance, except where endorsed by the courts, and a few (not many) of its interpretations have been queried.

In recent years, the law of contract has seen considerable change, whether effected by parliament or the judiciary. More general trends within these changes can be identified. For example, and *inter alia*, the age-old conflict between the value of predictability, provided by bright-line legal rules, and that of flexibility, provided by judicial discretion, has tipped very slightly in favour of the latter. Thus, and as will be seen, the recent case law governing both illegal contracts and penalty clauses has emphasised an assessment of wider factors than the narrow rules previously identified as governing such topics. Whether this is an entirely good thing is a matter of considerable academic and legal debate. It would have alarmed the eminent contract-law scholar Sir Guenter Treitel (1928-2019), who was opposed to wide-ranging discretion if it could reasonably be avoided, preferring the use of clear-cut rules.[1] Others take a much more positive view of such developments.

## History

The roots of English contract law go back centuries, a few to beyond the Norman Conquest of 1066. Nevertheless, its formative period, from the late eighteenth century to the early twentieth century, was highly influenced by the demands of the industrial revolution and the *laissez-faire* approach to freedom of contract that came with it. The judgment of Sir George Jessel MR in *Printing and Numerical Registering Co v Sampson* (1875) 19 Eq 462 is considered an almost classic enunciation of this doctrine. Sampson, the defendant, had made what might be considered a rather foolish contract with the claimant, giving the latter unlimited rights to one of his inventions. Jessel upheld the agreement, noting that public policy required that "men of full age and competent understanding shall have the utmost liberty of contracting, and that their contracts when entered into freely and voluntarily shall be held sacred and shall be enforced by Courts of justice. Therefore, you have this paramount public policy to consider—that you are not lightly to interfere with this freedom of contract". (As this comment suggests, even in the nineteenth century, children, drunkards, and the mentally impaired or ill were accorded a degree of protection, as will be discussed in Chapter 5.)

1 "Professor Sir Guenter Treiterl", Talk by Lord Burrows given on 7th May, 2021.

The late Victorian period and much of the twentieth century saw a gradual retreat from relatively untrammelled freedom of contract, as statutes such as the Sale of Goods Act 1893 (now 1979) and the Unfair Contract Terms Act 1977 and, to a lesser extent, case law, afforded more protections to contracting parties, especially consumers.[2] Arguably, the latter have benefitted from the presence of what has sometimes been termed a consumer-welfare ethos in much recent legislation.

Nevertheless, the foundation of contract law remains freedom of agreement, particularly when it comes to commercial contracts. As Lord Toulson observed in *Prime Sight Ltd v Lavarello* [2014] 2 WLR 84, parties are "ordinarily free to contract on whatever terms they choose and the court's role is to enforce them". For example, in *Retirement Villages Developments Limited v Punch Partnerships (Ptl) Limited* [2022] EWHC 65 (Ch), which involved a claim for declaratory relief by a developer who had made what appears to have been a very bad bargain, Lance Ashworth QC, sitting as a Deputy High Court Judge, noted that, even if the words of the contract led to a commercially absurd result (not, he felt, the situation in the instant case), if "the language is unambiguous (as I have found), I am bound to apply those words".

## Place of Contract in the Legal Corpus

The law of contract is part of private law--that is, that division of law that involves relationships between individuals, unlike public law, which deals with relationships between individuals and the state (such as constitutional, administrative, and criminal law). Of course, it also encompasses commercial relationships between the state and individuals, such as a contract between the government and a manufacturer from which the former is making a purchase of, for example, warships or medical supplies. Private law includes numerous subjects other than contract law, including family and property law. However, three of these subjects are grouped together in a branch termed the "law of obligations". This is made up of contract, tort, and (albeit of less significance) restitution or unjust enrichment (once termed "quasi-contract").

Sometimes, both tort and restitution can have a close relationship with contract, perhaps by providing a cause of action where one for breach of contract is not possible, or by providing an alternative to the latter action. For example, in *British Steel Corp v Cleveland Bridge and Engineering Co Ltd* [1984] 1 All ER 504, the claimant entered lengthy negotiations to sell cast steel nodes to the defendant which, unexpectedly, did not result in a formal contract being agreed. However, in the meantime, the defendants had requested that the claimant start work on the steel nodes, some of which had then been delivered and accepted. Although there was, ultimately, no contractual relationship between the parties, Goff J allowed restitutionary recovery for the value of the work done on the delivered nodes, something that meant that the defendant did not obtain a windfall benefit. More recently, in *Goodlife Foods Ltd v Hall Fire Protection Ltd* [2018] EWCA Civ 1371,

---

2 See generally, P.S. Atiyah, *The Rise and Fall of Freedom of Contract* (Oxford: Oxford University Press, 1985).

the claimant brought an action in negligence, alleging defective installation of a fire prevention system in his factory some years earlier, because he would probably have been time-barred if he brought one for breach of contract (the actions have different limitation periods).

A major difference between tort and contract is that obligations under the latter are normally voluntarily incurred, rather than being imposed by the general law, as is usually the case with the former. People are not obliged to provide a commercial service for money, but, if they do, they are obliged to carry it out with reasonable skill and care. By contrast, if they drive on the public roads they are obliged to do so with proper care and attention; they have no choice in the matter. Even so, there is sometimes an overlap between tort and contract, with potential actions in both resulting from the same incident and being open, simultaneously, to a claimant, as would have initially been the situation in *Goodlife*. For example, if a taxi driver steers his vehicle negligently, so that the passenger who hired him is injured, the passenger could sue him both for breach of the implied contractual term that he will exercise reasonable skill and care in providing the service and in the tort of negligence, although this will not permit "double recovery" of damages. In some situations, as *Goodlife* suggests, one such claim may be more beneficial than the other. The relationship of concurrent claims, at least when it comes to the precedence of their different tests for remoteness of damage, was considered by the Court of Appeal in *Wellesley Partners LLP v Withers LLP* [2015] EWCA Civ 1146, which involved an allegation of both breach of contract and negligence by a firm of solicitors involved in drafting a partnership agreement.

## Absolute Obligations and Contract

Contractual obligations are normally absolute; this means that there is no legally acceptable excuse for failing to perform them, unless (and unusually) it also constitutes a frustrating event (see Chapter 11).[3] To take a well-known illustration, in *Frost v Aylesbury Dairy Co. Ltd.* [1905] 1 KB 608 the claimant's wife contracted typhoid from infected milk supplied by the defendant dairy. He sued successfully for breach of the implied term under s.14(3) of the Sale of Goods Act 1893 (now replaced by SOGA 1979) that it would be fit for purpose; clearly it was not. It was not a defence to this action that no amount of skill or care would have allowed the defendant to identify its dangerous condition, as would have been the case with a tortious negligence claim. Of course, when it comes to express (rather than implied) terms, a party to a contract can sometimes limit his obligation, at least in some situations, to using his "best endeavours" or even "reasonable endeavours" to achieve a certain result, rather than the result itself.

Conversely, counterparties (the opposite party in a contract) are usually entitled to their "pound of flesh" if there is a breach of contract and can stick to the precise terms of an agreement, whatever their motivation. Thus, in the House of Lords

3 Albert Kiralfy, "Absolute liability in contract", *The Journal of Legal History*, v. 1, no. 1 (1980), pp. 89-93.

case of *Arcos v Ranaason* [1933] AC 470, the contract involved the sale of wooden staves for making barrels. The agreement stipulated that the staves were to be half an inch thick. However, some of the staves delivered were very slightly thicker. They could still readily be used for making barrels. Nevertheless, the purchaser rejected the goods under s.13 of the Sale of Goods Act 1893, for failure to correspond to description, as they were not of the specified size. This action was prompted not by eccentricity, but by an awareness that he could buy the staves cheaper elsewhere, *provided* he could avoid the initial contract. Even so, it was held that he was entitled to reject the goods as the law then stood, because they were not as described. His motivation was irrelevant. The similar case of *FW Moore & Co Ltd v Landauer & Co* [1921] 2 KB 519 was even more extreme. A sale of 3,000 tins of canned peaches, in cases of 30 tins, was avoided when half the cases contained only 24 tins, although the total number of tins delivered was still 3,000. The Court of Appeal held that, although there was no loss to the buyer, they could be rejected for a breach of s.13 SOGA 1893.

Much more recently, in *Monde Petroleum SA v Westernzagros Ltd* [2016] EWHC 1472 (Comm) Richard Salter QC, sitting as a Deputy High Court Judge, observed in *obiter* comments that an express right to terminate a contract did not need to be exercised in good faith. Provided that the conditions for doing so were satisfied, the exercising party was entitled to exercise that power, even if it was acting for some ulterior reason. In this case it had been alleged that a consulting contract had been terminated to deprive Monde of the chance to share in the profits of a deal with the Kurdistan government.

## Good Faith and Contract

As the above cases suggest, there is no general requirement of "good faith" when it comes to exercising contractual rights in English law. In this, it differs from civil law and even some foreign common law legal systems. (The courts of the United States and Australia have gone further in this regard).[4] Instead, England has developed piecemeal remedies for distinct forms of abusive behaviour, such as the action for pre-contractual misrepresentation. The general absence of a requirement of good faith helps explain why its very definition is somewhat nebulous in English law and has been subject to slightly different interpretations over recent decades.

For example, more than 30 years ago, Bingham LJ thought that it was best caught by colloquialisms such as "playing fair" or "coming clean": *Interfoto Picture Library Ltd v Stiletto Visual Programmes Ltd* [1989] 1 QB 433. In *CPC Group Ltd v Qatari Diar Real Estate Investment Co* [2010] EWHC 1535 (Ch), Vos J suggested that an obligation to act in good faith precluded a party from cynically resorting to the black letter of the law (arguably, this is what occurred in *Arcos v Ranaason*). He also found that it required observing reasonable commercial standards of fair dealing,

4 John Cartwright, *Contract Law: An Introduction to the English Law of Contract for the Civil Lawyer*, 3rd edn. (Oxford: Hart, 2016), p. 61.

being faithful to the common purpose of the agreement, and acting consistently with the justified expectations of the parties, although it did not require a party to subordinate their own interests in the way that would be required of a fiduciary. More recently, in *Essex County Council v UBB Waste (Essex)* [2020] EWHC 1581 (TCC), Pepperall J suggested that the key question to ask when deciding whether there had been a breach of good faith was whether the conduct would be regarded as "commercially unacceptable" by reasonable and honest people.

For a period in the early years of this century, it appeared that the need for good faith was expanding in English contract law. Like any other term, such a requirement might be implied as a matter of fact if necessary to give business efficacy to the contract or because it was so obvious that it went without saying (see Chapter 12). However, the process went further. Following the decision of Leggatt J in *Yam Seng Pte v International Trade Corp* [2013] EWHC 111 (QB), there was an increase in claims to an implied duty of good faith as a matter of law (rather than fact) in a category of "relational" contracts. These might cover joint ventures, in which the parties were committed to collaborating with each other, often on a long-term basis, and which, it was thought, required that the spirit of their venture be respected, even if all the ways in which this might happen had not been specified in the written contract.

Unsurprisingly, this special category of cases includes contracts of employment, where both employer and employee typically have mutual expectations, in terms of loyalty and cooperation. To protect those expectations, a term is implied into such agreements that neither party will act in a way that is likely to damage the relationship of trust and confidence between them. However, such relational cases have been held to extend further than those involving employment. For example, in *Bates and others v Post Office Ltd* [2019] EWHC 606 (QB) the court implied a duty to act in good faith into the contract between the Post Office and its sub-postmasters (who are not formal employees of the organisation). This meant that the Post Office was subject to duties of fair dealing, transparency, and cooperation, and was required to refrain from conduct which would be regarded as commercially unacceptable by reasonable people.

The court emphasized factors in the case that made *Bates* both a relational contract and one that also required good faith. For example, it was a long-term arrangement, involving close collaboration and a significant degree of investment by one or both parties in the venture. When the Post Office unsuccessfully sought leave to appeal from this decision, Coulson LJ observed that the trial judge had considered the circumstances of the case and found, for a variety of sound reasons, that a duty of good faith should be implied into such contracts. Nevertheless, and significantly, the judge also noted, "At no point did he [the trial judge] find that, because the contract could be described as 'relational', the good faith term somehow 'automatically' had to be implied."[5]

5 Case No: A1/2019/1387/PTA

Similarly, in *Essex County Council v UBB Waste (Essex)* [2020] EWHC 1581 (TCC), Essex CC entered a 25-year contract with UBB for the construction, operation, and maintenance of a biological waste-treatment plant. The contract provided for a commissioning period followed by tests to confirm that the facility could meet the performance requirements set out in the contract. If these were not passed, as proved to be the case, Essex CC was entitled to terminate the agreement, as they duly did. UBB contended, inter alia, that any failure to pass the tests was due to failures on the part of Essex CC and that these included the breach of an implied term of good faith. Pepperall J concluded that there was such a term in the contract because the agreement was long-term and required high levels of cooperation between the parties, so that "this 25-year PFI contract is a paradigm example of a relational contract in which the law implies a duty of good faith". (However, he decided that it had not been breached in the instant case.)

Nevertheless, in *Pakistan International Airline Corporation v Times Travel (UK) Ltd* [2021] UKSC 40 the Supreme Court firmly reiterated that there is no general principle of good faith in English contract law, and tacitly discouraged such a term from being lightly implied into agreements, putting a break on the doctrine's development. The number of relational contracts where a term requiring good faith must be implied as a matter of law appears to be very limited, while the requirements for implication by fact are (as always) extremely stringent and only rarely met.

For example, in *Morley (t/a Morley Estates) v The Royal Bank of Scotland plc* [2021] EWCA Civ 338, the Court of Appeal upheld the High Court's rejection of a borrower's argument that a bank had an implied duty to act in good faith towards it under a loan agreement. It held that this was not a relational contract of any kind. The bank's decision to call in the loan was simply the exercise of a contractual right.

Similarly, in *Candey Limited v Bosheh* [2022] EWCA Civ 1103 the Court of Appeal, like the High Court, found that a client was under no implied duty of good faith towards his lawyers, even where a contingency fee arrangement was in place. In this case, Candey, a firm of solicitors, were only entitled to payment if their client recovered damages from litigation. After they had done a significant amount of work, the client settled the proceedings on a "drop hands" basis, under which both parties agreed to withdraw their claims against one another with each bearing their own legal costs (where incurred). This meant that Candey's lawyers went unpaid. They unavailingly argued that in settling the litigation in this way, their client had breached an implied duty of good faith. However, the court held that such a term was not necessary for the retainer to work, nor so obvious that it went without saying, so that it was not implied by fact. Furthermore, the retainer was not a relational contract in which a duty of good faith would be implied as a matter of law, not least because the factors identified in *Bates* were absent. More specifically, there was no guarantee that the retainer would be a long-term contract, no commitment to collaboration, no required high level of communication between the parties, and no expectation of loyalty. The court noted that the concept of good faith did not justify a departure from the general tests required for implying terms and did not provide an opportunity to avoid clear and orthodox principles of contract law.

Of course, an express term requiring good faith can also be included in a contract. In *Berkeley Community Villages Ltd v Pullen* [2007] EWHC 1330 (Ch) Morgan J held that such a term, in an agreement between the owner of farmland and the claimant to maximise the land's potential for development and requiring that the parties act "with the utmost good faith towards one another", imposed an obligation to observe reasonable commercial standards of fair dealing and also required faithfulness to the agreed common purpose and the "justified expectations" of the claimant.

However, and more recently, in *Re Compound Photonics Group Ltd; Faulkner v Vollin Holdings Ltd* [2022] EWCA Civ 1371, the Court of Appeal, overturning a decision in the High Court, stressed that an express term requiring a party to act in good faith must be interpreted in the light of the wider agreement and all its underlying facts. As a result, previous decisions on similar clauses were of limited value. Snowden LJ acknowledged that, at the least, a duty of good faith would require a party to act honestly. It might, in some circumstances, also prohibit conduct that: "... reasonable and commercial people would regard as commercially unacceptable, but not necessarily dishonest". Nevertheless, the court rejected the lower court's finding that it would always be required to satisfy all the formulaic "minimum" standards of behaviour identified by the High Court in *Unwin v Bond* [2020] EWHC 768.

It should also be noted that the notion of good faith can be found in statutory form in s.62(4) of the Consumer Rights Act 2015, which (showing its EU and civil law roots) stipulates that a term regulated by the statute would be regarded as unfair and so not binding if it caused a significant imbalance in the parties' respective positions, to the detriment of the consumer, in a way that is "contrary to the requirement of good faith" (see Chapter 13).

## Interpretation of Contracts

Frequently the courts are required to interpret the wording employed in a contract. Ambiguity can produce different meanings, which might have very different results for the parties to an agreement. In the United States, it has been claimed that interpretation is the most common issue to come before contract lawyers, while interpretative disputes are the largest source of contractual litigation.[6]

It should be noted immediately that interpretation is made on an objective basis. As the Court of Appeal noted in *National Car Parks Ltd v Revenue And Customs* [2019] EWCA Civ 854: "English law, of course, generally adopts an objective approach

6 Joshua M. Silverstein, "Contract Interpretation and the Parol Evidence Rule: Toward Conceptual Clarification", *Chapman Law Review*, v. 24, no. 1 (2020), p. 91.

when deciding what has been agreed in a contractual context". This means that the courts do not attempt to determine what one party intended in their own mind, or what the other party understood to have been intended, but, to quote Lord Hoffmann in *Chartbrook Ltd v Persimmon Homes Ltd* [2009] UKHL 38, it seeks to establish "what a reasonable person having all the background knowledge which would have been available to the parties would have understood them to be using the language in the contract to mean".

This is sometimes easier said than done. As a starting point, the courts will follow the natural meaning of the clause. However, if this is at all unclear, other factors might creep into consideration. As was noted by the Supreme Court in *Wood v Capita Insurance Services Ltd* [2017] UKSC 24, it has long been accepted that interpretation is "not a literalist exercise focused solely on a parsing of the wording of the particular clause but that the court must consider the contract as a whole and, depending on the nature, formality and quality of drafting of the contract, give more or less weight to elements of the wider context in reaching its view as to that objective meaning".

When it comes to contractual interpretation, there is considerable debate as to where the balance should be struck between recourse to what is termed "textualism" (attributing the natural linguistic meaning of the words used in an agreement) and so-called "contextualism" (interpreting these words in the wider context of the contract), which might allow the meaning attributed to the words employed to be influenced by, *inter alia*, what would be common sense in the light of the particular business that forms the background to the agreement. In the past, the higher courts have placed a slightly different emphasis on these two factors.

In *Rainy Sky SA v Kookmin Bank* [2011] UKSC 50, the Supreme Court accepted that, if there were two possible constructions, the court was entitled to prefer that which was consistent with business common sense. Nevertheless, in *Arnold v Britton & ors* [2015] AC 1619, the same forum cautioned against commercial common sense overriding the ordinary natural meaning of a provision. In this case, recourse to the latter would oblige the tenants of a group of 25 holiday chalets to pay an annual service charge which increased by 10% each year, on a compound basis, irrespective of the cost to the landlord of providing such services. This meant that the annual charges would be over £500,000 by the end of the long leases, which would have very grave financial consequences for the tenants. The court held that commercial common sense should not be used to undermine the clear contractual wording of a clause, which should be the starting point in any assessment, even where that wording produces a very bad bargain for one of the parties. The court's task is to identify and give effect to their agreement, not make a different bargain because it thinks that the parties, or (more commonly) a party, would have been wiser to do so.

However, in *Arnold v Britton* the Supreme Court also emphasized that textualism and contextualism were not conflicting paradigms but complementary tools for ascertaining the objective meaning of the contractual language chosen by the parties. Where a dispute occurs as to the meaning of a particular provision, the courts will weigh the indications given by the language against the implications of rival meanings. Even so, the court also suggested that, for contracts where the parties are both more sophisticated and professionally (legally) advised, greater emphasis on a textual approach may sometimes be appropriate, reinforcing the importance of the natural meaning of the language, and so giving a boost to textualism. This has been evidenced in several subsequent cases.

Despite this, the growth in textualism has not been unqualified, especially outside the commercial sphere. For example, in *Grimes v The Trustees of the Essex Farmers and Union Hunt* [2017] EWCA Civ 361, the main issue was whether notice to quit an agricultural holding was validly served on the tenant, Mr Grimes, by his landlords. The tenancy agreement stated that notice had to be served at the address given on the lease "or such other address as has previously been notified in writing". The notice had been sent to the original address on the lease, although a new address had been notified in writing. The Court of Appeal, considering the meaning of "or" in this context, held that the judge at first instance had been overly literal in permitting service at the given address when a new one had been indicated. The "language can naturally be read as providing for an alternative which is not only exclusionary but also substitutive. ... [V]iewed objectively, this is what the parties must have intended".[7] The notice was not deemed to be effective.

More recently, in the Court of Appeal case of *Mashael Alebrahim v BM Design London Ltd* [2022] EWCA Civ 183, Coulson LJ opined that the relevant interpretive principles in such situations were now well-known. A contract must primarily be construed by reference to the language that the parties have used in the agreement, and that it is, "only if the meaning of the words used is uncertain or ambiguous that the court needs to have regard to other matters, such as commercial common sense, on the one hand, or excessive literalism, on the other."

It should be noted that only very limited use can be made of pre-contractual negotiations when it comes to interpreting the formal agreements that they produce. They can be employed to throw light upon what the parties meant where the language they used appears otherwise uncertain, this being part of the general background to an agreement. Otherwise, they are not admissible: *Chartbrook v Persimmon Homes* [2009] UKHL 38. No use at all can be made of post-contract dealings as an aid to interpretation. Although evidence of subsequent behaviour is admissible to determine if there ever was a contract (see Chapter 1), it cannot be adduced on the meaning of the terms within an agreement. As Lord Reid observed

7 See also Lord Sumption, "A Question of Taste: The Supreme Court and the Interpretation of Contracts", Harris Society Annual Lecture, Keble College, Oxford, 8 May 2017.

in *Whitworth Street Estates (Manchester) Ltd v James Miller and Partners Ltd* [1970] AC 583, "[I]t is now well settled that it is not legitimate to use as an aid in the construction of the contract anything which the parties said or did after it was made. Otherwise, one might have the result that a contract meant one thing the day it was signed, but by reason of subsequent events meant something different a month or a year later".

# Chapter 1: Agreement

## Introduction

All contracts require an agreement. As Leggatt J noted in *Blue v Ashley* [2017] EWHC 1928, this is normally reached by the parties signing a written document containing agreed terms or by one party making an offer (verbal or written) which the other accepts. In these situations, when an acceptance meets an offer, the "moment of contract" takes place--assuming valid consideration and an intention to create legal relations are also present--and what was fluid becomes rigid and binding. The parties cannot then unilaterally withdraw from the agreement or vary its terms.

However, it should be noted that this general situation is qualified by statute for consumers entering certain (far from all) contracts at a distance, by using the telephone, email, or internet etc., without any face-to-face contact with the vendor. They are granted a "cooling-off" period, usually seven days, during which they can change their mind and withdraw from the agreement, receiving a full refund of any monies already paid, by dint of the Consumer Protection (Distance Selling) Regulations 2000 (SI 2000 No. 2334).

Sometimes identifying a matching offer and acceptance, and so the moment of contract, can be difficult. As a result, a more flexible and holistic approach to contractual negotiations and reaching agreement was proposed by Lord Denning in several Court of Appeal cases during the 1970s. The distinguished judge thought that the traditional analysis of offer and acceptance was often out of date, and that in such cases it was better to look at all the documents passing between the parties and glean from them, or from the conduct of the parties, whether they had reached agreement on all material points: *Butler Machine Tool Co. Ltd* v *Ex-Cell-O Corporation (England) Ltd* [1979] 1 All ER 965. However, this approach found little favour with the House of Lords, as it appeared to occasion more problems than it solved.[1] Instead, and as Lord Wilberforce observed in *New Zealand Shipping Co. Ltd* v *A M Satterthwaite and Co. Ltd* [1975] AC 154, English law, having committed itself to a rather technical doctrine of contractual formation, frequently takes a practical approach to the issue, "often at the cost of forcing the facts to fit uneasily into the marked slots of offer, acceptance and consideration". As a result, the two parts of an agreement, offer and acceptance, need to be considered separately (consideration is dealt with in the next chapter).

## Offer

An offer is a statement expressing a willingness to enter a binding contract, on specified terms, without further negotiation as soon as an acceptance is received from the offeree. To cite an academic definition, it is an "expression of willingness

1 See generally Richard Stone, "Forming Contracts without Offer and Acceptance: Lord Denning and the Harmonisation of English Contract Law" [2012] 4 *Web Journal of Current Legal Issues* http://webjcli.ncl.ac.uk/2012/issue4/stone4.html

to contract on certain terms, made with the intention that it shall become binding as soon as it is accepted by the person to whom it is addressed".[2] An offer can be made verbally, in writing, or even by conduct.

It must be shown that the offeror "intended" to be bound by their statement. However, and as in many other areas of contract law, including acceptance, this is determined objectively, by regard to the parties' behaviour, rather than any subjective intention they might hold. As Lord Denning MR noted in *Storer v Manchester City Council* [1974] 1 WLR 1403, "In contracts you do not look into the actual intent in a man's mind. You look at what he said and did. A contract is formed when there is, to all outward appearances, a contract. A man cannot get out of a contract by saying 'I did not intend to contract' if by his words he has done so".

Similarly, in *The Leonidas* [1985] 1 WLR 925, Goff LJ observed that, "If the offeror so acts that his conduct, objectively considered, constitutes an offer, and the offeree, believing that the conduct of the offeror represents his actual intention, accepts the offer, then a contract will come into existence". In a gloss to this analysis, in *G Percy Trentham Ltd v Archital Luxfer Ltd.* [1993] 1 Lloyd's Rep. 25, Steyn LJ noted that, when determining how an offeror's words or conduct should be interpreted when made in a commercial context, it would be premised on the reasonable expectations of "sensible businessmen" who witnessed the statement (rather than the average man in the street).

As a result, an offeror will be bound if his words (whether written or oral) or conduct would induce a reasonable third-party observer to believe that he intended to be bound and (what is very important) the offeree did so believe, even if, in fact, he (the offeror) held no such intention subjectively. In practice, such situations will be very rare. Nevertheless, the principle became important in *Moran v University College Salford (No 2)* (1993) TLR Nov 23. In this case, the defendant college mistakenly offered a place to an intending student to study physiotherapy, due to a clerical error. The claimant (unaware of the error) accepted. Subsequently, when Mr Moran telephoned the course leader, he was informed that he had not been offered a place, but by then he had given up both his job and accommodation in London, while it was too late to make alternative arrangements for the forthcoming academic year. The college argued that no binding agreement had been made. The Court of Appeal, like the judge at first instance, applied the objective principle and held that a valid contract had been formed. Consequently, the claimant was entitled to damages to cover his detrimental reliance on their "offer". Nevertheless, the Court of Appeal refused to exercise its discretion to order specific performance by compelling the college to admit him to their course, one for which many others, who were better qualified, had been rejected. (See Chapter 16).[3]

---

2 Edwin Peel, *Treitel on the Law of Contract*, 13th edn. (London: Sweet and Maxwell, 2011), p. 8.

3 Magrath, Paul, "Law Report", *Independent* (London), 26 November 1993. No contract would have arisen if the had known or ought reasonably to have known of the university's mistake.

It should be noted that subsequent communications between the parties to an alleged contract can be adduced as evidence on the issue of whether the moment of contract has occurred, and a binding agreement been formed: *Global Asset Capital & anr v Aabar Block S.A.R.L. & others* [2017] EWCA Civ 37. In this case, the Court of Appeal decided that later exchanges, such as a reference to the "proposed transaction" and use of the phrase "upon your agreement that you are willing to proceed" were inconsistent with the existence of an earlier oral contract allegedly made by telephone, and persuasive in finding that such a contract had not been formed.

## Invitation to Treat

The language of an offer must be clear and unequivocal. Anything less risks becoming an "invitation to treat" (sometimes termed an "invitation to bargain" in North America), which is an expression of willingness to negotiate with the other party, and even an invitation to them to make an offer. As such, it is an important part of contract formation. Nevertheless, a person who makes an invitation to treat does not intend to contract and will not be bound if his statement is (purportedly) "accepted" by the counterparty.

For example, in the Privy Council case of *Harvey v Facey* [1893] AC 552 Harvey sent a telegram to Facey which asked, "Will you sell us Bumper Hall Pen? Telegraph lowest cash price--answer paid". Facey replied by telegram, "Lowest price for Bumper Hall Pen £900". Harvey then replied, "We agree to buy Bumper Hall Pen for the sum of nine hundred pounds asked by you. Please send us your title deed in order that we may get early possession". However, the Privy Council held that there was no agreement and so no contract. Facey had not committed himself to selling the property. He had not answered the initial question as to *whether* he would sell, and the price stated was merely an indication as to the lowest price that he would consider accepting *were* he minded so to do. He was providing information, not making an offer.

The quality of the language used in *Gibson v Manchester City Council* [1979] 1 WLR 294 was also vital. In this case, the defendant had adopted a policy of selling council houses to its tenants, including the claimant. In February 1971, the city treasurer wrote to him stating that the council "may be prepared to sell you the house". This letter also invited the claimant to make a formal application using an enclosed form. The next month, the claimant returned the completed form to the defendant. Following local elections in May of the same year, control of the council changed. The new Labour-dominated council's policy was that council houses would not be sold under the previous policy unless there was already a legally binding contract in force. They refused to sell to the claimant, who brought an action against them for breach of contract, which was successful at first instance and in the Court of Appeal. However, the defendant appealed to the House of Lords, which held that there was no contract, so that the defendant was not legally bound to sell the house. The original letter was an invitation to treat, not an offer. The claimant's response was the offer, one that had not been accepted by the council. The key phrase in the exchange was "may be". This left open the possibility that they might not be willing to sell the property.

By a neat symmetry, this case may be contrasted with the ostensibly similar *Storer v Manchester City Council* [1974] 1 WLR 1403, in which another newly returned Manchester council refused to proceed with the sale of a dwelling to its tenant (the claimant) under arrangements made by the previous council. In this case, the claimant had signed and returned the form sent to him by the council, and the courts decided that this form was sufficiently clear, firm, and precise to be an offer that was capable of acceptance, which the tenant had duly done.

### Special and Recurring Situations

In most cases, it is the quality of the words employed that determine whether a statement is an offer or an invitation to treat. However, there are certain commonly recurring situations where either this is not clear, or where there are strong policy reasons for deciding this question in a particular and consistent way. Sometimes both factors are present. In these situations, this is usually done by introducing a very strong, but not irrebuttable, presumption that the statement is an invitation to treat. Three situations, in particular, can be considered.

### Labelled Goods in Self-Service Shops

In *Pharmaceutical Society of Great Britain v Boots* [1953] 1 QB 401 Boots introduced a modern self-service system into their chemist shops. Customers would pick up labelled goods from a shelf, put them into a basket, and then take it to the till to pay. The Pharmaceutical Society of Great Britain challenged the legality of the new system, using a representative case from the Edgeware branch of Boots. They argued that the new system allowed poisons to be sold without the presence of a qualified pharmacist, which was contrary to s.18(1)(a)(iii) of the Pharmacy and Poisons Act 1933. In this case, there was a pharmacist near the cash till, but not by the shelves. If the contract came into existence at the till, the sales would be quite legal; if it occurred when the item was selected from a shelf and put into a basket, it would not. The Court of Appeal held that the labelled goods on the shelf constituted an invitation to treat, not an offer. (Otherwise, a purchaser could not change his mind and put an item back on the shelf.) The contract was concluded at the till (where there was a pharmacist), probably because the customer made an offer to purchase on the labelled terms when he tendered the goods, and this was accepted by the shop assistant ringing them up on the till. The assistant could still reject the offer up to this point.

### Labelled Goods in Shop Windows

In *Fisher v Bell* [1961] 1 QB 394 the defendant displayed a flick/gravity knife in his shop window labelled "Ejector knife – 4s". Section 1(1) of the Restriction of

Offensive Weapons Act 1959 made it a criminal offence to "offer" such knives for sale. At first instance, the magistrates held that displaying the knife was merely an invitation to treat, not an offer, and thus no liability arose. This was upheld when the prosecutor appealed their decision to the Queen's Bench Divisional Court, where Lord Parker observed that there was no "offer for sale". Although, to laymen, the labelled display of a knife might appear to be an offer, the relevant statute must be construed in the context of the general law. This clearly established a strong presumption that displaying an item in a shop window was an invitation to treat. (The wording of the statute was subsequently changed to accommodate such situations.)

A rare, albeit American, example of this presumption (which also applies in the USA) being rebutted can be seen in *Lefkowitz v Great Minneapolis Surplus Store, Inc* (1957) 86 NW 2d 689. In this case, the Great Minneapolis Surplus Store placed an advertisement in the window stating, "Saturday 9 A.M. Sharp. 3 Brand New Fur Coats Worth up to 100.00. First Come First Served 1 Each". Mr. Lefkowitz saw the notice and was the first person to enter the shop on the Saturday morning. He tendered 1 for a coat, but the shop owner refused to sell it to him, saying that the sale was for women only. (This had not been indicated.) The Supreme Court of Minnesota held that the advertisement constituted an offer, not an invitation to treat, as had been suggested by the defendant at trial, one that had been accepted by Mr. Lefkowitz by being one of the first three customers to tender a dollar for the garment. The wording was clear and definite.

### Advertised Goods in Newspapers, Magazines, and on the Internet

In *Partridge v Crittenden* [1968] 1 WLR 1204 the Queen's Bench Divisional Court considered a conviction from a magistrates' court in which Partridge had been found guilty of "offering for sale" a protected wild bird, contrary to the Protection of Birds Act 1954. In this case, an advertisement had been placed in the journal *Cage and Aviary Birds*, stating, inter alia, "Bramblefinch hens 25s". A Mr. Thompson wrote to Partridge asking him to send him a bramblefinch hen and enclosing a cheque. He eventually received the hen in the presence of an RSPCA inspector. Partridge was subsequently charged with the criminal offence by Crittenden, acting on behalf of the RSPCA.

Perhaps understandably, and despite being referred to *Fisher v Bell*, the magistrates decided that the advertisement was an offer for sale, so that Partridge was convicted and fined. He appealed against conviction by way of case stated. The court held that the advertisement did not constitute an offer for sale. It was analogous to the situation in *Fisher v Bell*, the insertion of a newspaper advertisement in the form adopted in the instant case being simply an invitation to treat. (The court rejected suggestions that there might be different meanings for "offer for sale" in contract and criminal law.) Lord Parker CJ also observed that "when one is dealing with advertisements and circulars, unless they indeed come from the manufacturers, there is business sense in them being construed as invitations to treat and not offers for sale".

Similarly, in contracts created on the internet, an advertisement on a website will not normally constitute an offer, rather than an invitation to treat, although, again, this presumption could be rebutted with the right (or wrong) wording. In a celebrated case from 1999, Argos accidentally advertised Sony televisions for sale on its website at £2.99 instead of £299.99. Subsequently, numerous orders were placed. However, no binding contract had arisen at this point between Argos and customers whose orders were (in reality) offers.[4] The situation was complicated by the fact that Argos sent a confirmation of receipt to some of these offers. Much might have depended on its wording, and whether it could have been interpreted as an acceptance. Nevertheless, the contracts would, in any event, very likely have been void *ab initio* for unilateral mistake as to terms given the huge under-pricing (see Chapter 9), and no actions against the company seem to have come for trial.

Since then, web commerce has grown exponentially. However, businesses have also become much more aware of the potential pitfalls of such trading and are usually careful to incorporate their terms and conditions into any agreement made on the internet. A standard method by which this is done involves the purchaser being required to click a box agreeing to them at some point in the process, before they place their order.[5] Typically, these might state, "I have read and agree to the website terms and conditions" (these terms being readily available on the site).

Internet transactions usually require the completion of a web order form by the customer, sometimes using a virtual basket, followed at some point by clicking a "complete order" type link. The customer's submission will normally be an offer, so that a contract will be formed once the supplier accepts it. However, the supplier will usually first send a confirmation email, noting receipt of the offer. Indeed, this is necessary in contracts between consumers and online traders made through websites, by dint of Regulation 11 of the Electronic Commerce Regulations 2002 SI 2002/2013. (This also provides that the order and acknowledgment are deemed to have been received when the recipient is able to access them.) The trader will normally set out what will constitute formal acceptance in his terms and conditions. It may even specify that this will take place only once the customer is notified that his goods have been shipped, giving it maximum discretion as to whether to contract or not.

## Advertising Offences

It should be noted that although an advertisement is not normally an offer that can be accepted, under s.8 of the Consumer Protection from Unfair Trading Regulations 2008 it can be a criminal offence for a person, acting in the course of a business, to

4 Richard Colbey, "When a snip turns out to be a slip-up," *The Guardian* (London), 18 September 1999

5 Andrew Burrows, *A Restatement of the English Law of Contract*, 2nd edn. (Oxford: Oxford University Press, 2020), p. 11.

give consumers misleading price indications about goods, services, accommodation, or facilities. This is punishable by a fine or, on indictment, (in theory) a custodial sentence, and acts as a powerful disincentive to making untruthful advertisements.

## Notices on Machines

The situation regarding notices in bilateral contracts is usually, and necessarily, rather different when they are appended to vending and car-park machines or self-service petrol pumps, which cannot refund money. This was considered in *Thornton v Shoe Lane Parking Ltd* [1970] [1971] 2 QB 163 where it was held that the notice on an automatic ticket machine in a car park was an offer, rather than an invitation to treat. Lord Denning noted that in these situations the customer paid his money and received a ticket. He could not then get his money back, so "[t]he contract was concluded at that time. It can be translated into offer and acceptance in this way: the offer is made when the proprietor of the machine holds it out as being ready to receive the money. The acceptance takes place when the customer puts his money into the slot".

The issue was also briefly discussed in *National Car Parks Ltd v Revenue and Customs* [2019] EWCA Civ 854, again in the context of machines in a car park, in which a tariff board set out hourly rates along with a statement that "overpayments" were accepted but no change given. A customer inserted cash and then elected to press the green button rather than cancelling the transaction. The Court of Appeal concluded that, in this situation, the best analysis would be that this was when the contract was brought into being, "On that basis, the pressing of the green button would represent acceptance by the customer of an offer by NCP to provide an hour's parking in return for the coins that the customer had by then paid into the machine".

As will be seen, the situation is also different when it comes to notices in unilateral contracts, which will usually be deemed to be offers (see below).

## Termination of Offers

Some offers are met by an acceptance to produce a binding contract. Others expire automatically, without acceptance, the original offer having been open for an expressly stated period which has passed. However, all offers that are not accepted, but not limited in time, come to an end via a variety of other mechanisms. Foremost amongst these are revocation, rejection, counter-offer, and effluxion of time.

## Revocation

An offer can be withdrawn or "revoked" at any point until it is accepted, although there are some qualifications to this statement when it comes to unilateral contracts and to offers contained in options (see below) or deeds (discussed in Chapter 2). For example, in *Payne v Cave* (1789) 3 TR 148, Cave made the highest bid (an offer) in an auction but changed his mind and withdrew his bid just before the auctioneer brought down his hammer. It was held that he was not bound to purchase the relevant lot, as he was still entitled to withdraw his offer. In the modern era, s.57(2) of the Sale of Goods Act 1979 expressly states that a bidder at an auction can retract his bid at any point until acceptance, with the latter being marked by fall of the hammer or in any other customary manner.

Obviously, if an offeror makes an offer stipulating that it will be open for a set period, such as a week, a purported acceptance made outside that time, such as after two weeks, will not be effective. However, there is (legally) nothing to prevent an offeror withdrawing his offer early, even if he has promised to keep it open for a longer period, *provided* that his offer was not itself made in a separate contract, usually known as an option, that is supported by consideration or, alternatively, that it was not set out in a deed (which does not need consideration to be binding). As Lindley J observed in *Byrne & Co v Leon Van Tien Hoven & Co* [1880] 5 CPD 344, normally "[t]here is no doubt an offer can be withdrawn before it is accepted, and it is immaterial whether the offer is expressed to be open for acceptance for a given time or not".

For example, in *Routledge v Grant* [1828] 4 Bing 653 the defendant offered to purchase the claimant's home. His (written) offer stated that it would remain open for a period of six weeks. However, during this period, the defendant wrote to the claimant once again, withdrawing the offer. After receiving this second letter, which was still within the six-week period, the claimant purported to accept the defendant's original offer. The court held that the offer had been withdrawn by the defendant, so that the claimant's "acceptance" was ineffective.

Similarly, in *Dickinson v Dodds* (1876) 2 Ch D 463, the defendant offered to sell some houses to the claimant for £800 and promised to keep the offer open until the following Friday. On the Thursday, the defendant accepted an offer from a third party to buy the buildings and (effectively) withdrew the offer through a friend. The claimant promptly "accepted" the original offer and then sought specific performance of the agreement. He was unsuccessful. The offer had been revoked, even though the purported acceptance occurred before the stipulated Friday deadline.

As suggested above, *Dickinson v Dodds* is also authority for the notion that an offer can be withdrawn via a "reliable" third party (in this case, the friend), rather than just by the offeror. In this, it differs from an acceptance, which can only be made by an offeree or his authorised agent: *Powell v Lee* (1908) 99 LT 284. (A school manager, acting without authority, could not accept a job applicant's offer to become headmaster). Who is a "reliable" person is a question of fact for the courts to determine. To take an extreme example, a severely mentally disturbed drug addict, who had a merely nodding acquaintanceship with the offeror, would probably not have this status. A neighbour and close friend, who was also a well-respected local bank manager, might well do.

Furthermore, *Dickinson v Dodds* is authority for the proposition that an offer can be revoked by implication, that is by conveying information that is incompatible with any other possibility, even though the revocation is not expressly enunciated, and was not necessarily intended. In this case, the friend simply told Mr Dickinson that the houses in the offer had already been sold to someone else. He did not say that the offer had been "revoked", but this was implicit in the information provided. Again, whether this has occurred is a question of fact for the courts. If an offeror is selling something that is (almost) unique, such as real estate or a particular painting by an old master, its sale to a third party will have this effect; if it is commonplace, such as a barrel of beer, it might not (he could well have more than one of them).

## Options

An option is a contract to keep an offer in another proposed contract open for a designated period. It precludes early withdrawal during this time. For example, in *Mountford v Scott* [1975] 2 WLR 114 the defendant granted the claimant a six-month option to buy his house for £10,000, for which he was paid £1 (legally "sufficient" consideration). The defendant purported to withdraw the option before the agreed period had expired, but the claimant subsequently exercised the option. When the defendant refused to sell, he successfully sued for specific performance. Options play a very important role in the commercial world, as companies seek to insure against unexpected price increases in, for example, both hard and soft commodities. Thus, in 2021, Virgin Atlantic took a fortuitous gamble that oil prices would soar, which paid off when Russia went to war in Ukraine the following year. The airline had locked in fuel prices by taking an option on purchasing oil for the year at 90 a barrel. This meant that the company did not have to buy oil on the spot market, saving it many millions of pounds.[6]

## Rejection

A rejection kills the offer to which it is a response. Any subsequent "acceptance" will, at most, be a fresh offer, putting the ball into the original offeror's court, and allowing them to accept or reject it as they wish. For example, in *Grant v Bragg* [2009] EWCA Civ 1228, the Court of Appeal had to consider, inter alia, whether an offer had been destroyed by a rejection, so preventing a subsequent purported acceptance from producing a contract. The case involved negotiations between the claimant and defendant for the sale of the former's shareholding in a company. These had, primarily, been conducted in an exchange of emails between 30 January and 2 February 2007. The judge at first instance decided the offer had not been rejected, but the Court of Appeal overturned this decision. Lord Justice Neuberger concluded that the discussions in the emails indicated that the offer *had* been rejected: "In the second email, Mr Jenkins [an agent] records the fact that, in the conversation following the first email, which, it can be remembered, contains the offer, Mr Grant [the offeree] indicated that he was 'not ready to transfer [his] shares

6 Oliver Gill, "Virgin Atlantic plots British Airways blitz after oil bet pays off", *The Telegraph* (London), 13 March 2022.

based upon the Dixon Ward wording unless he could be shown plans, and that was unlikely to happen'". The indication by Mr Grant that he was "not ready to transfer" constituted a rejection of the offer.

### Counter-Offers

A counter-offer has the same effect on an offer as a rejection. For example, in *Hyde v Wrench* (1840) 49 ER 132 the defendant offered to sell a farm for £1,000. The claimant responded by offering £950, which the defendant refused. The claimant then sought to "accept" the original offer of £1,000. The defendant, who had changed his mind by then, refused to sell and the claimant brought an action for specific performance (usually available for contracts for real estate). He failed, as the court decided that there was no contract. The counter-offer had destroyed the original offer, so that it could no longer be accepted. For this reason, counter-offers warrant more detailed consideration.

An acceptance must mirror the original offer to be valid. This is the so-called mirror image rule, although the phrase is more commonly used in the United States than in England. Clearly, a simple assent, without more, such as "agreed", "done", or "yes" will do this if used as a response to an offer. However, any variation to the terms of an offer that are contained in a purported acceptance risks becoming a counter-offer.

For example, in *Jones v Daniel* [1894] 2 Ch 332, the defendant wrote to the claimant offering to purchase some of the latter's land at a set price. The claimant's solicitors wrote back "accepting" the offer and enclosing a copy of the contract for the defendant to sign. This contained several additional terms, governing significant matters, such as the size of the deposit, that the defendant had not mentioned in his original offer. The defendant eventually wrote declining to purchase the land. The claimant sought specific performance of the sale, arguing that the initial exchange of letters constituted a valid contract. This was rejected by the court, which decided that the claimant had made a counter-offer, not an acceptance.

Nevertheless, a mere request for information or for a clarification of the terms of the original offer will not constitute a counter-offer. Thus, in *Stevenson, Jaques, & Co v McLean* [1880] 5 QBD 346 the defendants offered to sell the claimants iron for "40s., nett cash, open till Monday". Shortly afterwards, the claimant sent the defendant a telegram asking whether he would "accept forty for delivery over two months, or if not, longest limit you would allow". The question subsequently arose as to whether this was a counter-offer that extinguished the defendant's original offer. Lush J held that the claimant's telegram was not a rejection of the offer but a "mere inquiry" about its terms, which had no legal effect. However, although the distinction between a counter-offer and a request for information is easy to state, it can sometimes be difficult to apply in practice, and to distinguish between the two.

## Effluxion of Time

Offers, even if not expressly revoked, will eventually die of old age or, as it is often termed, through the "effluxion of time", even if no limit has been set on them. How long this will take is a question of fact for the courts to determine. Several factors appear to influence this decision. Most important, how volatile are prices for the subject matter of the contract? The less stable they are, the shorter will be the period required for the offer to expire. An offer to sell highly perishable goods, such as ripe bananas, will die much faster than one to sell bricks. Similarly, if the subject matter of the offer is traded on a highly volatile market, the period might be correspondingly short. Other factors could include the manner in which the offer was made. Was it done in an urgent fashion, such as a midnight telephone call, when a swift acceptance might be expected, or by a letter sent by second-class post, where more time might be allowed?

For illustrative example, in *Ramsgate Victoria Hotel v Montefiore* (1866) LR 1 Ex 109, the defendant offered to purchase shares in the claimant company at a specified price. Almost six months later the claimant accepted this offer, by which time the value of the shares had fallen. The defendant had not formally withdrawn the offer but refused to proceed with the purchase. The court held that the offer was no longer open, as it had lapsed after a reasonable period of time had passed, without its being accepted, which was less than six months. For a more recent example can be considered *LJ Korbetis v Transgrain Shipping BV* [2005] EWHC 1345, in which a defendant's offer was held to have expired after several months had passed, so that it could not be accepted.

## Acceptance

An acceptance constitutes a clear and unequivocal agreement by words or conduct to an offer, which (objectively) indicates that the offeree intends to be bound by the offeror's terms. To use an academic definition, it is a "final and unqualified expression of assent to the terms of an offer".[7] When this occurs, the moment of contract also takes place. For example, in *Athena v Superdrug* [2019] EWHC 3503 (Comm), the court held that a simple two-email exchange amounted to a binding contractual agreement. In the exchange, Athena asked Superdrug to confirm that a stated minimum number of orders was being placed. Superdrug responded, saying "Please go ahead with the below…". Superdrug's argument that there was no contract was rejected. It was not in dispute that "the below" referred to a preceding email chain, including an email of 23 May, which constituted an offer; their response was an acceptance.

An acceptance can also be made by gesture. A hypothetical example of this was provided by Lord Briggs in *Wells (Respondent) v Devani (Appellant)* [2019] UKSC 4. The judge considered the situation of a door-to-door seller of brooms: "He rings the doorbell, proffers one of his brooms to the householder, and says 'one pound

7 Peel, *Treitel on the Law of Contract*, 13th edn., p. 17.

50'. The householder takes the broom, nods and reaches for his wallet. Plainly the parties have concluded a contract for the sale of the proffered broom, at a price of £1.50, immediately payable".

Unsurprisingly, no party can be bound by an "offer" of which they were unaware, as they cannot be deemed to have accepted it. Similarly, because an offeree must be aware of the offer that he purports to accept, so-called cross-offers do not produce contracts. For example, in *Tinn v Hoffman* (1873) 29 LT 271, Hoffman wrote to Tinn offering to sell him 800 tons of iron and asking for a reply by post. At about the same time, but before he received Hoffman's letter, Tinn sent an offer with almost the same terms to Hoffman (they crossed in the post). The court found that a contract had not been created, not least because there had been no acceptance. There were two separate offers, one of which had to be accepted to produce an agreement. In like manner, performing a requested act in a unilateral contract, of which the performer is unaware, is not a valid acceptance (see below).

### Communication of Acceptance

Acceptance must normally be communicated to the offeror. As Lord Justice Lindley observed in *Carlill v Carbolic Smoke Ball Co* [1893] 1 QB 256, "Unquestionably, as a general proposition, when an offer is made, it is necessary in order to make a binding contract, not only that it should be accepted, but that the acceptance should be notified". This will usually be to the offeror or his agent. In the same case, Bowen LJ observed that "as an ordinary rule of law, an acceptance of an offer ought to be notified to the person who makes the offer, in order that the two minds may come together". This also usually decides where a contract is deemed to have been formed. As Birkett LJ noted in *Entores Limited v Miles Far East Corporation* [1955] 2 QB 327, when it comes to bilateral contracts, an acceptance of an offer must be communicated to the offeror and "the place where the contract is made is the place where the offeror receives the notification of the acceptance by the offeree".

### Stipulated Method of Acceptance

If the offeror has expressly stipulated the form by which it must be accepted (letter, etc.) and made it clear that no other means can be used, it will normally have to be accepted by the specified means to be effective. However, if he has stipulated a method of acceptance but not made it clear that *only* this method can be employed, a "no less advantageous" (to the offeror) means of acceptance might be effective: *Manchester Diocesan Council for Education v Commercial and General Investments Ltd* [1969] 3 All ER 1593. For example, in *Yates v Pulleyn* [1975] EWCA Civ J0224-4, an option to buy land was granted to the claimant, this being exercisable by notice sent by "registered or recorded delivery post". The claimant sent a letter via normal post, which was duly received by the defendant, who then refused to accept it as valid on the basis that it had not been communicated in the exact way required. The Court of Appeal held that it was valid, there being no disadvantage to the offeror, as the original method had been stipulated to ensure delivery, and that had happened via the normal postal system. The stipulation was directory, not mandatory.

Even so, an offeror cannot stipulate that the offeree's silence will amount to an acceptance. In *Felthouse v Bindley* (1862) 142 ER 1037, a nephew discussed buying a horse from his uncle. They reached a provisional agreement, but there was then a dispute as to whether they had settled on a price of 30 pounds or 30 guineas (31 pounds and ten shillings). Eventually, Paul Felthouse (the uncle) suggested that they halve the difference and wrote to his nephew stating that "if I hear no more about him, I consider this horse mine for £30 15s". The nephew did not respond to this offer but intended to accept it. He told an auctioneer, Mr. Bindley, not to include the animal with a batch of others that he (the nephew) was selling. Bindley subsequently forgot this instruction and sold the horse at auction to another man for £33. The uncle then sued Bindley in the tort of conversion, stating that he had sold his (Paul's) horse. This would only be the case if there was a contract between uncle and nephew, which in its turn required an agreement, which was absent. It was held that there was no contract, even though the nephew intended to sell the horse to his uncle.

### Exceptions to Communication of Acceptance

There are three exceptions to the general rule requiring communication of acceptance: acceptance in unilateral contracts, acceptance by conduct, and cases where the postal rule of acceptance applies.

#### 1. Unilateral Contracts

In unilateral contracts there is no requirement that the offeree communicate an intention to accept, since acceptance is through full performance. Thus, the Court of Appeal held that Mrs Carlill was entitled to the "Smoke Ball" reward as the advertisement constituted an offer in a unilateral contract which she had accepted by fulfilling the requirements stated, namely by contracting influenza after having used the ball three times daily for two weeks according to the printed directions supplied with each ball, even though she had not communicated acceptance to the Smoke Ball Company: *Carlill v Carbolic Smoke Ball Co* [1893] 1 QB 256. Unilateral contracts are dealt with more fully below.

#### 2. Acceptance by Conduct

A bilateral contract can be accepted by the conduct of the offeree, provided that, as a matter of objective analysis, it is deemed sufficient to indicate assent to proposed terms. For example, in *Brogden* v *Metropolitan Railway Co* (1877) 2 App Cas 666, the claimant supplied coal from Wales to the defendant railway company in London. Initially, they dealt using purely verbal agreements, but eventually decided to draw up a formal written contract. The defendant produced a draft agreement and sent it to the claimant. The latter made some minor amendments, effectively turning it into a counter-offer, signed it, and sent it back to the defendant. The latter then filed it without expressly communicating an acceptance. However, the claimant continued supplying coal, and this was accepted by the defendant in accordance with the terms of the new agreement. Subsequently a dispute arose, and the validity of the written contract was challenged. It was held that it was binding; the acceptance was made by performing the contract without objection to the terms in the written agreement, albeit not by the "mere private act" of putting the letter into a drawer.

More recently, this issue was considered again in *Reveille Independent LLC v Anotech International (UK) Ltd* [2016] EWCA Civ 443. In this case, the Court of Appeal upheld the Commercial Court's decision that a party had accepted the terms of a draft written agreement by subsequent conduct, which sufficiently indicated assent to its terms, even though it had not signed the relevant document and although the draft expressly stated that it was only binding when signed. Of course, in most situations, the offeror will be aware of the conduct that constitutes acceptance.

### 3. The "Postal Rule" of Acceptance

In *Entores Limited v Miles Far East Corporation* [1955] 2 QB 327, the postal rule of acceptance was identified as an important exception to the general situation when it comes to acceptance in bilateral contracts. Under the "rule", a letter of acceptance takes effect as soon as it is put into a post box or handed to a postal worker authorised to receive it, and where that occurs--for example, where the post box is situated--is also deemed to be the place where the contract is made. It should be noted that most postmen are authorised to deliver but not to receive mail: *Re London & Northern Bank, Ex P. Jones* [1900] 1 CH 220.

The postal rule is sometimes called the "Rule in Adams v Lindsell" after the case in which it originated. In *Adams v Lindsell* (1818) 106 ER 250 the defendant wrote to the claimant on 2 September, offering to sell them wool and asking for a reply by post. Delivery of this letter was delayed until 5 September. The claimants posted their acceptance on the same day, but it, too, was delayed, and not received until 9 September. However, on 8 September the defendants had sold their wool to somebody else. It was held that a contract had been made on the 5th, when the acceptance was posted, so that the defendants were in breach of contract when they failed to honour this agreement. The rule extended to telegrams and tele-messages, both of which are now of very little significance, but not (it seems) to other forms of electronic communication, including emails (see below).

The rationale for the "postal rule" has been a matter of some debate. A few observers have stressed commercial expediency. However, in *Byrne & Co v Leon Van Tien Hoven & Co* [1880] 5 CPD 344, Lindley J suggested, like several others before him, that it existed because the offeror "has made the post office his agent to receive the acceptance and notification of it". Whether either rationale is entirely satisfactory as an explanation is questionable, and it may be best to view it as an anomalous historical peculiarity, one that has now been abandoned by several foreign common law systems.

## Applies to Acceptance Only

It should be stressed that the postal rule applies only to acceptance. Revocation cannot be brought about by posting a letter containing a withdrawal of offer, which is effective only on receipt: *Byrne & Co v Leon Van Tienhoven & Co* [1880] 5 CPD 344. In this case, Van Tienhoven sent a letter from their office in Cardiff to Byrne in New York, on 1 October, offering to sell 1,000 boxes of tin plate at a certain price. A week later, on 8 October, Van Tienhoven posted another letter, withdrawing their offer, because tin plate prices had increased in the meantime, making it insufficiently profitable. The first letter arrived with Byrne on 11 October, and they immediately telegraphed an acceptance (the postal rule applies to telegrams), *before* the withdrawal arrived (but three days after it had been posted). Van Tienhoven & Co subsequently attempted to avoid the contract by relying on their posting of a revocation before Byrne and Co's receipt and acceptance of their offer. Lindley J held that although it was settled that, where an offer was accepted by post, the resulting contract was completed the moment it was posted, this principle was "inapplicable to the case of the withdrawal of an offer". The letter of 8 October was effective only when it was received in New York, by which time it was too late, as acceptance had already occurred. A similar decision was reached when a letter (not a telegram) was involved in *Henthorn v Fraser* [1892] 2 Ch 27.

## Not Always Operative

It is also clear that the postal rule will not *always* apply to an acceptance made by post. For example, it can be expressly or impliedly excluded. The former would merely require a short clause in the offer stipulating that the rule was not operative. An example of the latter can be seen in *Holwell Securities v Hughes* [1974] 1 WLR 155. In this case, Hughes granted Holwell an option to purchase his house, to be exercisable "by notice in writing" within six months. Five days before the six months was up, Holwell posted a letter exercising the option. However, this letter was never received by Hughes. Nevertheless, Holwell sought to enforce the option, on the basis that there was a valid acceptance when the letter was posted, something that happened before expiry of the time limit. In some ways, this would be similar to the situation in *Household Fire Insurance v Grant* [1879] 4 Ex D 216 (see below). However, in the instant case, Holwell failed. By requiring "notice in writing", Hughes had effectively specified that he had to physically receive the letter and so had impliedly excluded the postal rule. As Russell LJ noted, the language made clear that the usual contractual principle that acceptance must be received applied.

Furthermore, the postal rule will not apply where it is not reasonable to use the post as a medium of communication. As Lord Herschell noted in *Henthorn v Fraser* [1892] 2 Ch 27, it is only: "Where the circumstances are such that it must have been within the contemplation of the parties that, according to the ordinary usages of mankind, the post might be used as a means of communicating the acceptance of an offer, [that] the acceptance is complete as soon as it is posted". In this case, it was held that the postal rule applied, as it was reasonable to use a letter, and so within the contemplation of the parties objectively determined. However, this will not always be the case.

This is a question of fact for the court to decide. Much will depend on the subject matter of the contract and the urgency of the offer. If a man is telephoned in the middle of the night with an offer for a very volatile or perishable commodity, such as ripe bananas, an acceptance by post might well not lead to an application of the postal rule. Less drastically, in *Quenerduaine v Cole* (1883) 32 WR 185, an offer was sent by telegram. The offeree sent his acceptance by letter. It was held that, on the facts of the case, the postal rule did not apply, as it was not reasonable to accept by letter; in the circumstances, an offer made by almost instantaneous means (by the standards of the Victorian era) implied that an equally quick acceptance was required. That an offer was, itself, made by post will often be the firmest indication that acceptance by post, with the postal rule applying, is reasonable.

Additionally, in *Holwell Securities Ltd v Hughes*, Lawton LJ accepted that the postal rule "probably does not operate if its application would produce manifest inconvenience and absurdity". Thus, it is generally thought that the rule requires that the letter of acceptance is not incorrectly addressed due to the fault of the offeree and carries the right value in postage stamps. The rule will not apply if it is the sender's fault that the letter did not arrive. Although it involved a misdirected fax (to which the postal rule does not apply), this was the position reached in the broadly analogous situation in *LJ Korbetis v Transgrain Shipping BV* [2005] EWHC 1345.

An illustration of the strictness and potential harshness of the postal rule of acceptance, where operative, can be seen in *Household Fire Insurance v Grant* [1879] 4 Ex D 216. Grant applied by post for 100 shares in the Household Fire Insurance company, this being an offer. The latter allotted shares to him, and posted a letter informing him of this, this being the acceptance. Unfortunately, it was lost in the post. As a result, Grant did not pay for the shares. Sometime later, Household Fire went bankrupt. A liquidator was appointed and sought to identify all of the company's assets. He noticed that a cheque from Grant was outstanding and asked for payment for the now almost worthless shares. Grant refused to pay as he felt that there was no contract. However, at first instance, the court held that the liquidator was entitled to recover this money, as there was a binding agreement between the two parties, and this decision was upheld on appeal (Lord Justice Bramwell dissenting). The postal rule, where operative, applied even though the letter of acceptance letter did not reach Grant.

A strict application of the postal rule would also mean that retraction of a postal acceptance would not be effective if it reached the offeror *before* he received the letter of acceptance (as might be the case if it was sent by email or communicated orally). This was the position reached in the New Zealand breach of promise case of *Wenkheim v Arndt* (1873) 1 JR 73. There is a dearth of English authority on this point, and it has sometimes been criticised, while the rather unclear Scottish case of *Countess of Dunmore v Alexander* (1830) 9 Shaw 190 *might* lend some, albeit limited, support to such critics, and to a contrary view.

Overall, the position reached in *Wenkheim v Arndt* seems preferable, not least because it would be possible to envisage a situation in which any alternative analysis could be abused. For example, an offeree could accept an offer by second-class post in a fluctuating market (if this was deemed acceptable by the court) and then withdraw it the following day by an instant method of communication, before it arrived, if this seemed to his benefit. However, it could also be argued, following *Holwell Securities Ltd v Hughes*, that a strict application of the rule in these circumstances might sometimes produce absurdity, while it is also the case that there is some academic support for a more flexible approach.[8]

**Electronic Communications**

The postal rule does not apply to instantaneous forms of electronic documentary acceptance, such as those made by telex or facsimile. Thus, in *Entores v Miles Far East Corporation* [1955] 2 QB 327, the claimant sent a telex message from England offering to buy 100 tons of cathodes from the defendants in Holland. The defendant sent back a telex to the claimant's London office accepting that offer. The question for the court was at what point the contract came into existence. If acceptance was effective at the time the telex was sent, the contract was made in Holland and Dutch law would apply. If the acceptance took place when the telex was received in London, then the contract would be governed by English law. The Court of Appeal held that, to be effective, acceptance needed to be communicated to the offeree, so that the contract was made in England (where this occurred), not when it was sent.

A little more controversially, but very significantly, in *Thomas & Anor v BPE Solicitors (A Firm)* [2010] EWHC 306 (Ch), Blair J concluded that, contrary to the claimants' submissions, the postal rule was also inapplicable to emails, "[I]n my view the same principle [as for telex] applies to communication by email, at least where the parties are conducting the matter by email". This is now the generally accepted, if sometimes criticised, position, and has been matched in other common law jurisdictions, such as Singapore. In these situations, the contract is only complete when the acceptance is "received" by the offeror and (as is the general situation) is made where received, even though emails may, occasionally, take a short time to reach their recipient.

In *Brinkibon Ltd v Stahag Stahl GmbH* [1983] 2 AC 34 the House of Lords considered the wider impact of electronic means of communication on the formation of contracts. Brinkibon was an English company that bought steel from Austrian-based Stahag, using telex to send their acceptance of an offer from the latter. Their Lordships decided that this contract was formed in Vienna (place) when the

8 See A. Hudson, "Retraction of Letters of Acceptance", *Law Quarterly Review*, v. 82, (1966), p. 169.

telex acceptance was received (time). However, Lord Wilberforce noted that such situations could be complicated by messages being sent or received out of normal office hours, such as at night; a malfunction at the recipient's end which prevents receipt at the time contemplated by the sender; or the message having been sent or received through machines operated by third parties. In these (and some other) situations, the judge felt, "No universal rule can cover all such cases; they must be resolved by reference to the intentions of the parties, by sound business practice and in some cases by a judgement where the risks should lie".

**Constructive Receipt**

As Lord Wilberforce's comments above indicate, receipt itself can be problematic in an electronic context. Does it mean when the offeror reads it, or when it is available to be read? It appears that, at least when commercial bodies are involved, the courts favour a notion of constructive receipt, by which instantaneous or electronic forms of communication that arrive at business premises during normal working hours are taken to have been communicated to the recipient shortly after arriving, even if the recipient is not aware of the message or has not read it.

For example, in *Tenax Steamship Co v Owners of the Motor Vessel Brimnes* [1975] QB 929, the Court of Appeal decided that a communication of the withdrawal of an offer by telex sent to commercial premises was effective when it *could* have been read, rather than when it was in fact read. In this case, although the notice of withdrawal had been sent during ordinary business hours, the trial judge had been driven to the conclusion that the charterers' staff had either left the office early, well before the usual 6.30 pm, or that they had neglected to pay attention to their telex machine in the way that they claimed was their normal practice. As a result, he decided that the withdrawal telex must be regarded as having been "received" when it arrived at 5.45 pm, and that the withdrawal was effective at that time. The Court of Appeal, Edmund-Davies L.J. presiding, expressly supported this conclusion.

More recently, in *Mondial Shipping & Chartering BV v Astarte Shipping* BV [1995] 2 Lloyd's Rep 249, the charter (hire) party of a motor vessel named the *Pamela* required that the charterers pay the hire-fees on set dates. If they failed to do this, the owners of the vessel could give them 48 hours' notice of their failure. If the charterers had still failed to pay within that time, the owners could reclaim the vessel. When the first fee fell due, the charterers failed to pay. They were sent a notice, and duly paid within the 48-hour period. The next instalment was due on a Friday. Again, the owners sent a notice, the telex arriving at 11 pm that day. The charterers did not pay within 48 hours, and the vessel was reclaimed. There was a dispute as to whether the owners' notice was valid. The High Court concluded that the telex could only be "received" by the charterers during business hours. As the telex was sent outside such hours, the charterers received it at 9 am on Monday (the start of the next working day). Had it been sent on a Thursday evening it would have been received at 9 am on Friday.

Such an analysis would apply not just to a message sent by telex but also to an email or a message left on an answerphone. Of course, there can still be a debate as to what are normal office hours, as was the situation with a 6 pm email in *Thomas & Anor v BPE Solicitors (A Firm)* [2010] EWHC 306 (Ch). In this case, the email was deemed to have been received at 6 pm as this was held to be within normal office hours, even though the intended recipient had, in fact, already gone home. It is also uncertain how far the notion of constructive receipt applies to private contracts or even commercial agreements in which the messages are not sent to business premises.

## Battle of the Forms

Unsurprisingly, the parties to a negotiated contract, especially one that is made on a commercial basis, often wish to conclude an agreement on their own standard terms. If the contract goes to litigation, this can create a so-called battle of the forms as each argues that their own terms, contained in an exchanged series of contractual documents, acting as counter-offers, should take priority. The battle is usually won by the party who fired the "last shot" in the negotiations--that is, the last party who put forward terms that were not rejected, expressly or by implication, by the recipient: *Entores v Miles Far East Corporation* [1955] 2 QB 327. More recently, in *Transformers & Rectifiers Ltd v Needs Ltd* [2015] EWHC 269 (TCC), Edwards-Stuart J observed, "Where A makes an offer on its conditions and B accepts that offer on its conditions and, without more, performance follows, the correct analysis, assuming that each party's conditions have been reasonably drawn to the attention of the other, is that there is a contract on B's conditions".

The result of a battle of the forms can be enormously significant. For example, in *Trebor Bassett Holdings Ltd and The Cadbury UK Partnership v ADT Fire and Security plc* [2012] EWCA Civ 1158, Cadbury moved their popcorn production to a new factory and contracted with ADT to install a fire-suppression system. A fire subsequently broke out, and the building was destroyed. Cadbury claimed that ADT's failure to design an adequate system had caused losses that amounted to £110 million. However, ADT claimed that the contract had been entered on their standard terms and conditions which limited their liability to £13,000. At trial, the court had to resolve a "battle of the forms" and adopted a traditional "offer and acceptance" analysis.

ADT had provided a quotation to Cadbury in August 2003, offering to supply the suppression system for £9,000, but stating that it was subject to their standard terms and conditions, although a copy of these was not supplied. In September 2003, Trebor issued a purchase order accepting ADT's quotation. The purchase order stated that the contract was subject to Cadbury's standard terms and conditions which were "already supplied" and that additional copies were available "on request". Using the offer-and-acceptance analysis, ADT's quotation was an offer based on their standard terms and conditions; Cadbury's purchase order was a counteroffer based on their standard terms and conditions; by commencing work on the suppression system, ADT had accepted Cadbury's counteroffer. With no evidence to suggest otherwise, the last document in time (before work commenced), the purchase order, prevailed, so incorporating Cadbury's standard terms.

## Tenders

The general rule, as expounded in *Spencer v Harding* (1870) LR 5 CP 561, is that inviting tenders to be submitted, without any undertaking to accept the most competitive bid, is not an offer that can be "accepted". Instead, it is an invitation to treat. It is normally the tender that constitutes the offer, one that can then be accepted or rejected by the counterparty as they wish. In this case, the defendant sent out a circular asking for tenders for a large amount of stock warehoused at their Milk Street premises in London, which was to be sold as a single lot. The claimant sent in a tender, which turned out to be the highest of those submitted. Even so, the defendants refused to sell him the stock. Willes J held that the circular was merely an invitation to gather tenders. The absence of any specific wording, such as "and we undertake to sell to the highest bidder", rebutted any notion that the defendants had intended to be contractually bound by any tenders submitted.

Nevertheless, in certain circumstances an invitation for tenders *can* be an offer in a separate (or collateral) unilateral contract that is accepted by making the appropriate tender. In *Blackpool & Fylde Aero Club v Blackpool BC* [1990] 1 WLR 1196, the Court of Appeal decided that, in some situations, a request for tenders might impliedly include an offer in a collateral contract that the requestor would, at least, give due consideration to any timely bid, even if they did not accept it. In this case, Blackpool Borough Council, which ran Blackpool Airport, had licensed a single company to run pleasure flights to and from the airport. Blackpool & Fylde Aero Club had held this licence since 1975. In 1983 the existing licence was due to expire, and the council sent letters to seven organisations, including the Aero Club, inviting tenders, in a (complicated) designated form, for the licence to operate aircraft from the airport. The invitation required that the tender be at the Town Hall not later than 12 noon on a specified date. Three organisations replied.

The Aero Club sent in a significantly higher bid than the other two and placed their offer in the Town Hall letter box at 11 am on the specified date, an hour before the deadline. Unfortunately, the Town Clerk's staff failed to empty the letter box at 12 noon, as they were expected to do, the letter was not picked up until after the deadline, and so was not considered to have been "delivered" in time. As a result, the Aero Club tender was not considered. The licence was granted to one of the other bidders, Red Rose Helicopters. The council subsequently realised it had made a mistake, and considered running the tendering process again, but Red Rose Helicopters, which had taken legal advice, informed the council that they were contractually bound to grant them the licence.

The Aero Club then successfully sued the council for compensation in the High Court and the latter's appeal failed. The Court of Appeal held that while the party inviting tenders need not accept the highest tender, or indeed any tender, where tenders were solicited from selected parties and the local authority's invitation prescribed a clear, orderly, and familiar procedure, including the supply of special envelopes to preserve the anonymity of tenderers, these being subject to a strict deadline, the invitee was protected to the extent that if he submitted a conforming tender before that deadline he was "entitled, not as a matter of mere expectation but of contractual right, to be sure that his tender will after the deadline be opened and considered in conjunction with all other conforming tenders or at least that his tender will be considered if others are". The council's invitation to tender was, to this limited extent, an offer, and the club's submission of a conforming tender an acceptance (in a unilateral contract). Stocker LJ made clear that, "This would not preclude or inhibit the defendants from deciding not to accept any tender or to award the concession, provided the decision was bona fide and honest, to any tenderer. The obligation was that the claimants' tender would be before the deciding body for consideration before any award was made".

## Referential Bids

In *Harvela Investments Ltd. v Royal Trust of Canada (CI) Ltd.* [1986] 1 AC 207, the House of Lords concluded that referential bids, that is bids that are contingent and referenced to another bid, were invalid. In this case, Royal Trust (RT) owned shares in another company and invited bids for these securities. Of great significance, RT undertook to accept the highest compliant bid, so that the invitation for bids was an offer (unlike a normal invitation for tenders), that would be accepted by the submission of the highest bid. Harvela bid 2,175,000, while the business magnate Sir Leonard Outerbridge bid "2,100,000 or 101,000 in excess of any other offer expressed as a fixed monetary amount, whichever is higher." RT accepted Sir Leonard's bid as being 2,276,000 (Harvela's bid plus 101,000). Harvela then sued RT, arguing that such a referential bid was invalid. The Court of Appeal held in favour of RT, on the basis that expressing a fixed amount (the 2,100,000) along with the referential element made it valid. However, the House of Lords unanimously reversed this decision. Lord Templeman, citing *South Hetton Coal Co. v Haswell, Shotton and Easington Coal and Coke Co.* [1898] 1 Ch. 465, noted that it was illogical to say that Sir Leonard's unsuccessful but valid bid of 2,100,000 transformed his referential bid. The essence of sealed competitive bidding was the submission of independent, self-contained bids, and fair compliance to the process. Harvela had made the highest valid bid.

## Auctions

In *Payne v Cave* (1789) 3 TR 148, it was held that an auctioneer's request for bids was an invitation to treat, not an offer. This was reiterated in *British Car Auctions v Wright* [1972] 1 WLR 1519. The offer came from the bidder and was accepted by the auctioneer (as agent for the owner of the item being sold) by the fall of his hammer, gavel or other customary instrument (so forming a bilateral contract between owner and bidder). This has now been codified in s.57(2) of the Sale of Goods Act 1979.

Nevertheless, advertising an auction does not normally oblige the auctioneer to hold it. In *Harris v Nickerson* [1873] LR 8 QB 286, the defendant advertised a sale by auction of office furniture over a three-day period. The sale of furniture on the final day was withdrawn. The claimant attended the auction but was unsuccessful when he sued the defendant for breach of contract in not holding the sale, seeking to recover his expenditure in getting there and attendant expenses.

More significantly, in *Warlow v Harrison* [1859] 1 E & E 309, the majority of the Court of Exchequer Chamber concluded that, where an auctioneer put property up for sale "without reserve", he (personally) made a contract (separate to the contract of sale) with the highest *bona fide* bidder to sell to them. This case involved the sale of three horses without reserve. The claimant bid 60 guineas for one of the animals; another person, who, it transpired, was the horse's owner (not a *bona fide* bidder), immediately bid 61 guineas. The claimant, having been informed of the provenance of this bid, claimed that he was entitled to the horse. When this was denied, he sued the auctioneer. Although he failed on technical grounds, the Court of Exchequer Chamber held that, if the pleadings were appropriately amended, the claimant would be entitled to succeed on a retrial. Turner LJ observed that, "if an auctioneer says that a sale is without reserve, everyone must understand from that statement that no bidding is to be made on behalf of persons interested in the estate".

In *Barry v Davies* [2000] 1 WLR 1962, the Court of Appeal followed *Warlow v Harrison*, concluding that, in these situations, there was a collateral unilateral contract (to the contract of sale) between the auctioneer and the highest genuine bidder. This involved an offer by the auctioneer (not the owner of the item being sold) to sell to the highest bidder, which was accepted when the bid was made. An auctioneer could not then withdraw the sale because the price reached was too low. The measure of damages for a breach of this contract, was, prima facie, the difference between the bid value and the current market value of the goods, as also provided for in s.51(3) of the Sale of Goods Act 1979.

In *Barry v Davies* the lot consisted of two new Alan Smart engine analysers that were being sold by the Customs and Excise. The price of new machines of this type purchased from the manufacturers was about £14,000 each. Customs and Excise had instructed the auctioneer that the machines were to be sold without reserve, and he accepted them for sale on that basis. This was reiterated by the auctioneer to the claimant before he bid for the machines. His bid of £200 for each machine was the only one received. Even so, the auctioneer then withdrew the machines from the sale, on the basis that the bid was too low. The claimant successfully claimed the difference between the value of the machines, said to be about £28,000, and the bid of £400. (But see also Chapter 15 on this point.)

## Unilateral Contracts

Most (but not all) binding agreements are bilateral contracts, in which both parties come under a legal obligation. By contrast, a unilateral contract consists of an offer in exchange for an act, in which the act is both the acceptance and the consideration for the promise. Thus, one of the parties in a unilateral contract (the offeree) always provides purely executed consideration, as it is complete when the contract is made. (See Chapter 2 on the consideration aspect.) A unilateral contract is so called because only one party, the offeror, ever comes under a legal obligation. For example, if I offer £100 to anyone who returns my lost dog, Fido, to my home at 123 Acacia Avenue, when you appear at my door with Fido you have both accepted my offer and provided (executed) consideration for it. You are never under an obligation to look for and return Fido, even if you come across the dog while out walking, but, if you do, I am under an obligation to pay the reward.

In the celebrated Court of Appeal case of *Carlill v Carbolic Smoke Ball Co* [1893] 1 QB 256, the defendant placed a newspaper advertisement offering a £100 reward to anyone who contracted influenza after using their carbolic smoke ball three times a day for two weeks, in accordance with the directions supplied with each ball; essentially this required sniffing it. Mrs Carlill, the claimant, purchased some smoke balls and used them according to the directions but still caught flu. She then claimed the £100 promised. (That her husband was a solicitor reduced her litigation costs.) The defendant argued that there was no contract, for a variety of reasons, all of which were rejected by the Court of Appeal. The court held that Mrs Carlill was entitled to the money, as the advertisement constituted an offer in a unilateral contract which she had accepted by performing the conditions set out in that offer. In such contracts there is no requirement that the offeree communicate an intention to accept.

Many, but very far from all, offers in unilateral contracts are made to the world. Foremost amongst these are the so-called reward cases, in which offers are contained in advertisements that can be seen by any number of people, as in *Shuey v United States*, 92 U.S. 73 (1875). However, this is not necessarily the case. For example, the unilateral offer in *Errington v Errington and Woods* [1952] 1 KB 290 was made to two people, and others have been made to just one individual. A very important factor is that some of the rules and presumptions normally found in bilateral contracts do not apply to unilateral contracts. Thus, in the former, advertisements are usually considered to be invitations to treat, but in unilateral contracts they will normally be viewed as offers which are capable of acceptance, as was the case in *Carlill v Carbolic Smoke Ball Co*. The rules on revocation are also different (see below).

In most cases, the designated act asked for by such an offer, such as walking to York for £100, is performed as a conscious response to the offer. Nevertheless, this is not necessary, *provided* the acceptor is aware of the offer when he performs the act. In *Williams v Carwardine* (1833) 4 B. & Ad. 621 Mrs Williams claimed a reward of £20 offered by Mr Carwardine for providing information that led to the arrest of her husband for murdering Carwardine's brother. She did not do this immediately after she became aware of the reward. However, a while after the killing, following severe physical abuse from her husband, and fearing that she might die, she decided to give the requisite information to the authorities to "ease her conscience, and in hopes of forgiveness hereafter". This led to the conviction of her spouse and another man.

Unexpectedly, Mrs Williams made a full recovery and decided to claim the reward. Carwardine refused to pay, claiming that she was not induced by the reward to provide the information. At the trial of the issue at *nisi prius* (civil jurisdiction) at assizes it was found that she knew about the reward, but that she did not give information to secure it. Even so, Parke J held that she was entitled to the £20. The matter was referred to King's Bench, which upheld his decision. Two of the three judges sitting expressly stated that motive (unlike knowledge) was irrelevant in such cases. Mr. Justice Littledale opined that "[i]f the person knows of the handbill and does the thing, that is quite enough. It does not say, whoever will come forward in consequence of this handbill".

However, *Williams v Carwardine* was distinguished by the High Court of Australia, on appeal from the Full Court of Western Australia, in *R v Clarke* (1927) 40 CLR 227, in which a reward was offered for information that led to the conviction of those responsible for the murder of two policemen. Clarke, an experienced criminal, gave information that led to several arrests and subsequent convictions. His motive in giving evidence was to clear himself of the murders after he became a prime suspect in the killings. Only after the conviction of the true murderers did Clarke think of claiming the reward. It was held that he did not act "in reliance upon the offer or with the intention of entering into any contract". However, this would make the situation the same as that involving Mrs Carwardine. More pertinently, Higgins J decided that he had completely forgotten the offer of reward when he provided the information, unlike Mrs Carwardine, and "ignorance of the offer is the same thing whether it is due to never hearing of it or forgetting it after hearing". This was rather a nice distinction, perhaps best explained on policy grounds, and merely of persuasive authority in England.

### Constructive Revocation of Offers in Unilateral Contracts

The ability to make an offer to the world in unilateral contracts raises potential problems when it comes to their revocation. Unlike an offer in a bilateral contract, it is impossible to know who has seen such an offer when it is set out in a newspaper or handbill etc., and so can accept it by performing the sought-after act. This means that it would be impossible to communicate a revocation to all such persons, even if it was remotely practicable (often not the case where millions have seen an offer). The law gets around this problem by using the notion of constructive revocation.

In *Shuey v United States* (1875) 92 U.S. 73, it was held that where the offer of a reward in a unilateral contract had been made by public proclamation, it could be withdrawn (before it had been accepted) through the same channel and in the same manner as that in which it was made, even if not seen by someone who had been aware of the original offer. The case involved a reward of $25,000 that had been advertised in newspapers in April 1865 for the capture of one or more of those involved in the assassination of President Lincoln. In November 1865, the new President had an order revoking the reward published in the same fashion, at which time at least one fugitive was still at large. This was deemed to be effective, and the fact that the claimant of such reward was ignorant of its withdrawal, as was the situation when he subsequently provided information leading to the renegade's arrest, was irrelevant. Although this is an American case, it is considered by almost all commentators to be the situation that prevails in England and Wales.

### Timing of Revocation in Unilateral Offers

If strictly implemented, the normal rule of revocation in bilateral contracts--that it can be done at any point until acceptance--could occasion problems when it comes to unilateral contracts. As Goff LJ noted in *obiter* comments in *Dahlia v Four Millbank Nominees* [1978] Ch 231, in a unilateral contract the offeror is entitled to insist on full performance of the condition that he has imposed--whether finding a lost cat or walking to York--and short of that would not be bound. It is complete performance of the act that constitutes acceptance. However, as he also noted, allowing the offeror to withdraw their offer at any point until acceptance could create injustice in these situations. For example, suppose that I promise someone that, if they swim from Calais to Dover, I will give them £1,000. They are not entitled to the money if they give up 100 metres from Dover Harbour and finish the journey in a boat, but they would understandably be quite aggrieved if I shouted a revocation from the walls of the harbour at that distance while they were still swimming.

This issue was considered in *Errington v Errington Woods* [1952] 1 KB 290. In this case, a man purchased a house, in his own name, for his son and daughter-in-law to live in. He promised the couple that, if they paid the mortgage instalments, he would transfer the house to them when it was entirely paid off (an example of a unilateral offer to specific individuals rather than the world). They did not commit to doing so, but simply moved in and started making the payments. The owner of the house died, and his wife inherited the property. His son later went to live with his mother, but his wife, the dead father's daughter-in-law, refused to do so, and continued to pay the mortgage instalments. The mother then brought an action to evict the wife from the house. It was held that the woman was entitled to remain there. The father had made the couple a unilateral offer, which the wife was in the process of accepting by meeting the mortgage payments. Lord Denning held that, once performance had commenced, the mother could not revoke the unilateral offer, as doing so would be unconscionable. The daughter-in-law had to be given a reasonable opportunity to complete performance. What constituted embarking on performance and what was a reasonable opportunity was a question of fact for the court to decide. Subsequently, in *Dahlia v Four Millbank Nominees* [1978] Ch 231, Goff LJ suggested that in these situations there must be an "implied obligation on the part of the offeror not to prevent the condition becoming satisfied, which obligation it seems to me must arise as soon as the offeree starts to perform. Until then the offeror can revoke the whole thing, but once the offeree has embarked on performance it is too late for the offeror to revoke his offer".

Arguably, in such cases, there is an implied offer in a collateral contract to keep the offer open for a reasonable period, one that is accepted by embarking on performance, as in *Soulsbury v Soulsbury* [2007] EWCA Civ 969. In this case, it was held that the estate of the deceased former husband of the claimant was liable to pay her the £100,000 he had previously promised she would receive on his death if she did not enforce an order for periodical payments in her favour. Longmore LJ observed that it was a classic unilateral contract of the *Carlill v Carbolic Smoke Ball* type: "Once the promisee acts on the promise by inhaling the smoke ball, by starting the walk to York or (as here) by not suing for the maintenance to which she was entitled, the promissor cannot revoke or withdraw his offer. But there is no obligation on the promisee to continue to inhale, to walk the whole way to York or to refrain from suing. It is just that if she inhales no more, gives up the walk to York or does sue for her maintenance, she is not entitled to claim the promised sum".

# Chapter 2: Consideration and Promissory Estoppel

## Introduction

The presence of consideration is essential to the formation of a contract. Without it, an undertaking is not normally binding, becoming what is termed a bare promise or *nudum pactum*. For example, if I promise, whether verbally or in a letter, that I will give you £1,000, there is nothing (legally) preventing me from resiling from my promise and refusing to give you the money. The only way in which such a promise can be made legally binding, without the presence of consideration, would be for it to be made in a deed, this being a document that satisfies the requirements set out in section 1 of the Law of Property (Miscellaneous Provisions) Act 1989. In brief, this means that it must be in writing; make clear on its face that it is intended to be a deed (this might be done by the document describing itself as such); and be validly executed as a deed by the person making it, usually by signing the document, which signature must also be witnessed. (There is no longer any requirement that the document be "sealed".) However, if my promise to give you £1,000 is supported by consideration, it becomes enforceable, even if made verbally.

The doctrine appears to have developed as a way of distinguishing promises that were worthy of enforcement by the courts from those that were not. It is not found in most Roman law jurisdictions, such as Germany and France, which are more reliant on form(alities) to make promises binding. It has been the subject of some criticism over the years, by both legal academics and judges. For example, in *White v Jones* [1995] 2 AC 207, Lord Goff observed that the English law of contract was "perceived to be hampered by the presence of an unnecessary doctrine of consideration". However, it does, at least, help prevent casual promises from coming to court.

## Definition

The doctrine of consideration requires that, to produce a binding agreement, each party give or promise to give something of value in exchange for the other's promise. As a result, it has variously been described as the element of reciprocity, quid pro quo, mutuality, or bargain in a contract, or, as it is sometimes put, "the price on the other party's promise". In the leading case of *Currie v Misa* (1875) LR 10 Ex 153 Lush J defined it in the following terms: "A valuable consideration, in the sense of the law, may consist either of some right, interest, profit or benefit accruing to the one party, or some forbearance, detriment, loss or responsibility, given, suffered or undertaken by the other".

In practice, most contracts in developed market economies involve one party providing consideration in the form of money, and the other providing it in the form of goods or services. Thus, my promise to give you £1,000 tomorrow may not be enforceable, but if we agree that you will deliver a tanker of fuel oil in exchange for that sum, or will chop down my trees, it will become binding. Nevertheless, as Lush J's dictum also suggests, a huge range of things, going far beyond money or goods and services, can constitute valid consideration.

It is not necessary that the things tendered in the exchange be of even vaguely equal value. This is because the courts do not normally interfere with, or second-guess, the bargain made between the parties to a contract. As a result, in the words of an old maxim, consideration "must be sufficient but need not be adequate". In this context, "sufficient" means something that the law will recognise as capable of being consideration; "adequate" means "value for money". Some type of exchange must take place, but provided it is of value in the eyes of the law--which are not necessarily the same as those of the market--however small or nominal, it will be valid consideration.

This situation was illustrated in *Chappell & Co Ltd v Nestle Co Ltd* [1960] AC 87, in which a majority of the House of Lords held that the wrappers from 6d chocolate bars, although of almost no economic value, and despite being immediately thrown away by Nestlé (who requested them), were part of the consideration (and thus capable of being the whole consideration) in a promotion for a popular record. Lord Somervell observed: "It is said that when received the wrappers are of no value to Nestlé's. This I would have thought irrelevant. A contracting party can stipulate for what consideration he chooses. A peppercorn does not cease to be good consideration if it is established that the promisee does not like pepper and will throw away the corn".

As a result of these requirements, and as Lord Somervell's comment suggests, English law also saw the development of the notion of a "peppercorn rent". For example, a dying landlord wishing to provide a legally binding 12-month lease of a piece of land to a friend, in what is essentially a gift, rather than an easily revocable licence that may not be honoured by his children, can make it contingent on a peppercorn rental being paid for the property. Although a peppercorn is only worth a penny or so, it has *some* value, and so is sufficient, albeit, of course, not adequate, for such a rental. Historically, peppercorns were joined by other items of nominal worth such as a single red rose to be given on quarter days. More specifically, the rental for the Billingsgate fish market, provided by the Corporation of London, was one salmon annually.

Even so, in the modern era, the term "peppercorn" is often used in popular parlance for any rental that is far below commercial value, even when made in cash. For an example can be considered *Thomas v Thomas* (1842) 2 QB 851. In this case, an agreement was made that a woman be allowed to reside in a property for £1 a year. This was deemed to be sufficient consideration and prevented her late husband's executors from moving her out of the house. People sometimes also talk about a peppercorn consideration for one-off payments, such as the sale of a struggling company with heavy liabilities for just a pound. Unsurprisingly, this is found in other common law countries as well. Recently, the USS *Kitty Hawk*, a decommissioned aircraft carrier, was sold for a single American cent to scrap merchants who then had the legal responsibility for safely breaking up the huge vessel.[1]

---

1 Justin Vallejo, "Aircraft carrier sold for 1 cent", *Independent* (London), 19 January 2022

At common law, a person to whom a promise was made could enforce it only if he, rather than a third party, provided consideration for it (see also the discussion of privity in Chapter 6). For example, if A promises to pay B £800 if C will mend his car, and C does so, B cannot enforce A's promise unless B had procured C to do the repairs. However, it is enough that consideration moves from one party; it does not necessarily have to move to the other. Thus, if I agree to give you my car if you donate £10,000 to an educational charity, with which I have no connection, there is good consideration for my vehicle; your detriment in making the payment is enough.

Furthermore, consideration does not have to have market value. As Professor J.C. Smith observed many years ago, it will often be impossible to see any economic benefit in someone walking to York (a common Victorian illustration of consideration) in exchange for a promise of £100. Nevertheless, suffering a detriment in exchange for the counterparty's promise, even if it is of no benefit to the latter, is enough. A more realistic illustration might involve giving up the tenancy of a flat in exchange for a promise of accommodation elsewhere.

The "detriment" may even be of some benefit to the offeror. In the American case of *Hamer v Sidway* (1891) 27 NE 256, which cited *Currie v Misa*, a forbearance of legal rights by the offeree, in this case a nephew's refraining from drinking liquour, using tobacco, swearing, and playing cards or billiards for money until he was 21, was held to be consideration for his uncle's promise of 5,000 in exchange for such continence. The nephew had a legal right to engage in these activities (and had occasionally imbibed and smoked before the promise), and so provided valuable consideration by not indulging in them, even though it may have improved his physical and spiritual health.

Similarly, in *Shadwell v Shadwell* (1860) 9 CB NS 159, it was held that getting married could be consideration for a promise. As Byles J observed, "Marriage of the claimant at the testator's express request would be no doubt an ample consideration". Erle CJ agreed, "I am aware that a man's marriage with the woman of his choice is in one sense a boon, and in that sense the reverse of a loss: yet, as between the claimant and the party promising to supply an income to support the marriage, it may well be also a loss".

However, the detriment cannot be entirely nugatory. In *White v Bluett* (1853) 23 LJ Ex 36, the Exchequer Chamber identified consideration that was too intangible to be "sufficient". Mr Bluett had lent his son money prior to his death. After he died, the executor of his estate sued for its recovery. The son argued that his father had said he need not repay the money, provided he stopped complaining about the unequal way that he (the father) planned to distribute his property among his children in his will. Pollock CB held that no consideration had been provided for releasing the son from his obligation to repay the money. Not complaining was inherently vague and nebulous, and there were sound policy reasons for not allowing it, so that "the son's abstaining from doing what he had no right to do can be no consideration".

Likewise, it has been argued that refraining from something that the offeree has not the slightest interest in doing or (alternatively) the ability to do, such as flying to Pluto, would not constitute sufficient consideration. As was noted in *Arrale v Costain Civil Engineering Ltd* [1976] 1 Lloyd's Rep 98, it is not good consideration to "refrain from a course of conduct which it was never intended to pursue".

**Compromising Legal Claims**

The ability to pursue legal claims or defences before the courts is something of value, which can constitute valid consideration if exchanged for a promise (usually) for financial payment. It is this that allows people to compromise litigation with binding agreements, and most civil litigation does end in such compromises, so that it is vital to the entire process, and warrants further consideration as a result. It should be noted that it is the claim to such a legal right, rather than the legal right itself--which may or may not be valid, and whose existence remains untested at the time of any compromise--that provides consideration. However, there is a limit to how far this can go. In *Wade v Simeon* (1846) 2 CB 548, the claimant had claimed two sums of money, totalling £10,000, from the defendant, in exchange for promising not to bring a legal action against him. It was held that since the claimant knew his proposed claim was entirely ungrounded, and acted in bad faith, he had provided no consideration for the other party's promise, which could not be enforced as a result. Similarly, in *Cook v Wright* (1861) 1 B & S 559, it was noted that to be good consideration there must be "a reasonable claim on the one side, which it was bona fide intended to pursue".

The law on this area was reviewed by the Court of Appeal in *Simantob v Shavleyan* [2019] EWCA Civ 1105. Simon LJ, having considered the authorities, reiterated the traditional distinction between the two different situations. Where a person threatens to pursue a worthless claim or defence in which they have no belief or confidence, their forbearance to do so does not constitute good consideration for a promise (usually of money), if only on the grounds of public policy. By contrast, where a person makes a claim or defence which, even if they recognise that it raises a doubtful or undecided point, they believe in and intend to pursue in court if necessary, giving it up *can* constitute valid consideration, even if it subsequently transpires to be legally unfounded.

In *Simantob v Shavleyan* the parties dealt in valuable Islamic antiquities. They had a contractual dispute but reached a settlement which required Shavleyan to pay 1,500,000 by a particular date. If they did not do so on time, the agreement imposed liquidated damages of 1,000 for each day of delay. Shavleyan failed to pay all the money on time, triggering the liquidated damages clause. Shavleyan subsequently objected that the designated amount was an unenforceable penalty clause rather than an enforceable liquidated damages clause, and so was invalid. (See Chapter 15 on penalties). The parties renegotiated the settlement, agreeing that Shavleyan could settle the debt if he paid Simantob 800,000. In return, Shavleyan agreed not to challenge the validity of the "penalty clause" in court. Simantob later demanded full payment of the overdue money, arguing that the variation was not binding because the agreement not to challenge the validity of the damages clause had no real value, since there was almost no chance that it would succeed. However, the Court held in favour of Shavleyan, as he had reasonably believed he could challenge its validity when the parties reached their agreement, making it good consideration, even if he later turned out to be mistaken.

Of course, if the consideration for a contract or its variation is an agreement not to pursue a legal claim or defence, and there is any doubt about its validity, some additional consideration that is clearly "sufficient", even if of nominal value, such as a token chattel, could be specified to ensure that it was binding.

## Executory and Executed Consideration

Consideration can be either executory or executed. The former lies in the future; the latter is complete. Thus, executory consideration involves a promise to do something, this still being outstanding, and this is as much valid consideration as actually doing it. As Holt CJ observed in *Thorpe v Thorpe* (1701) 1 Ld. Raym. 235, "Where the doing a thing will be a good consideration, a promise to do that thing will be so too". For example, if I promise to give you £10 on delivery if you agree to deliver a sack of potatoes to my house tomorrow, and you do so promise, both of us have provided executory consideration. Once consideration has been provided it is executed. If on Wednesday I deliver a ton of carrots to you for which it is agreed you will pay me £500 on Friday, on the Thursday my consideration is executed, yours is still executory. More mundanely, if I requested and paid for a cup of coffee immediately upon ordering it in a café, my consideration would be executed, but until the café served the coffee theirs would be executory.

Executed consideration is always provided by one of the parties in a unilateral contract at the time the agreement is made. For example, if a promissor offers £1,000 to anyone who finds and returns his dog, the promisee both accepts this offer and provides consideration by giving the promissor what he has requested, the return of his dog. At this point, the promisee's consideration is executed, because it is complete. (See also Chapter 1). However, although executed consideration in a unilateral contract is complete when the contract is concluded, it still lies in the future when the offer for which it is given is made, which is not the situation with past consideration, from which it must be distinguished.

## Past Consideration

Although consideration can be "executory" or "executed", it cannot be "past". Consideration must be supplied in the present or future; something done *before* the promise for which it purports to be consideration is not legally sufficient. The reason for this is that, as it is complete by the time the promise is made, it cannot have been given in exchange for such an undertaking. A pair of old cases, from about the same time, provide simple illustrations.

In *Eastwood v Kenyon* (1840) 113 ER 482, a father died, having appointed Eastwood in his will as the guardian of his only child, a young girl named Sarah. Eastwood borrowed and spent a significant amount of money on her maintenance and studies. Sarah subsequently married Kenyon, the defendant, who on their union promised to reimburse Eastwood for the money he had spent on his future wife's education by paying off the loan he had taken out to do so. He subsequently refused to do this, and Eastwood sued on his promise. However, his action was unsuccessful. The promise was not in a deed, and so required consideration to make it enforceable. Unfortunately, as Lord Denman CJ noted, the "old common law" of England meant that past consideration was not good consideration. The money had been spent on her education before the promise was made and Kenyon had not even requested Eastwood to do this (see below).

Similarly, in *Roscorla v Thomas* (1842) 3 QB 234, the parties agreed the sale of a horse for £30. Subsequently, *after* the contract had been made, the seller made a promise that the animal was "sound and free from vice". Upon delivery, the buyer discovered that the horse was both vicious and physically defective. He sued on the promise, arguing that there had been a breach of an express term in the contract. He failed, because the assurance was not supported by consideration, and so was a bare promise. Had it been given *before* the contract was agreed, the purchase price for the animal would have provided the relevant consideration, and the promise would have been binding. As it was, the payment was past consideration. Lord Denman CJ observed that the promise must be co-extensive with the consideration, as "a consideration past and executed will support no other promise than such as would be implied by law".

The principle has been reiterated more recently in *Re McArdle* (1951) Ch 669. In this case, Marjorie McArdle voluntarily paid for repairs on her elderly father-in-law's bungalow. *After* the work had been concluded, and following the man's death, her brothers and sisters-in-law signed a document (that did not amount to a deed) stating that in consideration of her carrying out the repairs she would be paid £480 from the proceeds of sale. However, a change of heart ensuing, the payment was never made. The Court of Appeal held that the promise was not binding, as it was made after the purported consideration had been performed, making it past consideration.

### The Rule in *Lampleigh v Braithwaite*

An *apparent* but, in the eyes of the law, not true, exception to the rule on past consideration can be seen in the principle or 'rule' established in *Lampleigh v*

*Braithwaite* [1615] EWHC KB 117. In this case, the defendant killed a man and feared prosecution for the homicide. He asked the claimant to obtain a pardon from the King. In those days, this could be done prior to formal proceedings being instigated, and was not an uncommon legal procedure. However, it could be an expensive and onerous task, requiring the calling in of favours from those who had influence with the Monarch. Lampleigh rode regularly to Newmarket, where the court was then situated, and eventually managed to secure the desired pardon for Braithwaite. Subsequently, the latter promised to pay him £100 for his work. He then failed to honour this undertaking. It was held that, although the promise to make payment came after performance in this case, it was preceded by a request from the defendant to do the requisite act (obtaining a pardon), which was made with an understanding at the time it was made that payment would be forthcoming for this service. (It was to preclude such a possibility that Denman CJ noted that the defendant in *Eastwood v Kenyon* had not requested that the claimant pay for his ward's education). In these circumstances, the promise of £100 linked to the earlier request and was binding.

The principle in *Lampleigh v Braithwaite* was clarified in *Re Casey's Patents* [1892] 1 Ch 104. In this case, the defendant, Casey, managed some patents that were jointly owned by the two claimants. He had done a significant amount of work for the pair. As a result, the claimants later signed a document stating that "in consideration of your [earlier] services ... we hereby agree to give you one-third share of the patents". When Casey subsequently registered this document on the patent register, to secure his one-third interest, the claimants (who had changed their minds in the meantime) sought to have it expunged. They argued, *inter alia*, that, as the promise in the document was not a deed, it needed to be supported by consideration to make it enforceable, and the only potential consideration in the case was "past". The Court of Appeal held that Casey had been requested to do the work and had assumed, as would any manager in his situation, that it would be paid for. Bowen LJ observed that in such a situation the subsequent promise simply "fixes the amount of that reasonable remuneration". Casey's past work was good consideration and the agreement enforceable.

More recently, the principle was reiterated in *Pao On v Lau Yiu Long* [1980] AC 614, when Lord Scarman noted that an act done before a promise was made was good consideration for that promise if three essential prerequisites were satisfied (as was the situation in the instant case): it was done at the promissor's request, the parties understood the act was to be paid for at a later date, and the payment or benefit would have been enforceable had it been promised in advance. The existence of this "rule" has sometimes been explained by suggesting that, in these situations, the person who provided the allegedly past consideration has, by implication, traded a *quantum meruit* (as much as it is worth) claim that would otherwise have been open to him if a price had not been subsequently determined, in exchange for the agreed payment.

## Existing Duties as Consideration

In practice, provided it is not past or nebulous, consideration is rarely an issue and, as Leggatt J noted in *Blue v Ashley* [2017] EWHC 1928, agreements very rarely fail for lack of it. Even so, there have been difficulties when it comes to so-called existing duty situations. Normally, there must be "fresh" consideration to form a contract. If a party is already legally required to do something, whether by an earlier contract or the general law, there may be issues as to whether doing so in exchange for a promise constitutes valid consideration. This matter has been considered in the context of three different types of existing duty to perform the supposed consideration: an existing public obligation under the general law; an existing contractual obligation with a third party; an existing contractual obligation with the promissor. Different answers have been reached in these three situations.

## Existing Public Duty

Performing an existing public duty may not constitute fresh consideration. For example, in the historic case of *Collins v Godefroy* (1831) 1 B & Ad 950, the claimant, Mr Collins, had been subpoenaed to attend court as a witness in civil proceedings involving Godefroy. The latter subsequently promised Collins a guinea (£1.05) for each day he was at court. As it transpired, Collins did not give evidence, but was required to be at court for six days in case he was called. After the trial, Collins gave Godefroy an invoice for six guineas. When this was not paid, Collins sued on the agreement. It was held that Collins was under a public duty to attend court due to the subpoena, and, as a result, carrying out such a duty did not constitute fresh consideration for a promise from someone else. Godefroy was not required to pay Collins the six guineas. Lord Tenterden CJ observed, "If it be a duty imposed by law upon a party regularly subpoenaed, to attend from time to time to give his evidence, then a promise to give him any remuneration for loss of time incurred in such attendance is a promise without consideration".

In appropriate circumstances this principle can be circumvented by showing that the public duty has been exceeded. In *Glasbrook Bros v Glamorgan County Council* [1925] AC 270, the defendant owned a colliery and, in a period of industrial strife, asked the police to provide protection during a miners' strike. The police assessed the situation and concluded that it was sufficient that a vehicle-based mobile patrol should regularly call at the mine and check that all was in order and secure. The mine owners thought this inadequate, asked the police to garrison officers there on a permanent basis, and offered to pay for their presence. The council agreed and provided the manpower requested. At the end of the strike the council submitted an invoice to cover the extra costs of providing this protection. The defendants refused to pay, arguing that the police were under an existing public duty to provide such protection and keep the peace.

By a majority, the House of Lords decided that, in providing additional officers to those required (in their estimation), the police had gone beyond their existing duty.

They were therefore entitled to payment. In doing so they agreed with Bailhache J at first instance, who stated, "There is an obligation on the police to afford efficient protection, but if an individual asks for special protection in a particular form, for the special protection so asked for in that particular form, the individual must pay."

However, the general validity of the principle set out in *Collins v Godefroy* has also been questioned. In *Ward v Byham* [1956] All ER 318, after the relationship between an unmarried couple ended, the mother obtained custody of their infant daughter. The father promised her a £1 a week allowance "providing you can prove that she [the daughter] will be well looked after and happy". He stopped making these payments after the mother remarried, and the latter sought to enforce his promise. The mother was under a duty imposed by the general law to support the girl as she had legal custody of the child. The Court of Appeal had to decide whether she had given any consideration for the father's promise, so that it was enforceable. It held that there was consideration, and the contract was valid.

Slightly artificially, a majority of the Court of Appeal, Morris and Parker LJJ, considered that although the mother was required by statute to maintain her child, exceeding the basic requirement by ensuring the child was "well looked after and happy" and, more pertinently, was free to choose with whom she would live constituted consideration. However, Denning LJ was prepared to go further. He felt that a promise to perform an existing public obligation (in this case caring for the child) might be good consideration. Although the mother was only doing what she was legally bound to do, "Even so, I think that there was sufficient consideration to support the promise. I have always thought that a promise to perform an existing duty, or the performance of it, should be regarded as good consideration, because it is a benefit to the person to whom it is given". However, the other two judges refrained from agreeing with this view.

Denning LJ returned to this theme the following year in *Williams v Williams* [1957] 1 WLR 148, in which case a husband promised his estranged wife a weekly allowance of £1 10s if she did not "pledge his credit". Denning held that her promise not to do this, although it was a legal obligation as she was in desertion (and so not able to pledge her spouse's credit), was enforceable as it was not contrary to the "public interest". He also noted that it might mean the husband would avoid the stress of having to explain his position if she did pledge his credit (a tangible but not legal benefit). However, again, the other two judges on the bench declined to agree with Denning LJ's view and found consideration in the case. Although the wife had suspended her right to maintenance by being in desertion, she could, in *theory*, revive it until the divorce was granted by returning to him, so that a promise not to pledge his credit was valid consideration. As Morris LJ noted, that this was very unlikely to occur was a question of adequacy, not sufficiency.

There was some (albeit limited) support for Denning's view in several earlier decisions. For example, in *England v Davidson* (1840) 11 AD & E 85, a police constable claimed a £50 reward for providing information leading to the capture and conviction of a criminal who had broken into the offeror's house. The latter refused to pay the reward on the basis that the officer was only performing his existing public duty. It was held that the constable could claim the reward as it was in the "interest of justice", although, as Denman LJ noted, there was also an issue as to whether he was under any obligation to provide information to a private individual or had, in any event, exceeded his duty, "I think there may be services which the constable is not bound to render and which he may therefore make the ground of a contract". The matter remains slightly uncertain, although it is apparent that, at the very least, the position reached in *Collins v Godefroy* will apply where there is a strong policy justification for it doing so.

## Existing Contractual Duty to a Third Party

Performing an existing duty owed under a contract with a third party can be good consideration for a promise from someone else. Thus, in *Shadwell v Shadwell* (1860) 9 CB NS 159, the defendant was the estate of the claimant's uncle. The latter had, (a majority of) the court concluded, promised to pay his nephew £150 a year until the nephew's income as a chancery barrister reached 600 guineas per annum, provided the nephew married the woman to whom he was already engaged. Until 1971 an engagement was viewed as a contract and unilaterally breaking it off could lead to a special breach of contract action termed "breach of promise", so it meant that the nephew was already contractually bound to marry his fiancé, Ellen Nicholl (the third party).[2]

The uncle paid several instalments but then died, with some payments still outstanding. When the remaining instalments were refused by his executors, the nephew sued his uncle's estate for them. In response, the latter claimed that the nephew had provided no consideration for the uncle's promise. In reply, the nephew argued that going through with the marriage constituted consideration. In the Court of Common Pleas, Erle CJ agreed, and held that performance of a pre-existing contractual duty, so long as it was for a third party (rather than the promissor) was good consideration. Byles J dissented, but not on legal principle, disagreeing that the marriage was at the uncle's request, so that the offer was, at most, what would now be termed a conditional gift (a view of the facts supported by most modern observers). The principle established in *Shadwell v Shadwell* was reiterated the following year in *Scotson v Pegg* (1861) 158 ER 121, when Wilde B observed that "if a person chooses to promise to pay a sum of money in order to induce another to perform that which he has already contracted with a third person to do, I confess I cannot see why such a promise should not be binding".

---

2 For example, in August 1840 an action for breach of promise of marriage was tried at assizes in Norwich. Eliza Hastings, age 40, the daughter of a retired tailor, was the claimant, and Dr. Astley, a medical man, was the defendant. The jury returned a verdict of £100 damages for Miss Hastings. *London Evening Standard*, 5 August 1840.

Why this situation should differ from that in *Stilk v Myrick* (1809) 2 Camp 317, with its existing obligation to the same offeror (see below), has been a matter of some debate. One persuasive argument is that the third-party promissor does obtain a legal benefit that he did not have prior to the promise--the right to sue on a breach in his own right--so that there is extra or "fresh" and sufficient consideration for the promise, unlike the situation in the latter case. Such a notion was supported by Lord Wilberforce in *New Zealand Shipping Co Ltd v AM Satterthwaite & Co Ltd (The Eurymedon)* [1975] AC 154, who observed, "An agreement to do an act which the promisor [*sic*] is under an existing obligation to a third party to do, may quite well amount to valid consideration and does so in the present case: the promisee obtains the benefit of a direct obligation which he can enforce".

**Existing Contractual Duty Owed to the Offeror**

The historic case in this area of the law is *Stilk v Myrick* (1809) 2 Camp 317, which involved an action for a seaman's wages, after a voyage made from London to the Baltic and back. Prior to the journey, the ship's articles had stipulated that the claimant was to be paid £5 a month. During the voyage, two of the 12-man crew jumped ship while the vessel was moored in Cronstadt, and the master, having unsuccessfully attempted to recruit new sailors to replace them, promised the remaining men that the wages of the "deserters" would be divided up amongst them. They sailed back to London, but the master then refused to give them the extra money, although he did pay the sum originally agreed before departure. One of the sailors took this to court but failed in his action.

One reason for this decision--the court was also concerned about the potential for duress by crews at sea--was that the master's undertaking to pay extra money was a bare promise, and so void for want of consideration. Deserting crewmates, like bad weather, were part of the normal vicissitudes of the voyage that they were contractually bound to face when they signed on in England. Lord Ellenborough observed, "Before they [the crew] sailed from London they had undertaken to do all that they could under all the emergencies of the voyage. They had sold all their services till the voyage should be completed. [Of course] If they had been at liberty to quit the vessel at Cronstadt, the case would have been quite different". As a result, the claimant was limited to his agreed £5 a month.

This case is sometimes contrasted with *Hartley v Ponsonby* [1857] 7 EB 872. Ponsonby was the captain of a merchant vessel. Hartley, like his fellow sailors, had contracted to serve on the ship for three years. While in port, 17 out of 37 sailors deserted, almost half the crew, as opposed to a sixth in *Stilk v Myrick* (1809) 2 Camp 317, so that sailing the vessel became dangerous. To persuade the rest of the crew to continue manning it, Ponsonby promised them extra wages but then refused to pay them when the vessel returned to England. Hartley sued for the additional money promised. The defendant argued that the sailors had provided no extra consideration, only doing what they were obliged to do under the ship's articles, so his promise was *nudum pactum*. However, Lord Campbell CJ said that while a sailor was expected to complete a voyage if there was an emergency while at sea, the ship was in port at the relevant time, so that the claimant was within his legal rights to refuse to put to sea, as the vessel was *dangerously* undermanned (unlike the situation in *Stilk v Myrick*). Consequently, by agreeing to sail as crew, the claimant supplied fresh consideration, making Ponsonby's promise binding. As a result, the decision was not inconsistent with *Stilk v Myrick*, where just two men had deserted.

The principle set out in *Stilk v Myrick* was viewed as fundamental to English contract law for 180 years. For example, in *Atlas Express Ltd v Kafco (Importers & Distributors) Ltd* [1989] 1 All ER 641, a subsidiary ground for allowing the appeal (along with economic duress) was that Atlas Express had not provided any additional consideration for Kafco's enhanced offer of payment beyond what they were required to do under the original agreement. Atlas was merely performing their existing contractual duty, as in *Stilk v Myrick*. However, shortly afterwards, the law in this area was modified, but not abolished, by the Court of Appeal.

### *Williams v Roffey*

In *Williams v Roffey Bros & Nicolls* [1991] 1 QB 1, Roffey Bros contracted to refurbish 27 flats in a West London mansion block. As permitted under this agreement, Roffey subcontracted the attendant carpentry to Mr Williams for £20,000, payable in instalments. A significant amount of this work was done and paid for. However, Williams then experienced serious financial difficulties, in part because the price he had quoted was unrealistically low (his employees had also been poorly managed), something that reduced his ability to take on extra labour and so was also likely to occasion delay. Roffey Bros realized that, as a result, they were likely to face a liquidated damages clause for late completion under their contract. They called a meeting with Williams and promised him an extra £10,300--that is, £575 for each flat completed on time. Williams finished eight more flats but stopped when he did not receive the extra money promised. New carpenters were brought in to finish the project. Williams then sued for the additional money. At first instance, he succeeded, being awarded £4,600, this being eight times £575 with a few deductions then being made for various defects in the work (there had been "substantial" performance).

Unsurprisingly, in the light of *Stilk v Myrick*, Roffey challenged this in the Court of Appeal, on the grounds that no fresh consideration had been provided for the extra money. Even so, it was held that although Williams had promised to do nothing more than he was contractually obliged to do, the promise to pay the bonus was enforceable provided the defendant "obtains *in practice* a benefit or obviates a disbenefit". (A notion tentatively alluded to in the context of existing public duty by Lord Denning in *Williams v Williams* [1957] 1 WLR 148). In the instant case, in the words of Purchas LJ, there had been such consideration because "there was clearly a commercial advantage to both sides from a *pragmatic* point of view" (present author's italics). This was subject to the important proviso that the promise for extra remuneration must not have been obtained by fraud or duress. For example, had Williams been in possession of ample funds and lied about his financial situation to Roffey, or if Williams had deliberately "gone slow" on the work to pressure Roffey into agreeing to extra money, the situation might well have been different. Neither factor was present in the instant case. As a result, Williams was held to be entitled to the extra money, as Roffey had avoided the liquidated-damages clause, so obviating a disbenefit. Although *Stilk v Myrick* was not overruled, its importance was significantly "refined" and "limited" in some (but not all) situations.

Glidewell LJ thought that it was natural that a rule that was 200 years old should be subject to a "process of refinement and limitation in its application" in the modern era. He also thought that *Stilk* could be readily distinguished from *Roffey*, because the captain in the former case had not gained an extra benefit as a result of his promise of extra payment. (Although it could be argued that it discouraged further desertions). Nevertheless, it should also be noted that the modification established in *Williams v Roffey* has been criticised, with some observers complaining that it was contrary to principle and even urging that it be overturned.

In *South Caribbean Trading v Trafigura* [2004] EWHC 2676 (Comm), Colman J noted that, but for the fact that it was a decision of the Court of Appeal, he would not have followed it, saying, "The decision is inconsistent with the long-standing rule that consideration, being the price of the promise sued upon, must move from the promisee". Similarly, in *Adam Opel v Mitras Automotive* [2008] EWHC 3205 (QB), David Donaldson QC, sitting as a Deputy High Court Judge, applied the decision to the case before him, noting that the defendant had received a tangible benefit (albeit able to succeed on the separate issue of economic duress). Even so, he questioned the decision's "logical coherence". More specifically, it has been argued that, as a matter of public policy, the law of contract should encourage parties to price their contracts realistically in advance, rather than renegotiating [3]them later, and that the decision in *Williams v Roffey* has the opposite effect. An awareness that they will be held to their agreements discourages unrealistic quotations and so encourages fair and honest competition.

The decision in *Williams v Roffey* also had a potential but not, as it transpired (and as is currently the situation), an actual impact on the long-standing "Rule in *Pinnel's Case*", which needs detailed discussion.

## The Rule in *Pinnel's Case*

The general need for consideration explains the decision, and so-called 'rule', in *Pinnel's Case* [1602] 5 Co. Rep. 117 when it comes to settling debts (whether contractual or not). Pinnel sued Cole for a debt that had originally been £8 10s. The

3 For example, in August 1840 an action for breach of promise of marriage was tried at assizes in Norwich. Eliza Hastings, age 40, the daughter of a retired tailor, was the claimant, and Dr. Astley, a medical man, was the defendant. The jury returned a verdict of £100 damages for Miss Hastings. *London Evening Standard*, 5 August 1840.

latter argued that he had tendered £5 2s 2d, and the claimant had accepted this sum in full and final settlement of the entire amount. Pinnel subsequently brought legal proceedings to recover the balance of just over £3. In the Court of Common Pleas, Sir Edward Coke declared that "payment of a lesser sum on the day [it is due] in satisfaction of a greater, cannot be any satisfaction for the whole, because it appears to the Judges that by no possibility a lesser sum can be a satisfaction to the plaintiff for a greater sum". As a result, there was nothing to prevent Pinnel seeking the balance. There had been no fresh consideration for accepting the lesser sum, so the promise to release the debt was "bare" and not binding, unless set out in a deed.

The Rule in *Pinnel's Case* was restated as *ratio decidendi* at the highest level and clarified by the House of Lords in *Foakes v Beer* (1883-84) LR 9 App Cas 605. In this case, Dr Foakes owed Mrs Beer money. She went to court to secure its recovery and obtained judgement of £2,000 against him. Foakes then offered to pay £500 immediately and the rest by instalments. Beer agreed to this and said that she would not seek enforcement of the payment provided he kept up the instalments. No mention was made of interest being paid on the delayed payments, although judgment debts normally incur such interest automatically. Dr Foakes paid all the instalments as agreed. However, Mrs Beer then asked the interest on the debt and sued when it was nor forthcoming. It was held that Foakes was liable to pay this. Effectively, the agreement reached amounted to part payment of a debt--the debt rather than the debt plus interest--and under the rule in *Pinnel's Case* this did not preclude enforcement of the full amount due.

This analysis was subsequently reiterated by the higher courts on several occasions. For example, in *Vanbergen v St. Edmunds Properties Ltd* [1933] 2 KB 223, Lord Hanworth MR noted that it was a well-established principle that a "promise to pay a sum which the debtor is already bound by law to pay to the promisee does not afford any consideration". Similarly, in *D & C Builders Ltd v Rees* [1966] 2 WLR 28, the Court of Appeal observed that *Foakes v Beer* had "settled definitely the rule of law that payment of a lesser sum than the amount of a debt due cannot be a satisfaction of the debt, unless there is some benefit to the creditor added so that there is an accord and satisfaction".

However, the rule occasioned concern, even amongst some of the judges in *Foakes v Beer*, as it was arguably contrary to good business practice. Lord Blackburn expressly observed that "all men of business, whether merchants or tradesmen, do every day recognise and act on the ground that prompt payment of a part of their demand may be more beneficial to them than it would be to insist on their rights and enforce payment of the whole". This was especially likely if the debtor's solvency was in doubt. Blackburn admitted that he had originally intended to challenge Lord Coke's dictum in *Pinnel's Case* (technically it was *obiter*) but had yielded to his brother judges on the issue. In 1937, his concerns were reiterated by the Law Revision

Committee. Nevertheless, there are ways around the rule, at both common law and in equity.

## Circumventing the Rule in *Pinnel's Case* at Common Law

There are several common law "exceptions" to the Rule in *Pinnel's Case*. Most important, it might be circumvented by the provision of fresh consideration, although, of course, this must be given at the promissor's request. For example, this might be done by part payment *before* the contractually due date, or payment at a different place to that originally stipulated in the agreement (largely irrelevant in an era of banks and electronic transfers), or by the provision of an accompanying chattel such as, to use Edward Coke's words in *Pinnel's Case*, a "horse, hawk, or robe". How valuable this chattel is, is irrelevant, being a question of sufficiency rather than adequacy. A ballpoint pen could (at the creditor's request) take the place of half a debt of £10,000.

This situation has always been the subject of criticism. In *Couldery v Bartrum* (1881) 19 Ch D 394, Sir George Jessel MR observed, "According to English common law a creditor might accept anything in satisfaction of his debt except a less amount of money. He might take a horse, or a canary, or tomtit if he chose, and that was accord and satisfaction; but, by a most extraordinary peculiarity of the English common law he could not take 19 shillings and sixpence in the pound; that was *nudum pactum*".

It should also be noted that the rule does not apply if there is a genuine dispute about whether, and how much, money is owed. In these situations, accepting a lesser sum in settlement of the issue will be binding (see above). Furthermore, receiving a lesser sum from a third party, in exchange for a promise to discharge the debt, *does* preclude suing the original debtor for the balance, if only for policy reasons. In *Welby v Drake* (1825) 1 C. & P. 557 the claimant accepted part payment from the defendant's father in full satisfaction of a debt. He subsequently brought an action against the defendant for the balance but failed. Lord Abbott CJ gave as a rationale for this decision that allowing the son to be sued for the balance would mean the court facilitating a fraud on the father, who was induced by the claimant to advance the money on the basis that it would completely discharge his son from further liability.

This principle was reiterated by the Privy Council in *Hirachand Punamchand v Temple* [1911] 2 KB 330. In this case, the claimants were money lenders in India during the Raj. They lent money to the defendant, who was a young army officer. Subsequently, they unsuccessfully sought the return of their money, with attendant interest. As a result, they approached Temple's father. After negotiations through solicitors, the claimants asked how much the father would be prepared to pay to settle his son's account. A substantial, but not the entire, amount was agreed and duly paid in full settlement of the debt. The claimants had promised to send the father the promissory note relating to his son's debt once they had received payment. Instead, they retained it, and sued the son for the balance. It was held that the payment made by the father was sufficient to discharge the full balance, the need to avoid facilitating a fraud (again) being advanced as a justification by Vaughan Williams LJ, while Fletcher Moulton LJ observed that it would be "an abuse of the process of the court" to allow the creditor to recover under such circumstances.

### *Re Selectmove Ltd*

The principle established in *Williams v Roffey* (see above) has been followed in much of the common law world, including jurisdictions such as New Zealand, Canada, Australia, and Singapore. However, it was and is doctrinally problematic, especially when it comes to the Rule in *Pinnel's Case*, as a practical benefit (obtaining a guaranteed lesser payment) was rejected as valid consideration by the House of Lords in *Foakes v Beer*.[4] In *Re Selectmove Ltd* [1993] EWCA Civ 8, the Court of Appeal decided that the notion of a practical benefit, although used to modify the rule in *Stilk v Myrick*, should *not* be extended to part payment of debts, something that would undermine the Rule in *Pinnel's Case*. In the former case, Selectmove Ltd owed the Inland Revenue large amounts of tax and national insurance contributions. The company's managing director met with a representative from the Revenue and (he claimed) said that he would pay future tax as it fell due, and the arrears at £1,000 a month. The representative (allegedly) said that he would inform him if this was unacceptable. Selectmove Ltd heard nothing more, until they received a demand for £25,650, accompanied by the threat of a winding-up petition. The Court of Appeal held that even if the Revenue *had* said the company could pay less (it was denied), there was no consideration for the varied agreement.

Peter Gibson LJ observed that if the principle in the Court of Appeal case of *Williams v Roffey* was extended to debt it would leave the House of Lords case of *Foakes v Beer* without any application. As a result, although in situations where a creditor and a debtor reach an agreement to pay the debt by instalments, the creditor may see a practical benefit, due to a fear of not getting any money back at all, this could not be consideration in law, being a matter that had been expressly considered and rejected in *Foakes v Beer*. Peter Gibson LJ noted that, "*Foakes v Beer* was not even referred to in *Williams v Roffey Bros*, and it is in my judgment impossible, consistently with the doctrine of precedent, for this court to extend the principle of Williams's case to any circumstances governed by the principle of *Foakes v Beer*". However, the judge suggested that the matter might, at some point, be reconsidered by the highest Appellate Court (then the House of Lords, now the Supreme Court).

Nevertheless, the Supreme Court declined to take this opportunity when it arose in *MWB Business Exchange Centres Ltd. v Rock Advertising Ltd.* [2019] AC 119. In this case, the licensor (MWB) and the licensee (Rock) of office premises agreed to vary their agreement so that Rock, who had begun to suffer financial difficulties,

---

4 James C. Fisher, "Contract variation in the common law: A critical response to *Rock Advertising* v *MWB Business Exchange*", *Common Law World Review*, v.47, no.3 (2018), p.197 and. p.206.

could pay their arrears of fees in accordance with a revised schedule. Among the matters to be decided on appeal was whether Rock had provided any consideration for the variation. The county court judge at first instance, and the Court of Appeal, concluded that Rock had provided consideration in the form of the practical advantages entailed in their payment of the initial sum due under the schedule and their promise to keep up payments in future, even though they were obliged to pay these arrears in any event. Thus, the Court of Appeal appears, at first sight, to have extended the notion of practical benefit in a way that had been rejected in *Re Selectmove*.

However, somewhat complicating the matter, Kitchin LJ argued that, unlike that case, MWB *had* also received a practical benefit beyond accommodating the debtor's financial state, namely the retention of Rock as a licensee, so the property was not left empty at further loss. As a result, it could at least be argued that the Court of Appeal's decision, on its facts, was still consistent with *Foakes v Beer*. Whether there is a meaningful distinction from the latter case is debateable. As has been noted, it could have been argued that Mrs Beer obtained a "practical benefit" if she had, or could have, used the money to pay for a holiday, school-fees, the deposit for a house, to pay off a mortgage, or to finance any number of other ventures.[5] The Court of Appeal's decision would, in truth, have greatly undermined *Foakes v Beer*.

*MWB Business Exchange Centres Ltd. v Rock Advertising Ltd.* [2019] AC 119 then went to the Supreme Court (note the later case reference), but because that forum decided that a no-oral-modification (NOM) clause was binding (another of the grounds of appeal), it felt it "unnecessary" to deal with consideration. The court declined to engage with the inherent tension that exists between the decisions in *Roffey* and *Foakes* and to produce a view on the matter, feeling that, as it would lead to a reconsideration of the House of Lords decision in *Foakes v Beer*, and presumably recourse to the 1966 Practice Direction, it needed to go before more than a five-judge panel of the court, and be the *ratio decidendi* in a decided case.[6] As Lord Sumption observed: "It is probably ripe for re-examination. But if it is to be overruled or its effect substantially modified, it should be before an enlarged panel of the court and in a case where the decision would be more than obiter dictum." In the meantime, *Foakes v Beer* remains good law, and the decision in the Court of Appeal in *MWB* on the issue (slightly uncertain as it is) is merely of persuasive authority should the matter be reconsidered by the highest forum.

Although some legal observers have suggested that the law would be more satisfactory if it treated benefits obtained by part payment in the same way as the gift of a chattel, arguing that if a creditor was improperly pressured into agreeing to accept a smaller amount than that to which he was entitled he might seek a

5 Michael Woollcombe-Clarke, *"Case Note: MWB Business Exchange Centres Ltd v Rock Advertising Ltd"*, *Trinity College Law Review*, Online (2016), Accessed 19 December 2021.

6 James C. Fisher, "Contract variation in the common law: A critical response to *Rock Advertising* v *MWB Business Exchange"*, *Common Law World Review*, v.47, no. 3 (2018), p.197 and. p.206.

remedy in duress (see Chapter 10), not all are persuaded that such a change would be beneficial.[7] It has been argued that there is a fundamental difference between agreements to pay more and those to accept less, if only because, in the former instance, the instigator of the amendment is often the party to whom performance is owed, as was the situation in *Williams v Roffey*, while, in the latter, it is frequently the party who has yet to perform.

## Circumventing *Pinnel's Case* in Equity: Promissory Estoppel

Promissory estoppel is an equitable doctrine which in some tightly prescribed circumstances can prevent a contracting party going back on a contractual promise that is neither supported by consideration nor set out in a deed. As such, it can circumvent the Rule in *Pinnel's Case*. As the Court of Appeal noted in *MWB Business Exchange Centres Ltd v Rock Advertising Ltd* [2016] EWCA Civ 553 (it went on to the Supreme Court) the law and, more particularly Lord Denning "both at first instance and in this court, developed [it] to meet the hardship created by the rule in *Pinnel's* case".

The modern doctrine of promissory estoppel begins its life in *Central London Property Trust Ltd v High Trees House Ltd* [1947] KB 130. In this case, Denning J (as he then was) observed that, where operative, a "promise to accept a smaller sum in discharge of a larger sum, if acted upon, is binding notwithstanding the absence of consideration". It should be noted that the doctrine started as *obiter dicta* comments by a first-instance judge in the High Court, albeit one who was destined to become one of the most famous judicial figures of the twentieth century. This helps to explain its slightly uncertain status in ensuing years.

In 1937 High Trees House Ltd had taken a lease on a new-built block of flats in Clapham from the freeholder, Central London Property Trust Ltd., for a period of 99 years, this being for an annual ground rent of £2,500. It was intended that High Trees would make this money (and a profit) by subletting individual flats on short leases. Shortly afterwards, in September 1939, the Second World War broke out and, in (correct) anticipation of London being bombed, many tenants did not renew their leases and moved out of the city. High Trees quickly struggled to find tenants for the property, and so earn a satisfactory income. They approached Central London Property Trust in January 1940 to ask that their ground rent be lowered. A reduction of half, to £1,250 per annum, was eventually agreed in writing (but not put in a deed) to apply while "wartime conditions" prevailed. No consideration was provided for this change. High Trees paid the reduced rent from then onwards. In May 1945, the war in Europe ended, and the building, which had survived unscathed, very quickly returned to full occupancy.

In September 1945, Central London Property wrote to High Trees requesting a return to the full rent of £2,500 over forthcoming quarters, but also claiming arrears

7 Edwin Peel, *Treitel on the Law of Contract*, 12th edn. (London: Sweet & Maxwell, 2007), p. 136.

of £7,916 for the underpayment during the period from 1940 onwards. They then brought a legal action but (a very important point) confined this to recovering just the two quarters which had elapsed since June 1945. Unsurprisingly, they succeeded in this, as during this period "wartime conditions" (like the war) were clearly over, and the flats were commanding high rentals, due to the post-conflict shortage of housing in the capital and their non-rent-controlled status. Even so, as it was a test case, aimed at giving more general guidance, because accommodations on rent had been quite common during the war, Denning J considered what the situation would have been had the landlord sought repayment of the missing rent for the wartime quarters, as it had previously proposed to do (which explains why his comments were *obiter*). At common law, this would have meant applying *Pinnel's Case*, as reiterated in *Foakes v Beer*, so that although the owners of the building had accepted a lesser sum in full satisfaction of the whole, this would not preclude them from asking for the balance for those quarters on a later date.

However, Denning J thought that the common law situation could be circumvented by relying on what he termed the equitable doctrine of "promissory estoppel", which took precedence over common law (as equity normally does). He thought that this was applicable in situations in which a clear promise was made that was intended to affect the parties' legal relations, which was relied on by the person to whom it was made, in circumstances in which it would be inequitable to go back on it. In reaching this decision, Denning found authority in *Hughes v Metropolitan Railway Co* (1877) LR 2 App Cas 439, giving the case a significance that it had not attracted when it was decided.

In *Hughes*, Mr Hughes owned property that he leased to the Metropolitan Railway Company. He gave his tenant six months' notice to carry out repairs to various dilapidations, as was his right under the lease, which also provided that a failure to comply within this period could result in forfeiture. However, a month later, landlord and tenant entered extensive negotiations for the latter to purchase the freehold of the property from the former. Both parties thought that this would come to fruition. As a result, the tenant did not carry out the repairs, as they believed they would soon own the freehold, and the repairs were expensive and not necessary for their planned use of the property. At the last minute, negotiations broke down, and the six-month time limit fell due shortly afterwards. The landlord then gave the tenant notice to quit for failure to carry out the repairs. The tenant claimed the negotiation period should not count towards the six months. Even so, the Court of Common Pleas (shortly to become part of the new High Court) found in favour of Mr Hughes, the landlord.

However, the Court of Appeal reversed this decision, and on further appeal their interpretation was upheld by the House of Lords. The latter forum ruled that the initiation of the negotiations was accompanied by an implied promise by the landlord not to enforce his strict legal rights with respect to the time limit on the repairs, for the period that they were ongoing, and the tenant acted on this promise to their detriment (by not instituting the repairs). Lord Cairns CJ observed it was the first principle upon which all Courts of Equity proceed that if a party who has entered into distinct terms subsequently enter upon a course of negotiation that has the effect of leading the counterparty to suppose that the strict rights arising under the contract will be suspended, they "will not be allowed to enforce them where it would be inequitable having regard to the dealings which have thus taken place between the parties". In this instance the rights of the landlord were suspended temporarily, allowing the tenant more time to repair the dilapidations, the six months allowed for the repairs running from the date of the failure of the negotiations.

The situation in *Hughes* was not truly analogous to that found in *High Trees*. A precise parallel would have been if Central London Property had treated the wartime underpayments as repudiatory breaches of contract and sought to terminate the lease on that ground after the war. It is highly unlikely that the judges in *Hughes* thought that it would have any impact on the rule reiterated a few years later in *Foakes v Beer*, not least because two of the judges in the latter case had sat in the former. Even so, Denning opined (slightly artificially) that the fusion of common law and equity in the Judicature Acts produced the result seen in *High Trees*. He felt that, although the implication of *Hughes* was not considered in *Foakes v Beer*, given that "law and equity have been joined together for over seventy years, principles must be reconsidered in the light of their combined effect".

Despite this uncertain provenance, promissory estoppel has received enough judicial recognition over recent decades to have become a permanent feature of English law. For example, the House of Lords affirmed the doctrine's existence in *Tool Metal Manufacturing v Tungsten* [1955] 1 WLR 761. Even so, its prerequisites are sufficiently strict that it has not rendered the common law Rule in *Pinnel's Case*, as reiterated in *Foakes v Beer*, redundant or irrelevant.

### The Prerequisites for Promissory Estoppel

There are several prerequisites that need to be satisfied before promissory estoppel can be applied. Most importantly, it can only be used as a shield, to defend an existing cause of action, there must be a clear and unambiguous representation intended to affect the parties' legal relationship, there must be reliance on the promise, and it must be inequitable to go back on it. These will be addressed in turn.

#### 1. Shield Not A Sword

The first is that in England and Wales (at least) the doctrine operates to modify existing legal relationships, rather than to create new ones. It must act as a defence to a cause of action between the parties, making an otherwise unsupported contractual modification to an agreement binding. It cannot act as the basis of a new cause of action.

For example, in *Combe v Combe* [1951] 2 KB 215, the Court of Appeal rejected a first-instance judge's use of the (then) relatively new doctrine of promissory estoppel for this reason. In this case, a husband promised to provide maintenance of £100 per annum to his wife prior to their divorce, but then failed to make any payments. A very important point was that the wife was significantly wealthier than her husband; as a result, she had provided no consideration for his promise, such as forbearing to enforce legal rights to maintenance. Even so, she brought an action to enforce the promise, invoking promissory estoppel, and the trial judge acceded to this. Reversing this decision, Denning LJ observed that the principle never stands alone to create a new cause of action: "It only prevents a party from insisting upon his strict legal rights, when it would be unjust to allow him to enforce them, having regard to the dealings which have taken place between the parties". Birkett and Asquith LJJ both agreed, the former adopting the aphorism deployed by the husband's counsel, that the principle is "one to be used as a shield and not as a sword". The presence of consideration was still cardinal to the formation of contracts. The decision on this point was reiterated by the House of Lords in *Baird Textile Holdings Ltd v Marks & Spencer Plc* [2001] EWCA Civ 274.

### 2. Clear and Unambiguous Representation

Second, the promissor must make a clear and unambiguous representation that they will not insist on their strict legal rights to the other party to the contract. This representation may be express or (extrapolating from *Hughes*) implied, even if the latter is very unusual. Nevertheless, in *Woodhouse AC Israel Cocoa Ltd v Nigerian Product Marketing Co Ltd* [1972] AC 741, the statement was, it seems, implied when the seller and buyer, parties to a contract for the sale of coffee beans that was payable in pounds sterling, mistakenly sent and accepted (respectively) an invoice stating that the price was payable in Kenyan shillings. At the time the value of the pound and shilling was at parity, but subsequently the value of the former fell heavily against the latter. Even so, the buyer's acceptance of the shillings invoice amounted to an implied but unequivocal promise to pay on those terms, so that their attempt to return to the pound sterling was unavailing.

It is essential that the statement was intended to affect the legal relationship between the parties: *Combe v Combe* [1951] 2 KB 215. An inadvertent or casual remark will not constitute an estopping statement. In *Sabrina Soon Duck Park Kim v Chasewood Park Residents Ltd* [2013] EWCA Civ 239, a letter from a residents' association to its tenants about the benefits of buying the reversion on their property, including that of having "no ground rent to pay", was held merely to refer to a potential benefit and was not a clear enough representation that the management company was estopped from subsequently seeking to recover ground rent from the residents.

### 3. Reliance

Third, there must have been reliance on the promise by the promisee. Exactly what is entailed by reliance is a question of some debate; however, it is apparent from the case law that, when it comes to satisfying this prerequisite, the threshold is extremely low. Clearly, detrimental reliance, in which a party has changed their position as a result of the promise, will be sufficient: *Ajayi v Briscoe* (1964) 1 WLR 1326. However, in *Alan Co. Ltd v El Nasr & Import Co.* (1972) 2 QB 18, Lord Denning held that detriment is not an essential element of promissory estoppel; any form of reliance will be sufficient, such as making a reduced payment pursuant to the promise.

### 4. Inequitable to Go Back on the Promise

Fourthly, it must be inequitable to go back on the promise. Unsurprisingly, this will preclude its use where there has been active misconduct by the representee to obtain the supposedly estopping statement. For example, in *D & C Builders v Rees* [1966] 2 WLR 28, Mrs Rees instructed the claimant, one of a pair of jobbing builders, to do work on his home for £746. He paid £250 on account, and on completion the claimant reduced the cost of the work by £14, so that £482 was outstanding. The claimant wrote several times, unavailingly pressing for payment, although there had been no complaints as to the quality of the work he had done. He was in very serious financial straits, something that Mrs Rees was aware of. He offered £300 in full and final satisfaction of the whole debt, and threatened to pay nothing, eventually forcing the claimant to accept that sum "in completion of the account". The claimant subsequently brought an action to recover the outstanding amount. When promissory estoppel was considered by Denning as a possible defence, he concluded that Mrs Rees could not rely on the doctrine because he had taken advantage of the builder's situation and misled them as to his own financial position so that it would not be inequitable to go back on the promise. (Denning LJ was alone in considering promissory estoppel in this case; Danckwerts and Winn LJJ simply applied *Foakes v Beer*).

However, it seems that it might also not be inequitable to go back on a promise in other, much less drastic or reprehensible, circumstances. For example, and *inter alia*, *Chitty on Contracts* suggests that this could be the situation where the debtor had failed to perform his promise to pay even the smaller amount agreed. A sudden improvement in the debtor's financial position, shortly after the statement was made, might also come into this category. To consider another scenario, in *The Post Chaser* (1982) 1 All ER 19, a promise was withdrawn so quickly that the counterparty was held not to have suffered a disadvantage from their reliance on it, so that it was not deemed inequitable to allow the promissor to go back on it. This issue was also examined by the Court of Appeal stage of *MWB Business Exchange Ltd v Rock Advertising Ltd* [2016] EWCA Civ 553, which is discussed below.

### The Effect of Promissory Estoppel

In *High Trees House* Denning J thought that, when it came to future periodical payments, promissory estoppel, where operative, was normally merely suspensory, so that on reasonable notice the promissor could return to his strict rights under the contract. This notion was supported in *Tool Metal Manufacturing Co Ltd v Tungsten* [1955] 1 WLR 761, where the House of Lords held that Tool Metal was entitled to reinstate the licensing fees for its tungsten carbide patents, contained in a 1938 agreement, that they had forgone during the Second World War, *provided* reasonable notice was given to the defendant. In the instant case, this return to strict contractual rights was from January 1947, well after the end of the war, so that: "[O]n giving reasonable notice to the other party, [they were able to] revert to their legal entitlement to receive the compensation payments". What is reasonable notice is a question of fact that will, presumably, depend on the amount of time involved, the subject matter of the agreement, and the nature of the estopping statement or the circumstances that gave rise to it.

Nevertheless, in *High Trees House*, Denning was clearly of the view that the right to periodical past payments that have already accrued during the estopping period was permanently extinguished, and this is now generally accepted. What of a one-off payment? It is apparent that Lord Denning thought that promissory estoppel could, in the right circumstances, permanently extinguish the rights of the promissor. In *D & C Builders v Rees* [1966] 2 WLR 28, he expressed the view that, in this situation, the "promissor would not be allowed to revert to his strict legal rights and that the promissory estoppel will be final". Similarly, in *Collier v P & MJ Wright (Holdings) Ltd* [2008] 1 WLR 643 Arden LJ accepted, in principle, that *High Trees* could be used to extinguish a creditor's right to full payment of such a one-off debt. In this case, Mr Collier was one of three jointly liable business partners who agreed to a court order to pay £46,000 to Wright Ltd, in monthly instalments. In 2000, according to Collier, there was a meeting in which Wright said he would be severally liable for £15,600, rather than jointly as a partner. The other two partners subsequently went bankrupt. In 2006, after Collier had paid his third of the debt, Wright demanded the balance of the £46,000 from him. Collier alleged, inter alia, that Wright was estopped from enforcing the full payment. Arden LJ suggested in the Court of Appeal that although, ostensibly, *Foakes v Beer* applied to the facts of the case, the "brilliant dictum" of Denning J on promissory estoppel could aid Mr Collier. If a creditor made an unequivocal and clear promise to remit a debt, they would be prevented from resiling from their promise if it was inequitable to do so. To that extent, this, too, appears to be correct.

### Confusion in *Collier v Wright*

However, in *Collier v Wright* Arden LJ went much further and suggested that if a debtor offered part payment, the creditor voluntarily accepted that offer, and in reliance on that acceptance the debtor duly paid that part in full: "For him to resile will of itself [necessarily] be inequitable". In these situations, the creditor would be bound to accept that lesser sum in full and final satisfaction of the whole debt, the right to the balance being automatically extinguished. This approach would make such a promise of almost equal significance to the provision of consideration and reduce the latter to near irrelevance in such cases. For example, and by way of illustration, if the debtor came into a fortune immediately after the promise, it would be impossible to renege on it. Although, in *Collier v Wright*, the Court of Appeal had, effectively, reiterated *Re Selectmove*, by declining to extend the decision in *Williams v Roffey* so that it would affect *Foakes v Beer*, had Arden LJ's views on promissory estoppel gained traction they would have hugely reduced the significance of the latter.[8]

It should be noted that the other two Court of Appeal judges in Collier were more equivocal on this point, suggesting that it was not inevitable that Wright's demand would be deemed inequitable. Longmore LJ thought that there might be "much to be said" on this issue by the other side. Furthermore--and this is a very important point--the decision was merely an appeal from summary judgement, aimed at establishing whether there was an "arguable defence of promissory estoppel", not a final disposal after formal trial stating that such a defence would automatically be present. More generally, some critics of Arden LJ's position were mindful of an earlier warning by Roskill LJ that promissory estoppel should not be used as a backhanded way of abolishing the doctrine of consideration: *Brikom Investments v Carr* (CA) [1979] QB 467.

### Clarity in *MWB Business Exchange Ltd v Rock Advertising Ltd*?

The Court of Appeal sought to clarify this situation in *MWB Business Exchange Ltd v Rock Advertising Ltd* [2016] EWCA Civ 553. In this case, Rock was the licensee of managed office space owned by MWB. It had fallen into arrears with the monthly licence fees that it paid to the latter. As a result, MWB served a notice to terminate the licence. Rock argued that an oral agreement had been reached, on an earlier occasion, between MWB's credit controller and one of its directors, to reschedule the monthly fees, so that Rock would pay at a lower rate for several months and then at a higher rate for the remainder of the licence period.

As it transpired, the Court of Appeal found practical benefits in Rock's promise that could constitute fresh consideration, although these were questioned in the Supreme Court (see above). However, in *obiter* comments, the court took a much more traditional approach so far as promissory estoppel was concerned. Kitchin LJ suggested that it could not be argued that it would "necessarily be inequitable" for a creditor to go back on an agreement to accept payment of a debt by (for example) instalments, and insist on payment of the balance, even where an instalment had been accepted. Everything would depend on the circumstances. In the instant case, he thought that MWB were not estopped from resiling on the alleged agreement, as Rock had only agreed to defer payment and could easily be restored to the position it was in before the oral variation, not least because, in either case, it had to pay the full arrears. Although Rock had paid £3,500, it was already bound to do this. Furthermore, only two days had elapsed before MWB sought to re-impose its strict

8 Richard Austen-Baker, "A Strange Sort of Survival for Pinnel's Case: Collier v P & M J Wright (Holdings) Limited", *The Modern Law Review*, v. 71, n. 4 (2008), pp.619-620.

legal rights under the original agreement. As a result, Rock could not claim that it had suffered any prejudice by relying upon it, "In all these circumstances I have come to the conclusion that MWB would not have been precluded by the doctrine of promissory estoppel from taking the action it did". Arden LJ, who was also on the bench, agreed with Kitchin LJ, albeit asserting that there was no inconsistency with her comments in *Collier v Wright* on the facts of the case before the court, especially given the limited information that had been available in *Collier* due to the restricted nature of the appeal.

# Chapter 3: Intention to Create Legal Relations

## Introduction

An intention to create legal relations is the third part of the essential trinity of contract formation, along with agreement and consideration. It means that the parties to a contract must intend that their agreement will be legally binding. In turn, this means that they are willing to subject any disagreement about (for example) its terms to the jurisdiction of the courts, even if they think such a possibility is extremely unlikely when they enter the contract. As Salmon LJ observed in *Jones v Padavatton* [1969] 2 All ER 616, "The fact that a contracting party is in some circumstances unlikely to extract his pound of flesh does not mean that he has no right to it."

Not every agreement that is, ostensibly, supported by consideration falls into this category. More than 200 years ago, Lord Stowell observed in *Dalrymple v Dalrymple* (1811) 161 ER 665 that: "Contracts must not be the sports of an idle hour, mere matters of pleasantry and badinage, never intended by the parties to have any serious effect whatever". Suppose that someone agrees with a close relative that they will take them out to a restaurant on Saturday provided they babysit for them on Friday. It is unlikely (without more) that the courts would take cognisance of a failure to treat the relative to the appropriate meal, after they had given up their Friday to look after an infant, despite the presence of an agreement and apparent consideration. There may well be a moral duty to honour the agreement, but that is not the same as there being a legal requirement to do so. This is because the parties to such agreements do not normally intend to be legally bound by them. Similarly, and to consider a hypothetical offer in a unilateral contract, Leggatt J noted in *Blue v Ashley* [2017] EWHC 1928 that "if someone says at a party, 'I will give you a million pounds, if you can speak for a minute on [a random subject] without hesitation, deviation or repetition', this is unlikely to be interpreted as an offer despite the literal words used". It would be unreasonable to think that such a statement was meant seriously.

Whether an intention to create legal relations is present is always a question of fact for the courts to determine. However, this is done on an objective basis: would a reasonable person think the parties intended to create legal relations? In *Jones v Padavatton* Salmon LJ observed that the court must consider what the parties said and wrote in the light of all the surrounding circumstances, and then decide "whether the true inference is that the ordinary man and woman, speaking or writing thus in such circumstances, would have intended to create a legally binding agreement". This was reiterated by Lord Clarke in *RTS Flexible Systems Limited (Respondents) v Molkerei Alois Müller GmBH & Co (Appellants)* [2010] UKSC 14, when he noted that, "It depends not upon their subjective state of mind, but upon a consideration of what was communicated between them by words or conduct, and whether that leads objectively to a conclusion that they intended to create legal relations".

For example, in the celebrated case of *Carlill v Carbolic Smoke Ball Co* [1893] 1 QB 256 the Court of Appeal considered the case of a defendant who placed a newspaper advertisement offering a £100 reward to any person who contracted influenza after using the carbolic smoke ball as a prophylactic against the illness. One of the defendant's many grounds for arguing that there was no contract was that the advertisement was a mere sales puff and lacked the requisite intention to create legal relations. However, the contested statement had also referred to the deposit of £1,000 in the Alliance Bank in Regent Street to meet any claims, so "shewing our sincerity in the matter". This indicated the appropriate intention.

By contrast, in *Kleinwort Benson (KB) v Malaysia Mining Corporation BHD (MMC BHD)* [1989] 1 WLR 379, the Court of Appeal considered intention to create legal relations in the context of a commercial "letter of comfort". Malaysia Mining Corporation (MMC Metals) was a wholly owned subsidiary of the defendant (MMC BHD) but an entirely separate legal entity. MMC Metals approached the claimant bank (KB) for a loan. It was a relatively small and new corporation, lacking in the resources of its parent company, so that the bank approached the latter asking if they would act as guarantor for the loan. MMC BHD refused to do this but stated that it was their company policy to ensure that their subsidiaries were able to meet their debts. In partial reliance on this "letter of comfort" the bank advanced the money. However, MMC Metals subsequently went into administration, without having repaid the loan. The bank sought the money from the parent company, and when it was refused, brought an action against MMC BHD to recover it, based on their earlier assurance. It was held that the letter had no legal effect. The fact that MMC BHD had originally, and clearly, refused to act as guarantor demonstrated they did not intend to be legally bound. The letter of comfort merely referred to company policy at that time. There was nothing to prevent the company changing its policy.

In a different context, in *Blue v Ashley* [2017] EWHC 1928, the High Court found that Mr Ashley (the founder of Sports Direct) had not made a binding agreement during an alcohol-fuelled meeting with others in a public house, where he allegedly promised to pay Mr Blue £15m if he managed to double Sports Direct's share price, after the latter had been engaged to provide consultancy services to the company. (Essentially, it was claimed that this was the offer in a unilateral contract.) When the share price doubled, Mr Ashley paid Mr Blue £1m. However, after failing to persuade Mr Ashley to pay a further £14m, Mr Blue issued proceedings. The High Court decided, *inter alia*, that no agreement intended to be legally binding had been reached.

In part, this was because there was no evidence that Mr Ashley negotiated contracts (rather than dealing with more routine business matters) at meetings in licensed premises where drink had been taken. It would have been out of character for him to make such a promise with a view to it being legally binding. The promise was also very vague and made no business sense, being far larger than would have been necessary to motivate Mr Blue, given the latter's annual remuneration of, at most, £250,000. Furthermore, the witness evidence suggested that the nature of the conversation that night was jocular, with people laughing quite freely at what was said. Additionally, and very importantly, there was no written record or follow-up email of what had allegedly been agreed, as might have been expected if a serious, legally binding offer of this scale had been made. As Leggatt J observed, "It is rare in modern commercial litigation to encounter a claim, particularly a claim for millions of pounds, based on an agreement which is not only said to have been made purely by word of mouth but of which there is no contemporaneous documentary record of any kind". As a result, the court concluded that any statement that was made when it came to incentivising Mr Blue was "banter" and not intended to have legal effect.

A similar conclusion was reached in *Wright v Rowland and another* [2017] EWHC 2478 (Comm), which concerned another financial consultant claiming breach of a major oral contract that was, allegedly, made on a large yacht in the south of France. The defendant denied that any agreement had occurred, and successfully argued that, even if discussions had taken place, there was no intention to create legal relations. More generally, *Chitty on Contracts* suggests that if an agreement was reached in a social context, expressed in vague language, or made in anger or jest, these are all factors that tend to suggest that it was not meant to be legally binding.[1]

## Presumptions

To assist the courts in determining whether an intention to create legal relations is present on the facts of a case, the law has recourse to two presumptions, one pertaining to social and domestic agreements, the other to those made in a commercial context. In the former, there is a presumption against there being an intention to create legal relations, this becoming stronger as the social or domestic relationship becomes closer. In the latter, there is a strong presumption in favour of there being an intention to create legal relations. Both are presumptions of fact and so rebuttable, and there have been numerous cases in which they have been successfully rebutted: *Jones v Padavatton* [1969] 2 All ER 616. As was noted in this case, any competent contract draftsman would be able to draw up an agreement that would rebut the presumption that relations between close family members were not normally intended to be binding. A simple clause stating that the agreement was intended to have legal effect would normally be sufficient. (In many cases even this is not necessary.)

## Domestic Agreements

In *Jones v Padavatton* Salmon LJ, like his two fellow judges in the Court of Appeal, accepted that "as a rule when arrangements are made between close relations, for example, between husband and wife, parent and child or uncle and nephew in

1 *Chitty on Contracts*, 32nd edn. (London: Sweet & Maxwell, 2015), v. 1, paras. 2-177, 2-194, and 2-195.

relation to an allowance, there is a presumption against an intention of creating any legal relationship." This was based on experience of human nature, which indicated that in such circumstances men and women did not usually intend to create legal rights and obligations, but instead relied solely on family ties of mutual trust and affection.

A classic (if extreme) illustration of the presumption can be seen in *Balfour v Balfour* [1919] 2 KB 571, in which a colonial civil servant, who worked in Ceylon (now Sri Lanka) returned to England on leave with his wife. When he went back to Ceylon, his wife stayed behind in England for health reasons (she had arthritis), so he agreed to send her maintenance payments of £30 each month. At the time of the agreement the couple were (ostensibly) happily married. Their relationship later soured, and the husband wrote to his wife suggesting that they separate and stopped making the payments. She unsuccessfully sought to enforce the maintenance agreement in the courts. It was held that their arrangement was a purely social and domestic agreement, and therefore it was presumed that the parties did not intend to be legally bound. (There may have been problems identifying consideration as well).

However, for the presumption to apply to a married couple they must still be living in amity. In the Court of Appeal case of *Merritt v Merritt* [1970] 1 WLR 1211, a husband left his wife to live with another woman, after which the (former) couple met in a parked car to discuss the financial aspects of their separation. Part of the mortgage on their house, which was jointly owned by them, remained to be paid. At their meeting, the husband signed an agreement (not a deed) promising that he would pay the wife £40 per month to enable her to meet the payments on the mortgage, and that, if she paid it off, he would transfer his share of the house to her. When the mortgage was paid off, she brought an action for a legal declaration that the house belonged to her.

The Court of Appeal held that the agreement made in the car was binding. The court distinguished *Balfour v Balfour* on the grounds that the Merritts were already separated, not living in amity, and held that in these circumstances people normally did intend to be bound by their agreements. As Lord Denning MR observed, "They do not rely on honourable understandings. They want everything cut and dried. It may safely be presumed that they intend to create legal relations". The signing of a written agreement in this case was further (and strong) evidence of an intention to be bound. Similarly, in *Darke* v *Strout* [2003] EWCA Civ 176, the Court of Appeal found that an agreement for child maintenance set out in a letter following the breakdown of an unmarried couple's long-term relationship did not lack an intention to create legal relations given what Thorpe LJ referred to as the "due formality" of the written document. Indeed, the same judge thought that arguments to the contrary were "hopeless".

As was noted in *Jones v Padavatton*, the presumption also applies to agreements between uncles and aunts and their nephews and nieces (as it does to some other familial relationships), if not usually as strongly as it does between spouses or between parents and their children. For example, it was rebutted between nephew and uncle in *Shadwell v Shadwell* (1860) 9 CB NS 159, and by aunt and uncle and their niece in *Parker v Clark* [1960] 1 WLR 286. In the latter case, the Clarks were an elderly couple who invited their niece and her husband, the Parkers, to live with them. The Parkers indicated that, although they would like to do this, it would require them to sell their own house. The Clarks assured the Parkers that they would leave a share of their house to Mrs Parker in their will. The Parkers sold their house, lent the money released to their daughter so that she could buy a flat, and moved in.

Unfortunately, the Parkers subsequently fell out with the Clarks, who asked them to leave. They successfully sued for damages for breach of contract. Devlin J noted that they had relied on the assurance of the Clarks, to their detriment; the defendant could not really have thought that: "the law would leave him [Mr Clark] at liberty, if he so chose, to tell the [Parkers] when they arrived that he had changed his mind, that they could take their furniture away, and that he was indifferent whether they found anywhere else to live or not". The severe detriment suffered by the Clarks helped rebut any presumption that this might have been a social arrangement.

Whether or not a presumption has been rebutted can be a difficult decision to make, as can be seen in *Jones v Padavatton* [1969] 2 All ER 616. In this case, the three judges sitting in the Court of Appeal agreed on the law governing intention, and that the case before them was close to the borderline in this regard but were divided as to which side of this line it fell. A Trinidad-based mother, Violet Jones, had agreed with her daughter, Ruby Padavatton, a 34-year-old single mother to a young child, that if she gave up her well-paid and pensionable job as an assistant accountant at the Indian Embassy in Washington, and studied for the Bar in England, she (the mother) would pay her maintenance of 200 each month. (This was later varied to occupation of a London house, purchased by the mother, in which the daughter both lived and rented out rooms for income).

The arrangement between mother and daughter subsequently became acrimonious and ended in litigation. One question for the court was whether the original agreement between them had been legally binding, or whether it was merely a family arrangement. On this issue, two of the judges, Lords Justice Fenton-Atkinson and Dankwerts, thought that the presumption had not been rebutted, although they recognised it was close to the margin, while one, Lord Justice Salmon, thought that, on its "very unusual" facts, it had. The explanation for their disagreement on this issue (they agreed on the ultimate decision) lies in the different weight that they gave to aspects of the evidence adduced at first instance.

Like the Court of Appeal in *Parker v Clark*, Salmon LJ was very influenced by the amount that the daughter had given up. She was on the cusp of middle age in 1962, had been settled in Washington for 13 years in a comfortable flat, with a good and secure job as an embassy book-keeper. She had a son of seven years of age who was an American citizen and had already begun his education there. Salmon LJ could not envisage that a woman in this situation would risk such a life on an unenforceable agreement, even one made with her mother. He was also influenced by the mother's using her attorney to draw up a draft undertaking. By contrast, the other two judges placed more emphasis on, for example, the tearful way she had responded to her mother when a dispute arose, her lack of complaint when she discovered that the allowance was being paid in West Indian dollars rather than the (much more valuable) US dollars she had expected, and that she had been very close to her mother when the agreement was made. They felt that these factors were indicative of a family rather than a legal arrangement.

## Social Agreements

Social agreements also raise a presumption that the parties do not intend to create legal relations. The strength of this presumption depends on the closeness of the friendship or acquaintanceship, although it is rarely as strong as that involving intimate family relationships. For example, in *Coward v MIB* [1963] 1 QB 359, the husband of the claimant was regularly picked up as a pillion passenger by a friend and workmate on his motorbike and taken to their place of employment. In exchange, he helped with the cost of the petrol for the journey by paying a small sum of money each week. Sadly, there came a day when the two men were involved in a collision, and both were killed.

The crash was due to the negligence of Coward's friend, but his motorbike was not insured for accidents to pillion passengers. As the law then stood, this was not compulsory, *unless* the vehicle was being used to carry a passenger pursuant to a contract for hire or reward. In the latter situation, the Motor Insurance Bureau (MIB) would be required to cover an uninsured driver. Mr Coward's widow claimed that there was such a contract between the two dead men. However, the MIB argued that there was no binding contract, as there was no intention to create legal relations in the agreement, and so no obligation on the MIB to compensate Mr Coward's dependant. This was accepted by the Court of Appeal, which concluded that the arrangement was a social and domestic agreement between friends.

Nevertheless, the presumption against intention in a social context was successfully rebutted in *Simpkins v Pays* [1955] 1 WLR 975. In this case, a grandmother, her granddaughter, and a lodger regularly entered a monthly fashion competition in a Sunday newspaper. The costs of postage and the entry fee were shared. When the question of sharing winnings was considered by the lodger and grandmother, the latter said that they would "go shares" if anyone was lucky. The entry sent in for June 1954 was successful. It had been filled in by the lodger but was made out in the grandmother's name. The grandmother subsequently refused to pay a third of the prize money to the lodger, claiming that the arrangement to share any winnings was not intended to produce legal consequences. This was rejected by the court, which held that there was a binding agreement to share any proceeds three ways.

Conversely, in *Wilson & Anor v Burnett* [2007] EWCA Civ 1170 the Court of Appeal unanimously dismissed an appeal from a trial judge's decision that Burnett (the defendant), who had won a national bingo prize of £101,211 while playing with two work friends (the claimants), had not made a binding oral agreement with them that they would share any individual winnings equally. There was a dispute as to what had been agreed, although the judge accepted that there had been some chat about sharing winnings. However, the judge was not satisfied that the claimants had established that an intention to create legal relations could be inferred from the discussions leading up to the relevant bingo session.

**Commercial Agreements**

Where agreements are made between commercial bodies, or by a commercial body with an employee or consumer, there is a very strong presumption that they are intended to be legally binding. For example, in the Court of Appeal decision in *Edwards v Skyways* [1964] 1 WLR 349, the claimant was an airline pilot employed by the defendant, which decided to make some of its air crew redundant in the light of a challenging financial environment. Mr Edwards was one of those to be made redundant. As part of this, the defendants offered to match his contributions to the company pension fund, if he withdrew them, in what it termed an "*ex gratia*" payment. The claimant agreed and withdrew his contributions. However, the defendant company, experiencing worse financial difficulties than anticipated, subsequently sought to renege on its promise with regard to the *ex gratia* payment, on the basis that such words, by their nature, were not indicative of an intention to be legally bound. The Court of Appeal found for the claimant. It held that, despite the phrase employed (which indicates generosity rather than obligation), because the agreement had been made in a business context, there was a strong presumption that it was intended to be legally binding, and this had not been rebutted.

More recently, *Barbudev v Eurocom Cable Management Bulgaria Eood* [2012] EWCA Civ 548 provided another example of the courts' willingness to find that agreements negotiated in a commercial context evince an intention to create binding obligations. In this case, the issue in dispute was whether a side letter was a legally enforceable contract, or no more than an agreement to agree. In the High Court, Blair J held, *inter alia*, that the parties did not intend to create legal relations. The Court of Appeal upheld the High Court's decision that the side letter was unenforceable for *uncertainty* but were unanimous in overturning the first-instance finding that the parties did not intend to create legal relations. In this context, Aikens LJ pointed to the fact that the letter was drafted by City lawyers and contained legal language, such as referring to the parties' providing consideration. The onus of proving a lack of intention to create legal relations was on the party asserting it, not easily discharged, and this had not occurred in the instant case.

Nevertheless, although strong, it is not an irrebuttable presumption. A suitably worded clause in an agreement, for example, could easily do just that. In the House of Lords case of *Rose & Frank Co v Crompton Bros* [1925] AC 445 the parties entered into an agreement for the supply of carbonised tissue paper under which the claimants were to be the defendant's sole agents in America for a set period. The agreement contained an 'honourable pledge' clause which stated that it was not a legally binding agreement and could not be subject to the jurisdiction of the courts in either England or the United States. The defendants terminated the agreement early, prompting the claimants to bring an action for breach of contract. They failed in this as the honourable pledge clause clearly rebutted the (strong) presumption that the parties to commercial agreements intend to be legally bound.

It should be noted that honourable pledge clauses are not confined to commercial contracts. In *Jones v Vernon Pools* (1938) 2 All ER 626, Mr Jones appeared to have won a large sum of money after playing the football pools. On the back of his receipt there was an honourable pledge clause from the pools company stating that the entry of the relevant coupon "shall not give rise to any legal relations". The company claimed not to have received the coupon and, in any event, asserted that it was not a binding contract because of the clause. The court held that the "binding in honour only" clause demonstrated that the parties did not intend to be legally bound, so that Mr Jones's claim was dismissed. This decision was reiterated half a century later in the very similar case of *Ferrera v Littlewoods Pools* [1998] EWCA Civ 618. Again, the claimant filled in what would have been a winning entry and sent it to Littlewoods Pools. The latter denied receiving it but, again, also claimed that they would not be legally obliged to pay out, even if they had, because of a binding in honour only clause. The claimant unsuccessfully challenged the decision reached in *Jones v Vernon*. Littlewoods were not required to pay out because of the clause, which demonstrated an intention not to be legally bound.

### Executed Agreements and Intention

Once an agreement has, ostensibly, been performed, rather than being executory, the courts will be very reluctant to find that the parties did not intend to contract. As Steyn LJ observed in *G Percy Trentham Ltd v Archital Luxfer Ltd* [1993] 1 Lloyd's Rep. 25, "The fact that the transaction was performed on both sides will often make it unrealistic to argue that there was no intention to enter into legal relations". This can be significant, because commercial pressure can sometimes mean that work will start on a project before the terms of a contract have been fully and formally drawn up, let alone executed, even though the Supreme Court has stressed its perils: *RTS Flexible Systems Limited (Respondents) v Molkerei Alois Müller GmBH* [2010] UKSC 14. Thus, had one of the parties failed to pay for tissue paper that had been delivered and used in *Rose & Frank Co v Crompton Bros*, rather than their refusing to honour future orders, the court may well have enforced the agreement. (Alternatively, they could have made a *quantum meruit* order).

## "Subject to Contract"

The phrase "subject to contract" is often placed as a heading on letters or emails during contractual negotiations. It is well established that dealing on this basis negates contractual intention in any apparent agreement prior to a formal contract being executed. Thus, in *Winn v Bull* (1877) 7 Ch D 29, the defendant made a written agreement to take a lease on a house. However, this was stipulated to be "subject to the preparation and approval of a formal contract". The claimant subsequently sought specific performance of the agreement. This was rejected, Sir George Jessel MR observing that "where you have a proposal or agreement made in writing expressed to be subject to a formal contract being prepared, it means what it says; it is subject to and is dependent upon a formal contract being prepared".

In *Joanne Properties Ltd v Moneything Capital Ltd* [2020] EWCA Civ 1541 the Court of Appeal overturned a decision at first instance that concluded that the parties had reached a binding agreement despite employing "subject to contract" communications. The Court of Appeal reiterated the long-standing and traditional meaning of the phrase to mean that neither party intends to be bound by any "agreement", and each reserves their right to withdraw from negotiations at any point, until a formal contract is executed. In this case, the Court of Appeal held that the trial judge had "seriously undervalued" the force of using "subject to contract" wording in written correspondence. The court emphasised that once negotiations are begun that are subject to contract the court will not conclude that such a qualification has been withdrawn unless it is expressly agreed by the parties, or if this is the necessary implication of their words or conduct, even of the phrase is not always used in subsequent correspondence. The waiving of "subject to contract" status needs to have been unequivocally agreed by the parties, as occurred in *RTS Flexible Systems Limited (Respondents) v Molkerei Alois Müller GmBH & Co (Appellants)* [2010] UKSC 14.

# Chapter 4: Certainty and Formalities

## Introduction

This chapter will consider two separate contractual issues: certainty and the requirement for formalities. The need for the former applies to all contacts, while the latter affects only a small number of agreements.

## Certainty

The notion of freedom of contract means that it is for the parties, not the courts, to draft the terms of their agreement. As a result, if sense cannot be made of an agreement, it will fail for uncertainty. As Sir Andrew Morritt VC observed in *Baird Textile Holdings Ltd v Marks & Spencer Plc* [2001] EWCA Civ 274, "All contracts, to be enforceable, must be sufficiently certain to enable the courts to give effect to the parties' intentions rather than to give effect to a contract which the court has had to write for them". More recently, Alexander Nissen QC, sitting as a Deputy High Court Judge, observed that a contractual provision will be void for uncertainty if the court "cannot reach a conclusion as to what was in the parties' minds or where it is not safe for the court to prefer one possible meaning to other equally possible meanings": *Buckingham Group Contracting Limited v Peel L&P Investments And Property Limited* [2022] EWHC 1842 (TCC).

However, it is not every minor uncertainty that will have this effect. As Maugham LJ observed in *Foley v Classique Coaches Ltd* (1943) 2 KB 1, to make a contract unviable, the vagueness or complete absence of a term must normally relate to a significant matter. Nevertheless, all material terms must either be agreed or there must be a mechanism for determining what they are: "An agreement to agree in the future is not a contract; nor is there a contract if a material term is neither settled nor implied by law and the document contains no machinery for ascertaining it".

For example, a contract failed for uncertainty of terms in *G Scammell and Nephew Ltd v HC & JG Ouston* [1941] 1 AC 251. The claimants in this case wished to trade in their old van for a new vehicle purchased from the defendants. They agreed a specific price for the old van's trade-in value, but only that they would pay for the new van "on hire purchase terms" (hire with the option to purchase the vehicle) over a two-year period. The defendants subsequently withdrew from the agreement, and when the claimants attempted to sue, argued that the agreement was too uncertain to be enforced. The House of Lords agreed. Hire purchase terms varied enormously, there was no evidence that there were any well-known "usual terms" in the industry, and there was no way the court could know what price was intended or appropriate, and this was vital to the contract, as were several related matters. For example, there was no mention of interest payments in the agreement. As Viscount Maugham observed, "In order to constitute a valid contract the parties must so express themselves that their meaning can be determined with a reasonable degree of certainty". Otherwise, identifying a consensus *ad idem* would be a matter of mere conjecture.

In like manner, in *May and Butcher v The King* [1934] 2 KB 17, the Government's Disposals Board had arranged by written agreement to sell surplus government military tentage that was left over from the First World War to the claimants, at prices and times to be agreed, as and when the tents became available. May and Butcher Ltd left £1,000 as a security deposit for their purchases. In 1923, a new Disposals Board took over and refused to sell the tents. The House of Lords found that the original agreement to agree was not a legally binding contract. Price was, and is, fundamental to a contract for the sale of goods and had not been determined. Although s.8 SOGA 1893 (and 1979) provides that a reasonable price can be implied by the courts if it is not mentioned in a binding agreement, this particular contract was not silent on how price was to be determined, which was to be by the parties agreeing it from time to time, so that the statutory provision was not operative. (Section 15 of SGSA and s.51 of CRA import similar implied terms to those set out in s.8 SOGA).[1] More generally, in many (but not all) cases, the courts will decide that a failure to agree a price is indicative that the parties had not yet entered a binding agreement.

More recently, in *Mamidoil Jetoil Greek Petroleum Company SA v Okta Crude Oil Refinery AD* [2001] EWCA Civ 406, Rix LJ noted that where the parties have used the phrase "to be agreed" in relation to an essential term, it is unlikely that a contract has been formed, as there must normally be consensus on all vital parts of the transaction. Similarly, in *Barbudev* v *European Cable Management Bulgaria Eood* [2012] EWCA Civ 548, a communication that offered investment on "terms to be agreed" was unenforceable for uncertainty. Nobody could tell what the terms might have been. The court reiterated that there is no such thing as a legally binding "agreement to agree".

In *Blue v Ashley* [2017] EWHC 1928, Leggatt J noted that even if he had not found the alleged agreement lacking in any intention to create legal relations, he would have found that it failed for uncertainty, because it lacked an essential term. The relevant payment of £15 million was, it was claimed, contingent on the claimant's doubling the share price of the defendant's company. However, nowhere was it stipulated as to how long he had to do this, and the gap was "not one which the court can fill". The judge observed that although. in many cases, such as a contract for the carriage of goods, a term could be implied that performance must occur within a reasonable time to make sense of the agreement and avoid fatal uncertainty, this was not possible in the instant case. In part this was because there was no yardstick available to determine such a period; there was no previous course of dealing between the parties or any ordinary commercial usage that could be consulted on the issue.

---

1 Under section 8 SOGA 1979, with regard to ascertainment of price: (1) The price in a contract of sale may be fixed by the contract, or may be left to be fixed in a manner agreed by the contract, or may be determined by the course of dealing between the parties. (2) Where the price is not determined as mentioned in sub-section (1) above the buyer must pay a reasonable price. (3) What is a reasonable price is a question of fact dependent on the circumstances of each particular case.

## Reluctance to Find Uncertainty

In the modern era the courts have been keen to preserve contracts, especially commercial agreements, wherever possible, and some modern observers even feel that *May and Butcher* manifests an excessive reluctance to find ways of making sense of uncertainty and might not be followed today. Certainly, the courts will try to give legal force to the parties' attempt to make a contract unless it is legally or practically impossible: *Scammel* v *Dicker* [2005] EWCA Civ 405. They are aware that, if any potential ambiguity allowed an agreement to fail, commercial life would quickly become very difficult, if not impossible, while also appreciating that parties seeking to avoid contracts for uncertainty are often doing so because they regret entering the agreement, perhaps because a better opportunity has arisen elsewhere.

As a result, and as was noted in *Hillas v Arcos* (1932) 147 LT 503, "even if the construction of the words used may be di cult, that is not a reason for holding them too ambiguous or uncertain to be enforced if the fair meaning of the parties can be extracted". Similarly, in *Baird Textile Holdings Ltd v Marks & Spencer Plc* [2001] EWCA Civ 274, Sir Andrew Morritt VC observed that the courts do not incline towards a "nit-picking" attitude to such matters and will endeavour, where possible, to construe the obligations in a way which gives effect to the parties' bargain. In like manner, in *Openwork Ltd v Forte* [2018] EWCA Civ 783, the Court of Appeal reiterated that courts should strive to give some meaning to contractual clauses agreed by the parties, if it is at all possible, not least because businessmen often record very important agreements in a crude and summary fashion and they must have meant something by them when they did so.

For an example of this approach at work can be considered *Durham Tees Valley Airport Ltd v Bmibaby Ltd* [2010] EWCA Civ 485. In this case, an airline entered an agreement with Durham Tees Valley Airport (DTVA) to operate two aircraft from their airfield for ten years from 2004. After incurring heavy losses, the airline abandoned its operation in 2006. The airport then brought an action for breach of contract. The airline contended that the agreement was insufficiently certain to be enforceable. For example, it did not specify a minimum number of passengers or flights that were to be flown to or from the airfield each week or year. As a result, they argued that it merely provided the airline with the permissive right to conduct operations from Durham, not a mandatory obligation to do so. Nevertheless, the Court of Appeal concluded that the agreement contained sufficiently clear terms to determine Bmibaby's required minimum level of performance, and this had been breached. Patten LJ, considering the issue of certainty in these situations, thought that for a contract to be enforceable the court must be able to say whether any particular standard of performance is a breach of contact. This test had been met in the instant case.

Similarly, in *Vinci Construction UK Ltd v Beumer Group UK Ltd* [2017] EWHC 2196 [TCC], Vinci was carrying out construction work at Gatwick Airport and subcontracted some of the building tasks to Beumer. However, there was no definition in the documents of several important terms, such as "Baggage" or "Remaining Works". Beumer subsequently argued that the provisions were so uncertain as to render the contract void. Even so, citing *Arnhold & Co Ltd v Attorney General of Hong Kong* (1989) 47 BLR 129, the High Court reiterated that a contract will be void for uncertainty only if the court cannot reach a conclusion as to what was in the parties' minds, or where it is not safe for the court to prefer one possible meaning to other equally plausible meanings. In the instant case they were able to attribute meanings to the words and uphold the agreement.

**Aids to Preserving Contracts**

The courts have identified several aids that can be used to make sense of, and so preserve, contracts in which there is apparent uncertainty. As already indicated with regard to s.8 SOGA 1979, some are statutory. Thus, under s.52 Consumer Rights Act 2015, if a time is not stipulated for completion of a service, it must be carried out within a reasonable period, this being a question of fact for the court to determine. However, others have been developed by the courts. For example, in *Nicolene v Simmonds* [1963] 1 QB 543, a contract for the sale of iron bars stated that "we are in agreement that the usual conditions of acceptance apply". There were no such "usual conditions", and it was argued that this rendered the contract unenforceable for uncertainty. However, this was rejected by the Court of Appeal, Lord Denning noting that, in the right circumstances, an uncertain but meaningless phrase, that could be deleted without impairing the sense or reasonableness of the contract, might simply be ignored or severed from the agreement, this being the so-called blue-pencil test (also used elsewhere in the law of contract).

Sometimes, the contract itself will provide a mechanism for determining price or other matters, if agreement is not reached, and the courts will ensure that this is effective. Thus, in *Foley v Classique Coaches Ltd* (1943) 2 KB 1 Foley owned a petrol station and its surrounding land. He sold some of this land to Classique Coaches Ltd. As part of this agreement, Classique was required to purchase all the fuel for their buses from Foley's petrol station, provided the latter was able to supply it. It also contained an arbitration clause, but not a stipulated price for the petrol, which was to be sold at a price to be "agreed by the parties in writing and from time to time". The agreement operated smoothly for three years, until Classique received legal advice suggesting that it might be unenforceable for uncertainty, and stopped buying fuel from Foley, which sued them for breach of contract.

The Court of Appeal concluded that the agreement was not void for uncertainty, even though the price for the fuel had not been set out in it. There was an implied term that, in default of agreement, the fuel was to be of reasonable quality and sold at a reasonable price, and the contract contained an arbitration clause to resolve disputes as to what this might be, which was also something that could be determined on an objective basis by the court. In this case, the judges were influenced by the fact that the second agreement was part of the consideration provided for the land being transferred to the defendant, something that made it particularly undesirable to hold it void for uncertainty. Classique Coaches was in breach of contract by failing to purchase its fuel from Foley.

Similarly, in *Sudbrook Trading Estate v Eggleton* [1983] AC 444, a lease on an industrial property gave the tenant an option to purchase the freehold of the property at such price "as may be agreed upon by two valuers one to be nominated by the lessor and the other by the lessee". The tenant sought to exercise this option, but the landlord refused to appoint a surveyor and argued that, as a result, the purchase clause was too vague to be enforced, as it did not specify a price. The House of Lords rejected this argument. The agreement specified a mechanism to establish a fair and reasonable price. This rendered the option sufficiently certain. Because the mechanism had broken down due to the landlords refusing to appoint a valuer, the court could intervene to set a fair price and grant an order for specific performance if the defendants failed to proceed with the sale.

Referring to industry norms or special trade definitions provides another way of making sense of apparently uncertain terms, while taking cognisance of other, similar, executed contracts between the parties can also give guidance. For example, in *WN Hillas & Co Ltd v Arcos Ltd* [1932] 147 LT 503, Hillas were large-scale timber merchants. In 1930, they agreed to purchase 22,000 units (or standards) of timber of "fair specification", on condition that they should also have the option of entering a contract with Arcos to purchase 100,000 units the following year with a 5% reduction in price. The initial 22,000 standards of timber were delivered and paid for without issue. However, the following year, Arcos refused to sell them the 100,000 standards, on the grounds that the term as to their quality was too uncertain. (In reality, they had already sold the requisite timber elsewhere.) They lost on this basis at first instance, won on appeal (the Court of Appeal feeling that too much in the agreement was left unsettled), but lost on final appeal to the House of Lords, which rejected the argument as to uncertainty. The previous year's contract had also included the requirement of "fair specification", and timber of a certain standard had been tendered and accepted as satisfying that requirement. This could be used as indicative of the necessary quality required for the 100,000 units of timber under the option. Lord Wright noted that it was clear that both the parties originally intended to contract, and both thought they had done so. Businessmen often recorded important agreements in a crude fashion, and, where possible, it was the court's duty to construe them fairly but without being too zealous or subtle in finding defects.

In like manner, in *MRI Trading AG v The Erdenet Mining Corporation LLC* [2013] EWCA Civ 156, the Court of Appeal was able to uphold a contract containing an agreement to agree on the price for copper concentrates, despite the decision in *May v Butcher*, by considering the wider context of the agreement. The Court read the disputed contract in the light of two other contracts for the same concentrates, seeing them as parts of a wider whole.

Unsurprisingly, and as with intention to create legal relations (see below), once an agreement has been (largely) carried out, the courts will be particularly reluctant to decide that it fails for uncertainty. In *G Percy Trentham Ltd v Archital Luxfer Ltd*. [1993] 1 Lloyd's Rep. 25, Steyn LJ noted that "the fact that the transaction is executed makes it easier to imply a term resolving any uncertainty, or, alternatively, it may make it possible to treat a matter not finalised in negotiations as inessential". This avoids the inconvenience of *quantum meruit* claims for completed work where the courts ultimately decide that there was no binding contract, as was the case with the manufacture and delivery of steel work for a construction project in *British Steel Corp* v *Cleveland Bridge and Engineering Co Ltd* [1984] 1 All ER 504.

## Formalities

At common law, all contracts can be made informally. There is no requirement that they be made or even evidenced in writing, let alone in a particular form of writing, such as a deed. All the exceptions to this general rule are statutory. As a result, "form", unlike agreement, consideration, and intention, is not an essential prerequisite for all contracts. Furthermore, the number of exceptions to the general principle is very limited, so that most contracts can be made by a purely oral agreement, whatever their value. Thus, a diamond dealer and one of his customers could have a purely verbal contract to buy/sell a huge ruby worth £10 million. Of course, it would be very foolish to do so, because if there was a dispute it might be difficult to persuade the courts that there had been such a contract if this was denied by one of the parties to the alleged agreement--not least because, as Leggatt J has noted, to anyone with business experience its absence might tend to suggest that there was no contract--and precisely what its terms were, even if it was not. However, these "are matters of proof they are not legal requirements": *Blue v Ashley* [2017] EWHC 1928.

For another illustrative example can be considered the alleged, but firmly denied, and ultimately not proven existence of multi-billion-pound oral contracts between two Russian oligarchs that the court had to examine in *Berezovsky v Abramovich* [2012] EWHC 2463 (Comm). More recently, in *Moorgate Capital v Sun European* (2020) EWHC 593 (Comm), the High Court concluded, inter alia, that there was insufficient evidence of a consensus being reached to conclude that an oral contract arose from a ten-minute telephone conversation between two directors from Moorgate and Sun European. It had been alleged that the former's offer of advisory services for £1 million had been accepted by the latter. In part, this decision was reached because the court felt that it was unlikely that a contract of this type and magnitude would be agreed in a telephone conversation without being put into writing, something that was supported by expert evidence at trial. Furthermore, there had been no follow-up correspondence confirming what had (allegedly) occurred, while the fee itself was unusually large for this kind of transaction. Additionally, a subsequent email did not refer to a contract having been concluded, and some later emails spoke of a "proposal".

Nevertheless, such an oral contract would be entirely valid and binding *if* its existence and terms could be proved in a manner that satisfied the court. In this, common law differs from many Roman-law countries, where there is often a requirement that, to be enforceable, even comparatively small contracts must be in, or evidenced by, writing. "Evidenced in writing" means that, for example, an oral contract of which there is later confirmation by a memorandum in writing could satisfy the requirement.

### Statutory Exceptions to the General Rule

One of the most important statutory exceptions to the general situation, when it comes to formalities, involves contracts for the sale or disposition of an interest in land. These must be "made in writing" by virtue of s.2 of the Law of Property (Miscellaneous Provisions) Act 1989. Even more demanding, a lease for more than three years must be made by deed, not just in writing, by dint of s.52 and s.54(2) of the Law of Property Act 1925.[2] It should be noted in this context that s.91 of the Land Registration Act 2002 provides that a document in electronic form that purports to effect a disposition, and which meets certain requirements, is to be regarded for the purposes of any enactment as a deed. Less demandingly, section 4 of the Statute of Frauds 1677 requires that for contracts of guarantee (surety for another's debt) to be enforceable "some Memorandum or Note thereof shall be in Writing and signed by the party to be charged therewith or some other person thereunto by him lawfully authorised." In *Golden Ocean Group Ltd v Salacia Mining Industries PVT Ltd and Another* [2012] EWCA Civ 265 the Court of Appeal decided that a lengthy exchange of authenticated emails between two parties, without any single formal document being signed, satisfied the requirements of section 4 of the Statute of Frauds 1677. They could be put together to form a complete agreement which not only constituted a guarantee but also complied with the Act. Section 4 does not require an agreement to be evidenced in a single document.

Contracts of consumer credit, for the transfer of shares in a limited company, for the assignment of the benefit of some contractual rights, between seamen in a UK registered ship and those employing them, and for some intellectual-property rights, amongst several others, also normally require some type of writing (depending on the type of contract) to be binding. Again, this can normally be provided by electronic communication, as well as in paper and ink. Occasionally disputes as to whether these requirements have been met come before the courts.

---

2 Deeds are sometimes used for ordinary or "simple" contracts (those supported by consideration) where they are not legally required, because agreements made in this manner have a statutory "limitation period" of 12 years, unlike the six years found in simple contracts under the Limitation Act 1980. This means that a party to the contract can bring a claim for breach up to 12 years after it took place, without being time-barred.

## No Oral Modification (NOM) Clauses

"No Oral Modification" (NOM) clauses are sometimes included in written contracts to impose a degree of formality on future changes to the agreement. They are often found in the "boilerplate clauses" of commercial contracts. (These are ready-made, all-purpose, clauses that are inserted into different kinds of agreement). NOMs forbid the parties from orally agreeing an amendment to their contract, requiring any changes to be made in (usually signed) writing. Holding that NOM clauses are binding occasions creates theoretical problems in contract law. It might be argued that, as the parties to an agreement have freedom of contract, provided they both agree that the relevant clause be disregarded, it can properly be ignored, and the contract changed verbally, the original contract not being able to restrict such freedom, especially as English law rarely requires "form". However, upholding them also brings benefits. For example, NOMs avoid the risk of disagreements as to precisely what the oral variation was, if any, given that oral discussions can readily give rise to misunderstandings.

In recent decades the status of NOM clauses has been a matter of some legal debate, with theoretical and practical arguments vying with each other. Nevertheless, in *MWB Business Exchange v Rock Advertising* [2019] AC 119, the Supreme Court settled this issue when (albeit with one partially dissenting voice) it reversed the decision of the Court of Appeal in the same case and held that they *were* binding. In this case, MWB contracted with Rock to use its office premises as a licensee for one year at a monthly rental. The licence agreement contained a NOM clause, Clause 7.6, which provided that the written contract set out all the terms agreed between MWB and Licensee and stated, "All variation to this Licence must be agreed, set out in writing and signed on behalf of both parties before they take effect". Rock subsequently encountered financial difficulties and claimed that MWB had *orally* agreed to vary the license agreement. Even if this was true (it was disputed), it raised the question as to whether the variation could be effective given the existence of the NOM clause.

The Supreme Court decided that any alteration to the contract, including the abandonment of Clause 7.6, could not be effective unless first put in writing and signed by both parties. An "informal" variation (one that was not compliant with the relevant clause) was invalid. Lord Sumption observed that the law "should and does give effect to a contractual provision requiring specified formalities to be observed for a variation". They were commonly found in commercial agreements, and there were legitimate reasons for upholding them, not least because they avoided the misunderstandings often produced by oral variations. The objections to enforcing NOM clauses were largely conceptual, the argument being that it was impossible to prevent the parties orally changing their agreement. However, the same judge also observed that once a NOM clause had been formally abandoned by a written agreement, future variations could be made orally.

It should be noted that several common law countries have rejected this (English) approach and held that NOMs are not binding. Thus, the courts in Singapore were influenced by criticism of the decision in *MWB Business Exchange* from both academics and practising lawyers and preferred the Court of Appeal analysis in that case: *Charles Lim Teng Siang v Hong Choon Hau* [2021] SGCA 43. They favoured a more liberal approach, deciding that NOM clauses merely create a rebuttable presumption that oral modifications are not effective.

# Chapter 5: Capacity and Illegality

## Capacity to Contract

In English law there is a presumption that all (natural) legal persons have the capacity to contract. However, where those who are minors, lack the necessary mental ability, are drunk, or (it is thought) under the influence of mind-altering drugs enter a contract, this presumption can, in certain circumstances, be rebutted so that the agreement will not be enforceable. In all cases, the onus is on the person seeking to rebut the presumption of capacity to establish that they belong to one of the three protected classes due to infancy, mental incapacity, or intoxication. It should be noted that s.3 of the Sale of Goods Act 1979 expressly states that the ability to buy and sell goods is regulated by the general law concerning capacity to contract.

## Minors

A minor is someone under 18 years of age, by dint of s.1 of the Family Law Reform Act 1969 (which reduced it from 21). Minors can enter contracts. However, most such contracts are "voidable". This means that they can be avoided (terminated) by the minor at any point before the minor reaches 18 years, or within a reasonable time thereafter. What is a reasonable time is a matter for the court to determine and will depend on the facts of each case. The purpose of the rule is to protect the minor, so that it is irrelevant that an adult is unaware that the person they are dealing with when they enter an agreement is below 18 years of age. This means that, for example, if goods are supplied to a minor he will not normally have to pay for them, although he will usually be required to return them. Thus, in the modern era, s.3(1)(b) of the Minors' Contracts Act 1987 expressly provides that if a contract is unenforceable against a minor the court may, if it is just and equitable to do so, require him to return to the claimant any property acquired under the agreement, or any property representing it. (This is a rare statutory intervention in a field that is largely dominated by common law).

There are only two types of contract that are binding on a minor, and so constitute exceptions to the general rule: those for "necessaries" (especially when the contract has been executed) and contracts of service that are deemed to be for the minor's own benefit, such as those involving apprenticeship, training, or education.

## Necessaries and Instructional Contracts

Necessaries involve the basic goods and services required for daily living. However, the notion extends beyond food and the protective clothing needed to keep warm and dry, being influenced by the minor's needs, age, means, and even, perhaps a little anachronistically, their 'station' in life, something that was put into statutory form by s.3(3) SOGA 1979, which provides that "'necessaries' means goods suitable to the condition in life of the minor or other person concerned and to his actual requirements at the time of the sale and delivery". To consider an old and unusual example, in *Chapple v Cooper* (1844) 13 M&W 252, an "infant" (under 21 in those days) widow was bound by her contract with an undertaker to pay for the funeral of her husband. It was necessary for the woman's spouse to be buried in an appropriate and seemly fashion.

Necessaries will not extend to what are clearly luxury items, but even here there can be an element of uncertainty. Thus, in *Peters v Fleming* (1840) 151 ER 314, a gold ring and watch chain were viewed as necessaries for the eldest son of a wealthy MP. By contrast, in *Ryder v Wombwell* (1868) LR 4 Exch 32 a pair of jewelled cufflinks worth £25 and an antique goblet valued at 15 guineas (£15.75) were not considered necessaries, even though the minor concerned had an income of £500 per annum. (This case also noted that it was for the claimant to establish that the contract with the minor was for a necessity). In *Nash v Inman* [1908] 2 KB 1, it was held that 11 expensive, "fancy", waistcoats supplied to an 18-year-old Cambridge undergraduate (the age of majority at that time being 21) for two guineas each by a Savile Row tailor *might* have been considered as necessaries in the right circumstances, not least because he was the son of a very well-to-do architect. However, in the instant case this was not the situation, because his father had given uncontradicted evidence that he had already provided his son with an ample wardrobe. The student did not have to pay for the garments but was required to return them. Of course, it must be remembered that these cases usually involved young adults under 21 rather than juveniles under 18 years of age, as would be the case today with any such claim, helping to explain why relatively expensive items might be deemed necessaries in the right circumstances.

It should also be noted that a minor is required only to pay a reasonable price for goods, even if they are considered necessaries, which might be deemed to be below the contract price if he has made a bad bargain. (This was put into statutory terms by s.3(2) of the Sale of Goods Act 1979). Thus, if a hungry 15-year-old contracted to buy a pork pie for £50, when it normally sold for £1, he would be required only to pay (something like) the latter sum, even though the pie might be viewed as a necessary. Furthermore, even a contract for necessaries will not be binding if it contains other terms (to price) that are deemed to be oppressive so that, taken as a whole, it is not deemed to be beneficial for the minor: *Fawcett v Smethurst* (1914) 84 LJKB 473.

When it comes to contracts of service for a minor's benefit, such as an agreement for employment that involves education or training, everything will depend on the facts of the specific case that has come before the court. The assessment is based on the contract taken as a whole, with the potential benefits and disadvantages for the minor being weighed up against each another. For example, in *Clements v London & North Western Ry. Co.* [1894] 2 QB 490, a newly appointed railway employee who was under the age of majority was required to join an insurance society to which the railway company contributed, and agreed to accept compensation from this society in lieu of any claim he might have under the Employers' Liability Act of

1880. It was held that, overall, the contract was for the infant's benefit, so it was binding. The rights he gained under the insurance scheme were more beneficial to him than those given up under the statute. Similarly, in *Doyle v White City Stadium* [1935] 1 KB 110, an agreement with a minor to train him as a professional boxer was held to be enforceable, because the training involved could allow him to earn a living, even if it denied him a prize for hitting below the belt. Overall, it was deemed to be for his benefit, although this might not apply to "any one particular stipulation" in the agreement.

By contrast, in the case of *De Francesco v Barnum* (1890) 45 ChD 430, a 14-year-old girl contracted to train as a stage dancer under a seven-year apprenticeship. However, the contract had few terms that were beneficial to the minor and several that were not. She received no guaranteed payment under the agreement, could not take on other engagements without written permission, and could not marry during its duration. Furthermore, the counterparty could terminate the contract unilaterally at any point, while the minor could not. These outweighed the benefits so that she was not bound by the agreement.

More recently, one of the issues in the first instance decision in *Proform Sports Management Ltd v Proactive Sports Management Ltd & Stretford* [2007] 1 All ER 542 was whether a football agent's representation contract with the then 15-year-old player Wayne Rooney fell within the class of contracts that were enforceable against a minor. As the contract in issue did not involve matters deemed essential to a football player's training or livelihood, not being for necessaries, it was held not to be binding on Mr Rooney, who was entitled to avoid the agreement.

**Mental Incapacity**

Mental incapacity might relate to either sanity or cognitive ability. In the leading historic case of *Imperial Loan Co Ltd v Stone* [1892] 1 QB 599, Mr Stone was sued on a promissory note that he had signed as surety. The jury found that he was insane when he signed the note but made no finding as to the creditor's knowledge of his mental state. The judge entered a verdict against the creditor, Imperial Loan, who then appealed the decision. It was held that a contract that was entered into by such a person was not void, but could be avoided by them, *provided* the counterparty knew or ought to have known of his incapacity. Lord Esher MR stated that: "When a person enters into a contract, and afterwards alleges that he was so insane at the time that he did not know what he was doing, and proves the allegation, the contract is as binding on him in every respect, whether it is executory or executed, as if he had been sane when he made it, unless he can prove further that the person with whom he contracted knew him to be so insane as not to be capable of understanding what he was about". In the same case, Lopes LJ observed that a defendant who seeks to avoid a contract on the ground of his insanity, must "plead and prove, not merely his incapacity, but also the claimant's knowledge of that fact, and unless he proves these two things he cannot succeed".

The decision in *Imperial Loan Co* was upheld in the Privy Council case of *Hart v O'Connor* [1985] AC 1000, the court accepting that a contract made by a party of unsound mind who appears sane, with the counterparty having no knowledge (or reason to know) of his true mental state, is valid. In this somewhat controversial case--some argued that the counterparty's awareness of mental incapacity should be irrelevant--the vendor of a farm in New Zealand sold it at a significant but not enormous undervalue while suffering from senile dementia, although this was unknown to both his own solicitor and the purchaser. The sale was later challenged by his siblings but was upheld by the Privy Council. Lord Brightman observed that the "validity of a contract entered into by a lunatic who is *ostensibly* sane is to be judged by the same standards as a contract made by a person of sound mind, and is not voidable by the lunatic or his representatives by reason of 'unfairness'".

What degree of intellectual capacity is needed to enter a contract? This is not fully defined by s.2(1) of the Mental Capacity Act 2005 which merely states that a person "lacks capacity in relation to a matter if at the material time he is unable to make a decision for himself in relation to the matter because of an impairment of, or a disturbance in the functioning of, the mind or brain." This definition is insufficient when it comes to contractual matters, so that case law must be consulted when considering the issue. In *Fehily v Atkinson* [2016] EWHC 3069 [CH], a debtor entered an Individual Voluntary Arrangement (IVA) but then failed to comply with its terms, claiming that she had lacked the mental capacity to enter such an arrangement. Stephen Jourdan QC, sitting as a Deputy High Court Judge, took the opportunity to review the authorities relating to the assessment of mental capacity, including those that are relevant to determining whether a party has sufficient capacity to enter a contract.

The judge reiterated that people should be assumed to have such capacity unless the person alleging its absence is able to prove otherwise. The key issue to be determined is whether they had the ability to understand the transaction, not whether they understood it, at the time that they entered the agreement. The court expressly noted that capacity might vary over time, and that this must be allowed for: for example, some mentally disturbed people had lucid intervals. The test required that the individual should have more than an ability to understand the "general nature" of what he was doing but did not need him to be able to understand the minute or peripheral details of a proposed contract: "In my view, there is a distinction between the key features of a transaction, and ancillary, incidental or procedural aspects of it. I think that the requisite capacity is to understand the key features". It should be noted that, as with drunkenness (see below), if someone enters a contract during a period of mental incapacity, but subsequently ratifies the agreement, either expressly or through their conduct, after they recover their faculties, the contract will become binding.

## Intoxication

Intoxication poses special problems to the law of contract. Unlike insanity or mental disability, it is normally a voluntary and short-lived condition, one that occurs in varying degrees of severity. It also raises difficult questions of contractual autonomy and personal responsibility.[1] Writing in 1826, Joseph Chitty identified a change in the way that English law dealt with contracts made by the inebriated that had occurred since the start of the nineteenth century, and by the 1840s this new position had become relatively settled. Thus, and typically, in *Gore v Gibson* (1845) 13 M & W 621 it was held that where a person entered a contract when they were so intoxicated as not to know the consequences of their act, it would not be binding on them if their condition was known (or ought to have been known) to the other party to the agreement.

Such a contract is not void, but merely voidable. In *Matthews v Baxter* (1873) LR 8 Ex 132 it was held that, as with mental incapacity, if the drunken party, upon coming to his senses, ratifies the contract, he is bound by it, even if he subsequently repents of his affirmation. It is likely that the same rules would be applied to persons intoxicated by drugs other than alcohol.

## Contracts that are Illegal or Contrary to Public Policy

Some contracts will be deemed to be illegal, or contrary to public policy, from their very formation, and so void or at least unenforceable. These two types of agreement will be considered in turn.

## Illegality

Contracts that are contrary to a specific statute when formed or that are tainted by criminality may be deemed to be illegal. In the old case of *Holman v Johnson* (1775) 1 Cowp 341, Lord Mansfield observed, "No court will lend its aid to a man who founds his cause of action upon…an illegal act". Various rationales have been advanced for why such contracts should be unenforceable--for example, that it would be harmful to the integrity of the legal system and so contrary to the public interest, while a person should not benefit from his own wrongdoing. In *K/S Lincoln v CB Richard Ellis Hotels Ltd* [2010] EWHC 1156 (TCC), the High Court suggested that deterrence was another important factor behind the rule, along with a desire not to encourage illegal acts by allowing claims that are based upon them. More recently, in *Patel v Mirza* [2017] 1 All ER 191 Lord Toulson felt that there are two broad, discernible, policy reasons for the common law doctrine of illegality as a defence to a civil action: "One is that a person should not be allowed to profit from his own wrongdoing. The other, linked, consideration is that the law should be coherent and not self-defeating, condoning illegality by giving with the left hand what it takes with the right hand". Many of these rationales, especially the importance of deterrence, were also identified by the Law Commission in its report on *The Illegality Defence* of 2010 (No 230).

1 Warren Swain, "Without the Power to Drink or Contract", <i>Edinburgh Law Review</i>, v. 24, no. 1 (2020), p. 27..

## Statutory Illegality

Some statutes or statutory instruments expressly prohibit certain contracts. Others do so by implication--for example, by imposing a penalty upon those who enter a particular type of agreement. Such agreements will not be enforced, not least because to do so would undermine the purpose of the statute, even where it does not make the proscribed behaviour a specific criminal offence. Thus, in *St John Shipping Corporation v Joseph Rank* [1957] 1 QB 267, Devlin J observed that the courts will "not enforce a contract which is expressly or impliedly prohibited by statute. If the contract is of this class it does not matter what the intent of the parties is; if the statute prohibits the contract, it is unenforceable whether the parties meant to break the law or not". This was reiterated in *Phoenix General Insurance Co of Greece SA v Administratia Asigurarilor de Stat* [1987] 2 All ER 152 by Kerr LJ, who also viewed it as settled law that any contract that is prohibited by statute, whether expressly or by implication, is "illegal and void".

For example, in *Re Mahmoud and Ispahani* [1921] 2 KB 716 an order was made under the Defence of the Realm Act 1914 which provided that a person should not buy, sell, or otherwise deal in linseed oil without a licence. The claimant had such a licence and sold 150 tons of oil to the defendant. The latter had wrongly told the claimant that he, too, had a licence to deal in linseed oil. Later, he refused to accept delivery of the oil, and when the claimant sued for damages argued that as he had no such licence the contract was illegal and so void, preventing the claimant from suing for damages for its breach. The Court of Appeal agreed. Banks LJ observed that "it is open to a party, however shabby it may appear to be, to say that the Legislature has prohibited the contract, and therefore it is a case in which the court will not lend its aid to the enforcement of the contract".

Similarly, in *David Taylor & Son v Barnett Trading Co* [1953] 1 Lloyd's Rep. 181, Barnett Trading agreed to sell a very large quantity of stewed steak to David Taylor, both parties being meat wholesalers. At the time, a government order was in force preventing the buying or selling of meat over a certain price, which the contract for the steak very clearly exceeded. When Barnett Trading failed to provide the meat, Taylor claimed damages for non-delivery. At first instance, the arbitrator ordered that Barnett Trading pay Taylor compensation of £11,000. The Court of Appeal held that as the contract had been illegal when made, due to the specified price exceeding government limits, it was void and the arbitrator's order would be set aside.

More recently, in *Mohammed v Alagi & Co (A Firm)* [2000] WLR 1815, the claimant was a member of the Somali community living in the United Kingdom who, allegedly (it was denied), made an agreement with the defendant solicitors that he would introduce newly arrived Somalis to them, who would in turn apply for legal aid on their behalf and, if it were granted, represent them in their applications for asylum. In exchange, it was claimed that the defendant agreed, inter alia, to pay commission of one half of any fees received from the Legal Aid Board to the claimant within four weeks of the introduction of clients and the application for legal aid. However, this was contrary to regulation 7 of the Solicitors Practice Rules 1991, as established pursuant to the Solicitors Act 1974, albeit not a criminal offence. When Mr Mohammed was not paid, and sued for his fees, he failed because, even if there had been such an agreement, were he to succeed the court would be sanctioning agreements for payment that are expressly forbidden by law and would be requiring solicitors to do what statute forbids.

**Tainted by Criminality**

Where an agreement necessarily involves one or both parties committing some form of criminal activity, it may be unenforceable at common law. In many of these cases, the defendant in a breach-of-contract action argues that the claimant should not be entitled to a contractual remedy because of criminal conduct linked to the claim. Sometimes this can create an inherent tension. If he succeeds, and the courts accept such an argument, they will grant an (often) unjustified windfall to the defendant, even if the latter is equally implicated in the relevant criminality. However, if the courts refuse to accept such a defence, they may be seen to be condoning criminal behaviour.

In the recent past, defendants could succeed in pleading this defence only if they could show that the claimant would need to rely on his own criminal conduct as part of his pleaded case: *Tinsley v Milligan* [1994] 1 AC 340. (In this case, it was held that a woman who had transferred her share of a jointly purchased house to her partner as part of a social security fraud could reclaim her equitable interest in the property because it did not require her to rely on the illegal purpose behind the transaction.) Thus, and to take an extreme example, a contract between drug traffickers and buyers would be invalid because the terms of the agreement itself are illegal; indeed, it would amount to the criminal offence of conspiracy to contravene one or more provisions of the Misuse of Drugs Act 1971 and would necessarily have to be relied on by the claimant. In such a case, neither party could apply to the court for its enforcement.

However, the Law Commission in its final report on *The Illegality Defence* in March 2010, cast doubt on reliance as a test for enforcement, and argued that it was difficult to establish strict, universally applicable rules in this area of the law. Instead, it suggested that the underlying policy should be considered in the light of the specific factors raised by each case. After some incremental caselaw developments, the Supreme Court ushered in major change in *Patel v Mirza* [2017] 1 All ER 191, which is now the leading case on the subject, and renders older authority of very limited significance.

In *Patel v Mirza*, Mr Patel transferred £620,000 to Mr Mirza, a finance professional. This was for the purpose of speculating on Royal Bank of Scotland (RBS) shares, for their common benefit, using inside information that Mr Mirza expected to obtain from contacts at RBS regarding an anticipated government announcement. As a result, the agreement between the two men amounted to a conspiracy to commit insider dealing contrary to s.52 of the Criminal Justice Act 1993 and if carried out would, of course, have amounted to the substantive offence.

However, Mr Mirza's expectation of a government announcement proved to be mistaken, so that the intended speculation did not occur. He then failed to repay the £620,000 to Mr Patel, despite repeated requests and promises to do so. The latter eventually brought an action to recover the money on various grounds, including breach of contract. In response, Mr Mirza argued that, in view of the illegality of their transaction, Mr Patel should not succeed in his claim. This argument was accepted at first instance but rejected by both the Court of Appeal and the Supreme Court, which ordered that the money be returned. The latter forum took the opportunity to reconsider the complicated maxims and principles governing illegality for criminal conduct.

A majority of the nine judges in the Supreme Court rejected the principle whereby relief was refused to parties who had to rely on their own illegal behaviour to establish their case in court. Instead, they thought that the deployment of illegality as a defence should be more flexible, best served by a principled and transparent assessment of identified considerations, and dependent on a range of policy factors.

Giving the leading judgment, Lord Toulson (with whom Lady Hale and Lords Kerr, Hodge, and Wilson agreed) argued that the court should ask itself three questions: whether enforcing the claim would lead to inconsistency that is damaging to the integrity of the legal system, something that might involve considering the purpose of the rule that has been broken and whether it would be strengthened by a denial of the claim; whether there were other relevant public policy considerations that might be affected by denying the claim; and whether denying the claim would be a proportionate response to the illegality. In the circumstances of the instant case, these favoured the claimant, not least because the illegal contract was not, in the end, carried out. The money could be recovered.

In *Stoffel & Co v Grondona* [2020] UKSC 42 the Supreme Court concluded that the Court of Appeal had correctly applied the policy-based approach adopted in *Patel v Mirza* [2017] 1 All ER 191, so providing further guidance. In this case, the court decided that a firm of solicitors, Stoffel & Co, could not escape liability to Ms Grondona for their negligent failure to register documents effecting a transfer of property, even though it formed part of an illegal mortgage fraud in which the claimant had agreed to make false representations to a bank to procure a mortgage for an associate. The mortgage was to be secured against other properties, legal title to which would be transferred to Ms Grondona, something that her solicitors negligently failed to do. When her associate defaulted on the mortgage repayments, the bank pursued Ms Grondona for the unsecured debt. In turn, Ms Grondona claimed against the solicitors, who unsuccessfully advanced the defence of illegality.

The Supreme Court analysed the case according to the *Mirza* considerations, asking itself whether denying the claim for illegality would enhance the purpose of the relevant prohibitions, and concluding that it was difficult to see how refusing the respondent a civil remedy against her solicitors would deter mortgage fraud. There were other policy considerations supporting their decision, albeit that these were of secondary importance. Upholding legal professional standards was one. Lord Lloyd-Jones noted that denying Ms Grondona's claim on the grounds of illegality might discourage proper diligence amongst solicitors and be "inconsistent with the policy that the victims of solicitors' negligence should be compensated for their loss". He also felt that it would not be proportionate to deny Ms Grondona's claim because it was conceptually entirely separate from the mortgage fraud.

As these cases suggest, diverse issues, including, *inter alia*, how seriously criminal the relevant conduct is, the respective degree of involvement of the parties in that conduct, the deterrent value of refusing a remedy where a particular form of illegal activity has occurred, and, most important, the effect of a decision on the integrity of the wider legal system, might all influence a decision on illegality. Some have welcomed the flexibility that this "range of factors" approach produces. However, critics have argued that it will create excessive uncertainty because of its wide formulation. Thus, in *Mirza*, Lord Sumption (who was in the minority) suggested that the new test was too vague, and likely to produce unpredictable results. He felt that it was wrong for the courts to be required to weigh up the various consequences of granting or refusing relief. Doing so would mean that decisions would sometimes depend on the individual judge hearing the case, which would make it harder for lawyers to advise their clients on their prospects of success. He preferred the traditional reliance rule and feared that the court would be doing no service to the coherent development of the law if it "simply substituted a new mess for the old one".

## Public Policy

In some identified situations the courts will refuse to enforce contracts on the grounds of public policy, so subordinating private rights to what is deemed to be the wider general interest. Historically, it has often been very difficult to determine when this should occur, so much so that Asquith LJ thought that the courts should "use extreme reserve in holding such a contract to be void as against public policy, and only do so when the contract is incontestably and on any view inimical to the public interest": *Monkland v Jack Barclay Ltd* [1951] 2 KB 252.[2]. As a result, the courts have demonstrated a reluctance to lightly increase the number of such cases.

Nevertheless, and for example, in *Foster v Driscoll* [1929] 1 KB 470 the Court of Appeal held that contracts made in England with a distiller and a ship broker to supply whisky to the United States in breach of that country's prohibition policy and

2 Angus Macauley, "Contracts Against Public Policy: Contracts For Meretricious Sexual Services", <i>Sydney Law Review</i>, v. 40, no. 4 (2018), p. 527.

laws was unenforceable, although it would have been legal in the UK. Lawrence LJ held that a partnership: "...formed for the main purpose of deriving profit from the commission of a criminal offence in a foreign and friendly country is illegal". Similarly, in *HIH Casualty and General Insurance Ltd v Chase Manhattan Bank* [2003] UKHL 6 the House of Lords held that, as a matter of public policy a party could not exclude liability for personal fraudulent (rather than negligent) misrepresentation, although it might be possible to exclude liability for an agent's fraud.

Three especially important areas where the courts have been willing to intervene for public policy reasons can be identified: those that involve contracts that are deemed to be in restraint of trade; those that seek to oust the jurisdiction of the courts and, albeit of increasingly marginal significance in the modern era, those that promote sexual immorality or undermine the status of marriage. These will be considered in turn.

## 1. Contracts in Restraint of Trade

Contracts or contractual provisions that are deemed to be in restraint of trade are normally found in agreements made between the buyer and seller of a business, or between an employer and an employee. They usually prevent the seller or employee from engaging in, or setting up, a similar business, or from working in the same trade, within a specified geographical area and inside a designated time. Historically almost all contractual restraints of trade were thought to be contrary to public policy and so void. This was because they inhibited trade and so, it was thought, the well-being of the wider society. Thus, in *Dyer's case* (1414) 2 Hen. V, fol. 5, pl. 26, a London master prohibited his apprentice from pursuing his trade in the same city for six months following his apprenticeship. The court ruled against this covenant in very firm terms. However, after the Elizabethan period, this approach was relaxed, the law evolving to accommodate changing business conditions. For example, in the early-17th-century case of *Rogers v Parry* (1614) 2 Bulst 136, it was held that a promise by a landlord not to trade as a joiner from his house for 21 years after he let out part of the property was enforceable, since the time and place were both certain and limited.

The House of Lords took the opportunity to reconsider such clauses in *Nordenfelt v Maxim Nordenfelt Guns and Ammunition Co Ltd* [1894] AC 535, and the modern law on restraint of trade stems from their decision. In this case, a Swedish armaments manufacturer, Thorsten Nordenfelt, sold his business to an American company engaged in the same trade for £200,000. (Both manufactured early machine guns). As part of the contract, they agreed that Nordenfelt "would not make guns or ammunition anywhere in the world, and would not compete with Maxim in any way for a period of 25 years". The House of Lords held that the first point of the restraint clause was enforceable (if very unusual) because in the limited world of armaments sales (where sales were normally made to governments) it was reasonable to "not make guns or ammunition anywhere in the world". This was especially so given the very high payment made for the business. In this case, Lord Macnaghten observed that although restraints on trade were contrary to public policy, and so prima facie void, this would not be the case "if the restriction is reasonable—reasonable, that is, in reference to the interests of the parties concerned and reasonable in reference to the interests of the public".

Essentially, a restraint-of-trade clause will be enforceable if three conditions are met, namely that the claimant can show that he has a legitimate interest that requires protection; the clause does no more than is reasonably necessary to provide this protection; and the same term is reasonable from the viewpoint of public policy (the public interest). In making this decision, the courts consider the extent of the geographical and temporal constraints contained in the clause as well as the scope of the vendor or employer's business.

Each case turns on its particular facts, so that very different lengths of time, geographical limits, and stringencies of restraint might be allowed in any given situation. Thus, and for example, in *Mason v Provident Clothing & Supply Co Ltd* [1913] AC 724, the defendant had been employed by the claimant as a canvasser in the Islington district of North London. His contract included a clause that he would not work as a canvasser within 25 miles of London for three years after he left his employment. The court held that the requirement not to work within this 25-mile radius was excessive. Had it been confined to Islington it would have been upheld; the court recognised that the employer had a legitimate concern that the (former) employee should not abuse contacts he had made, and information he had secured, as part of his work for them in this particular borough.

Similarly, in *M & S Drapers (a firm) v Reynolds* [1957] 1 WLR 9, the defendant took up employment with the claimant firm, who sold drapery on credit and then received payments for it. When doing so, he entered a restrictive covenant that required him not to canvass or solicit orders from anyone with whom he had had professional dealings on behalf of his employer for three years before leaving the latter's employment, for a period of five years afterwards. It was held that this was unreasonably restrictive, not least because Mr Reynolds had introduced many of these clients to the firm himself when he originally entered the claimant's employment.

By contrast, in *Law By Design Ltd v Ali* [2022] EWHC 426 (QB), the High Court held that a non-compete clause in the defendant's agreement with a niche firm of solicitors, which applied across the North West of England for a year after the end of her employment, legitimately prevented Ms Ali, an experienced lawyer with access to a great deal of transportable information, from joining a much larger but directly competing firm of solicitors as a partner until the prescribed period was over. The clause was not drawn too widely geographically and did not last for too long. By contrast, the court also held that a wider restriction, contained in a separate shareholder agreement, which prohibited Ms Ali from competing with any other part of LBD's business was unenforceable and void.

### Divisibility of Restraint Clauses

Where possible, the courts can sever unreasonable parts or words from a restraint clause and enforce what remains, provided the unenforceable provision can be removed without varying or adding to the remaining wording, which must remain viable in its own right. This is the so called "blue pencil test" (also found in other areas of contract law). Thus, in the *Nordenfeldt* case itself, the second part of the restraint clause was severed, as it was considered unreasonable that the defendant could "not compete with Maxim in any way". Similarly, in *Goldsoll v Goldman* [1915] 1 Ch. 292 the defendant sold his imitation-jewellery business to the claimant, who was in a similar line of business, and covenanted that for two years he would not deal in either real or imitation jewellery in, *inter alia*, any part of the United Kingdom, France, the United States, Russia, Spain, or certain areas of Germany. The claimant subsequently sought an injunction against the defendant for an alleged breach of this covenant. The Court of Appeal held the covenant was only good to the extent that it restrained the defendant from carrying on business in imitation (rather than real) jewellery in the UK (rather than abroad). However, the offending provisions could be severed, leaving a viable contract.

This issue came before the Supreme Court in *Tillman v Egon Zehnder Ltd* [2019] UKSC 32. Ms Tillman had been employed by Egon Zehnder, an executive recruitment consultancy. Her contract contained a non-compete clause preventing her from being "concerned or interested in any business carried on in competition" with that of Egon Zehnder for a period of six months after leaving his service. Ms Tillman decided to move to a rival firm. Her former employer sought an injunction to prevent her from doing so for the relevant period. This was granted at first instance by the High Court. However, the Court of Appeal allowed Ms Tillman's appeal, on the basis that the clause was in unreasonable restraint of trade, not least because "interested in" might restrict Ms Tillman from purchasing even a minor shareholding in a competing company, and so was wider than was reasonably required for the protection of the employer's legitimate business interests. In unanimously allowing the further appeal, the Supreme Court found that the "blue pencil" test could be applied, so that these words were removed rendering the remainder of the clause enforceable (because reasonable). The words could be severed without additional words having to be added, there was adequate consideration for the remaining terms, and the character of the restriction was not fundamentally changed.

### 2. Contracts to Oust the Jurisdiction of the Courts

A contract that includes a clause that purports to oust the jurisdiction of the courts from the agreement is deemed to be contrary to public policy and so void and unenforceable. For example, in *Baker v Jones* [1954] 1 WLR 1005, a dispute arose over an agreement pertaining to an unincorporated weightlifting association. Words in the agreement that purported to make its council the sole interpreter of any legal issues flowing from it were held to be void. More recently, in *Aribisala v St James Homes (Grosvenor Dock) Limited* [2007] EWHC 1694 (Ch) the High Court held that it was not possible for the parties to a contract for the sale of land to agree to exclude the operation of s.49(2) of the Law of Property Act 1925, which gives the court a discretion to order repayment of a deposit to a buyer, as this was deemed to be an attempt to oust the jurisdiction of the court.

However, such contracts must be differentiated from those that contain provisions that stipulate that an agreement is not to be legally binding, so called "honour only" clauses which, where operative, preclude any contract coming into force, although the distinction can sometimes be quite subtle: *Rose & Frank Co v Crompton Bros* [1925] AC 445. Furthermore, they must also be distinguished from those that provide that no right of legal action shall accrue until a third person or arbitrator has decided on any issue between the parties to the agreement, such clauses being legally binding: *Scott v Avery* (1855) 5 HLC 811.

In *Scott v Avery*, Avery took out a policy of marine insurance from Scott. A clause in the policy stated that if there was a dispute about an award under the agreement the matter should be referred to arbitration before it could go to court. Subsequently, a dispute arose, but Avery refused to go to arbitration and took the matter directly to court. He argued that the clause requiring referral to arbitration was unenforceable for public policy reasons. The House of Lords found for Scott, the insurer, distinguishing between a clause that ousted the jurisdiction of the court where a cause of action had already risen, and the instant case, which stated that there was no cause of action until an arbitration decision on the issue had been made. Campbell J noted that where it is expressly and "unequivocally agreed upon between the parties that there shall be no right of action whatever till the arbitrators have decided, it is a bar to the action that there has been no such arbitration". In the same case, Lord Cranworth observed that he could not envisage the slightest ill consequences that could flow from such an agreement but could see great advantages that might arise from it. Such clauses did not offend against public policy and were enforceable.

In the modern era, some contracts, especially those for commodities, still include *Scott v Avery* clauses. Thus, the Federation of Oil, Seeds and Fats Association's arbitration clause states that neither party to an agreement "shall bring any action or other legal proceedings against the other of them in respect of any such dispute until such dispute shall first have been heard and determined by the arbitrators ... [which] shall be a condition precedent to the right of either party hereto or of any person claiming under either of them to bring any action or other legal proceedings".[3]

It should also be noted that an arbitration clause can quite properly stipulate that the arbitrator will, *prima facie*, have the final say on questions of fact. However, this is not the case on questions of law, where, under s.69 of the Arbitration Act 1996,

3 Andrew Tweeddale and Keren Tweeddale, <i>"Scott v Avery</i> Clauses: O'er Judges' Fingers, Who Straight Dream on Fees", <i>Arbitration</i>, v. 77 (2011), pp. 423-427

decisions can be appealed to the courts, with the latter's permission (or that of the counterparty). Very significantly, under s.69(3) legal issues will include a claim that the decision of the arbitrator on a finding of fact is "obviously wrong" or "open to serious doubt", so that even when it comes to questions of fact, the arbitrator does not have *carte blanche*.

### 3. Contracts in Restraint of Marriage or Promoting Sexual Immorality

Traditionally, contracts that were considered prejudicial to the status of marriage or which promoted sexual immorality were held to be void for reasons of public policy. Thus, and considering the former issue, a condition in a contract intended to procure marriage or to prevent someone from marrying would not be effective. For example, in *Lowe v Peers* (1768) 4 Burr. 2225 the defendant covenanted that if he married any person other than the claimant, Catherine Lowe, he would pay her £1,000 within three months of that marriage. Some years later the defendant married another woman, and the claimant brought an action for breach of contract. It was held that the contract was void and so unenforceable, something that would still be the case today.

However, when it comes to contracts that promote sexual immorality, there has been considerable change in legal attitudes since the end of the Second World War. Historically, in *Girardy v Richardson* (1793) 1 Esp Cas 13, Lord Kenyon CJ held that a contract under which a claimant who had let rooms to a prostitute for use in her trade was *contra bonos mores*, and so unenforceable when he sued for arrears of rent. Similarly, in *Pearce v Brooks* (1865) LR 1 Exch 213 the defendant was a prostitute who rented a small carriage from the claimant, a coachbuilder. She wanted the carriage specifically for the purpose of attracting clients in a local park. The defendant returned the carriage in a damaged condition, in breach of the agreement. The coachbuilder sued for non-payment of rental and for the significant cost of repairing the carriage. At trial, the jury found that, at the time the contract was made, the coachbuilder knew the purpose for which the defendant sought the carriage, and that he expected to be paid out of the profits of prostitution. As a result, the court decided the contract was illegal on the grounds of sexual immorality, and so the coachbuilder should not be allowed to recover on the agreement.

Nevertheless, this was subject to an important caveat. In *Pearce*, Bramwell B distinguished between a contract to supply a prostitute with a carriage that was to be used specifically for the purpose of attracting customers and an agreement to supply her, for example, with a pair of shoes, as these were one of the necessities of life. This followed from *Appleton v Campbell* (1826) 2 Car & P 347, in which the claimant brought an action for the recovery of board and lodging after renting a room to the defendant. The court held that the claimant could not succeed if he knew that the defendant was a prostitute and that she was using the room to entertain her clients, but "if the defendant had her lodgings there, and received her visitors elsewhere, the claimant may recover, although she be a woman of the town, because persons of that description must have a place to lay their heads".

Moving on to the early twentieth century, in *Upfill v Wright* [1911] 1 KB 506, the claimant let a flat to the female defendant for three years, knowing that she was the mistress of a particular man, and assuming that as a kept woman her rent would be funded by the man. The court held that, as the flat was let for an immoral purpose, the claimant was not entitled to recover this rent.

Even so, nowadays, following major changes in social mores, and *pace* Chief Baron Pollock's belief that no distinction could be drawn between an illegal and immoral purpose, it seems that an act will *normally* have to be criminal rather than what some observers might view as simply immoral before the courts will invoke the doctrine. Thus, in the light of several cases, including *Tanner v Tanner* [1975] 1 WLR 1346, in which an unmarried woman was given contractual rights in (vaguely) similar circumstances, the decision in *Upfill v Wright* would not be followed today.

More generally, the Court of Appeal decision in *Armhouse Lee Ltd v Chappell and another* [1996] EWCA Civ J0723-3 can be considered. In this case, an advertising agency had placed very lewd and often graphically illustrated advertisements in pornographic magazines for premium telephone sex lines run by the defendants. The latter resisted the claimant's claim for £700,000 for this work, on the grounds that their promotional material was such that the courts should decline to enforce the contracts on public policy grounds, if only because they tended to promote sexual immorality.

The court rejected this argument and enforced the agreements. Lord Justice Simon Brown noted that the defence advanced was limited to the advertisements, and that these were not related to prostitution, as at no point were the women who provided salacious conversations in the presence of their clients. No generally accepted moral code (in the modern era) condemned such sex lines, which were subject to an independent regulatory body and even had their own code of practice. Although such advertisements might be distasteful, they were not so bad that the court should feel morally obliged to renounce its usual jurisdiction over contractual disputes.

This does not *necessarily* preclude the possibility of such a defence being raised, in all circumstances, in the future. However, nowadays the "immorality" might have to be quite extreme, if it was technically legal, before it could be invoked. Of course, actively soliciting for prostitution is still an offence (although prostitution is not) and contracts that facilitate it might well be deemed illegal for this reason.

# Chapter 6: Privity and Agency

## Introduction

The common law doctrine of privity provides that only parties to a contract, rather than its beneficiaries (if different from the former), can enforce an agreement. As part of this rule, they must also have provided consideration for it. As was noted in *Dunlop Pneumatic Tyre Co Ltd v Selfridge Ltd* [1915] AC 847, if a "person with whom a contract has been made is to be able to enforce it consideration must have been given by him". Nevertheless, the doctrine was a comparatively late arrival in the canon of English contract law. It was not firmly settled until the middle of the nineteenth century, although its roots are very much older.

In the case of *Tweddle v Atkinson* (1861) 1 B&S 393, the fathers of a young man and woman who had become engaged entered into an agreement to pay sums of money to the couple on their marriage. The father of the bride died before he had paid his part of the money, and the father of the groom died before he could sue on the agreement between the parties, although he may have been restricted to nominal damages had he done so (see below). However, the fathers' contract expressly stipulated that the groom could personally sue on the agreement. As a result, the groom brought proceedings against the executor of his father-in-law's will, asking for the payment that he had been promised. Nevertheless, it was held that, as a "stranger" to the contract, one who had neither been party to it nor provided consideration for it, he could not enforce it, even though it was for his benefit and the contract had expressly stipulated that he could do just that. As a result, the court found in favour of the executor.

Within 50 years, the House of Lords viewed this principle as fundamental to English contract law. In *Dunlop Pneumatic Tyre Co Ltd v Selfridge and Co Ltd* [1915] AC 847, the claimant (Dunlop) sought to enforce a resale price maintenance (RPM) scheme (legal in that era). The claimant had sold tyres to a distributor, Dew & Co. In their contract with the latter, they specified that the tyres should not be sold to consumers at below their list price, and that if the distributor sold them on to retailers they should include a similar clause, one that entitled Dunlop to sue the retailer on any failure to keep to the RPM. Dew sold tyres on to a retailer, Selfridge, including the appropriate clause in their agreement. However, Selfridge failed to comply with the condition, selling below the list price, and Dunlop sued them for breach of contract.

The House of Lords held that because Dunlop was not a party to the agreement between Dew and Selfridge, it had no contractual relationship with the latter, and could not sue them. Viscount Haldane LC observed that in English law certain principles are fundamental, "One is that only a person who is a party to a contract can sue on it. Our law knows nothing of a *jus quaesitum tertio* arising by way of contract. Such a right may be conferred by way of property, as, for example, under a trust, but it cannot be conferred on a stranger to a contract as a right to enforce the contract *in personam*".

The rule was reiterated by the House of Lords in *Beswick v Beswick* [1968] AC 58, and attempts by Lord Denning to circumvent it, in the same case in the Court of Appeal, were rejected. Peter Beswick was an elderly (and increasingly unwell) Lancashire coal merchant who purchased coal from the National Coal Board, bagged it up, and took it around his neighbourhood in a lorry, to sell to private individuals. His nephew, John Beswick, assisted him. In March 1962, Peter Beswick assigned his business to his nephew in consideration of the latter employing him for the remainder of his life and then making a weekly payment of £5 to his widow. After Peter's death the nephew made just one payment of the agreed weekly amount to Mrs Beswick and then stopped. The House of Lords refused to broaden the doctrine of privity to allow third-party beneficiaries (Mrs Beswick in her personal capacity in this case) to enforce benefits under a contract.

However, and fortunately, Mrs Beswick could sue in her capacity as Mr Beswick's appointed administratrix (a woman representing the estate of someone who dies without making a will) to enforce the nephew's promise to pay Mrs Beswick (in her personal capacity) an annuity. She could, in Lord Pearce's words, "stand in his shoes". Furthermore, she was also granted specific performance of the contract, which was fortunate, given that, if awarded, damages to the estate *may* have been nominal, although Lord Pearce doubted this (see below).

**Privity and Contractual Defences**

The privity rule applies to the use of defences that are available under a contract, such as exemption clauses, just as it does to causes of action. For example, in *Adler v Dickson* [1955] 1 QB 158, the claimant, Mrs Adler, was a passenger on the cruise ship *Himalaya*, having booked a ticket with Thomas Cook in England. She was injured in a fall from a defective gangway, breaking her legs in the process. The passenger ticket she had been issued contained clauses excluding the shipping company from any liability in respect of injury to a passenger (this would now be void under the CRA 2015). This prevented Mrs Adler from suing the steamship company for breach of contract. Instead, she sued the ship's master and bosun personally, in the tort of negligence. The two defendants sought to rely on the exclusion clause in Mrs Adler's ticket. In response, she argued that they could not rely on the terms of an agreement to which they were not privy. The Court of Appeal, Denning LJ presiding, agreed, and held that the men could not take advantage of the clause.

Similarly, in *Scruttons Ltd v Midland Silicones Ltd* [1962] AC 446, the House of Lords applied the Privity Rule to prevent a firm of stevedores from relying on a limitation clause in a bill of lading. A shipping company (the carrier) had agreed to transport a drum of chemicals belonging to the claimant. The bill of lading in the contract limited their liability for damage to £179. The drum was damaged by the negligence of the defendants, who had been engaged by the carriers to unload their vessel.

The claimants sued the defendants in the tort of negligence for the full extent of the damage, which amounted to £593. The defendants sought the protection afforded by the limitation clause. The House of Lords held in favour of the claimants; as the defendants were not parties to the contract of carriage, they could not take advantage of it.

However, in *Scruttons* Lord Reid also suggested that stevedores or similar workers, might be covered by such an exemption clause if four pre-conditions were satisfied, these being that: the bill of lading made it clear that the stevedore was intended to be protected by the exemption clause; the bill of lading made it clear that the carrier, in addition to contracting for these provisions on his own behalf, was also contracting as agent for the stevedore; the carrier had authority from the stevedore to do that (later ratification might suffice); and that any difficulties about consideration moving from the stevedore were overcome. A rare illustration of these requirements being satisfied can be seen in *New Zealand Shipping Co. Ltd. v A. M. Satterthwaite & Co. Ltd., (The Eurymedon)* [1975] AC 154, in which the Privy Council found that all four aspects of the "Lord Reid test" had been met, so that a negligent stevedore could rely on such an exemption clause.

**Third Party Damages**

Compounding the problems occasioned by the doctrine of privity at common law was that, although a contracting party might be able to sue for breach of a contract that they had entered for the benefit of a third party (unlike the third party), they could often only recover nominal damages for any loss sustained by the proposed beneficiary. Damages compensate a claimant for his own loss; if a third party has sustained the loss, the claimant's loss is, potentially, non-existent, limiting him to a token sum. As Lord Diplock observed in *The Albazero* [1977] AC 774, the "general rule of English Law [is] that apart from nominal damages a claimant can only recover in an action for breach of contract the actual loss he has himself sustained." This produces what is sometimes referred to as a legal black hole, in which the party who has suffered loss is not privy to the contract and cannot sue, while the party who is privy to the agreement has suffered no loss and so cannot claim substantial damages. It helps explain why securing an order of specific performance, rather than damages, was (potentially) important in *Beswick v Beswick*.

However, in *Jackson v Horizon Holidays Ltd* [1975] 1 WLR 1468, Lord Denning MR appeared to challenge this general principle. In this case, the claimant booked a luxury package holiday in Sri Lanka from Horizon Holidays for himself and his wife and two children. He paid £1,200. When they arrived, the facilities were fairly unhygienic and quite run-down, and the catering was very poor. The trial judge followed *Jarvis v Swan Tours Ltd* [1972] 3 WLR 954 (see Chapter 15), and awarded damages of £1,100, including a significant measure for mental distress and loss of enjoyment. Nevertheless, in the latter case, only Mr Jarvis had gone on the holiday. In the instant case, the defendant appealed against the substantial damages awarded to Mr Jackson on behalf of his wife and children, who were not parties to the agreement. Lord Denning held that Mr Jackson could recover damages of £600 for defective performance and £500 for disappointment or "mental distress" for himself and his family, even though this would have been excessive for his own personal loss. Denning suggested that other situations in which such a claim might allow substantial damages to be recovered on behalf of third-party beneficiaries would include a vicar contracting for a coach trip for a church choir and a host booking a restaurant dinner for himself and his friends.

Nevertheless, Lord Denning's reasoning was doubted as the basis for a more general rule by the House of Lords in *Woodar Investment v* Wimpey *Construction* [1980] 1 WLR 277, which suggested that the decision, although right in itself, was limited to a narrow category of consumer cases. Wimpey had contracted to buy 14 acres of land from Woodar for a payment of £850,000 to the latter and £150,000 to a linked (owned by Woodar but legally separate) third party, Transworld Trade Ltd. The contract allowed the purchaser to rescind the contract if, before completion, a statutory authority started compulsory purchase of the land. Relying on this provision, Wimpey subsequently purported to terminate the agreement, while Woodar sought damages alleging wrongful repudiation of the contract. Their claim included the £150,000 loss suffered by Transworld. The Court of Appeal found no entitlement to terminate and, albeit with evident reluctance, decided that that they were bound by *Jackson v Horizon Holidays* into holding that substantial damages for the payment due to Transworld could also be recovered. Ultimately, on further appeal, the House of Lords decided that the termination *was* justified, so that the issue of damages did not arise. Even so, in *obiter* comments, the court was sceptical about the general applicability of the decision in *Jackson v Horizon Holidays*, confining it to its facts and analogous situations, such as meals ordered in restaurants on behalf of guests. Thus, Lord Wilberforce thought that the award of substantive damages for Transworld's loss was a question of "great doubt and difficulty".

Despite this case, another exception to the general rule (to that seen in *Jackson*) has been identified in contracts for goods or land where the parties contemplated that the loss in respect of such property would be suffered by a third party, and the latter does not have a right against the promissor to recover their own loss. This exception was based on *The Albazero* [1977] AC 774 and older cases and developed and expanded in *St. Martin's Property Corporation Ltd. v. Sir Robert McAlpine Ltd.* [1994] 1 AC 85 and *Alfred McAlpine Construction Ltd* v *Panatown Ltd* [2001] 1 AC 518. However, the advent of the Contracts (Rights of Third Parties) Act 1999 limits its significance (see below), not least because in these situations they will usually have a right to sue the original promissor under the statute.

Ignoring such exceptions, the general proposition, that a contracting party can only sue for damages in respect of his own loss, and not those suffered by a third person, has been restated in several cases over recent years. Thus, the Court of Appeal has held that, where a buyer wrongly terminated a two-year contract, the seller could claim only its own loss of profit and not that of a sister company that was supplying half the products in question: *BV Nederlandse Industrie Van Eiprodukten v Rembrandt Enterprises, inc* [2019] EWCA Civ 596. At a more elevated level, in the Supreme Court case of *Swynson Ltd v Lowick Rose LLP* [2018] AC 313, large loans had been made by Swynson Ltd to a borrower (EMSL) based on negligently produced due diligence reports provided by Lowick Rose LLP (then called HMT). The loan would not have been made but for these reports. EMSL subsequently defaulted on the loan. Mr Hunt, Swynson's controlling mind and primary shareholder, did not want the bad loan to be on Swynson's books, so he personally loaned EMSL money to repay Swynson. In Swynson's subsequent claim for negligent breach of contract against HMT, the latter argued that, as a result, of EMSL's repayment Swynson had suffered no loss and so were confined to nominal damages. The Supreme Court agreed, concluding that although HMT's duty was owed to Swynson, the loss had been suffered by Mr Hunt in his personal capacity. The repayment of the loan had extinguished HMT's liability to Swynson.

## Circumventing the Privity Rule

Throughout its existence, the doctrine of privity has been viewed as problematic. In *White v Jones* [1995] 2 AC 207, Lord Goff observed that the English law of contract had been "stunted through a failure to recognise a jus quaesitum tertio". Even so, it was not until 1999 that it was subject to major reform, in the form of the Contracts (Rights of Third Parties) Act (see below), and even this statute created a very major qualification to the rule, rather than abolishing it outright. The belated nature of reform, despite decades of criticism, is itself significant and cannot be attributed purely to parliamentary indolence. It could suggest that the rule was, perhaps, not as problematic as might at first appear, perhaps because there were ways to circumvent it, and that reforming it raised serious difficulties of its own, helping to explain the lack of alacrity.

Several specific, and limited, statutory exceptions to the privity rule were passed in the years before more general reform in 1999, many involving insurance policies (for obvious reasons). Among them, and for example, was the Third Parties (Rights Against Insurers) Act 1930 (now replaced by the 2010 iteration of the statute), which, under certain situations, allowed potential claimants a direct right to claim against the insurers of an insolvent party. Similarly, s.148(7) of the Road Traffic Act 1988 allowed third parties to claim on drivers' mandatory insurance policies.

However, several techniques were also identified at common law to get round the privity rule. Some of these have largely been abandoned. Thus, artificially creating a "trust of the promise" to circumvent the rule was hugely undermined by the decision in *Re Schebsman* [1944] Ch 83, which required the court to find evidence of a deliberate intention to create a trust rather than creatively inventing it. Others, such as finding a collateral contract, have proved slightly more durable, even if their prerequisites are only rarely satisfied.

## Collateral Contracts

In *Shanklin Pier Ltd v Detel Products Ltd.* [1951] 2 KB 854 the claimants owned a pier in the Isle of Wight that had been damaged by weathering and enemy action during the Second World War. After the war, they contracted with builders to have the pier repaired and repainted. Under the agreement, they had the power to specify the paint to be used by the builders. A representative of the defendant company went to Shanklin and suggested to the claimants that one of their paints was eminently suitable, claiming that it would last for at least seven years. The claimants specified that this, rather than the paint originally suggested by the builders, should be employed on the project. It was duly purchased and used by the latter. It proved to be manifestly unsuitable for a harsh salt-water environment and started to flake off after just three months. The claimants could not sue their builders as they had, themselves, specified the paint to be used. The builders had suffered no financial loss, and so could not sue Detel for substantial damages. Shanklin Pier had not purchased the paint directly from Detel, so there was no contract of sale between them. Even so, they succeeded in a breach of contract action against Detel because there was a collateral contract between the two parties. The defendant (the paint company) was found to have provided an express warranty about the durability of their paint to the claimants, who in turn provided consideration for that guarantee by specifying their paint to the contractor.

Similarly, in *Andrews v Hopkinson* [1957] 1 QB 229, the claimant acquired a car from the defendant's garage, which described the vehicle as a "good little bus. I would stake my life on it". However, the claimant had to purchase the vehicle on hire-purchase terms so that the defendant sold it to a finance company who then made a hire-purchase agreement with the claimant. When the car was delivered, the claimant signed a note saying he was satisfied with its condition. Shortly afterwards, due to a defect in the steering, the car crashed. The claimant could not sue the finance company because of the delivery note (as the law then stood). Instead, he sued the garage owner, although he had no contract of sale with them. Nevertheless, it was held that he had a collateral contract with him. The defendant had promised that the car was in good condition in exchange for the claimant's promising to make the hire-purchase agreement. As a result, he was liable. Of course, such a collateral contract, like any other agreement, is contingent on the courts' being able to identify an offer and acceptance and an intention to create legal relations, and this will not be a common occurrence, especially in the modern era, when the courts are less willing to be creative about finding such prerequisites.

It should also be noted that, in certain circumstances, a party to a contract may "assign" (transfer) his right to benefits (not burdens or detriments) under the agreement to a third party, who then has the power to enforce it. It is possible for this to be done without the consent (or even knowledge) of the party in the main contract against whom those rights are held, this being brought about by the formation of a separate contract between assignor and assignee. As a result, assignment can sometimes circumvent the privity rule. However, there are limits on assignment, greatly restricting its significance. For example, the right to the benefits from a contract of personal service cannot be assigned if it would be detrimental to the party required to provide them: *Don King Productions Inc v Warren* [2000] Ch 291. Thus, it is very unlikely that the agreed weekly services of a gardener could be assigned to another person and garden. Furthermore, contracts often restrict a party's ability to transfer their rights under the agreement, either by prohibiting assignment outright or by requiring the consent of the counterparty who is providing the benefit before an assignment will be effective. Additionally, assignments that involve unliquidated damages or which are deemed to be contrary to public policy will not usually be permitted.[1]

However, despite the exceptions and stratagems discussed above, demands for wider reform to the privity rule continued. Some 60 years after the Law Commission's first suggestions for change, the commission produced its Report No. 242 of 1997, *Reform of the Privity Rule in English Contract Law*, with an attendant draft parliamentary bill. Many of its recommendations came to fruition two years later.

### The Contracts (Rights of Third Parties) Act 1999

Section 1 of the Contracts (Rights of Third Parties) Act 1999 provides that a person who is not a party to a contract may enforce rights under the agreement if he or she is identified by name, as a member of a class, or as answering to a particular description, and the contract either expressly provides that the third party may enforce it (as in *Dunlop v Selfridge*) or, alternatively, it simply purports to confer a benefit on the third party. Thus, the act, where operative, overrides the common law rule that a third party cannot enforce the terms of an agreement. Furthermore, s.1(6) of the 1999 Act provides that contracts may confer the benefit of the defence provided by an exclusion or limitation clause on a third party, not just a cause of action. As a result, the sailors in *Adler v Dickson* might now be able to take the benefit of the exclusion clause under the statute were a similar case to recur.

However, and crucially, unless the conditions set out in s.1 are met, the common law doctrine of privity remains operative, although s.7(1) makes clear that the Act does not affect earlier statutes or identified situations that allowed third parties rights under an agreement (which continue in force). Furthermore, under section 6 of the 1999 Act, a small number of contracts are excluded from the ambit of the statute, so that, for example, a third party cannot enforce any term of an employment contract against an employer. Additionally, under s.1(2), the parties to a contract can expressly or impliedly exclude the statute from their agreement. As a result, the 1999 Act operates as a huge exception to, not an abolition of, the privity rule.

1 Andrew Burrows, *A Restatement of the English Law of Contract*, 2nd edn. (Oxford: Oxford University Press, 2020), pp. 255-260.

In some cases, like *Tweddle v Atkinson*, it will be obvious that the third party has been expressly identified by name, class, or description. However, this provision has been interpreted quite broadly by the courts. For example, in *Nishin Shipping Co. Ltd v Cleaves & Co. Ltd* [2004] EWHC 2602 the parties to a contract agreed they would pay commission to third-party brokers. The court held that the contract was for the benefit of the brokers, and that as there was nothing in it stipulating that they would not be able to enforce the agreement, they could sue under it. More recently, in *Chudley & Ors v Clydesdale Bank PLC* [2019] EWCA Civ 344, in the Court of Appeal, Flaux LJ, with whom Longmore and Moylan LJJ agreed, found that a "letter of instruction" created rights and purported to confer a benefit for third-party investors for the purposes of the statute, even though the investors were unaware of the letter at the time they invested, and it simply referred to a "Segregated Client Account". The court found that the reference to a client account was an express identification of the class (clients of the investment company who were investing in the scheme), and the investors were within that class. The opening of a segregated client account was clearly intended to provide a benefit to these investors by ensuring that their monies were held separately by the bank. They could take advantage of the statute.

Nevertheless, and by contrast, in *Dolphin Maritime & Aviation Services Ltd v Sveriges Angfartygs Assurans Forening* [2009] EWHC 716 the parties to a contract agreed that one of them would pay money to the other via the latter's agent. It was agreed between the agent and his principal that the former would receive commission on this payment. However, the paying party was not involved in this agreement. Subsequently the contracting parties decided that the payment should be made directly between them (so that the agent could not get commission). The agent sued the recipient party for this money. The High Court concluded that the *purpose* of the contracting parties was not to benefit the agent, and so held that s.1(1)(b) of the 1999 Act would not apply. Christopher Clarke J observed, "A contract does not purport to confer a benefit on a third party simply because the position of that third party will be improved if the contract is performed".

The Contracts (Rights of Third Parties) Act 1999 had to address the situation in which the parties to an agreement to benefit another (both) subsequently changed their minds about doing so. This difficult issue helps explain the belated nature of major reform. Section 2.1 of the Act deals with tit by providing that where a third party is aware that they have been given a right under s.1 to enforce an agreement, and has communicated assent to it to the promissor, or the promissor is aware that the third party has relied on it, or ought reasonably to have been aware that this would occur, and the third party has in fact relied on it, the contracting parties cannot end or alter his entitlement without the third party's agreement. However, it should be noted that under s.2.3 of the Act the contracting parties, in their original agreement, can expressly exclude the operation of s.2.1, and reserve the right to vary the contract between themselves without limitation.

## Agency

At first sight, an agency agreement may appear to be a circumvention of the privity rule. However, this is not the reality. Under an agency relationship, one person (the agent) has the power to create legal relationships on behalf of (and binding) another (the principal) with a third party. An agent does not contract in his own right, so that normally he has no liability under such an agreement. For example, at an auction, when a sale is concluded, the contract is made between the purchaser and vendor, and not between the purchaser and auctioneer, who is the vendor's agent. Once the contract is created between the principal and the third party, the agent normally falls away from the agreement. Thus, the agent is really an extension of the principal. It should be noted that not all parties who refer to themselves as "agents", such as estate and recruitment agents, are true legal agents, as they often do not have authority to bind other parties contractually.

Agents come in two forms, those with actual authority and those with apparent or ostensible authority. Actual authority refers to specific powers that have been expressly conferred by the principal on an agent to act on his behalf. Such arrangements can be tailored to the principal's commercial needs. Thus, agency can be limited by time, to particular transactions (such as those up to a set value), or to a specific geographical area (such as Greater London). Apparent or ostensible (the words are synonymous) authority is more complicated. Under the traditional doctrine, as Lord Diplock observed in *Freeman and Lockyer v Buckhurst Park Properties (Mangal) Ltd* [1964] 2 QB 480, "apparent authority is created by a representation, made by the principal to the third party, that the agent has authority to enter on behalf of the principal into a contract of a kind within the scope of the 'apparent' authority, [rendering] the principal liable to perform any obligations imposed upon him". These representations can be made in words or by conduct, whether expressly or by implication. The latter might involve permitting the agent to act in such a way in the conduct of the principal's business with others as to give the impression that he had actual authority. For example, a sales representative who wears a company uniform might bind his company even if he enters a transaction of higher value than allowed by his actual authority.

Of course, apparent authority can be relied upon only by a person who does not *know* that the agent lacks actual authority. As was noted in the Privy Council case of *Russo-Chinese Bank v Li Yau Sam* [1910] AC 174, a "person who deals with an agent, whose authority he knows is limited, does so at his peril, in the sense that should the agent be found to have exceeded his authority his principal cannot be made responsible". (It may, sometimes, be possible to establish liability if the principal subsequently ratifies his involvement in a contract that was made by his agent in excess of his actual authority.)

More significantly, in *Morris v Kanssen* [1946] AC 459, Lord Simonds noted that the principle of ostensible authority cannot be invoked by a person where it should have been apparent that it was questionable as to whether the agent had such authority. The notion of apparent authority is designed to protect those who are entitled to assume, because they cannot know, that the agent has the authority which he claims, "the rule cannot be invoked if the condition is no longer satisfied, that is, if he who would invoke it is put upon his inquiry. He cannot presume in his own favour that things are rightly done if inquiry that he ought to make would tell him that they were wrongly done." This was reiterated by Lord Scott in *Criterion Properties plc v Stratford UK Properties LLC* [2004] UKHL 28, who also observed that, if a person dealing with an agent knows or has reason to believe that the transaction is not in the commercial interests of the agent's principal, it is likely to be very difficult to assert with any credibility that he (the third party) believed that the agent had actual authority, and lack of such a belief would be fatal to a claim of apparent authority.

For example, in *Armagas Ltd v Mundogas SA* [1986] AC 717, a ship was sold by the defendants to the claimants, this being followed by a three-year charter of the vessel back to the defendants. One of the issues before the court was whether a senior employee of the latter had ostensible authority to enter the charter on their behalf. The Court of Appeal, in a decision upheld by the House of Lords, decided that he did not. In part, this was because unusual features of the charter party should have put the claimants on inquiry as to this employee's lack of authority. (Unsurprisingly, the House of Lords also stressed that any representation indicating apparent authority must come from the principal, not the agent.)

By contrast, in *CRJ Services Limited v Lanstar Limited* [2011] EWHC 972 (TCC) the lessee disputed liability under three long-term lease agreements for plant on the grounds that the signatory did not have authority to enter them on their behalf. However, although the signatory was not an employee of the lessee, he was engaged as a consultant and given the title "Landfill Manager" to run a site operated by them. It was common ground that in this capacity he had actual authority to enter into short-term hire agreements for plant, although it was the lessee's case that he had no actual or apparent authority to enter long-term hire contracts. The court quickly rejected the lessee's arguments that the signatory to the agreements lacked the necessary authority to bind the lessee. There was no suggestion that the lessee had taken any steps to inform the counter party that there were limits on the signatory's authority. Although the signatory had no actual authority to contract for long-term hire, he clearly had apparent authority.

For a recent illustration of agency, there can be considered *Athena v Superdrug* [2019] EWHC 3503 (Comm). In this case, a question arose (there were other issues as well) as to whether a Mr Sisson was an agent for Superdrug for the purposes of agreeing a minimum commitment for the purchase of cosmetic products from the claimant. It was accepted that there was no real prospect of showing that he had actual authority to do so--Mr Sisson expressly denied it--so that the focus was on his apparent or ostensible authority. On the face of it, he had been held out by Superdrug as the person with whom terms of trading were to be discussed and agreed. This was made clear in the supplier pack sent to the claimant, which did not contain an indication of any limits on the terms that he might agree, or state that such terms required ratification or confirmation by another member of staff. Indeed, it was the sort of normal commercial term that a buyer might be expected to discuss. As a result, the court found that the buyer did have apparent authority to give the minimum purchase commitment, and it was not unreasonable for the claimant to rely on that authority.

# Chapter 7: Puffs, Representations and Express Terms

## Introduction

During pre-contractual negotiations various statements may be made by the parties to an agreement, whether orally or in writing contained in non-contractual documents, such as an exchange of letters or emails. Some of these may attain the status of full express terms, which, if broken, might be the subject of an action for breach of contract. (Considered in Chapter 12). By contrast, some statements will have no legal significance at all, and so no legal consequences, even if the person to whom they were made feels that they were very inaccurate. Foremost amongst the latter are instances of obviously exaggerated or very vague sales talk, so-called mere puffs.

Yet other statements will not necessarily attain the status of express terms but, unlike puffs, will still have legal significance as so-called mere representations, and if untrue might lead to an action for misrepresentation, a separate legal action from that for breach of contract. (Discussed in the next chapter). However, and complicating matters, it should be noted that some statements can be both representations and terms. For example, sometimes, an untrue representation will (subsequently) become an express term but continue to co-exist (with that term) as an actionable misrepresentation. Thus, in *Naughton v O'Callaghan* [1990] 3 All ER 191 the claimant formulated their claim in misrepresentation, rather than breach of contract (also open to him), following a negligent misstatement as to the pedigree of a racehorse, because the latter was more likely to allow recovery of the extensive expenses that had resulted over ensuing years when the animal failed to win any races. Nevertheless, and limiting such situations, in *SK Shipping v Capital VLCC* [2022] EWCA Civ 231, the Court of Appeal reiterated that, in the "absence of words of representation, the mere offer of contractual terms will not amount to any representation".

Distinguishing between the three categories (express terms, representations, and puffs) can be difficult, but case law has identified various tests and guidelines that can be employed when doing so. Fortunately, if there is any doubt when it comes to the key distinction between express terms and mere representations, as there often will be, a claimant can advance both possibilities simultaneously in litigation, as alternative scenarios in their statement of case ("further or in the alternative") and leave it to the trial judge to decide which (if any) is appropriate. Similarly, and as was the situation with a charter party in *SK Shipping v Capital VLCC*, the allegedly injured party (the charterer in this case) might simultaneously purport to rescind the contract for misrepresentation and, alternatively, to terminate the agreement for repudiatory breach of an express term, so covering both eventualities.

## Distinction Between Puffs and Representations

Mere puffs are not actionable, unlike (some) untrue representations, the next step up in the legal hierarchy of significance. For example, in *Dimmock v Hallett* (1866–67) LR 2 Ch App 21, an advertisement for the sale of a farm described the property as having "fertile and improvable land". This failed as a representation, being deemed to be nothing more than a sales puff that did not entitle the buyer to rescind. As Turner LJ observed, "I think the statement is to be looked at as a mere flourishing description by an auctioneer". All land is improvable and, at the least, sufficiently fertile to produce a crop of weeds.

When it comes to the distinction between mere puffs and representations the court must be able to identify a statement of fact, upon which the representee was entitled to rely, for it to fall into the latter category. In *MCI WorldCom International Inc v Primus Telecommunications Inc* [2004] EWCA Civ 957, Mance LJ approved Professor John Cartwright's view on this issue, which had been set out in his academic work on misrepresentation. Professor Cartwright suggested that the key question was whether the representee was entitled to take the statement seriously and so rely on it when deciding whether to enter the contract. This should be judged by the impact that whatever was said might be expected to have on a reasonable person with the known characteristics of the actual representee involved.[1] This was expressly reiterated in *Cassa di Risparmio della Repubblica di San Marino SpA v Barclays Bank Limited* [2011] EWHC 484 (Comm), where Hamblen J stated that a representation is a statement of fact made by the representor to the representee "on which the representee is intended and entitled to rely as a positive assertion that the fact is true. ... [It is to be interpreted] according to the impact it might be expected to have on a reasonable representee in the position and with the known characteristics of the actual representee".

## Distinction Between Representations and Terms

The distinction between mere representations and express terms is vital, as only a breach of the latter will allow the injured party to sue for breach of contract, although, if the former turn out to be untrue, they *might* have an action for misrepresentation. In the Court of Appeal case of *Oscar Chess Ltd v Williams* [1957] 1 WLR 370, Lord Denning reiterated the traditional test for distinguishing between a term and a mere representation, one that had been identified by Lord Chief Justice Holt in *Crosse v Gardner* (1689) Comb.142, when he noted that "an affirmation at the time of sale is a warranty, provided it appear on evidence to have been so intended". In Lord Denning's words this became "Was it [the statement] intended as a warranty [a term in this context] or not?"

However, as Denning also noted, "intended" did not mean that the tribunal should try to look into the parties' minds to see what they had meant subjectively. As with several other areas of the law of contract, their intention is determined objectively,

1 John Cartwright, *Misrepresentation* (London: Sweet and Maxwell, 2002), para. 2.12.

from the totality of the extrinsic evidence, and "depends on the conduct of the parties, on their words and behaviour, rather than on their thoughts. If an intelligent bystander would reasonably infer that a warranty [term] was intended, that will suffice".

Of course, this then raises the question as to how an intelligent bystander would judge such matters. It is not always an easy question to determine. Indicative of this, in Oscar Chess itself, Morris LJ delivered a dissenting opinion on the issue. Nevertheless, to help answer this question, and to give a degree of judicial consistency to such determinations, the courts have identified factors or benchmarks that they feel might properly influence an intelligent bystander's decision on the issue. These are not the test, merely indicators as to how an answer to the test identified by Holt and Denning might be reached. Sometimes more than one will be present, and they might be conflicting, with factors going both ways, for and against a statement being a term, leaving it to the court to decide which is more significant, or whether they cancel each other out.

### Reduced to Writing

In *Oscar Chess Ltd v Williams* it was noted that, where a contract is written down in a formal contractual document, it is very likely that any earlier statements repeated in the written agreement are intended to be contractual terms, and probable that any that are omitted will be representations (at most), since the parties are likely to record only statements that they want to form part of the contract. This is an illustration of what is sometimes termed the "parol evidence rule" which is discussed in detail in Chapter 12.

### Importance Placed on the Statement

The more significance that is placed on a statement by one of the parties to an agreement, the more likely it is to be viewed as an express term. In *Bannerman v White* (1861) 10 CBNS 844, the claimant contracted to purchase hops for brewing beer. He asked the seller if they had been treated with sulphur (used to deal with pests) and told him that he would not give them a second glance if they had, as it would make them unsuitable for his form of high-quality brewing. The seller assured him that the hops had not been so treated. This transpired to be partially untrue (some of them had been so treated), and the question arose as to whether the statement that the hops had not been treated with sulphur was a term or a mere representation. This was a vital issue as, on the facts of the case, at this time, the latter would not provide an effective remedy for the injured party. It was held to be a term as the claimant had made its crucial importance to his decision to purchase the hops quite clear. Of course, if such importance is placed on a statement that it becomes a term, it is also likely to be a condition, or at least an innominate term, rather than a warranty (lesser term).

## Relative Degrees of Knowledge

The degree of knowledge possessed by the maker of the statement is also very significant. A statement made by an expert or specialist, within his field of knowledge, especially to a layman who does not have such expertise, is more likely to be considered a term. Conversely, a statement made by a layman, especially to a specialist about a matter that is within the latter's area of expertise, is more likely to be viewed as a representation, although everything turns on the words used. This point was considered by Lord Denning in *Oscar Chess Ltd v Williams* [1957] 1 WLR 370. He observed, "When the seller states a fact which is or should be within his own knowledge and of which the buyer is ignorant, intending that the buyer should act on it and he does so, it is easy to infer a warranty. ... But if the seller, when he states a fact, makes it clear that he has no knowledge of his own but has got his information elsewhere, and is merely passing it on, it is not so easy to imply a warranty".

In the instant case, Mr Williams's mother had purchased a second-hand Morris car having been told that it was a 1948 model, something that was supported by the vehicle's logbook, and then given the car to her son. The following year it was used as a part-trade-in for a brand-new Hillman Minx, from Oscar Chess Ltd, a firm of car dealers. Mr Williams stated that it was a 1948 model, and on that basis Oscar Chess offered him £290 off the purchase price of the new vehicle. Some eight months later Oscar Chess Ltd discovered from engine block and chassis numbers that the car was, in fact, a 1939 model (the design had barely changed during WW2 so that this was not obvious), with a cleverly altered logbook, and so worth just £175. They brought an action for breach of contract arguing that the statement as to the date of the vehicle was an express term of the agreement, giving them grounds to claim damages.

It was held that the statement relating to the age of the car was not a term but a representation. The representee, as a professional car dealer, would be in a better position to know the age of manufacture than the defendant, could easily have ascertained it by looking at the chassis or engine block numbers (far too low for a 1948 vintage), and would also know that having purchased it second-hand the vendor was basing their knowledge on the logbook and what they (or their mother) had been told when buying it. It was unlikely that such a person would warrant the year of manufacture, although, of course, they could do so if they made this sufficiently clear.

By contrast, in *Dick Bentley Productions Ltd v Harold Smith (Motors) Ltd* [1965] 1 WLR 623, Dick Bentley, the owner of the eponymous company, sought a "well-vetted" second-hand Bentley car. Harold Smith were car dealers and offered them one that they said had done only 20,000 miles since having a replacement engine and gearbox fitted. It subsequently transpired that the Bentley that they tendered had done nearer 100,000 miles since these parts had been replaced. Dick Bentley sued Harold Smith for breach of contract and was successful at first instance. The Court of Appeal also held that the statement of mileage was a term of the contract, because Harold Smith (Motors) Ltd were car dealers and in a better position than the claimant to know the truth of the statement. Lord Denning observed that the dealer, Mr. Smith, "was in a position to know, or at least to find out, the history of the car. He could get it by writing to the makers. He did not do so. ... He ought to have known better. There was no reasonable foundation for it".

### Propinquity

The closer a statement is to the making of a contract, the more likely it is to be a term. If there is a lengthy gap between the statement and the formation of the agreement, during which it is not reiterated, it is less likely to be given this status, if only because it is taken as indicative of a lack of importance. For example, in *Routledge v McKay* [1954] 1 WLR 615 the claimant purchased a motorbike. The registration documents falsely stated that it was a 1942 model, as a previous owner (to the defendant) had wrongly registered it as being of that vintage. The seller gave that date to the purchaser during negotiations, but there was then a delay of almost a week before the contract was agreed, without any further discussion of the motorbike's age. In the written contract, signed a week later, no mention was made of the model's date. It transpired that the motorbike was made in 1936, and worth much less than one from 1942. It was held that the statement as to its age was a mere representation and not a contractual term. In part, this was because of the delay between the negotiations and the making of the contract (the failure to include it in the written agreement was also a factor). If it was fundamental to the agreement the purchaser would have asked for it to be restated.

### Assumption of Responsibility

If a party assumes responsibility for the veracity of their statement, it is more likely to be viewed as a term. In the Irish case of *Schawel v Reade* [1913] 2 IR 81, the claimant purchased a horse from the defendant after telling the latter that he wished to use the animal for stud purposes. Whilst the claimant was examining the horse, the defendant told him that it was "perfectly sound", and that if there was anything wrong with it, he would tell him. He also advised him that there was no need to get a vet to examine the animal. Relying on this, the claimant purchased the horse, which turned out to have a hereditary eye disease making it unsuitable for breeding. It was held that the statement that the animal was sound was a contractual term. The defendant had assured the purchaser he could rely on it, and actively discouraged him from seeking professional advice on the issue.

By contrast, in *Ecay v Godfrey* [1947] 80 Lloyds Rep 286, the defendant sold a small yacht to the claimant. He stated that, as far as he was aware, it was structurally sound, but advised the claimant to have a marine survey carried out on the vessel. The claimant went ahead with the purchase without doing this. Unfortunately, the yacht turned out to be defective. It was held that the statement that it was sound was merely a representation, not an express term. By advising the purchaser that it should be surveyed, the vendor had indicated that he was not taking contractual responsibility for his statement. (There would be no need for a survey in such a situation.)

# Chapter 8: Misrepresentation

## Introduction

An actionable misrepresentation is a false statement of existing fact, made by one party to another, which, whilst not necessarily becoming a term, induces the representee to enter a contract with that other party. (See Chapter 7 for the distinction between terms and representations). It is subject to its own regime of remedies, distinct from those for breach of contract(ual term). The prerequisites for such a legal action, and the qualifications to them, must be considered in detail.

## 1. A Statement Made by One of the Parties

The statement must be made by or on behalf of one of the contracting parties; thus, a party may be liable for a statement made by himself or by his agent. However, if a contracting party relies on an untrue statement made by a third party (for example, one made by a casual but officious observer), it will (unsurprisingly) not be actionable. The statement can be made by words (written or oral) or even by conduct (discussed below).

### Statements and Silence

The need for a statement means that silence will not *normally* constitute a misrepresentation. There is usually no obligation on a potential party to a contract to disclose adverse information to the counterparty prior to the conclusion of an agreement, even though they know that it might affect the latter's decision as to whether, or on what terms, to enter the contract. For example, in the old case of *Keates v The Earl of Cadogan* (1851) 10 CB 591, the defendant contracted with the claimant for the lease of one of the former's properties for use as a family residence. The property proved to be in an extremely poor structural condition, and in danger of collapse. The defendant had known about this during negotiations without informing the claimant. Even so, it was held that a landlord had no obligation to inform a potential tenant as to the state of a property prior to entering a lease (as opposed to actively deceiving him about its condition). The contract could not be rescinded for misrepresentation.

In like manner, in *Peek v Gurney* (1873) LR 6 HL 377, promoters issued a prospectus for a planned company without mentioning the heavy liabilities of a business that the company was set to purchase, which would be transferred to the new company. The appellant bought shares in it and, when it went into liquidation, lost almost £100,000. He alleged misrepresentation by the directors. Although he failed, in part, because he had not relied on the prospectus (see below), Lord Cairns reiterated that silence was not normally sufficient for such an action: "Mere non-disclosure of material facts, however morally censurable ... would in my opinion form no ground for an action in the nature of an action for misrepresentation".

More recently, it has been held that there was no obligation to disclose a forthcoming marriage in a divorce settlement, even though it might well have affected the husband's willingness to pay £13,000 to his former spouse, so that his action to rescind the agreement on the grounds of misrepresentation was rejected: *Wales v Wadham* [1977] 1 WLR 199. Very gruesomely, in *Sykes v Taylor-Rose* [2004] EWCA Civ 299, the defendants owned a house in which a previous resident had murdered and dismembered his adopted daughter in 1985, concealing some body parts on the premises. They sold the property to the claimants without telling them about its history. The latter discovered its past from a television programme and sought damages from the defendants for misrepresentation. The High Court concluded that the respondents were not under a duty to disclose that a recent murder had taken place there, and there was no appeal on this point.

### Exceptions to the Silence Rule

There are, however, several exceptions to the general rule, in which silence *can* constitute a misrepresentation. These include misleading half-truths that misrepresent the true situation by omitting vital information; contracts of the utmost good faith (in Latin, *uberrimae fidei*); those where a change of circumstances mean that a statement that was true when made has become false by the time a contract is concluded; and contracts between those who are in a fiduciary relationship.

### i. Misleading Half-Truths

Misleading half-truths were considered in *Oakes v Turquand* (1867) LR 2 HL 325, when Lord Chelmsford observed that although everything stated in a prospectus in the case before him was literally correct, the objection to it was "not that it does not state the truth as far as it goes, but that it conceals most material facts with which the public ought to have been made acquainted, the very concealment of which gives to the truth which is told the character of falsehood".

More famously, and at about the same time, in *Dimmock v Hallett* (1866–67) LR 2 Ch App 21, the sale of an estate included a statement in the relevant particulars that two of its main farms were let, one at £130 per annum and the other at £160 per annum. There was no mention that both tenants had given notice to quit, which would expire shortly after the sale went through. As a result, the buyer would be led to suppose that he was acquiring property that was fully let out, although he would have to find tenants immediately after completing his purchase. The silence on this issue was especially significant, as the serving of a notice to quit *had* been expressly disclosed with regard to another farm that was offered for sale at the same time.

In *Nottingham Patent Brick & Tile Co v Butler* (1886) 16 QBD 778 a solicitor's statement that he was not aware of any restrictive covenant on a parcel of land that was being sold, although technically true, was misleading because he had not examined the title deeds. Such a statement, made by a lawyer in these circumstances, impliedly suggested that he had grounds for his belief. (It was a negligent not a fraudulent misrepresentation as he genuinely did believe that there were no covenants).

### ii. Contracts of the Utmost Good Faith

Certain contracts, deemed to be of the utmost good faith, require that parties volunteer information that might affect the other's decision to enter the agreement and on what terms. Historically, and very significantly, these include insurance contracts. When taking out a contract of insurance, information must be disclosed if it would influence the decision of a hypothetical "prudent insurer" (rather than any specific insurer) in deciding whether to issue a policy, or the level of the premium charged for the insurance if they did: *T Brit UW Ltd v F&B Trenchless Solutions Ltd* [2015] EWCA 2237 (Comm). This rule can be traced back to the case of *Carter v Boehm* (1766) 1 Blackstone W 593, in which Lord Mansfield noted that in insurance contracts "special facts usually lie in the knowledge of the insured only. The underwriter trusts to him, that he conceals nothing, so as to make him form a wrong estimate. [Even] If a concealment happens without any fraudulent intention by mistake of the principal or his agent, still the policy is void". This issue was considered in *Lambert v Co-operative Insurance Society Ltd* [1975] 2 Lloyd's Rep 485, in which Mrs Lambert insured her jewellery with the defendant under an all-risks policy, and had done so for more than nine years. When her jewellery was stolen, her claim was rejected on the grounds that she had not disclosed that her husband had been convicted of two offences of dishonesty, one relating to the theft of cigarettes, even though the insurer had not asked her about such matters. The Court of Appeal sympathised with Mrs Lambert, but thought the law was clearly established and found for the insurer.

Nevertheless, s.14(1) of the Insurance Act 2015 has abolished any rule of law permitting a party to a contract of insurance to automatically avoid the contract solely on the ground that the utmost good faith has not been observed. A range of alternative remedies is provided. For example, negligent non-disclosure that would only have resulted in an increase in the premium charged for an insurance contract will no longer give rise to the right to avoid the agreement altogether. Instead, the insurer will be entitled to a proportionate reduction in the value of the claim.

### iii. Statements That Have Become Untrue Prior To Contract

A representor is required to correct a statement that was true when made, but which has become untrue by the time the contract is concluded. This is particularly significant where there have been prolonged pre-contractual negotiations. In *With v O'Flanagan* (1936) CH 575, the defendant was selling his private medical practice, which he previously said had received about £2,000 each year in fees. This was true at the time he made the statement, but in the meantime the doctor had fallen seriously ill, which led to a very significant decrease in income, as his patients transferred to other practices. The Court of Appeal held that there had been a misrepresentation because he had not told the purchaser of the change.

### iv. Fiduciary Relationships

Where a fiduciary relationship exists between the parties to a potential agreement there is a duty on the fiduciary to disclose all material facts of which they are aware to their principal if they propose to contract with each other. As was noted in *Bristol and West Building Society v Mothew* [1996] EWCA Civ 533, a fiduciary must act in good faith and not place himself in a position where his duty and his personal interest may conflict. This might affect contracts between, inter alia, solicitor and client, doctor and patient, and the partners in a partnership. Similarly, the promoters of a company stand in a fiduciary relationship to that company. It was for this reason that, in *Erlanger v New Sombrero Phosphate Co* (1878) 3 App Cas 1218, the defendant promoters of the claimant company, who sold them an island from which to extract phosphate for £110,000, committed an actionable non-disclosure when they failed to tell the claimant that they had purchased the island for half that amount just a few days earlier.

### Conduct to be Distinguished from Silence

Although silence is not normally actionable, a misrepresentation can be made by conduct, without express statements having to be made orally or in writing. Thus, in *St Marylebone Property v Payne* (1994) 45 EG 156, the use of a photograph taken from the air in auction particulars that was printed with arrows, one of which misleadingly indicated the extent of a property boundary and suggested that a large door belonging to adjacent premises was part of the sale property, was held to convey a statement of fact and so amounted to an actionable misrepresentation. Unsurprisingly, in *Walters v Morgan* (1861) 3 DF & J 718, Lord Campbell also noted that silence did not include a "nod or wink, or a shake of the head, or a smile from the purchaser intended to induce the vendor to believe the existence of a non-existing fact, which might influence the price of the subject to be sold".

However, this notion was taken much further in *Gordon v Selico Ltd* (1986) 278 EG 53, which held that active concealment can constitute a fraudulent misrepresentation, albeit in fairly extreme situations. In this case, Selico owned a flat that was in poor condition, and which the company intended to sell. Selico instructed some decorators to prepare it for sale, which involved concealing patches of dry rot from view by painting over them, prior to sale. Gordon, the claimant, obtained a detailed survey of the flat which concluded that no dry rot had been found, although only one floorboard had been lifted, and its absence could not be guaranteed elsewhere in the flat. Gordon purchased the flat believing it to be sound, before discovering the extensive dry rot. The court concluded that painting over the rot was a statement of fact and, in the circumstances, a (fraudulent) misrepresentation. This must be a matter of degree. Prudent prospective house purchasers know that, for example, Ingrain (woodchip) wallpaper often covers cracks and flaws of some type.

Less dramatically (and not fraudulently), in *Spice Girls Ltd v Aprilia World Service* [2000] EWHC Ch 140, the claimants were the managing company of a five-woman pop group. The defendants signed a sponsorship agreement with them to assist in the sale of their scooters after being sent promotional materials that depicted all five group members taking part in the filming of a TV commercial for the scooters, something that suggested that membership of the group was not about to change. Subsequently, Aprilia resisted making payment, saying that one of the five, Ginger Spice, had already given notice to leave the group when they entered the agreement, departing just three weeks later, substantially reducing the campaign's impact. It was held that the claimants knew that the defendants were relying on what was, effectively, a representation by conduct that the group would be intact at the time the campaign went out. The claimants had also circulated a draft agreement referring to the Spice Girls as "currently comprising" the five named individuals, without going on to say that one of them was set to leave within the period of the agreement, so that, arguably, the statement was also a misleading half-truth (see above).

## 2. A Statement of Existing Fact

To be actionable, a misrepresentation must normally involve a statement of existing fact. An incorrect statement of opinion or of future intention (that is not ultimately carried out) is not in itself actionable. For example, in *Bisset v Wilkinson* [1927] AC 177, the claimant purchased land to use as a sheep farm after asking the seller how many sheep it would support. The land had not previously been used for such animals, but the seller estimated that it would graze 2,000 sheep. This turned out to be a serious over-estimate; in reality, there was grass for less than half that number, and the claimant brought an action for misrepresentation. The Privy Council held that the statement was only a statement of opinion, and not one of fact, so that it was not actionable.

However, as was noted at first instance in *BV Nederlandse Industrie van Eiprodukten v Rembrandt Enterprises* [2018] EWHC 1857 (Comm), "A statement of opinion is invariably regarded as incorporating an assertion [of fact] that the maker does actually hold that opinion". This was certainly not new law, being recognised by Bowen LJ as far back as *Smith v Land and House Property Corporation* (1884) LR 28 Ch D 7. In this case, Land and House contracted to buy the freehold title of a hotel from Smith. The latter had advertised that it was currently let to a "most desirable" tenant. In reality, the tenant was long overdue in paying his rent for the hotel. He went bankrupt shortly before the freehold title was transferred. Land and House refused to complete the transaction, and resisted Smith's claim for specific performance on the basis that the description of the tenant was a misrepresentation (so that he lacked "clean hands").

Although, at first sight, the phrase a "most desirable" tenant might appear to be merely one of opinion rather than fact, Bowen LJ held that such a statement, especially by someone who best knows the facts, frequently involves an implied statement of fact that he knows things which justify his opinion. The judge went on to note, "The state of a man's mind is as much a fact as the state of his digestion. ... A misrepresentation as to the state of a man's mind is, therefore, a misstatement of fact". In the judge's opinion a tenant who had paid his previous quarter's rent by driblets, under considerable pressure from his landlord, and was in arrears, could not be regarded as a desirable tenant. Specific performance of the contract was refused.

Similarly, a statement as to future intention will also contain an implied statement of fact, namely that such an intention is held when stated. In *Edgington v Fitzmaurice* (1885) 29 Ch D 459, the claimant purchased newly issued shares in the defendant company after reading the latter's prospectus, which stated that they were being issued to raise money to expand the company. In truth, the business was experiencing serious financial difficulties and it was always intended that the money raised from the sale of the shares would be used to pay some of its debts. Although the statement was one of future intention (expansion of the company), it was an actionable misrepresentation, as the defendant had no intention of using the money for this purpose when they made the statement. Of course, proving this will often be very difficult, and in the instant case was possible only because the true intention was entered into the company minutes. Nevertheless, as Bowen L.J observed in *Edgington v Fitzmaurice*, "It is true that it is very difficult to prove what the state of a man's mind is, but, if it can be ascertained, it is as much a fact as anything else".

## Materiality

Traditionally, it was thought necessary for an actionable misrepresentation to be "material", in the sense that it would have induced a reasonable person to enter the contract. It could not be for a trivial or inconsequential matter, this being viewed as an independent element of the prerequisites necessary for such an action.[1] Thus, if the vendor of an expensive motorcar told the purchaser that it had a pair of pink fluffy dice hanging from the rear-view mirror, and it transpired that these were absent, it might not constitute an actionable misrepresentation, as the presence of such ornaments would not influence a reasonable person.

Nevertheless, in *Museprime Properties v Adhill Properties* [1990] 36 EG 114, it was suggested by Scott J that any misrepresentation which induces a person to enter a contract might be a ground for rescission. However, if it was of a type that could induce a reasonable person to enter an agreement, the court would be more likely to presume that the representee had, in fact, relied on it, and the onus would be on the representor to show that the representee did not do so. By contrast, if the representation would not have had this effect (it was not material), the onus would be on the representee to show that it had induced him to enter the agreement, something that might, sometimes, be quite difficult. In *SK Shipping v Capital VLCC* [2022] EWCA Civ 231, the Court of Appeal reiterated that a misrepresentation was

1 Gareth Spark, *Vitiation of Contracts: International Contractual Principles and English Law* (Cambridge: Cambridge University Press, 2013), pp. 170-211.

"material" if it was "likely to induce the contract". Such a representation gave rise to a rebuttable inference of fact that there was inducement, unlike a non-material representation.

### 3. Falsity

To be actionable, a misrepresentation must, of course, be false. However, to a modest extent, this is a matter of degree. Rix J has observed that a representation may be deemed to be true without being entirely correct "provided it is substantially correct and the difference between what is represented and what is actually correct would not have been likely to induce a reasonable person in the position of the claimants to enter into the contracts": *Avon Insurance plc v Swire Fraser Ltd* [2000] 1 All ER (Comm) 573.

### 4. Reliance

For a misrepresentation to be actionable, it must have induced the representee to enter the contract, that is, it must have been relied on by the person to whom it was made. The key issue is whether he would have entered the agreement had the representation not been made, not whether he would have done so if told the true position: *SK Shipping v Capital VLCC* [2022] EWCA Civ 231. This is a question of fact. In cases of innocent and negligent misrepresentation, the claimant has the onus of proving his reliance on the statement. However, a misrepresentation need not be the only reason or inducement behind the representee's decision. It is sufficient if it can be shown to have been *one* of the reasons for his decision, "but for" which he would not have entered the agreement. Thus, in the case of *Edgington v Fitzmaurice* (1885) 29 ChD 459, the claimant was induced to purchase a financial instrument partly because of a misrepresentation in the prospectus, but also because of a mistaken personal belief that the instrument had certain rights of security attached to it. The court found reliance and held that "it is not necessary to show that the misstatement was the sole cause of his acting as he did".

By contrast, in *JEB Fasteners Ltd v Marks Bloom & Co* [1983] 1 All ER 583, JEB took control of another company. Marks were the auditors for the latter business. One of JEB's primary motivations behind taking over the company was that they would be able to acquire the services of two of its (well-regarded) directors. JEB understood at the time that they assumed control of the company that there were errors with the accounts that had been audited by Marks. However, they proved to be more inaccurate than JEB had realised, and JEB subsequently sued for damages. Their claim was dismissed, and this decision was upheld by the Court of Appeal. There was ample evidence to show that JEB would have proceeded to take control of the company and its directors irrespective of the representations, even if they knew the true situation.

Unsurprisingly, in these circumstances, a representation will not be actionable if the representee was entirely unaware of it, knew it was false, or relied purely on his own judgment or investigations when deciding to enter a contract. For example, in *Horsfall v Thomas* [1862] 1 H&C 90, although the active concealment of a defect in a gun was held to be a misrepresentation, as the buyer did not inspect the gun, he did not know about it, so that it could not have induced him to enter the contract. More recently, in the case of *Hartelid v Sawyer & McClintock Real Estate Ltd* [1977] 5 WLR 481, an estate agent made a false statement about the size of a garage to a potential buyer, but prior to purchasing the relevant property the buyer visited the garage and saw its true size for himself. It was held that there was no actionable misrepresentation because the representor's false statement had no causal impact; the representee had carried out his own investigations and knew the true position prior to signing the contract.

Changing scenario, in *Attwood v Small* [1838] 6 Cl & F 232, the claimant purchased an estate from the defendant for £600,000, including land that was intended for mining. The defendant made several statements about the property and provided various reports and accounts to support them. The claimant agreed to purchase the property but made this subject to being satisfied that they were accurate. He then had his own accountants and agents thoroughly examine the books and property, and they concluded that this was indeed the case. The claimant then went ahead with the purchase. Unfortunately, it transpired that the pre-contract statements had greatly exaggerated the income from the estate. The claimant sought to rescind the contract for misrepresentation but was unsuccessful. After getting his own experts to scrutinize the reports he had relied purely on their judgment rather than the statements.

It should be noted that *Attwood v Small* is, factually, slightly unusual; if a claimant had partly relied on his own agents, but also partly relied on the misrepresentation, as will often be the case, it would still be actionable. Furthermore, it seems that the principle in *Attwood v Small* may not apply to a fraudulent misrepresentation: *S. Pearson & Son Ltd v Dublin Corporation* [1907] AC 351.

Much more recently, in *Ahuja Investments Ltd v Victorygame Ltd* [2021] EWHC 2382 (Ch), the High Court rejected a claim for misrepresentations about the duration of the leases of retail units in a shopping centre and their attendant rental income, because they had not induced the claimant to enter the transaction. Ahuja knew the true terms of the leases before exchanging contracts because the original leases were in their possession or that of their solicitors.

However, there can still be an inducement if the misrepresentee is given an opportunity to discover the truth of a statement but does not take advantage of it. In *Redgrave v Hurd* (1881) 20 Ch D 1, Redgrave, an elderly solicitor, advertised for a partner to join his business. He told Hurd, a more recently qualified lawyer, that the practice brought in £300 a year. Redgrave then showed him summaries of work that accounted for an average of £200 per annum and said that the balance of about

£100 was evidenced by other letters and papers available in his office, and that Hurd could go through them to confirm this if he wished. In reality, these letters showed almost no business. Hurd chose not to inspect them, but realised the true situation just before completion of the agreement. Although he had signed the contract, he refused to go through with it. Redgrave sought specific performance (see Chapter 16), and Hurd counterclaimed for rescission based on fraudulent misrepresentation. It was held at first instance that, because Hurd had not taken the opportunity to check the papers, he could not be taken to have relied on the statement. This decision was reversed in the Court of Appeal and the contract rescinded on grounds of innocent (not fraudulent) misrepresentation. Relying on the representation was enough, and there was no duty on the representee to inspect the papers.

When it comes to inducement in cases of fraudulent misrepresentation the standard of causation is lower, and the test weaker. It is sufficient if there is evidence to show that the representee was materially influenced by the misrepresentation in the sense that it had some impact on his thinking, was a reason for entering the contract, or was "actively present to his mind": *Hayward v Zurich Insurance Co plc* [2016] 4 All ER 441. In *Raiffeisen Zentralbank Osterreich v Royal Bank of Scotland* [2010] EWHC 1392, Christopher Clarke J suggested that it is enough to show that but for the representation he *might* (not would) have acted differently, and this approach has found favour with the Court of Appeal.

Thus, in *BV Nederlandse Industrie van Eiprodukten v Rembrandt Enterprises* [2018] EWHC 1857 (Comm), an outbreak of avian flu in the US in April 2015 led to millions of hens being slaughtered. As a result, Rembrandt Enterprises had to import Dutch dried egg-based products from NIVE to satisfy customer demand. The Dutch supplier subsequently described a proposed price increase to its American customer as reflecting the increased cost of complying with US regulatory requirements for such products. Their customer agreed to the increase on this basis, and a new contract was signed. In fact, the new price merely reflected a desire for increased profit. Rembrandt's case was that it was induced to enter the revised contract by a fraudulent misrepresentation about the additional costs of complying with the US requirements. In the High Court, Teare J agreed with this analysis, and rejected NIVE's argument that Rembrandt needed the egg product so badly that it would have agreed to the increased price, even if it had been told that it was motivated by profit and did not reflect real regulatory costs.

The Court of Appeal dismissed NIVE's appeal. The court asked itself whether, but for the misrepresentation, the customer "might have acted differently" and came up with a positive answer. Longmore LJ held that the representee merely had to show that the fraud was .actively present to his mind.. Once this had been done, a presumption of fact arose that he was induced to enter the contract, one that the representor then has the onus to disprove, something that was difficult to do.

The difficulty entailed in rebutting this presumption can be seen in *Richard Edwards v Jahid Ahmet Ashik* [2014] EWHC 2454 (Ch). In this case, Mr Edwards purchased a nightclub owned by Mr Ashik. The trial judge found that in answer to pre-contractual enquiries, Mr Ashik had deliberately and dishonestly failed to confirm that there had been a complaint about the club, and that recommendations made by the Local Authority had not been implemented. Mr Edwards, who was the only person to make an offer for the business, contended that he would not have proceeded with the purchase if he had been alerted to the true position. As the misrepresentation was found to be fraudulent, it was then for Mr Ashik to show that it did not play a significant part in the other party's decision to enter the agreement, and he failed to do this.

Nevertheless, in *Leeds City Council and others v Barclays Bank plc and another* [2021] EWHC 363 (Comm), the High Court concluded that a claimant must prove not only that a representation had been made, but that the representee's awareness of it amounted to a *conscious* factor in their decision to enter a contract. In this case, several local councils sought to rescind LIBOR-referenced loan agreements with Barclays Bank, alleging that there had been a fraudulent implied misrepresentation that LIBOR rates were being set in a proper fashion. The claimants argued that it was sufficient to show that the implied representations about LIBOR operated on their minds subconsciously. The court accepted the bank's argument that it was not possible to rely on a statement without being consciously aware of it. More was needed than "subconscious operation".

## Contractual Provisions Preventing Claims for Misrepresentation

Any attempt in non-consumer contracts to exclude or restrict liability for a misrepresentation must satisfy the reasonableness test set out in s.11(1) of the Unfair Contract Terms Act 1977 (UCTA), by dint of s.3 of the Misrepresentation Act 1967 (as amended by s.8 UCTA), and it is for those claiming that the term satisfies that requirement to show that it does. (The 1977 statute is discussed in Chapter 13). Although this section does not (now) apply to consumer contracts, section 62 of the Consumer Rights Act 2015 will have the same effect.

For example, in *Cremdean Properties Ltd v Nash* (1977) 244 EG 547, Cremdean contracted to buy property from Nash for commercial development, following representations by Nash's agents that it had planning permission for 17,900 square feet of offices. In reality, the figure was very much lower. When Cremdean subsequently brought an action for misrepresentation, Nash sought to rely on a clause in their original invitation to tender that said that although such statements were believed to be correct, their accuracy was not guaranteed and that errors would not annul any sale. The Court of Appeal held that this was an exclusion clause within the terms of s.3 MRA and, on its facts, unreasonable under s.11 UCTA.

The use of "non-reliance" clauses in written contracts has become increasingly common in recent years. These usually stipulate that the parties to a contract do not rely on any statement or representation that is not set out in the agreement itself, such as a pre-contractual statement that would otherwise be an actionable misrepresentation, rather than excluding liability for such a misrepresentation. (They are often combined with entire agreement clauses). However, any clause that has the effect of avoiding liability in these circumstances must *still* satisfy s.3 of the Misrepresentation Act 1967, in the same way that a clause expressly excluding liability for such a misrepresentation would: *First Tower Trustees Ltd and other v CDS (Superstores International) Ltd* [2018] EWCA Civ 1396.

In *First Tower Trustees*, the landlord had leased warehouse premises. By a clause in the agreement, the tenant acknowledged that it had not entered the lease in reliance on any representation made by the landlord. In its replies to pre-contract enquiries, the landlord had stated that it was unaware of any environmental problems relating to the property. Nevertheless, the landlord *was* aware of asbestos contamination in the warehouse. Remedial works were necessary to deal with it, and the tenant had to lease alternative premises while these were carried out. The trial judge found that the tenant had entered the lease in reliance on the misrepresentation, that the clause was an attempt to exclude liability for such misrepresentation, and as a result, it was required to satisfy the test of reasonableness under s.11(1) UCTA, which it failed to do.

The Court of Appeal dismissed the defendant's appeal. The clause was not held to be reasonable, even though it had been negotiated by equally matched commercial parties with the benefit of legal advice. In part this may have been because the case involved commercial conveyancing, in which pre-contractual enquiries play a vital role. In some other situations this might not necessarily be the case. However, and unsurprisingly, any purported exclusion of fraudulent misrepresentation will be deemed to be unreasonable: *Thomas Witter Ltd v TBP Industries Limited* [1996] 2 All ER 573.

It should be noted that a simple entire agreement clause will only exclude extrinsic contractual terms from being added to a written document. It will not preclude liability for misrepresentation based on extra-contractual representations unless these are expressly included in a 'combined' clause or a dedicated clause dealing solely with misrepresentation. Thus, considering such a clause in *MDW v Norvill* [2021] EWHC 1135 (Ch), HH Keyser QC observed that: "It is an 'entire agreement' clause, the purpose of which is to make it clear that nothing said, written or done prior to the SPA creates contractual obligations or liabilities. It has nothing to do with reliance on prior statements, far less their existence, or with excluding claims of a non-contractual nature".

**Types of Misrepresentation**

Not all misrepresentations are the same, especially when it comes to their consequences, and particularly to the remedies that are open to a representee.

Broadly speaking, three types have been identified: fraudulent, negligent, and purely innocent misrepresentations. These will be dealt with in turn.

## 1. Fraudulent Misrepresentation

Fraudulent misrepresentation is the most serious form of misrepresentation, being founded in the tort of deceit. The historical definitional case is *Derry v Peek* (1889) 5 TLR 625. In this case, the defendant issued a company prospectus stating that it had the right to use steam- (rather than horse-) powered trams, although the former required the approval of the Board of Trade. This had been applied for but was, unexpectedly, subsequently refused. The claimant purchased shares in the company, allegedly relying on the statement, and subsequently brought a claim for fraudulent misrepresentation against the defendant. In the instant case, it was held that the statement was not fraudulent, but made in the honest belief that approval was forthcoming. Lord Herschell took the opportunity to define fraudulent misrepresentation, noting that it was a statement that was made knowing it to be false, without belief in its truth, or recklessly as to whether it was true or false. However, he also noted: "I think the third is but an instance of the second, for one who makes a statement under such circumstances can have no real belief in the truth of what he states. To prevent a false statement from being fraudulent, there must, I think, always be an honest belief in its truth".

The implications of this definition have been considered and refined in subsequent decisions. For example, in *Goose v Wilson Sandford & Co.* [2000] EWCA Civ 73 Morritt LJ observed that, to establish liability in deceit, and unlike other forms of misrepresentation, it is necessary to show that the representor "intended his statement to be understood by the representee in the sense in which it was false". However, the defendant's motive in making the false representation, or that there was no intention to injure the person to whom it was made, is irrelevant. In *AIC Ltd v ITS Testing Services (UK) Ltd (The "Kriti Palm")* [2007] 1 Lloyd's Rep 555, Buxton LJ adopted a similar definition of deceit, one taken from *Clerk & Lindsell on Torts*, when noting, "Where a defendant makes a false representation, knowing it to be untrue, or being reckless as to whether it is true, and intends that the claimant should act in reliance on it, then in so far as the latter does so and suffers loss the defendant is liable for that loss."

The Court of Appeal, when handing down its judgment in *Eco 3 Capital Ltd v Ludsin Overseas Ltd* [2013] EWCA Civ 413, reconsidered the prerequisites for making out a claim based on the tort of deceit, and reiterated that it required that the defendant made a false representation to the claimant, knew that it was false or was reckless as to its truth; that he intended that the claimant should act in reliance on it; the claimant did so act, and in consequence suffered loss. "Intention to deceive" was not a separate element of the tort, but merely another way of describing the second and third conditions, its mental element.

The courts do not lightly make findings of fraudulent misrepresentation, not least because the allegation might amount to an offence if prosecuted in a criminal court. Although, like any civil matter, the standard of proof is only on the balance of probabilities, in *AIC Ltd v ITS Testing Services (UK) Ltd ('the Kriti Palm')* [2007] 1 Lloyd's Rep 555 the Court of Appeal accepted Lord Nicholls' reasoning on standard of proof in civil cases, made in *re H (Minors)* [1996] AC 563, and its implications for allegations of fraud. The court noted that where a serious allegation such as deceit is in issue, its inherent probability or improbability can be considered when deciding whether it occurred. Frequently, the graver the allegation, the less likely it is to have happened, and the stronger the evidence must be. Fraud is a very serious allegation. Furthermore, since the advent of the Misrepresentation Act 1967, there are far fewer benefits in making an allegation of fraudulent, as opposed to negligent, misrepresentation than previously, while the latter is very much easier to establish (see below), discouraging ready recourse to the former.

## 2. Negligent Misrepresentation

Although a negligent misrepresentation, one made carelessly rather than deliberately, could lead to rescission, unlike fraudulent misrepresentation, it could not lead to an award of damages until the 1960s. In 1963, in *Hedley Byrne & Co Ltd v Heller & Partners Ltd* [1964] AC 465, the House of Lords held that in the correct (and quite restrictive) circumstances, a negligent misstatement that occasioned financial loss could give rise to an action for damages. There was no inherent reason that this should not cover negligent misrepresentations in contractual negotiations. This was considered in *Esso Petroleum v Mardon* [1976] QB 801, where an alleged contractual misrepresentation made in 1963 was in issue. However, developments at common law were swiftly overtaken by statute in the form of the Misrepresentation Act 1967. The new statute rendered the decision in *Hedley Byrne & Co Ltd v Heller* of relatively minor significance for contractual misrepresentation, not least because it put potential claimants in a superior position to that found at common law.

Most important, s.2(1) of the Misrepresentation Act provides that where a person has entered into a contract after a misrepresentation has been made to him by another party to the agreement, and as a result has suffered loss, if the person making the misrepresentation would be "liable to damages in respect thereof had the misrepresentation been made fraudulently, that person shall be so liable notwithstanding that the misrepresentation was not made fraudulently, unless he proves that he had reasonable ground to believe and did believe up to the time the contract was made that the facts represented were true". Effectively, this provision does two things once the claimant has proved that the defendant made a representation that was untrue, that it induced him to enter the relevant contract, and that as a result he has suffered loss.

First, it introduces the so-called 'fiction of fraud', whereby negligent misrepresentations will be treated like fraudulent ones, something that allows the recovery of damages on the same basis as those secured for deceit. (See below). Second, s.2(1) presumes that any misrepresentation was made negligently, *unless* the person making it proves that this was not the case (on the balance of probabilities). This means that the normal onus of proof in civil litigation (on the claimant) is reversed. It is not a burden that is easily discharged. For example, in *Howard Marine v Ogden* [1978] QB 574, the claimant, Ogden, hired a dredging barge from the defendant, Howard Marine, to carry out excavation works for the Northumbrian Water Authority. Ogden had first asked Howard the capacity of their barge. Howard checked the very well regarded (in the shipping industry) and normally reliable *Lloyds Register* and, relying on this source, stated it to be 1,600 tonnes. In fact, this was wrong, and the capacity was just 1,055 tonnes, as the ship's own documents made clear. As a result, the work carried out by Ogden took much longer and cost much more to complete. The claimant brought an action for negligent misrepresentation. In response, Howard argued that they had reasonable grounds for believing that their statement as to capacity was true, as they had checked an authoritative work, *Lloyds Register*. This argument was rejected by the court (Lord Denning MR dissenting). Howard had ready access to the vessel's registration document which contained the correct capacity and was a superior source of information; he should have consulted it.

### 3. Innocent Misrepresentation

Of course, some misrepresentations are still made entirely innocently and non-negligently, the defendant proving that he believed, and had reasonable grounds to believe, up to the time that the contract was made, that the false statements represented were true. In these situations, the primary remedy remains rescission, and there is still no *right* to damages, although, under s.2(2) of the Act the court can sometimes award damages in lieu of rescission (see below).

## Remedies for Misrepresentation

To some extent, the remedies available for misrepresentation depend on whether the statement was made fraudulently, negligently, or innocently (non-negligently in this context). However, rescission is the traditional or, as Longmore LJ has observed, the "normal" remedy for all forms of misrepresentation: *Geoffrey Alan Salt v Stratstone Specialist Ltd* [2015] EWCA Civ 745. In some situations, an indemnity might be awarded, as might damages. These will be dealt with in turn.

### 1. Rescission

The primary aim of rescission is to put the parties back into the position they were in before they entered the contract, as if there had been no agreement. It is "unstitched". This means that it is a retrospective remedy. It is usually done by making a mutual restoration of benefits, with the parties returning any property or money that they received under the contract. For this reason, rescission is often attractive to claimants who have struck a "bad bargain" and are seeking to reverse it.

Rescission is brought about by the victim of the misrepresentation expressly or impliedly informing the other party that he is setting aside the contract. It can be brought about informally, without using technical language. As Roch LJ observed in *TSB Bank v Camfield* [1995] 1 WLR 430: "The right to set aside or rescind the transaction is that of the representee, not that of the court". However, although there is no need for a court order to effect rescission, it might be necessary to have recourse to the courts to enforce it, provided they decide that the representee truly was entitled to rescind the agreement. A judicial order for rescission will be backdated to the date of a party's election where relevant. In *TSB Bank v Camfield*, Roch LJ concluded that there was no discretionary power to declare a contract that had been properly rescinded for misrepresentation to be subsisting other than that provided for by s.2(2) MRA 1967 in cases of innocent misrepresentation (see below).

Of course, where fraudulent misrepresentation is alleged, informing the other party of a decision to rescind will sometimes be impossible, as the person who made the misrepresentation will have hurriedly disappeared. In these circumstances, the victim of the misrepresentation may be able to rescind the contract constructively, something that might be vital to pre-empt the intervention of third-party rights.

For example, in *Car & Universal Credit v Caldwell* [1964] 2 WLR 600, Caldwell sold his car to a rogue (as they are often termed in such cases) who called himself Norris, who paid a £10 cash deposit and left a cheque for £965. The following day, when Caldwell attempted to cash the cheque, he discovered that it was fraudulent. He immediately reported the incident to the police and cooperated with them in their search for Norris and the vehicle. He also reported the incident to the Automobile Association (AA). Norris, of course, had acquired a defective or voidable title to the car, as the contract had been induced by a fraudulent misrepresentation (about his identity). He sold the car on to a Bona Fide Purchaser for Value or BFPV (Car and Universal Credit) three days after acquiring it. The court decided that Caldwell had constructively rescinded the contract by informing the police and AA, and cooperating with the former, so that rescission was effective when this was done, which was *before* the BFPV acquired the car. (For further discussion of BFPVs see below). As a result, the rogue's voidable title had become void by the time the transaction occurred, so that the maxim *nemo dat quod non habet* applied ("no one gives what they do not have"), and Car and Universal Credit acquired no title, allowing Caldwell to recover the vehicle. Upjohn LJ observed that if a party to an agreement deliberately absconded, so that the other could not communicate a rescission, he could not insist on his right to be made aware of it. In these circumstances, an innocent party could rescind by "overt measures falling short of communication". Whether these are sufficient will, of course, be a matter of fact for the court to determine.

It should be noted that there is no power to award partial rescission. For example, a misrepresentee who thought that he had guaranteed a transaction to the sum of £15,000 when (in reality) it was unlimited, had his guarantee fully rescinded, rather than being limited to £15,000: *TSB Bank plc v Camfield* [1995] 1 WLR 430. This was reiterated by Colman J in *De Molestina v Ponton* [2002] 1 All ER (Comm) 587, who thought that allowing partial rescission would conflict with the remedy's requirement that the parties are (within reasonable limits) to be restored to their pre-contractual position.

**Losing the Right to Rescind**

The representee can lose the right to rescind if one or more of the "bars to rescission" is present. These occur if it is impossible to return the parties *substantially* to their original position, the representee has affirmed the contract, or a third-party bona fide purchaser for value (BFPV) has acquired legal rights over the subject matter of the contract. Until recently, the right to rescind in cases of non-fraudulent misrepresentation could also be lost by simple effluxion of time, via what might be viewed as a form of constructive affirmation, although this is now open to question (see below). These bars to rescission will be dealt with *seriatim*.

It will be impossible to order rescission if the parties cannot be put back into their pre-contractual positions: *Thomas Witter Ltd v TBP Industries* [1996] 2 All ER 573. For a simple illustration, rescission will not be possible following a misrepresentation made prior to the sale of a herd of cattle--for example that they are two-year-old Angus cows when they are six-year-old Friesians--if the animals have since been slaughtered and turned into cuts of meat. Returning a pile of steaks is not the same as giving back live animals. More specifically, in *Clarke v Dickson* (1858) EB & E 148 Mr Clarke purchased shares in a lead and copper mining company after fraudulent representations by the defendants, who were the directors of the company. A few years later, the company went into liquidation. Mr Clarke sought rescission and the return of the purchase price in exchange for giving up his shares. Crompton J held that the contract could not be rescinded, as the shares had become worthless, and rescission required that the claimant "must be in such a situation as to be able to put the parties into their original state before the contract".

Nevertheless, since the nineteenth century, and especially in recent years, the courts have often taken a pragmatic approach to this issue. It is not necessary that the parties be returned *precisely* to their pre-contractual position. It will be sufficient if substantial and fair restitution can be achieved, even if it involves an element of financial adjustment. For example, in *Salt v Stratstone Specialist Ltd* [2015] EWCA Civ 745 the defendant car dealer (mis)represented that a vehicle was brand new when, in fact, it was two years old (albeit never registered and barely used) and had been damaged in a collision. He subsequently sought to avoid rescission by arguing that the car had depreciated in value during the significant period that had elapsed since its sale, and therefore it was no longer possible to put the parties back into their original position, if only because the car could not be returned in its original condition. The Court of Appeal ruled that the depreciation of the vehicle did not render it impossible to restore them to their original position and that rescission would be available if "practical justice" could be done. In some situations, this might involve the claimant returning the vehicle and receiving a refund of his money, but then compensating the defendant for relevant depreciation costs.

Another bar to rescission occurs where a third party has acquired rights to the subject matter of the contract *before* any purported rescission; for example, where it has been sold on. This remains the case even if the original misrepresentation was made fraudulently. However, for this to apply, the third party must be a *bona fide* purchaser for value (BFPV) without notice. This phrase is used to describe an innocent person, sometimes known as "equity's darling", who purchases property in good faith without being aware of another party's claim over that property or the seller's defective title to it. As this suggests, a BFPV must *pay* for the property rather than receiving it as a gift--that is, as a "volunteer". If these requirements are satisfied, a BFPV will take good title to the property despite the competing claims of the other party.

It was for this reason that the claimant in *Phillips v Brooks* [1919] 2 KB 243 sought to rely on mistake, rather than fraudulent misrepresentation, to avoid a contract. In this case, a rogue purchased a ring from the claimant's jewellery shop after fraudulently claiming to be Sir George Bullough and paying for it with a dishonoured cheque in the same name. The rogue had immediately sold on the ring to the defendant pawnbrokers before the claimant was even aware of the misrepresentation. Any form of rescission, constructive or otherwise, would have come too late. The claimant had to show that the contract was void *ab initio*, not voidable, to succeed.

Furthermore, the right to rescind will be lost if a contract has been affirmed by the representee--that is, the claimant knows of their right to rescission and nevertheless either takes no action within a "reasonable period of time", to quote Upjohn LJ, or actively indicates an intention to continue with the contract, rather than rescinding it: *Car & Universal Credit v Caldwell* [1964] 2 WLR 600. For example, in *Long v Lloyd* [1958] 1 WLR 753, the claimant purchased a lorry from the defendant. It had been advertised in a newspaper which described the vehicle as being in exceptional condition. At a subsequent viewing, the claimant was also told that it could reach a speed of 40 miles an hour and do 11 miles to a gallon of petrol. On the first journey the purchaser noted various faults with the lorry and saw that its speed and fuel efficiency had been exaggerated. He contacted the defendant, who offered to pay half the cost of repairs. The claimant accepted this. However, on a further lengthy journey the lorry broke down completely, and the claimant decided to rescind the agreement for (innocent) misrepresentation. Pearce LJ held that by accepting the offer of payment for half the repairs, after he became aware of the defects, and continuing to use the vehicle, the defendant had affirmed the contract and lost his right to rescind.

The situation in *Edwards v Ashik* [2014] EWHC 2454 (Ch) was more complicated. Mr Edwards claimed that he had been induced into purchasing a nightclub following a fraudulent misrepresentation made by the seller, Mr Ashik. The latter argued, *inter alia*, that, even if Edwards had had the right to rescind, he had lost it after affirming the contract by continuing to make use of the property on a commercial basis for six weeks after he believed the right had arisen before commencing proceedings. The Deputy Judge in the High Court agreed with the preliminary ruling in the County Court that the continued business use of the property by Mr Edwards would probably have amounted to an affirmation of the contract *if* taken alone. However, he concluded that, in the instant case, the legal correspondence between the parties during this time clearly indicated that legal action for fraudulent misrepresentation was about to be taken and, accordingly, there was no affirmation. The delay was purely to see what Mr Ashik had to say about the allegations. The deputy judge stressed that the test for affirmation was an objective one, and did not depend on the claimant's personal intention, or the impression made on the defendant, but on what was communicated.

In *SK Shipping v Capital VLCC* [2022] EWCA Civ 231, the Court of Appeal reconsidered affirmation in the context of a charterparty, and reiterated that any decision to affirm a contract must be communicated unequivocally to the other party, but this could be done by conduct or by necessary implication; the test for determining affirmation is objective, what would a reasonable person think was intended; in *some* (but not all) situations expressly reserving the right to rescind might prevent conduct that would otherwise amount to an affirmation, from having that effect (as can be seen in *Edwards v Ashik*).

Until recently, it was thought that substantial delay would prevent rescission in cases of non-fraudulent misrepresentation, even though the claimant had acted swiftly once he had, belatedly, become aware of the misrepresentation. Thus, in *Leaf v International Galleries* [1950] 2 KB 86, the claimant bought a painting from the defendant gallery following an innocent misrepresentation that it was by the famous painter John Constable. After five years he realized his mistake, and immediately attempted to rescind the contract. However, it was held that he had lost the right to do so. Effectively, when it came to innocent (not fraudulent) misrepresentations, long delay operated as a form of constructive affirmation, even if the representee was unaware of the misrepresentation.

Nevertheless, this must now be seen in the light of *Salt v Stratstone Specialist Ltd* [2015] EWCA Civ 745. In this case, Longmore LJ noted that *Leaf v International Galleries* had been decided before the 1967 Misrepresentation Act had been passed, and concluded that lapse of time, on its own, could not be a bar to rescission. Mr Salt had only become aware of the availability of rescission during first instance proceedings relating to defects in a car that he had purchased, when he discovered that the vehicle was not new, as had been represented to him. Mr Justice Roth (sitting in the Court of Appeal) emphasised that, as an equitable remedy, and in the absence of a statutory bar, an objection to rescission must rest on an equitable basis, so that it was wrong to say that rescission could be barred by lapse of time per se. It was only where the lapse of time was such that it would be inequitable to grant rescission that it could constitute a bar to the remedy.

## 2. Financial Remedies: Indemnity

The courts have always been able to order payment of an "indemnity" for costs that were *necessarily* incurred in complying with the terms of the contract after an agreement has been rescinded for misrepresentation, of whatever type. It should be stressed that what can be claimed under an indemnity is very limited, as can be seen in *Whittington v Seale-Hayne* (1900) 82 Lt 49. In this case, a poultry farm was leased to the claimant to raise chickens, following a representation from the defendant (Seale-Hayne) that it was in good sanitary condition. It was not, being extremely unhygienic, and, as a result, the claimant's stock of chickens died while his manager was made ill and required expensive medical treatment. Under the lease, the claimant was legally *required* to make necessary repairs to the farm as well as to pay council rates and (of course) rent.

Mr Whittington rescinded the contract and claimed compensation for the repairs he had been required to make, the rent paid, rates on the premises paid to the council, medical expenses for his manager, the original value of his dead chickens, and loss of profit on the birds. It was held that Whittington could claim indemnity for repairs to the farm, rates, and rent, as these were *necessarily* incurred under the lease. He had no choice about paying them. However, there was no *requirement* that he raise chickens or employ a manager (he could have left the farm unused), so that these were not covered by the indemnity. Compensating them would require an award of damages, something that was only available for fraudulent misrepresentation at the time (and until the 1960s). As Farwell J observed, "The defendant admits liability so far as regards anything which was paid under the contract, but not in respect of any damages incurred by reason of the contract; and I think the defendant's view is the correct one".

## 3. Financial Remedies: Damages at Common Law

Historically, at common law, damages were only available for fraudulent rather than negligent or innocent (non-negligent) misrepresentation: *Heilbut, Symons & Co Ltd v Buckleton* [1913] AC 30. If a misrepresentation was fraudulent, the claimant could claim both rescission and/or damages. Damages in such cases were and are assessed on tortious principles, so that they are aimed at placing the claimant into the position he would have been in financially if the misrepresentation had not been made, and the contract not created, rather than the prospective basis that is normally used for breach-of-contract actions. So, and for example, if someone purchased an antique bureau for £10,000, following a fraudulent misrepresentation that it was authentic Louis Quinze, which, if true, would mean that it should be worth £20,000, but it was, in reality, a Victorian copy worth just £5,000, the measure of damages would be £5,000, if they retained the bureau, not £15,000. This would put them in the same financial position they were in before entering the agreement.

However, putting the injured party into the position that he would have been in if the misrepresentation had not been made will not *always* mean simply putting him back into his precontractual position. Allowance will sometimes be made for benefits that would otherwise have been gained from any money utilised in the contract. For example, in *East v Maurer* [1991] 2 All ER 733 the defendant sold one of his two hair salons to the claimant. The latter was partly induced to buy the business by a representation from the defendant that he planned to go abroad and did not intend to work in the second salon except in emergencies. Instead, he continued to work there, and many of his clients from the salon he had sold followed him. As a result, the claimant's salon saw a steady decline in business, and never made a profit. Eventually, the claimant sold the business for considerably less than he had paid for it. East then sued Maurer for deceit. The Court of Appeal held that damages for the fraudulent misrepresentation should be awarded on a tortious basis, that is, placing the claimant in the same position he would have been in had the wrong not been committed. As a result, East could recover the price paid for the business minus the selling price, plus expenses entailed in buying and selling the business, and in carrying out improvements. However, he could also claim forgone profits that he might otherwise have made with the money.

Nevertheless, although these were recoverable, the claimant in *East v Maurer* could only claim damages for the loss of profit he might have expected to make in respect of another, similar, hypothetical, hairdressing business, in which he could have invested his money but for the misrepresentation, rather than the unusually high profits which he would have made after purchasing the defendant's business in the instant case, *if* the representation relating to it had been true. As a result, the Court of Appeal reduced damages for loss of profit by one-third from the £15,000 awarded at first instance to £10,000. A breach of contractual term would have been necessary to recover the former level of profits.

Against this, and favouring claimants, damages are awarded for all losses, including consequential losses, flowing from a fraudulent misrepresentation, even if they could not be foreseen: *Doyle v Olby (Ironmongers) Ltd [1969]* 2 QB 158. In this case, Doyle bought a business from Olby after being told that all its business was done "over the counter". In reality, half of it came from their travelling sales representative, and Doyle sustained heavy losses. In the Court of Appeal Denning MR awarded £5,500 in damages. He noted that the claimant's position before the fraudulent inducement should be compared with his position at the end of the transaction. In this regard, damages for fraudulent misrepresentation were to be assessed on a different basis to those for breach of contract: "The defendant is bound to make reparation for all the actual damages directly flowing from the fraudulent inducement. … it does not lie in the mouth of the fraudulent person to say that they [the damages] could not reasonably have been foreseen".

## 4. Financial Remedies: Damages Under the Misrepresentation Act 1967

The advent of the so-called 'fiction of fraud', established under s.2(1) of the Misrepresentation Act 1967 (MRA), meant that a negligent misrepresentation would be treated in the same way as a fraudulent misrepresentation, which then allowed damages to be recovered in such cases, whether instead of, or in addition to, rescission. Both might be appropriate where there has been consequential loss because of the misrepresentation, so that, for example, returning an asset that was the subject matter of the agreement and recovering the payment made for it, would still leave the representee out of pocket. By way of illustration can be considered the situation in which a representation about the quality of a second-hand van turns out to be untrue. As a result, shortly after the sale it breaks down in a remote part of Dartmoor. Although the purchaser rescinds the contract, returns the van, and recovers his payment, he might also want to obtain damages for the expense of repairing the broken-down vehicle so that he can get home. In *Naughton v O'Callaghan* [1990] 3 All ER 191 the claimant successfully claimed the wasted livery and training costs that had followed the defendant vendor's negligent misrepresentation as to the pedigree of a potential racehorse.

The 'fiction of fraud' under s.2(1) of the Misrepresentation Act was pursued to its logical conclusion in *Royscot Trust v Rogerson* (1991) 2 QB 29, in which the Court of Appeal held that the wording of the statute meant not just that damages could be awarded, but that they are assessed in the same way as those available in the tort of deceit, rather than under general contractual principles, even in the total absence of fraud. Thus, the aim of an award of damages is to restore the claimant to his pre-misrepresentation position. Additionally, and as with deceit, rules on foreseeability of damage do not apply (see below), unlike the situation in *Hedley Byrne v Heller* (discussed above), so that all damages flowing from the misrepresentation are recoverable. Rix J subsequently suggested that because of the broad measure of damages available in the light of the decision in *Royscot v Rogerson*, misrepresentations should not be found too easily, where there was room for doubt: *Avon Insurance Plc v Swire Fraser Limited* [2000] 1 All ER (Comm) 573.

Although damages cannot be recovered as of right for purely innocent misrepresentations (those that are neither fraudulent nor negligent), section 2(2) of the MRA gives the court power to declare a contract subsisting and to award damages in *lieu* of rescission, where it feels that it would be more equitable to do so than making an order for rescission or upholding a rescission made personally by the claimant.

Hoffman LJ (as he then was) considered some of the factors that might influence the court in exercising this discretion in *obiter* comments made in *William Sindall plc v Cambridgeshire County Council* [1993] 3 ALL ER 932. For example, he thought that the significance of the misrepresentation to the wider contract would be an important factor. Thus, in the case at hand, an alleged misrepresentation involving the presence (or absence) of a buried pipe that would cost £18,000 to remedy was of relatively minor significance compared with a sale worth £5,000,000, suggesting that an award of damages, rather than rescission, might be appropriate. This confirmed long-standing suggestions by academic and legal observers that s.2(2) will often be employed to prevent a major contract being unstitched for a comparatively minor and innocent misrepresentation (perhaps because the claimant has identified a better commercial opportunity elsewhere).

However, it should also be noted that in *Government of Zanzibar v British Aerospace (Lancaster House) Ltd* [2000] 1 WLR 2333 it was held that the wording of s.2(2), that the claimant must "be entitled, by reason of the misrepresentation, to rescind the contract", meant that the award of damages under the provision is dependent on the right to rescission still being present. In this case, the Government of Zanzibar (GoZ) purchased an executive jet from British Aerospace (BA). The plane was faulty. The GoZ brought an action against BA to rescind the contract or, alternatively secure damages under either s.2(1) or s.2(2) MRA 1967, on the grounds that representations were made that the plane was airworthy, reliable, and without design or construction defects. However, BA claimed that putting the parties back in their original position had become impossible because the finance company had sold the jet on, so restitution was impossible. This acted as a bar to rescission, so that damages under s.2(2) were precluded. Raymond Jack QC, sitting as a deputy judge in the High Court, accepted this argument and held that because the GoZ had no right to rescission they had no right damages. This approach was followed in *Geoffrey Alan Salt v Stratstone Specialist Ltd* [2015] EWCA Civ 745, when the Court of Appeal concluded that the courts had no discretion to award damages under s.2(2) as an alternative remedy to rescission, if rescission itself was no longer available, because one of the bars to rescission applied.

# Chapter 9: Mistake

## Introduction

Where operative, mistake renders contracts void *ab initio*; essentially, there is no contract. In this it contrasts with (for example) misrepresentation, which renders contracts voidable, and so operative until they are rescinded. This difference can have very significant effects on the rights of third parties who have acquired property that was the subject of a (purported) contract. Mistake is a common law doctrine, the notion of a lesser form of equitable mistake having now been abandoned, although it merits brief discussion.

## The Demise of Equitable Mistake

In *Solle v Butcher* [1950] 1 KB 671 Denning LJ (as he then was) suggested that there was a separate category of "equitable mistake", that involved less drastic mistakes than those recognised at common law, and which did not have such severe consequences when operative. Most important, and like misrepresentation, they made a contract voidable, rather than void *ab initio*. The case in question involved a mistake by both landlord and tenant as to whether statutory rent control applied to a particular flat. The claimant leased this property to the defendant for £250 per annum, on the basis that it did not. They later found out that this was wrong, and that the rent was legally limited to £140. When Mr Solle realized the mistake they had (both) made, he asked for the return of the overpaid rent from Mr Butcher. The latter counterclaimed, asking to rescind the whole agreement for common mistake. The Court of Appeal held that the claimant could rescind the contract on equitable terms. According to Denning, "A contract was liable in equity to be set aside, if the parties were under a common misapprehension either as to the facts or as to their relative and respective rights, provided that the misapprehension was fundamental and that the party seeking to set it aside was not himself at fault."

The notion of equitable mistake troubled lawyers for decades after *Solle v Butcher*, periodically being alluded to, albeit only rarely applied in practice. The validity of the whole doctrine was, rather bravely, questioned at first instance by Toulson J in *Great Peace Shipping Limited v Tsavliris Salvage Limited* [2002] EWCA Civ 1407. The Court of Appeal supported his analysis, Phillips LJ declaring that Toulson had reached the bold conclusion that the view "expressed by Denning LJ in *Solle v Butcher* was 'over-broad', by which he meant wrong". It upheld the trial judge's decision that a contract could not be rescinded on the grounds of a mistake where the contract was otherwise valid and enforceable at common law, effectively bringing the notion of equitable mistake to an end.[1]

1 GP McMeel, "Equitable Mistake Repudiated--The Demise of *Solle v Butcher*? (The Great Peace)", *Lloyd's Maritime and Commercial Law Quarterly*, 2002, pp. 449-453.

## The Categorisation of Common Law Mistake

Although terminology and categorisation sometimes differ, three main types of mistake have been identified in English contract law: common mistake, mutual mistake, and unilateral mistake. (Some observers place mistakes relating to identity in their own category, while others subsume them under unilateral mistake, as will be the case in this book). To these can be added the specialist doctrine of *non est factum*, under which a party who signs a written contract is not bound by their signature, contrary to the normal rule. It should be stressed that the various forms of mistake lack coherence as a uniform doctrine, and many of the situations in which operative mistake have been identified can be explained by recourse to other contractual principles, such as consideration and agreement. The four situations will be discussed in turn.

## 1. Common Mistake

Common mistake occurs where both parties have entered a contract under the same "fundamental" misapprehension. In *Great Peace Shipping Limited v Tsavliris Salvage Limited* [2002] EWCA Civ 1407, Lord Phillips MR, identified the prerequisites necessary for such a mistake to be operative and so render a contract void *ab initio*: (i) there must be a common assumption as to the existence of a state of affairs; (ii) there must be no warranty [guarantee in this context] by either party that that state of affairs exists; (iii) the non-existence of the state of affairs must not be attributable to the fault of either party; (iv) the non-existence of the state of affairs must render performance of the contract impossible; (v) the state of affairs may be the existence, or a vital attribute, of the consideration to be provided, or circumstances which must subsist if performance of the contractual adventure is to be possible.

Several situations where there has been deemed to be an operative common mistake can be considered. They include a common mistake as to the (continued) existence of the subject matter of the agreement, which is sometimes termed *res extincta*. In the historic case of *Couturier v Hastie* (1856) 5 HLC 673, a buyer bought a cargo of Indian corn from its owner's agent in London. At the time, both parties believed it to be at sea, on its way from the Mediterranean to England. In reality, it had already been disposed of because it had started to decay. The seller argued that the purchaser had acquired title to the corn and therefore bore the risk of its being damaged or lost. However, the court held that the contract was void, as its subject matter had ceased to exist at the time the contract was made. The principle was subsequently codified in s.6 of the Sale of Goods Act, which in its 1979 iteration provides, "Where there is a contract for the sale of specific goods, and the goods without the knowledge of the seller have perished at the time when the contract is made, the contract is void".

Even so, common mistakes of this and other types will not be operative where, for example, one of the parties is taken to have guaranteed the existence of the subject matter of the contract, whether expressly or, more commonly, impliedly, this being the second point in Lord Phillips' definition in *Great Peace*. (It should be noted that there are some similarities here to the doctrine of frustration.) As Steyn J observed in *Associated Japanese Bank (International) Ltd v Credit du Nord SA* [1989] 1 WLR 255, before considering mistake it was first necessary to "determine whether the contract itself, by express or implied condition precedent or otherwise, provides who bears the risk of the relevant mistake. It is at this hurdle that many pleas of mistake will either fail or prove to have been unnecessary". More recently, the High Court has noted that one of the reasons that mistake is rarely invoked successfully is that the contract, or general legal principles, will usually allocate the risk of an assumed state of affairs turning out to be wrong to one of the parties: *John Lobb S.A.S v John Lobb Ltd* [2022] EWHC 2306 (Ch).

For an example of such a warranty can be considered the Australian case of *McRae v Commonwealth Disposals Commission* (1951) 84 CLR 377, in which the Commonwealth Disposals Commission (CDC) sold McRae the salvage rights to the shipwreck of a tanker that was supposedly on the "Jourmand Reef" off Samarai in Papua New Guinea. The vessel was thought to contain oil. McRae fitted out an expensive salvage operation and sailed to Samarai. However, not only did they not find a tanker, but they also discovered that there was no such place as the Jourmand Reef. It transpired that a CDC employee had made a "reckless and irresponsible" mistake in relying on what was merely a rumour when deciding that there was a tanker to sell.

The McRae brothers brought an action against the Commission for breach of contract to sell a tanker that was located at the place specified, seeking their reliance loss, that is the cost of fitting out the salvage expedition (as discussed in Chapter 15) as the measure of damages. The Commission argued, *inter alia*, that the contract was void *ab initio*, given that the subject matter did not exist. The High Court of Australia rejected this argument. *Couturier v Hastie* was distinguished because there the parties, who had equal knowledge as to the existence of the subject matter of the agreement, had shared the assumption that the corn existed. In the instant case, the Commission, the only party that had knowledge of the subject matter of the contract, had impliedly guaranteed that the tanker existed and therefore had assumed the risk that it did not.

Another scenario where a contract will be void for common mistake involves situations in which a buyer already owns property he is purchasing from a vendor, and neither party is aware of this. Such (very rare) situations are sometimes termed *res sua*. Thus, in the House of Lords case of *Cooper v Phibbs* (1867) LR 2 HL 149, a nephew leased an Irish fishery from his uncle. On the latter's death, he renewed the lease with his aunt. Subsequently, it transpired that the uncle had left the nephew riparian rights for life in his will, so that he effectively paid for rights that he already owned. The lease was held to be void for mistake.[2]

2 P. Matthews, "A Note on Cooper v. Phibbs", *Law Quarterly Review*, v. 105 (1989), p. 599.

The same principle can apply where the parties contract on the basis of a shared but mistaken assumption that is fundamental to the agreement. Thus, in *Griffith v Brymer* (1903) 19 TLR 434, the claimant had entered an agreement to hire a room overlooking King Edward VII's coronation procession and paid a deposit. Unfortunately, by then, the monarch had developed appendicitis, and a decision to operate on him, which rendered the procession impossible, had been taken about an hour before the contract was made. In these circumstances, Wright J held that the contract was void for mistake so that the claimant was entitled to recover his deposit. As this case suggests, sometimes the distinction between mistake and a frustrating event will be purely a matter of timing, the tests mirroring each other, a point that was also made in *Great Peace*. Had the decision on the King's operation been taken two hours later, the latter doctrine would have been relevant, although as the law then stood the deposit would not have been recoverable (see Chapter 11).

Similarly, in *Scott v Coulson* [1903] 2 Ch 439, the parties entered a contract for insurance on the life of the appropriately named Mr Death, who both parties believed was still alive. In fact, he was already dead. The contract was void for a common mistake (that Death was alive). In like manner, in *Galloway v Galloway* (1914) 30 TLR 531 both parties, while under the assumption that they were married to each other, made a separation agreement. It was later discovered that their marriage was invalid because, unexpectedly, the husband's former wife was still alive. As a result, a separation agreement for the second "marriage" was void because it was entered into in the mistaken belief that the parties were lawfully married and so needed a formal separation.

It should be noted that both *res extincta* and *res sua*, as well as cases such as *Scott v Coulson*, could also be explained by recourse to the doctrine of consideration, which was, as it transpired, absent for the promised payments. However, common mistake as to the quality of the subject matter of a contract is much more problematic.

### Common Mistake as to Quality

The starting point for considering common mistake as to quality is the historic House of Lords decision in *Bell v Lever Bros* [1932] AC 161. In this case, Lever Brothers had appointed the two defendants as chairman (Mr Bell) and vice-chairman of their subsidiary company, Niger, for a term of five years. However, Lever subsequently decided to merge Niger with another subsidiary company, which already had its own executives, and so make the defendants redundant, long before this period had expired. As a result, Lever bought out their contracts of employment, providing substantial compensation (some £30,000 and £20,000 respectively) in exchange to the two men. Lever later discovered that, some time before, the defendants had committed repudiatory breaches of contract by trading on their own account using inside information on future price reductions to sell cocoa, something that would have entitled the company to summarily dismiss them without compensation. It should be noted that it was held that both the managers were unaware of the repudiatory nature of their private dealings when negotiating the compensation package (hence it being a common, not a unilateral, mistake).

Lever brought an action to recover the payments made to the two men. This was based, *inter alia*, on their mistaken belief that they were under an obligation to pay substantial compensation. They failed. It was held that a "contract may be void if the mistake is as to the existence of some quality which makes the thing without that quality essentially different from the thing it was believed to be". This was not the situation in the instant case. Lever had paid to buy out contracts of employment and had done just that. This case is indicative of the very high bar set before a mistake as to quality will be operative. Lever Brothers had spent £50,000 buying out what were, essentially, worthless contracts, but this was not held to be sufficient.

This high standard was applied less than twenty years later, in *Leaf v International Galleries* [1950] 2 KB 86. In this case, the claimant purchased a painting of Salisbury, viewed from across water meadows, from the defendant gallery. Both parties believed that it was by the famous artist John Constable. Some five years later, the claimant discovered that the painting was not, in fact, a Constable, but a work painted in a similar style by an obscure Victorian artist, something that greatly affected its value. The purchaser brought an action asserting, *inter alia*, common mistake. This failed, as the mistake related to the quality of the painting and was not of a type that rendered it essentially different from what it was believed to be. The purchaser thought he was buying a painting of Salisbury, and that is what he got. Many non-legal observers might feel that he thought that he was buying an authentic Constable.

The same analysis was reiterated, albeit in slightly less extreme circumstances, in *Great Peace Shipping Ltd v Tsavliris Salvage (International) Ltd* [2002] EWCA Civ 1407. In this case, a ship named the *Cape Providence* suffered serious structural damage in the Southern Indian Ocean. A tug was chartered to assist the stricken vessel by the defendants (who were salvagers) but was still six days' sailing-time away. Fearing for the safety of its crew in the meantime, and as is common maritime practice in such situations, the defendants sought another merchant vessel to "stand by" and render assistance if necessary. They were given the names of four vessels that were reported to be in the vicinity of the damaged vessel, and selected one, the *Great Peace*, that was believed by both parties to be about 35 miles away from it. They then contracted with this ship's owners to stand by the damaged vessel for a minimum of five days. It was subsequently discovered that the two vessels were, in fact, 410 miles and many hours' sailing time apart. The defendants then sought a nearer vessel to assist and, having found one, cancelled the contract with the claimants and refused to make any payment for the hire of their vessel. When the claimants brought an action for US 82,500, this being the minimum five days' rental, the defendants argued that the contract was void for common mistake, namely their shared belief that the *Great Peace* was only 35 or so miles away from the vessel she was to assist.

At first instance, the judge found for the claimants, and this was upheld on appeal. The contract was not void for mistake. The court reiterated that common mistake was a mistaken assumption of fact, held by both parties, that rendered the subject matter of the contract essentially different from what the parties contemplated. In the instant case, both the trial judge and the Court of Appeal, when deciding that the *Great Peace* was not so far away from the *Cape Providence* at the time of the contract to turn it into something essentially different from what the parties had agreed, were influenced by the fact that the defendants on learning the true position of the vessels did not seek to cancel the agreement until they knew they could find a nearer ship. This suggested that it was not (quite) entirely devoid of purpose. The situation *may* have been different if, for example, the vessels were in different oceans.

A more recent, but equally unsuccessful attempt to use common mistake as a defence can be seen in *Triple Seven Msn 27251 Ltd and another v Azman Air Services Ltd* [2018] EWHC 1348 (Comm). The claimant was the owner of two Boeing 777-200 aircraft which were leased to the defendant airline. The latter tried to cancel the agreement, arguing that it was void for common mistake, this being their shared assumption that the airline would be approved to participate in the 2006 Hajj airlift, although (unknown to them) their application had already been rejected. The trial judge in the High Court determined that the contract was not void for mistake, as the parties' error did not change the nature of their agreement. He also reviewed the authorities on operative common mistake and condensed them into general principles. These were that there must have been, at the time of the agreement, an assumption as to the existence of a state of affairs substantially shared between the parties that was fundamental to the contract; it must have been wrong, as a result of which the contract or its performance would either be essentially and radically different or, alternatively, impossible to perform in accordance with the common assumption; the party relying on the common mistake would not have entered into the contract had they been aware of it; the contract must not have made provision for the common assumption being mistaken. This last point encompasses that made in *Great Peace Shipping* (discussed above). For mistake to be operative, there must be no warranty, express or implied, by either party, that the mistaken state-of-affairs exists.

It is not easy to find common mistakes as to quality that *have* been deemed sufficiently fundamental to render a contract void. In *Nicholson and Venn v Smith-Marriott* (1947) 177 LT 189 Hallett J suggested, in *obiter* comments (the case was decided under s.13 SOGA 1893), that there might have been such a mistake where table napkins were sold as having been the personal property of Charles I, but turned out to be Georgian, with no connection to the Stuart monarch. The judge thought that if the parties' intention was to buy and sell table linen, the mistake would not be operative. However, if they intended to trade a relic belonging to Charles I, their mistake might be fundamental. Even so, the judge himself admitted that he had reservations about the correctness of his opinion, and in the light of *Leaf v International Galleries* this view might be doubted.

More pertinently, in *Associated Japanese Bank (International) Ltd v Credit du Nord SA* [1989] 1 WLR 255, funds were raised by a fraudster on the sale of four packaging machines for £1 million to the claimant bank, which then immediately leased them back to him, without taking possession of them. The defendant bank guaranteed the payments due under the lease. In reality, the packaging machines did not exist, although both parties thought that they did. When the fraudster absconded with the money, the claimant bank sought to enforce the contract of guarantee with the defendant, one that had been based on their mistaken belief in the existence of the machines on which it was secured. Steyn J reiterated that the common law rules on mistake must relate to facts as they existed at the time the contract was made and render the subject matter of the contract "essentially and radically different from the subject matter which the parties believed to exist". However, he felt that this was the situation in the instant case, so that the contract was void *ab initio*. A guarantee with security over four (real) machines is radically different to one without. The judge also noted that the matter was close to the classic *res extincta* cases.

More recently, in *British Red Cross v Werry* (2017) [2017] EWHC 875 (Ch), after a Mr Harding died, apparently intestate, there was a dispute as to the division of property between his longstanding (unmarried) partner, Ms Deeley, and his relatives. An agreement was reached whereby she received a life interest in (but not ownership of) Mr Harding's home. However, after her death, a will made by Mr Harding was (very belatedly) discovered. This left the property to Ms Deeley outright. The charities who were the beneficiaries under Ms Deeley's own will then applied for the original agreement to be set aside for common mistake, this being the shared belief that Mr Harding had not made a will. This would greatly increase Ms Deeley's assets, which would now include the home, and so what they received under her bequests. The High Court agreed, holding that this mistake was fundamental to the original agreement, so that the settlement was void *ab initio*.

### 2. Mutual Mistake

Mutual mistake involves a misunderstanding between the parties as to each other's intentions so that they are, essentially, at cross-purposes, with neither party's interpretation being objectively more plausible than the other. This means that no agreement is formed. In the historic case of *Raffles v Wichelhaus* (1864) 2 H. & C. 906, Raffles contracted to sell Wichelhaus bales of cotton that were to be carried on a ship named the *Peerless* from Bombay to Liverpool. Unknown to either party, and by a considerable coincidence, there were two ships, both named *Peerless*, leaving the Indian port over a twelve-week period, and both were bound for Liverpool.

One of them was due to leave Bombay in October and the other in December. The defendant believed the contract to mean that the cotton he purchased would be on board the vessel sailing in October. The claimant believed the contract to mean that he would ship the cotton on the *Peerless* leaving in December. The cotton arrived in Liverpool on the later shipment, but the defendant refused to accept delivery, claiming that their agreement was for cotton to be shipped on the October sailing. The claimant sued the defendant for breach of contract.

Ultimately, the issue to be determined in *Raffles v Wichelhaus* was whether the ambiguity was sufficient to prevent a proper meeting of minds. It was held that it was. Even after considering parol evidence, it was impossible for an observer to make objective sense of the contract in a way that would favour one interpretation over the other; either vessel could have been covered by the wording. As a result, there was no agreement on terms and, as such, no contract. Of course, if a reasonable man, considering the contract and extrinsic events, would have concluded that one of the two vessels was indicated in the agreement, whatever the subjective belief of one of the parties, the situation would have been different, and that interpretation would have constituted the (binding) agreement.

### 3. Unilateral Mistake

A unilateral mistake occurs where only one party is mistaken, and the other party is, or ought to be, aware of this, and then takes advantage of the former's error. However, an operative unilateral mistake must relate either to the terms of the contract or to the identity of one of the parties to the agreement; otherwise, huge numbers of contracts might be avoided. As with other forms of mistake, it will render an apparent contract void *ab initio*. The two situations, identity and terms, need to be considered separately.

### Unilateral Mistake as to Identity

Where an error as to the identity of the other party to a contract is made in dealings that are conducted at arm's length (*inter absentes*) rather than face to face (*inter praesentes*) the agreement might be deemed to be void *ab initio* for unilateral mistake, *provided* that person truly exists and their existence is considered fundamental to the contract. In the historic case of *Cundy v Lindsey* (1878) 3 App Cas 459, a rogue named Blenkarn rented a room at 37 Wood Street in Cheapside. The reputable firm Blenkiron & Son was situated a few doors down in the same street. The rogue then ordered a large quantity of linen handkerchiefs on credit from the claimant, obscuring his signature to make it appear as Blenkiron. The handkerchiefs were duly dispatched to Blenkiron & Son, but at 37 Wood Street (the rogue's address). Blenkarn then sold them on to the defendant, who purchased them in good faith, so becoming a Bona Fide Purchaser for Value (BFPV).

The claimant subsequently brought an action against the BFPV in the tort of conversion to recover the value of the handkerchiefs, which the latter had already sold on (otherwise he could have sought the handkerchiefs themselves). Everything turned on whether the contract between the rogue and the claimant was void *ab initio* for unilateral mistake as to identity. If so, title would not pass to the rogue, so he would have no title to pass on to the defendants, the maxim *nemo dat quod non habet* applying. Instead, ownership of the goods would remain with the claimant, and the defendant would be liable. It was held that the contract was void for unilateral mistake as the claimant was able to demonstrate the existence of a real business, Blenkiron and Co., with whom they always intended to contract. They would not have dealt with Blenkarn the person.

This approach was upheld by a (bare) majority of the House of Lords in *Shogun Finance Ltd v Hudson* [2003] 3 WLR 1371. In this case, a rogue purchased a car on HP terms from a dealer through a finance company. To do so, he produced a false driving licence in the name of Durlabh Patel (not his name but that of a real person). The car dealer faxed the driving licence to the claimant finance company and phoned through the details on the application form. The claimant then did a credit search on Durlabh Patel and being satisfied told the dealer to let the rogue have the car. (The rogue's dealings with Shogun were all by electronic correspondence.) The rogue then quickly sold it on to a third party (the defendant, Mr Hudson), and reneged on the finance agreement. The claimant (the finance company) brought an action in conversion against the defendant, claiming to be the owner of the car on the basis that their contract with the rogue was void for mistake.

The House of Lords held that the contract was, indeed, void. It had been made *inter absentes*, as the rogue had not purchased the car from the dealer (whom he met in person) but from the finance company (whom he did not meet). The identity of the (real) person that he claimed to be was crucial to the contract, as it was for Durlabh Patel that the credit check had been carried out, and the claimant would not have allowed the car to go without a satisfactory answer to that check.

In this case, the two dissenting judges were uncomfortable with the result produced by following the traditional approach to mistake in these circumstances. Instead, Lord Millet and Lord Nicholls suggested that *Cundy v Linsey* should be overruled and that there should be no distinction between contracts made *inter absentes* and those made *inter praesentes* (discussed below). Conversely, Lord Hobhouse firmly believed that following the traditional approach was best, and the rest of the bench agreed with him.

It is very important that the mistake in such cases be to the person rather than his attributes. In *Kings Norton Metal co ltd v Edridge, Merrett & co ltd* (1897) 14 TLR 98 a rogue ordered goods from the claimant using a letter with an elaborately printed, embossed, and illustrated heading. This claimed that it was from a company called Hallum & Co, which allegedly had offices in Belfast, Lille, and Ghent. In fact, no such company existed. The claimant sent the goods to the rogue on credit. He swiftly sold them on to the defendant, who purchased them in good faith, so becoming a BFPV. The rogue then disappeared without (of course) paying for them. The claimants brought an action for conversion against the BFPV, demanding the return of the goods, based on their unilateral mistake as to identity. However, in this case, the contract was held not to be void for mistake. There was no company called Hallum & Co, so they must have intended to contract with the author of the letter, even if they had made a serious mistake as to his attributes; he was a rogue, not a limited company with offices around Europe. Again, of course, the contract would have been *voidable* for fraudulent misrepresentation (see Chapter 8), but it had not been rescinded before title passed to the BFPV.

### *Inter Praesentes*

By contrast, where the parties negotiate in person, or *inter praesentes*, there is a very strong presumption that their intention is to deal with the person who is physically in front of them, rather than anyone they claim to be, even if their claimed identity is fundamental to the agreement and such a person truly exists. As a result, it is unlikely that a contract will be void for mistake in these circumstances.

The "historic" case on this issue is *Phillips v Brooks* [1919] 2 KB 243, in which a rogue purchased some items from the claimant jeweller's shop, claiming to be Sir George Bullough. He gave the address of (the real) Sir George, and the jewellers checked the name matched that address in a directory. The rogue paid by cheque and persuaded the jewellers to allow him to take home a valuable ring from the selected items before it cleared. He then swiftly pawned the ring at the defendant pawnbrokers under another false name and received £350 for it. The rogue then disappeared without trace. The claimant brought an action for conversion against the pawnbroker, arguing that he had made a unilateral mistake as to identity, making the agreement with the rogue void *ab initio*, so that the rogue acquired no title to give the pawnbroker (the maxim *nemo dat quod non habet* applying). Nevertheless, this was rejected by the court, which held that, in such situations, there is a very strong presumption that they intend to deal with the person physically in front of them, not the person they claim to be. The jewellers were unable to demonstrate that they would only have sold the ring to Sir George Bullough, and so failed to rebut this presumption.

The decision reached in *Phillips v Brooks* is still good law, although the decision of the Court of Appeal in *Ingram v Little* [1961] 1 QB 31 occasioned a degree of uncertainty for several decades. In this case, two elderly sisters, Hilda and Elsie Ingram, agreed to sell their car to a rogue who falsely identified himself (in person) as a Mr. Hutchinson of Caterham. When the rogue offered a cheque, Elsie said that it had to be a cash sale. The rogue then provided his full assumed name and address, which Hilda checked for veracity at a local post office. She informed Elsie that the details were accurate, and the sisters let Mr. Hutchinson take the car. Before the cheque was dishonoured, the rogue sold the car on to the defendant. The sisters brought an action to recover the vehicle from the latter. The Court of Appeal held that the contract was void for mistake as the sisters only intended to deal with Mr. Hutchinson and were not willing to offer a sale for payment by cheque to anyone else. This case received widespread criticism, even at the time, and was not subsequently followed. The House of Lords concluded that it was wrongly decided in *Shogun Finance Ltd v Hudson* [2003] 3 WLR 1371.

The traditional (*Phillips v Brooks*) analysis was reasserted in *Lewis v Averay* [1972] 1 QB 198. In this case the claimant, Mr Lewis, agreed to sell his car for £450 to a rogue who claimed that he was the actor Richard Greene. The rogue asked to pay by cheque. Mr Lewis agreed to accept the cheque after the rogue presented a (stolen) pass for Pinewood Studios with Greene's name and photograph on it. The rogue quickly sold the car on to the defendant, Mr Averay, for £200. The cheque was, of course, dishonoured. The claimant argued that the mistake as to the identity of the buyer meant that there was no contract with the rogue, so that the latter had no title to pass to Mr Averay, which meant the car was still his property. However, it was held that this did not prevent a valid contract being created between the rogue and Mr Lewis at their *inter praesentes* meeting. The contract was not void for mistake or set aside for fraudulent misrepresentation before Mr Averay purchased the car in good faith so that he was entitled to retain it. In the light of *Shogun Finance v Hudson*, this remains the correct interpretation of the law.

**Unilateral Mistake as to Terms**

As Singleton J noted in *Hartog v Colin & Shields* [1939] 3 All ER 566 when an offeree knows, or ought to have known, that the offeror has made a mistake as to the terms (not the subject matter) of their offer, he cannot "snap it up" by accepting it and expect to enforce the agreement that (ostensibly) results. For example, and to use a simple and blatant illustration, this might occur if an offeror sends a letter offering to sell something very valuable for £100 when it should really have been £100,000, and all previous negotiations have been at or around this sum. In this situation, the offeree knows (or ought to know) that there has been a typographic error, so that his purported acceptance of the "offer" would not be valid.

In *Hartog v Colin &* Shields the facts were a little less extreme. The defendants, Colin & Shields, were London hide merchants. Hartog was a Belgian furrier. In verbal discussions Colin & Shields provisionally agreed to sell 10,000 Argentinian hare skins at "10d per skin" to Hartog. However, when the firm sent their offer in writing to the latter it mistakenly wrote "10,000 skins at 10d per lb". This was not the usual way of pricing skins in the fur industry, where skins were priced individually rather than by weight. As hare skins average around five ounces (less than a third of a pound) the offer was far below the market rate, and the price previously discussed. Mr Hartog immediately accepted the "offer" and then tried to hold Colin & Shields to it. The latter pleaded that their offer was mistaken, that they intended throughout to offer the goods per piece, and not by pound weight, and that Hartog was aware of this. The trial judge found in Colin & Shields' favour, on the grounds that the claimant must have been aware of the error, which, as it concerned a term of the contract, rendered the contract void: "[T]he defendants by their evidence, and by the correspondence, have satisfied me that the claimant could not reasonably have supposed that that offer contained the offerors' real intention".

The more plausible or reasonable the mistaken offer, the more likely an acceptance is to produce a binding contract, because it will be harder to show that the defendant knew or ought to have known that it was a mistake. For example, in *Centrovincial Estates Plc v Merchant Investors Assurance Co Ltd* [1983] Com LR 15, the defendants, Merchant Investors, had held the lease on an office building for over a decade. In 1982, the claimants, Centrovincial Estates, acquired the freehold to the property and wrote a letter to the defendants, offering them a renewed lease at a rental of £65,000 per annum. At the time, they were paying £68,000 a year, and quickly sent back a letter of acceptance. However, it subsequently transpired that a mistake had been made in the original offer, which, it was intended, should have been for £126,000 per annum. The defendants rejected any correction to the figure of £65,000 and held the claimants to the "agreement" that, they felt, had been concluded by their letter of acceptance. The claimants argued that this was void for unilateral mistake as to its terms.

The key issue in this (type of) case was whether the offeree knew or ought to have known that the offer in the renewal letter contained a mistake. The court concluded that this was not the situation. Although the claimants argued that no reasonable tenant could have expected their rent to be reduced at a time of inflation, the defendants claimed that this was reasonable, in the light of their earlier and communicated dissatisfaction with the terms of the previous letting. There was no evidence to show that the defendants knew of the claimant's error. As a result, the latter were bound by the acceptance of their offer. Ironically, if their mistaken offer had been ridiculously low, for example, £1,260, they would have been very much more likely to have succeeded, as in these circumstances it would, or ought to have been, obvious that they had made a mistake.

Case law suggests that, when it comes to commercial contracts, the test as to whether an offeree is entitled to rely on a mistaken offer is that of a hypothetical and reasonable businessman in his position: *Dhanani v Crasnianski* [2011] All ER 799 (Comm).

## Personal Mistakes as to Subject Matter

It should be stressed that, unlike a mistake as to terms, a vendor or purchaser's personal mistake as to the subject matter (rather than the offer) of what he is selling or buying is irrelevant, even if the counterparty is aware of it. Parties are allowed to take advantage of their superior knowledge in negotiations, and this commonly occurs. Thus, in *Smith v Hughes* (1871) LR 6 QB 597 Blackburn J observed that if a vendor was aware that the purchaser had entered a contract mistakenly believing that the article he was purchasing possessed a certain quality, without thinking that this quality was part of the offer, he was not obliged to enlighten him as to the correct position: "[T]here is no legal obligation on the vendor to inform the purchaser that he is under a mistake, not induced by the act of the vendor". Similarly, Lord Hoffman observed in *Bank of Credit and Commerce International SA v Munawar Ali, Sultana Runi Khan and Others* [2001] 2 WLR 735, "there is obviously room in the dealings of the market for legitimately taking advantage of the known ignorance of the other party". For example, if a vendor sells an old table for £200, although it is worth just £50, but realises that the purchaser thinks he is buying a valuable antique worth £2,000 (the value of which the vendor is ignorant), albeit that the vendor has done nothing to encourage such a belief, the contract will be valid, just as a purchaser who knowingly buys a valuable antique from a dealer who thinks that it is a commonplace item has a valid contract.

*Smith v Hughes* (1871) LR 6 QB 597 involved a horse trainer, Hughes, who bought a quantity of oats that matched a sample he had been shown. However, Mr Hughes had misidentified the kind of oats that had been tendered. His animals could not eat them, and when he realised this, he refused to pay for them. Mr Smith, the oat supplier, successfully sued for breach of contract. That Mr. Hughes had made a personal mistake about the nature of the oats he was purchasing was his own fault. He had not been misled by Mr Smith, and did not think, to Mr Smith's knowledge, that it was an express term that the oats being offered were of the type that he believed them to be (old oats). (In reality, he was also unaware of Mr Hughes' personal mistake).

## Objective Interpretive Principle

In *Smith v Hughes* (1871) LR 6 QB 597 Blackburn J neatly summed up the objective interpretive principle (also alluded to in Chapter 1) that is fundamental to mistake: "If, whatever a man's real intention may be, he so conducts himself that a reasonable man would believe that he was assenting to the terms proposed by the other party, and that other party upon that belief enters into the contract with him, the man thus conducting himself would be equally bound as if he had intended to agree to the other party's terms". For another example, can be considered *Tamplin v James* (1880) 15 CH D 215. In this case, Mr Tamplin wanted to purchase the Ship Inn when it was sold at auction. Through his own carelessness he thought the property being offered for sale was much larger than it was, believing that it extended to two adjacent fields that he had seen the vendor of the property use in the past, unaware that this was by permission of their owners. He failed to check the plan properly in the sale room, which would quickly have made it apparent that this was not the case. After he bought the property, he asked for the contract to be set aside for mistake. He failed; the auctioneer did not know, and had no reason to believe, that Tamplin thought he was bidding for more than the advertised property, rather than the advertised property and the adjacent fields.

## 4. *Non Est Factum*

In exceptional circumstances, a party may avoid being bound by their signature, contrary to the principle in *L'Estrange v F Graucob Ltd* [1934] 2 KB 394, after signing a contractual document by mistake, under the doctrine of *non est factum.* ("It is not my deed".) The prerequisites necessary for this to apply are very strict, as it reduces a signature's value as the basis for contractual liability. As Lord Wilberforce noted in the leading decision on the subject, *Saunders v Anglia Building Society (Gallie v Lee)* [1970] AC 1004, the rules exist to protect innocent third parties who may rely upon a document that has, apparently, been signed correctly.

It is a long-established doctrine, with its prerequisites being identified in Victorian cases such as *Foster v Mackinnon* (1869) LR 4 CP 704. In this case, a senile man who was induced to sign a document after being told it was a guarantee, when it was really a bill of exchange, succeeded in his plea of *non est factum*. Byles J observed that "if a blind man, or a man who cannot read, or who for some reason (not implying negligence) forbears to read, has a written contract falsely read over to him, the reader misreading to such a degree that the written contract is of a nature altogether different from the contract pretended to be read from the paper which the blind or illiterate man afterwards signs; then, at least if there be no negligence, the signature so obtained is of no force".

In *Saunders v Anglia Building Society (Gallie v Lee)* [1970] AC 1004 the leading modern case on the issue, the House of Lords reiterated that, to apply, the signatory must (first) have made a "fundamental mistake" as to the contents of the signed document, which must be radically different in nature from the one he intended to sign, and (second) they must not have been careless when doing so. This means that the person pleading *non est factum* must belong to a class of persons who, through no fault of their own, are unable to read or understand the relevant document. This might be because of blindness, illiteracy, or some other disability, such as extreme old age or senility. The disability must be one requiring their reliance on others for advice as to what they are signing. A simple failure to read a contract before signing it will never be enough.

In *Saunders v Anglia* Mrs Gallie was a woman of 78 who wished to transfer her house to a nephew as a gift on condition that he allowed her to remain there rent free for the remainder of her life. However, her nephew and a friend of his named Lee prepared a document that, instead, assigned the property to Lee. She signed it unread as she had lost her glasses. Mr Lee then used the document to obtain a mortgage on the property for £2,000. He failed to keep up repayments on the mortgage and the building society sought possession of the property. In the action with the building society, Mrs Gallie raised the plea of *non est factum*. The House of Lords found against her on both disqualifying grounds. The document was not radically different to what she believed it to be, in that she thought that she was relinquishing her rights to the property, albeit not to Lee. Additionally, she was not blind or illiterate but careless in not reading it.

By contrast, in *Lloyds Bank v Waterhouse* [1993] 2 FLR 97, a father acted as a guarantor to his son's debt when purchasing a farm. The father was illiterate and allegedly signed the bank document under the belief that he was signing a guarantee that was limited to the money borrowed to purchase the land when, in reality, it was for *all* the debt accumulated by his son. When the son defaulted, the father refused to pay under the guarantee, on the basis that its scope was wider than he had understood at the time he signed. In the Court of Appeal, he relied on two grounds, *non est factum* and negligence or breach of duty by the bank. The Court of Appeal allowed the father to escape liability, with a majority of the judges agreeing with the *non est factum* submission (some also agreed with the second ground). Conversely, in *Avon Finance Co. Ltd. v Bridger* [1985] 2 All ER 281, *non est factum* was successfully pleaded at first instance by an elderly couple who had guaranteed a loan but rejected by a majority in the Court of Appeal, which felt that they had not acted with sufficient care (the decision was upheld on other grounds).

# Chapter 10: Duress and Undue Influence

## Introduction

The notion of freedom of contract requires that an agreement be entered into voluntarily, albeit that this can be a rather vague concept. Nevertheless, if entering a contract is not the result of a voluntary decision, it may be voidable, and might be rescinded under the common law doctrine of duress or the equitable doctrine of undue influence. As Lord Hoffman has noted, both are "based upon the principle that a transaction to which consent has been obtained by unacceptable means should not be allowed to stand": *'R' v Attorney General for England and Wales* [2003] UKPC 22. However, although attempts have been made to see these doctrines as part of an over-arching whole, and there is a limited degree of overlap between them, where both might be applicable on certain facts, they are very different in nature, and properly viewed independently.

It should also be noted at the outset that although contracts can be avoided using undue influence or duress, damages cannot be awarded as a remedy in such situations, albeit that money that has been paid over might be recovered where they are found to be present. Furthermore, even when present, the right to rescind that these doctrines have engendered can be lost by delay (*laches*).

## Duress

Historically, duress involved threats of violence, whether to persons or (eventually) their property, which could render a contract voidable. A classic modern example of such duress can be seen in the Privy Council case of *Barton v Armstrong* [1976] AC 104. Armstrong was the chairman of, and held the largest shareholding in, Landmark Corporation Ltd., a property-development company in New South Wales. Barton was its managing director and had a substantial shareholding in the company. There were two other directors. There had been a long history of discord between the four men. The three other directors sought the removal of Armstrong, as they believed that he was putting the company at risk of insolvency. Armstrong was only prepared to resign on his own terms, and made several death threats to Barton, with a view to pressuring him into signing an agreement that included the purchase of Armstrong's shares at a substantial over value.

Barton agreed to this, in *part* due to the threats of violence, but also because it would mean that Armstrong would no longer have a controlling interest. However, the company became insolvent shortly afterwards and Barton sought to have the contract with Armstrong set aside for duress. He succeeded, a majority in the Privy Council holding that physical duress did not need to be the only or even the main reason, rather than merely *one* reason, for the threatened party entering a contract. Lord Cross held that that if Armstrong's threats "were . reason for Barton's executing the deed he is entitled to relief even though he might well have entered into the contract if Armstrong had uttered no threats to induce him to do so".

The issue of duress to the person was briefly considered in *Holyoake v Candy* [2017] EWHC 3397(Ch). In this case, the defendant allegedly warned that if the claimant, Mr Holyoake, did not sign a supplemental agreement rescheduling a loan, it would create an extremely stressful situation for him and his pregnant wife, saying that he (the defendant) would "feel terrible if anything were to go wrong during the pregnancy for her or the baby". (She had previously suffered a miscarriage.) It was claimed that this amounted to duress, as it encompassed a physical threat to a close relation of the counterparty. In the High Court, Nugee J held that although these remarks were ill-judged, the defendant was not threatening to do anything specific, and was merely referring to the possible consequences if agreement could not be reached. As such, it did not constitute duress to the person.

In the early nineteenth century there were doubts as to whether the doctrine extended to "duress of goods", which might involve a threat to damage, destroy, seize, or detain goods whilst demanding a change to contractual terms. In *Skeate v Beale* [1840] 11 Ad & El 983 a landlord who was owed money by his tenant seized goods owned by the latter, and threatened to sell them immediately, unless the tenant agreed to repay the sums owned. The tenant agreed to the suggested terms, but then sought to have the agreement set aside for duress. The court rejected this, as the threat had been directed towards property (the seized goods) rather than the person. However, judicial attitudes subsequently changed in this regard, as can be seen from the consequences of an unlawful threat to seize the claimant's goods if he did not pay money in *Maskell v Horner* [1915] 3 KB 106. In *Occidental Worldwide Investment v Skibs (The Sibeon & The Sibotre)* [1976] 1 Lloyds Rep 293 the court reiterated that serious threats to property could be considered as duress. Kerr J observed that it would, for example, apply to an "imminent threat of having my house burnt down or a valuable picture burnt through without any threat of physical violence to anyone".

## Economic Duress

During the 1970s, the doctrine was greatly extended to cover instances of economic duress, making it a much more important and regularly advanced defence. The first case to consider this possibility was *Occidental Worldwide Investment v Skibs (The Sibeon & The Sibotre)* [1976] 1 Lloyds Rep 293. In this case, the defendants chartered two vessels from the claimant. Subsequently, they told the claimants that they would go bankrupt if they did not lower the cost of the charter, although this was untrue. The claimants feared that they would lose valuable customers, and they were also owed substantial amounts of money by the defendant which they feared they would lose if the latter did become insolvent. As a result, they agreed to renegotiate the contract to lower the cost of the charter. They later sought to have the renegotiated contract set aside. The court recognised that it *would* be possible to render a contract voidable for economic duress in the right circumstances but concluded that it was not established in the instant case.

In *North Ocean Shipping Co Ltd v Hyundai Construction Co Ltd* [1979] QB 705, the court went further. Hyundai were South Korean shipbuilders who contracted with North Ocean Shipping to build an oil tanker, the *Atlantic Baron*. It was to be paid for in US dollars, in five instalments. In 1973, after the first instalment was paid, the US dollar was devalued against the Korean won. Hyundai said they would not deliver the vessel unless the price was increased by 10 per cent to allow for this devaluation. North Ocean was worried that they would lose a favourable charter with Shell if the vessel was not delivered on time and so agreed to this. The ship was subsequently delivered in November 1974. In July 1975, North Ocean took legal action over the increased price.

In the instant case, Mocatta J found that because Hyundai had increased a letter of credit there was good (i.e. "sufficient") consideration for the price variation, so that the agreement could only be challenged on the basis of duress, this being the threat to break the original contract. He concluded that there was such a thing as economic duress, and that the agreement in the instant case was the result of such duress, which meant that the contract was a "voidable one which can be avoided and the excess money paid under it recovered". However, because of the eight-month delay in bringing the case to court, economic duress could not be found, as the inaction of the owners could only be regarded as an affirmation of the variation. Subsequently, in the Privy Council case of *Pao On v Lau Yiu Long* [1980] AC 614, Lord Scarman also recognised the concept of economic duress, and identified some of its prerequisites and limitations, noting that it was a coercion of the will that vitiated consent, and that this was different from normal (and acceptable) commercial pressure, a point that was to become well-established in subsequent cases.

In *DSND Subsea Ltd v Petroleum GeoServices ASA* [2000] BLR 530 and *Carillion Construction Ltd v Felix (Ltd)* [2001] BLR 1, Dyson J produced a now generally accepted tripartite test when he observed that the three necessary ingredients for a successful claim of economic duress were that there must be pressure which is illegitimate; that it was a significant factor in the claimant's decision to enter into or vary the contract; and that its effect was to create a lack of practical choice or realistic alternative for the innocent party. Subsequently, in *Adam Opel v Mitras Automotive* [2008] EWHC 3205 (QB), Dyson J's observations were accepted by both parties to the litigation and the trial judge as an accurate reflection of the law on this issue. Much more important, they were confirmed by the Supreme Court in *Pakistan International Airline Corporation v Times Travel* (UK) Ltd [2021] UKSC 40. The three aspects of this test will be considered *seriatim*.

### 1. An "Illegitimate" Threat

The pressure used in cases of economic duress must be illegitimate. In this context, and as Dyson J observed in *DSND Subsea Ltd v Petroleum Geo Services*, "Illegitimate pressure must be distinguished from the rough and tumble of the pressures of normal commercial bargaining". Many contractual negotiations, especially those conducted in a commercial context, are conducted under some degree of pressure, between parties who are not of equal bargaining power. Most of this is (legally) quite legitimate. Thus, in *Holyoake v Candy* [2017] EWHC 3397 (Ch) the High Court dismissed a property developer's claim of economic duress. The plea arose from Candy's threats of litigation if Holyoake did not sign various supplemental agreements. The essential question was whether this amounted to illegitimate pressure. It was held that Candy was justified in taking a hard line on negotiations and could properly threaten litigation if Mr Holyoake did not sign, and therefore there was no economic duress. However, if the pressure becomes too extreme, there is a danger that, in some situations at least, the weaker party *might* be able to set aside a contract, or the variation of an existing agreement, on the grounds of economic duress.

This raises the obvious question as to *when* legitimate commercial pressure becomes illegitimate duress. It is not always an easy question to answer. As Tucker J noted in *Atlas Express Ltd v Kafco (Importers & Distributors) Ltd* [1989] 1 All ER 641, "The borderline between the two may in some cases be indistinct". Nevertheless, almost all cases where economic duress has been advanced successfully at trial have involved the threat to do something unlawful, whether it was to break a contract or commit a tort. A selection of cases can be considered in this regard.

In *B&S Contractors v Victor Green Publications* [1984] ICR 419, a contractor agreed to erect stands for a fire-safety exhibition at Olympia in London. Less than a week before the exhibition was due to open, the contractor told his client that the work would not be done unless he paid an additional sum to meet extra claims which were being made against him (the contractor) by his own employees. This would have been disastrous for the client, inflicting reputational damage and potentially exposing him to legal claims from exhibitors who had already rented space on the stands. In the Court of Appeal, Kerr LJ, like the judge at first instance, held that the extra payment was made under duress and could be recovered.

Similarly, in *Atlas Express Ltd v Kafco (Importers & Distributors) Ltd* [1989] 1 All ER 641, Kafco had a contract to supply Woolworths with decorative Christmas baskets. They contracted with Atlas Express to deliver consignments of the baskets to the various shops in the Woolworth chain. Having entered this contract, Atlas realised that it had underestimated the size of the consignments, making it much less profitable than they had anticipated. However, Kafco refused to agree to their proposed minimum order of £440 per trailer load. In response, Atlas sent an empty lorry to Kafco to pick up the festive baskets, with a letter saying that if a higher charge was not agreed, the lorry would return to its depot without a load. They reluctantly agreed to the increased charges. The agreement continued until Kafco sent Atlas a letter stating that they had signed the contract under duress and refusing to pay the further sums involved. Atlas then sued for the extra money. Kafco argued, *inter alia*, that there was economic duress. Tucker J agreed; Kafco's manager had signed the new agreement "unwillingly and under compulsion," and had acted without delay to avoid it when he could. The variation was unenforceable. It should be noted that where duress has led to a contractual variation, as in the instant case, it is only the variation, not the main (original) contract, that is voidable.

In *Carillion Construction Ltd v Felix (UK) Ltd* [2001] BLR 1 Carillion was the main contractor for the construction of an office building in London. They engaged Felix as subcontractor to supply specialist cladding for the building, this work to be completed by January 2000. At the end of February, although it had still not been completed, Felix asked for a payment of £3,314,000. Carillion assessed their entitlement at only £2,756,000. By then, a lack of cladding meant that areas of concrete were still exposed, and other work on the building was being delayed. Felix then wrote to Carillion and stated, "Without the figure being agreed, [we] cannot predict when the project will be complete". Carillion eventually agreed to pay £3.2 million. Once this settlement was agreed the deliveries began again and proceeded as originally scheduled. Subsequently, Carillion claimed that the extra money had been secured by economic duress. Dyson J applied the criteria he had set out in *DSND Subsea* and found that such duress to be present. Felix had threatened not to make any deliveries until settlement was reached, which was a threat to commit a breach of contract, as the agreement did not allow them to do this. Felix was claiming more than they were entitled to under the agreement and were obviously aware that Carillion had no realistic alternative but to concede to their demands for payment.

To take another example, in *Adam Opel v Mitras Automotive* [2008] EWHC 3205 (QB), Mitras was a manufacturer of car parts and (at the time) the sole supplier of one specific part to Adam, a car manufacturer. The latter decided to source this part from a new supplier and advised Mitras that they would be terminating their supply contract in the future (as they were entitled to do). Mitras then made several demands for payment based on an amortisation of their development costs. Adam offered substantially less than they were claiming. Mitras provided Adam with the option of either accepting their demands or immediately sourcing the special part elsewhere, which was not at all practical. Adam paid for fear of not being supplied with the essential part for the remainder of the year, which would have had grave commercial consequences. Subsequently, they successfully claimed duress. It was held that Adam had been compelled to pay the money to secure the vital part. They were unable to find an alternative provider, as Mitras was, at the time, the sole supplier of the item.

To consider a non-contractual civil wrong, in the House of Lords case of *Universe Tankships v International Transport Workers Federation, The Universe Sentinel* [1983] 1 AC 366, the ITWF "blacked" (took extreme industrial action against) a vessel to prevent it from leaving port. They made several demands in relation to pay and conditions and further demanded that the ship owners pay a large sum of money to the Seafarers International Welfare Fund. The owners agreed so that the *Universe Sentinel* could leave port, and then sought to recover the sum paid to the welfare fund. It was held that the money had been extracted by economic duress and so could be recovered.

Very similarly, in the Court of Appeal case of *Dimskal Shipping v ITWF (The Evia Luck)* [1991] 4 All ER 871, the ITWF threatened to 'black' the *Evia Luck* merchant vessel unless certain demands were met. This would have had serious consequences for the claimant, so they agreed to the demands. They later sought to have the agreement set aside for duress and any monies paid under it returned. The main question before the court was the legitimacy of the pressure. At the time of the threatened strike the *Evia Luck* was in Sweden. Under Swedish law such a strike would be lawful, so that, if it applied, there would be no illegitimate pressure. However, under English law the strike would be unlawful, and the threat regarded as illegitimate. It was held that English law applied to the agreement, so that the threat did constitute duress.

**Lawful Act Duress**

Can threatening to commit an otherwise lawful act ever amount to economic duress? In *theory*, the answer seems to be yes, albeit that cases where this occurs will be quite exceptionally rare. In the Court of Appeal case of *CTN Cash & Carry v Gallagher* [1994] 4 All ER 714 the defendant sent a consignment of cigarettes to the wrong address, where they were stolen. He mistakenly believed that the cigarettes were at the claimant's risk and sent an invoice for their cost, threatening to withdraw the claimant's credit facility unless it was paid. The claimants needed the credit facilities and so paid the invoice and then sought to reclaim the money on the grounds of economic duress. It was held that the threat to withdraw the credit facility was lawful since, under the terms of the parties' agreement, it could be withdrawn at any time. As a result, the threat was legitimate and, on the facts of the case, economic duress could not be established.

Nevertheless, the Court of Appeal accepted, in principle, that illegitimate pressure need not *necessarily* constitute unlawful conduct, suggesting that the appropriate test is "not whether the conduct is lawful but whether it is morally or socially unacceptable". As a result, a threat to commit what would otherwise be a lawful act might be improper if it was coupled with a demand that went far beyond what was normal in commercial arrangements, so that it was tantamount to blackmail. Even so, the court also noted that this would be an exceptionally rare situation when commercial contracts were involved.

In *Progress Bulk Carriers Limited v Tube City IMS LLC* [2012] EWHC 273, which involved an appeal from the ruling in an arbitration between the owners of a cargo vessel and its charterers, the Commercial Court hinted at a slightly more liberal interpretation of lawful-act duress. The trial judge rejected an argument that such cases required conduct that was so extreme and so "manifestly beyond the norms of ordinary commercial practice that it could be considered on a par with conduct that the law does expressly recognise as illegal or criminal". Unfortunately, the decision did not give much general guidance on what constituted morally or socially unacceptable conduct.

In any event, in *Times Travel (UK) Ltd v Pakistan Airlines Corporation* [2021] UKSC 40 the Supreme Court reconsidered the issue and set a very high bar for those seeking to establish lawful act duress. It clarified and (arguably) restricted the decision in *Progress Bulk Carriers Limited.* In this case, Times Travel (TT) was a small business selling tours to Pakistan and dependent on an agency agreement with Pakistan International Airlines Corporation (PIAC), which was the sole operator of direct flights between the UK and the Asian country. PIAC gave notice that it was terminating its existing contract with TT. It then offered a new contract on condition that TT waived its (contested) claims for unpaid commission, allegedly worth around £1.1 million, under a previous agreement. PIAC genuinely believed that the commission had ceased to be payable.

In the High Court, TT successfully challenged the validity of the new contract on the grounds of economic duress. However, the Court of Appeal allowed PIAC's appeal. The matter then went to the Supreme Court. In a judgment handed down in 2021, the court confirmed the existence of lawful-act economic duress but emphasised the narrowness of its scope, citing just two specific sets of circumstances in which, to date, a remedy had been provided for such duress. These were where the defendant has either threatened to report criminal activity by the claimant or a family member to the police or, alternatively, where they had used illegitimate means to manoeuvre the claimant into a position of weakness to force him to waive his claim. The Supreme Court accepted that there could be other situations but indicated that the courts should approach any extension of the doctrine with caution. Lord Hodge observed that lawful-act economic duress was particularly limited when it came to commercial transactions. In the instant case, PIAC had not used any "reprehensible means" to exploit Times Travel's vulnerability, nor did he find any bad faith on their part. The airline's actions were simply those of a hard-nosed commercial negotiator who, quite legally, exploited PIAC's position as a monopoly supplier. The appeal was dismissed.

## 2. A Significant Inducement

The second of Dyson J's pre-requisites for economic duress identified in *Carillion Construction Ltd v Felix (UK) Ltd* [2001] BLR 1 was that the pressure exerted was a significant cause or inducement behind the claimant's decision to enter the contract/ agree the contractual variation. In the instant case, the judge felt that it was clear from the facts that Carillion would never have entered into the settlement agreement on the new terms but for the threat not to deliver. There was no legitimate commercial reason for them to do so. Furthermore, Carillion indicated in contemporaneous correspondence their "extreme displeasure at being required to enter into such an agreement". This pre-requisite overlaps heavily with Dyson J's third requirement.

### 3. A Lack of Practical Choice

Whether a threat amounts to economic duress is highly context, and so case, specific. Nevertheless, in *Pao On v Lau Yiu Long* [1980] AC 614 Lord Scarman thought that, in determining this question, it was relevant to ask whether the person involved protested and whether, at the time he was allegedly coerced into making or altering a contract, he had a realistic alternative course of action. For example, in most cases, a party faced with an unwarranted demand for an increase in the price to be paid pursuant to a contract can source its subject matter elsewhere, whether it be goods or services, and if they pay significantly more, sue the party in breach of contract for the difference. In this situation, they would not be under operative economic duress if they agreed to the additional demand. As Kerr LJ observed in *B&S Contractors v Victor Green Publications* [1984] ICR 429, a threat to break a contract unless extra money was paid would only constitute duress where there was "no reasonable alternative open, such as by legal redress".

However, sometimes alternative suppliers (for example) are not readily available within a reasonable time at an affordable price, and the pressured party has no practical option but to agree to the new terms being imposed. In these circumstances they are acting under duress. Those who are being threatened into accepting an unfavourable contractual variation can strengthen their future position when it comes to economic duress by: making it clear in writing that they are acting under protest, obtaining and preserving evidence that the relevant contract could not readily be fulfilled elsewhere (for example by requesting and preserving quotations or rejections from alternative potential providers), and by seeking to avoid the contract as soon as possible after the pressure ceases to operate.

For illustrative example, in *Atlas Express Ltd v Kafco (Importers & Distributors) Ltd* [1989] 1 All ER 641, discussed above, Kafco was financially dependent on the success of their Christmas-basket venture, hoped that it would lead to future business from a potentially lucrative customer (Woolworths), and knew that so close to Christmas it would be very difficult if not impossible to make affordable alternative arrangements for transporting the baskets. In *Carillion Construction Ltd v Felix (UK) Ltd* [2001] BLR 1, also discussed above, Carillion were under pressure to complete the job as soon as possible. Without it, other trades could not start on the building work, and the overall project would be delayed. The cladding provided by Felix was bespoke, and Carillion could not go anywhere else for it. Furthermore, adjudication was not an option because it would still have taken at least six weeks to obtain a decision.

## Undue Influence in Equity

The notion of duress is aimed at preventing direct, but illegitimate, pressure from influencing contracting parties. By contrast, the equitable doctrine of undue influence is more subtle, and primarily aimed at preventing those with a dominant influence over others from abusing it, even where there is an absence of overt acts of pressure. As Sir James Wilde observed in *Hall v Hall* [1868] LR 1 P&D 481, "Persuasion is not unlawful, but pressure of whatever character if so exerted as to overpower the volition without convincing the judgment ... will constitute undue influence, though no force has been either used or threatened". More recently, the issue was considered in *Daniel v Drew* [2005] EWCA Civ 507 by Ward LJ, who felt that in all cases of alleged undue influence the critical question was whether the persuasion or advice "in other words the influence, has invaded the free volition of the donor to accept or reject the persuasion or advice or withstand the influence. The donor may be led but she must not be driven and her will must be the offspring of her own volition, not a record of someone else's". In the right circumstances, the doctrine can extend to transactions carried out with third parties, such as a bank, who are independent of the person exercising the undue influence but deemed by the courts to have had notice of it and (effectively) been contaminated by it. The doctrine allows the courts to set aside transactions that have been carried out as a result of such influence, which are voidable. However, and as with duress, this right can be lost by, *inter alia*, delay.

As *Daniel v Drew* suggests, many, indeed a majority, of reported cases relating to undue influence do not involve contracts. Undue influence may apply to a wide variety of other transactions, such as gifts, loans, and testamentary dispositions. However, the principles are normally the same, so that cases on the latter areas are also important when considering those involving contracts. For example, if someone exercises undue influence to get someone else to sell them a new Rolls-Royce for £100, it is a contract; if they use it to persuade the person to give it to them for nothing, it is a gift. Both can be challenged using the doctrine.

Although many such cases involve situations that a layman might view as immoral, such as someone exercising undue influence to secure personal financial advantage, this is not *necessarily* the case. As was noted by Cotton LJ in *Allcard v Skinner* (1887) 36 Ch D 145, the "court interferes, not on the ground that any wrongful act has in fact been committed by the donee, but on the ground of public policy, and to prevent the relations which exist between the parties and the influence arising therefrom being abused". In this historic, but still very important, case, the Mother Superior of an Anglican religious order was not exercising influence for her own personal benefit, but rather for the wider convent and its spiritual and charitable work, but it was still deemed to be undue influence.

Unsurprisingly, the legal burden of proving undue influence is placed on the person alleging it. In *Randall v Randall* [2004] EWHC 2258 (Ch), in which an executor sought to set aside gifts made by the deceased (an elderly aunt) to his brother, alleging undue influence, the trial judge, Edward Bartley Jones QC, reiterated, "Here, as elsewhere, the general principle is that he who asserts a wrong must prove it. The burden of proof in an allegation of undue influence rests upon the person who claims to have been wronged". As will be seen, he can be aided in this by various presumptions, but its presence is a question of fact for the court to determine.

Traditionally, the law has distinguished between "actual undue influence" and "presumed undue influence". However, cases of presumed undue influence can themselves be subdivided into two further categories. As a result, in *Bank of Credit and Commerce International v Aboody* [1990] 1 QB 923, the Court of Appeal set out, and numbered, three classes of undue influence. Class 1 constituted "actual undue influence"; Class 2(a) involved "presumed undue influence" flowing from certain specific types of relationship; Class 2(b) involved "presumed undue influence" based on the presence of a relationship of trust and confidence, proven on the facts of the individual case. This categorisation and numbering was criticised in *Royal Bank of Scotland v Etridge (No.2)* [2002] 1 AC 773, where Lord Clyde opined that it might lead to confusion. This danger was aggravated because, the judge felt, the terminology employed in *Aboody* was misleading, confusing definition and proof. Nevertheless, the division does have some residual value for the purposes of academic analysis, provided it is recognised that it no longer attracts support from the courts and, as a result, forensic use.

## Actual Undue Influence

As Lord Nicholls noted in *Royal Bank of Scotland v Etridge No. 2* [2002] 1 AC 773, actual undue influence has the closest similarities to duress; indeed, he felt that there was now "much overlap" between the two. In *Holyoake v Candy* [2017] EWHC 3397 (Ch), Nugee J even declined, on the facts of the case before him, to consider the issue of actual undue influence because he had rejected the same factual allegations in relation to Mr Holyoake's failed plea of duress. In *Etridge*, Lord Nicholls described actual undue influence as "Overt acts of improper pressure or coercion, such as unlawful threats". However, they do not *necessarily* involve a threat to do anything illegal, unlike most cases of duress. By contrast, presumed undue influence (discussed below) involves relationships where one party has acquired ascendancy over another which they take unfair advantage of "without any specific acts of coercion". In *Daniel v Drew* [2005] EWCA Civ 507 it was claimed that, very broadly, the difference between the two classes is that in the case of actual undue influence, "something has to be done to twist the mind of a donor whereas in cases of presumed undue influence it is more a case of what has not been done, namely ensuring that independent advice is available to the donor."

In practice, it is unusual for a contract to be set side on the grounds of actual undue influence. As Lloyd LJ observed in *Smith v Cooper* [2010] EWCA Civ 722, it must be proved positively by the evidence, and such cases are rare. The question is whether the innocent party's free will has been overborne by pressure, hectoring, coercion, or threats (even if falling short of duress) to bring about the transaction at the time they entered an agreement. The vulnerability of one party and the forcefulness of the other are highly relevant when determining this question. In the old case of *Wingrove v Wingrove* (1885) 11 P.D. 81, it was noted that a "person in the last days or hours of life may have become so weak and feeble, that a very little pressure will be sufficient to bring about the desired result". More recently, in *Daniel v Drew*, that the influenced party was a frail and elderly woman, and the influencer a very much younger, and highly assertive, man was held to be highly significant.

Strictly speaking, and unlike presumed undue influence, it is not necessary to prove a pre-existing relationship between the parties for actual undue influence to occur, although, in practice, it is usually present. As Nugee J observed in *Holyoake v Candy*, "actual undue influence need not consist of abuse of an existing relationship, although it commonly does". It is no longer necessary that the challenged transaction be manifestly disadvantageous to the party relying on the doctrine (as was once the case) or even that it calls for an explanation, unlike current cases of presumed undue influence (see below).

The notion of actual undue influence originated during the nineteenth century, when threats that fell short of the then very limited doctrine of duress were first considered. For example, in *Williams v Bailey* (1866) LR 1 HL 200, a son forged his father's signature on promissory notes and gave them to the bank where both were customers. This was a very serious offence, and, at a meeting with the bank and its solicitor, the father was (effectively) obliged to honour the notes if he did not wish to see his son prosecuted for a crime that, as was pointed out to him, carried a potential sentence of transportation for life. The father agreed to make an equitable mortgage of his property to the bank in exchange for the return of the promissory notes. He subsequently succeeded in an action to cancel the agreement. Lord Westbury observed that he had not acted with the freedom of deliberation necessary for such a transaction to be binding.

More recently, in the Court of Appeal case of *Bank of Credit and Commerce International v Aboody* [1990] 1 QB 923, it was held that a husband had exerted actual undue influence over his wife to get her to sign a charge securing the family home on the debts owed by the family company in which the husband and wife owned shares. The couple were unable to repay the mortgage, and the bank sought to repossess the home. The wife attempted to have the mortgage set aside on the grounds that he had bullied her until she signed to get some peace. This was accepted by the court, although the defence failed on other grounds. More successfully, in *Daniel v Drew* [2005] EWCA Civ 507, the elderly Mrs Drew disliked confrontation, and was nervous, if not frightened, of her overbearing nephew. He told her to sign an agreement resigning from a family trust, under the threat of taking court action against her if she failed to do so. Mrs Drew signed, feeling cornered and unable to refuse. Again, it was held that there was actual undue influence.

## Presumed Undue Influence

In cases of presumed undue influence (and unlike actual undue influence) two factors must be present. First, there must be a relationship in which the presumption of influence arises, whether because it falls within a recognised and protected class or because it is established on the particular facts of the case. Second, there must be a transaction that calls for an explanation. In *Royal Bank of Scotland v Etridge No. 2* [2002] 1 AC 773, Lord Nicholls noted that once both have been established it will normally be sufficient, failing satisfactory evidence to the contrary, to discharge the burden of proof, "In other words, proof of these two facts is prima facie evidence that the defendant abused the influence he acquired in the parties' relationship ... the evidential burden then shifts to him. It is for him to produce evidence to counter the inference which otherwise should be drawn". This has been reiterated on numerous occasions since the landmark decision.

However, and complicating matters, the two factors are not hermetically sealed. Although a transaction that calls for an explanation will not, without more, be conclusive of a relationship of undue influence between donor/granter/maker and beneficiary, it will be a *factor* in deciding whether there was such a relationship when it was made, especially where it is extreme. As was observed in *Moursi v Doherty* [2019] EWHC 830 (Ch), they "reflect upon each other, since the greater the bounty which is conferred upon the disponee [the transaction calling for an explanation], the more likely it is that there was a relationship of trust and confidence".

Furthermore, the weight of the presumption will vary from case to case and depend both on the nature of the relationship and the value of the impugned transaction. As a result, the cogency of the evidence needed to rebut such a presumption will also vary. Thus, in *Moursi v Doherty*, it was also noted that, "The greater the disadvantage caused by the transaction, the more cogent must be the explanation before the presumption is rebutted". For example, because the presumption in *Allcard v Skinner* (1887) 36 Ch D 145 was very strong, given the rigid rules of the convent in which the donor resided, and the size of the donation, correspondingly strong evidence would have been required to rebut it.

Nevertheless, that a transaction might well have proceeded, in any event, without the undue influence, is irrelevant. In *Hewett v First Plus Financial Group* [2010] EWCA Civ 312, it was noted, "It has never been part of the proof of undue influence that, but for the relevant abuse of trust, the impugned transaction would not have been entered into. The right to set aside the transaction arises not because, on a but for causation analysis, it would otherwise have been avoided, but because the equitable wrong constituted by the abuse of confidence was part of the process by which the victim's consent to it was obtained".

## Protected/Recognised Relationships

As the House of Lords observed in *RBS v Etridge*, in certain protected relationships the "law presumes, irrebuttably, that one party has influence over the other." As already mentioned, for a time, these were called Class 2(a) cases. Amongst them are those of religious leader and acolyte, parent and child (until shortly after the latter comes of age), guardian and child, trustee and beneficiary, doctor and patient, lawyer and client, and (traditionally) a fiancé and his female betrothed (but not vice versa), although this last may now be challenged in light of changing social mores. In theory, the list is not closed, but it appears that no new relationship has been added in recent years. Thus, it has been held that the presumption does not apply to an accountant and his client, while in *Birmingham City Council v Janet Beech* [2014] EWCA Civ 830, the Court of Appeal decided that a relationship between a landlord's agent and a tenant under a contractual periodic tenancy was not inherently one of trust and confidence, such that a presumption of influence would automatically arise.

Perhaps strangely, there is not, and never has been, such a presumption between husband and wife, although the basis for the presumption applying to a fiancée, as Maugham J noted in *Re Lloyds Bank* [1931] 1 Ch 289, was that a young woman necessarily "reposes greatest confidence in her future husband, otherwise she would not marry him ... [and] would sign almost anything he put before her". Presumably, this would not apply once she was married! As was noted in *RBS v Etridge*: "It is now well established that husband and wife is not one of the relationships to which this latter principle applies".

By way of specific illustration, the position of spiritual leader and acolyte was considered in *Allcard v Skinner* (1887) 36 Ch D 145. In this historic case, a spinster in her late twenties sought a clergyman as her confessor. The following year she became an associate of an Anglican order of nuns of which he was spiritual director and, in 1871, took full vows of poverty, chastity, and obedience. Having done this, and without independent legal advice, she made very substantial gifts of her inherited money, stocks, and shares to the mother superior, to whom strict obedience was owed under the rules of the order, who received it on behalf of the wider sisterhood. However, the claimant left the convent in 1879 and subsequently became a Roman Catholic. In 1884, and keen to benefit her new Church, she asked for the return of any securities that had not been liquidated and the proceeds then spent. The following year, when they were not returned, she commended legal proceedings to recover them. It was held by the Court of Appeal that, had she brought such an action promptly after leaving the convent, and being freed from the undue influence of the mother superior, she would have succeeded, her gifts being voidable. However, in the instant case she had lost her right to recover them, because of her substantial delay.

In these situations, once the claimant has shown that he was in such a recognised relationship, influence is assumed, and all he must do is establish a transaction that calls for an explanation (see below) to create a presumption of undue influence. The onus is then on the defendant to show that this presumption has been rebutted. Although, as Lord Nicholls observed in *RBS v Etridge*, the law is "sternly protective" in such situations, it could be argued that there is a lack of intellectual coherence to the system of presumptive relationships. For example, why distinguish between wives and fiancées? In the case of an underage child, why should there be a presumption where the ascendant party is a parent, but not a very regularly seen grandparent? Nevertheless, the categories are well established.

## A Relationship of "Trust and Confidence"

The second form of presumed undue influence, what used to be referred to as Class 2(b), arises out of a relationship between two individuals in which one of them, on the particular facts of the case itself, has acquired a very high measure of influence, ascendancy, or dominance over the other. This is sometimes described as a relationship of "trust and confidence". Thus, in *RBS v Etridge*, Lord Nicholls noted that this part of the presumption would be established on proof that the complainant "placed trust and confidence in the other party in relation to the management of the complainant's financial affairs". As Buxton LJ noted in *Turkey v Awadh & Anor* [2005] EWCA Civ 382, this would "usually spring from a historic relationship between the parties of a general nature that precedes the impugned transaction". Indeed, it is very difficult to envisage a situation in which this would not be the case.

Many (but very far from all) examples of such cases are provided by spouses. Although there is no presumption of undue influence in cases involving wives (see above), the courts are well aware of the potential for abuse in marital relationships. As Dixon J observed in the Australian case of *Yerkey v Jones* (1939) 63 CLR 649, they are not blind to the opportunities open to a husband to obtain and exploit influence over his wife. Similarly, in *RBS v Etridge*, Lord Nicholls noted, following an older case, "Where there is evidence that a husband has taken unfair advantage of his influence over his wife, or her confidence in him, 'it is not difficult for the wife to establish her title to relief'".

Old and frail people have provided another major source of cases on undue influence, using the doctrine to set aside gifts, contracts, and guarantees which in hindsight were not in their best interests.[1] The elderly, especially those who are dependent on younger, fitter, or more alert relatives, friends, or employees, are likely to be susceptible to such a relationship taking root. For example, in *Re Craig (deceased)* [1971] Ch 95, an 84-year-old widower employed a much younger woman as his secretary and companion. After the start of their work relationship in January 1959 she held a position of trust, running the man's house and becoming intimately

1 Fiona Burns, "The elderly and undue influence inter vivos", *Legal Studies*, v. 23, no. 2 (2003), pp. 251-283.

involved in arranging his affairs. This lasted until the elderly man's death in August 1964. During this period, he gave her gifts worth £28,000 from his total assets of about £40,000. The High Court held that the gifts could not be accounted for by the normal motives by which men ordinarily act (i.e., they called for an explanation in modern parlance) and that the relationship between the two people involved such confidence being placed by the elderly Mr Craig in the woman as to place her in a position to exercise undue influence over him. She failed to rebut the resulting presumption. As a result, the gifts were set aside.

Similarly, in *Lloyd's Bank v Bundy* [1975] QB 326 a guarantee was given to a bank by an elderly farmer for his son's company's very pressing debts. Both were long-standing clients of the same bank and, more particularly, of one of its assistant managers. The assistant manager appreciated that Bundy senior relied on him solely and implicitly for financial advice. The guarantee was secured by placing a mortgage on Mr Bundy senior's house in favour of the bank. This was later extended at the bank's suggestion, although a solicitor (had he been consulted) would have advised Mr Bundy not to enter the transaction, as the house was his sole asset and his son's company was in a parlous state. The Court of Appeal set aside the guarantee and charge. The relationship between a banker and customer is not, *per se*, one in which undue influence is presumed, unlike that between lawyer and client. Nevertheless, Lord Denning held that, in the instant case, and on its facts, the relationship between the bank and the father was clearly one of trust and confidence.

Nevertheless, everything turns on the facts of the individual case. For example, and in contrast to *Re Craig (deceased)*, can be considered *Re Brocklehurst (deceased)* [1978] Ch 14. Sir Philip Brocklehurst was a slightly eccentric, very generous, and rather elderly man who had been educated at Eton and Cambridge, the latter of which he represented as an amateur boxer. He had had a successful period in the army during two world wars and been an Antarctic explorer, who was awarded the Polar Medal, as well as driving across the Sahara Desert in the 1930s. In his eighties he lived alone, and became friendly with the defendant, who owned a local garage, and with whom he shared a keen interest in field sports. Sir Philip wrote to the defendant saying that he wished to give him the shooting rights over his estate. He pressed the latter to instruct a solicitor to draw up a 99-year lease of such rights, which he then executed. This occasioned a major diminution in the freehold value of the estate. After Sir Philip died, his executors brought an action against the defendant, seeking to have the grant of the shooting rights set aside on the grounds of undue influence. The Court of Appeal rejected this and held that the nature of the relationship between Sir Philip and the defendant was not one of trust and confidence that would give rise to such a presumption. Instead, the evidence suggested that it was one of simple friendship. Indeed, it was the very forceful deceased who had tended to dominate the much less educated and socially advantaged defendant.

The physically and intellectually vulnerable were considered in the first-instance case of *Hackett v CPS & D Hackett* [2011] EWHC 1170 (Admin). The trial judge noted that the claimant was "deaf, dumb, barely educated and illiterate". Since the death of her husband, she had become reliant on the alleged influencer to manage her affairs and to care for her. As a result, she satisfied the burden of establishing that she had a relationship with the defendant from which a potential claim of presumed undue influence arose. Similarly, in *Smith v Cooper* [2010] EWCA Civ 722, the relationship between a man and a woman had quickly become one in which the former had complete ascendancy over the latter. This finding was assisted by the woman's vulnerable condition, especially her mental state (she acted in the legal proceedings by the Official Solicitor as her litigation friend), the man's awareness of this, and his decision to run her finances.

Physical vulnerability and age were combined in *Moursi v Doherty* [2019] EWHC 830 (Ch), where a claimant successfully had a transaction set aside on the basis of presumed undue influence. In this case, a widowed 78-year-old woman met the 33-year-old defendant when he did some gardening and repairs for her. They quickly formed a close friendship, and less than two years later the disputed transaction occurred. The elderly woman, who was on the cusp of dementia, thought the defendant was her boyfriend or fiancé (denied by Mr Doherty), consulted him on most matters, and telephoned him several times each day at the time the transaction occurred. Clearly, there was a relationship of trust and confidence.

However, it is certainly not just spouses and elderly or infirm people who become involved in relationships that fall into this category. For example, in *O'Sullivan v Management Agency & Music Ltd* [1985] QB 428, the claimant, Gilbert O'Sullivan, successfully sought to set aside a number of sole agency recording and publishing contracts he had entered as a very young musician and composer, on the grounds of undue influence. Similarly, in *Credit Lyonnais Bank Nederland NV v Burch* [1997] 1 All ER 144 Miss Burch had gone to work for an English-based Italian businessman, who was a decade older, when she was just 18 years of age. She became close to him, trusted him implicitly, often visited his home to do babysitting, and even went on holiday with his family to Italy. At the age of 21 she purchased a flat. Some years later, she was still working for him, but his company was experiencing financial difficulty. Mr Pelosi asked her to put up her flat as security for a loan taken out by the company. He told her that his home and villa in Italy were also secured on the debt, but that the bank would not accept a 100 per cent mortgage on these properties and needed another £20,000. She agreed to allow her home to be used as security, mistakenly believing that it was only for £20,000 and also that Mr Pelosi's properties would be sold first (so that there was no risk to her). The Court of Appeal held that the agreement of Miss Burch had been obtained by the exercise of undue influence. (How this affected the bank is discussed below). In like manner, in *Leeder v Stevens* [2005] EWCA Civ 50, a close, long-term, romantic relationship between a woman and her boyfriend, in which the former had been given a ring that she thought was almost analogous to an engagement pledge, was held to be one of trust and confidence. (Had they been engaged this would have been presumed). She had demonstrated this trust by allowing her boyfriend to draw up the deed that transferred half of her house to his name.

## A Transaction That Calls For An Explanation

There must be a basis for suggesting that the relationship of trust and confidence has been abused. This used to be expressed in terms of the need for a "manifest disadvantage" to the person against whom the alleged undue influence has been exercised. However, this had the potential to lead to confusion, particularly where a wife had some interest in her husband's business and guaranteed a loan in its favour. As a result, in the House of Lords case of *Royal Bank of Scotland v Etridge (No 2)* [2002] 2 AC 773, it was decided that the second prerequisite for establishing undue influence should be a "transaction that calls for explanation". This wording alluded to *Allcard v Skinner*, where Lindley LJ had observed that a questionable transaction was one that "cannot be reasonably accounted for on the ground of friendship, relationship, charity or other ordinary motives on which ordinary men act". This requires a transaction that appears inexplicable or irrational on the facts of any given case.

It is always a matter of degree. In *Turkey v Awadh* [2005] EWCA Civ 382, the Court of Appeal observed that a trial judge ought to exercise his common sense "to consider whether, given the circumstances and nature of the transaction, it says to the unbiased observer that absent explanation it must represent the beneficiary taking advantage of his position". Obviously, where the transaction is clearly not to the benefit of the vulnerable party but confers a major advantage on the party who is in a fiduciary position, this will be the case. Thus, in *Leeder v Stevens* [2005] EWCA Civ 50 the Court of Appeal noted that giving a boyfriend a half interest in a house worth £70,000 for just £5,000, something that also put her home at risk, was obviously the "sort of thing" which calls for an explanation. Indeed, it "cried out" for it.

Similarly, in *Hackett v CPS & D Hackett* [2011] EWHC 1170 (Admin), when considering whether a transaction--in this case, the gift of a house--called for an explanation, Silber J concluded that, even if the beneficiary was her son, any transaction by which the donee of a Power of Attorney subsequently obtains the gift of a substantial asset from the donor, "calls for some form of justification, especially if, as in this case, the donor is old, infirm, deaf and dumb and the donee himself organises the transaction".

By contrast, In the first instance decision of *Libya Investment Authority v Goldman Sachs International* [2016] EWHC 2530 (Ch) Rose J decided, *inter alia* (there were several other issues at trial), that a disputed transaction did not call for an explanation. The case involved trades made by Goldman Sachs on behalf of the

Libyan government. It was decided that Goldman Sachs' profits on these trades were commensurate with the work involved and so were not unconscionable. Much more mundanely, normal fees or modest Christmas gifts from a client to their doctor or solicitor will not be called into question. The status of larger but not enormous gifts might depend, in part, on the means of the donor. A gift of £10,000 by a billionaire to his religious leader would be very different from one for the same value by someone on who was on the breadline.

### Rebutting The Presumption of Undue Influence

Once a presumption has arisen, both prerequisites having been satisfied, someone accused of exercising undue influence may rebut it by demonstrating that the vulnerable party exercised free will when entering the transaction. However, and as was expressly noted in *Leeder v Stevens* [2005] EWCA Civ 50, this cannot be done simply by establishing that they knew what they were doing. This will always be the case. It is also irrelevant that they appeared happy with the transaction, even some time after it occurred. The question to ask is whether, at the time a woman (for example) entered the transaction, she was in a position where, "because of her vulnerability, financial and perhaps otherwise, she agreed to something which, if she had been fully alert in her own interest and advised by an independent adviser, she would not have done or may not have done".

As this suggests, free will is usually established by the defendant proving that the influenced party was made fully aware of the risks involved by receiving appropriate independent advice from a suitable third party *before* agreeing to the transaction. As was noted in *Coomber v Coomber* [1911] 1 Ch 723, "All that is necessary is that some independent person, free from any taint of the relationship, or of the consideration of interest which would affect the act, should put clearly before the person what are the nature and the consequences of the act".

In *practice*, as Buxton LJ observed in *Turkey v Awadh* [2005] EWCA Civ 382, this normally means that fully informed independent legal advice from a solicitor or other qualified legal adviser, given in the right circumstances, can be expected to bring home to the influenced party a proper understanding of the transaction, so that their "will [is] fully unconstrained", and so discharge the burden. Thus, in *Re Brocklehurst (deceased)* [1978] Ch 14, the court held that, even if there had been undue influence, contrary to their finding (see above), it had been rebutted by proof that Sir Philip had received independent legal advice. What this advice should entail was considered, in the context of third parties, in *Etridge* (see below). Nevertheless, in very general and simplistic terms, the solicitor and client should have a fully informed, face-to-face meeting, in the absence of the potential influencer, discussing the relevant transaction and its attendant documentation, with the former pointing out the seriousness of any risks, especially the "worst-case scenario".

However, that a lawyer was involved in some way will not, on its own, automatically have an emancipating effect. For example, in *Smith v Cooper* [2010] EWCA Civ 722, a vulnerable woman who was under the undue influence of a cohabiting man made several property disposals in the latter's favour within a relatively short time of their moving in together. The solicitor who had dealt with these disposals had been jointly instructed but had not spoken to the woman on her own. Although, as Lloyd LJ noted, he had advised quite competently in his capacity as the solicitor jointly representing two clients, "What he did not do, or purport to do, was to give any advice to Miss Cooper from her own separate point of view and for her own separate benefit. This is therefore not a case in which Miss Cooper had any independent advice". The Court of Appeal concluded that the presumption of undue influence had not been successfully rebutted.

To rebut the presumption, the lawyer instructed to advise in such cases should consider the specific state of the client, refusing to proceed if anything raises special concern, and taking extra precautions where necessary. For example, in *Hackett v CPS & D Hackett* [2011] EWHC 1170 (Admin) the High Court noted that, where the subject of alleged undue influence is suffering from a mental impairment the court must take special care to ensure the decision taken by the donor was really based on full, free, and informed thought. The trial judge cited the case of *Williams v Williams* [2003] WTLR 1371, where it was held that the presumption was not rebutted in the case of a claimant suffering from severe mental impairment, who was dependent on the defendant, even though it was accepted that he had been "independently advised and that advice would have brought [home] to an ordinary person the implications of what he was doing".

## A Case of Summary Judgment

Allegations of undue influence turn heavily on the evidence and, as such, are not commonly associated with summary judgment, where the claimant's case must be so overwhelming that a full trial is not considered justified. Nevertheless, one such case shows how presumptions can be used effectively to make out undue influence. In *Moursi v Doherty* [2019] EWHC 830 (Ch), an elderly woman sold the freehold of her home to a handyman for £70,000 and a declaration of trust on the property for her benefit for the rest of her life. Expert evidence subsequently established that the property was worth £191,500 when subject to the woman's life interest. This meant that she had sold at an undervalue of over £121,000. She had also given him a watch and bracelet that had belonged to her late husband that were, together, worth £63,800, and what appears to have been a significant amount of cash as gifts. The woman died five years later from pneumonia and dementia, with medical evidence suggesting that the latter may have been taking hold when the transaction occurred. After her death, her daughter, Mrs Moursi, received legal advice and sought to have the transaction set aside on the grounds of undue influence.

An application for summary judgment was heard by Master Price in the High Court. A relationship of trust and confidence and a transaction that called for an explanation were readily established in the instant case. The presumption this created then had to be rebutted by the defendant if the transaction was not to be set aside. Unfortunately for the defendant, the solicitors who acted for Mrs Gurney in the sale also acted for him and failed to advise her properly that the transaction was highly disadvantageous, despite knowing that the sale was at a severe undervalue. Further investigations revealed that the £70,000 purchase price for the house was, in part, derived from the settlement of previous litigation relating to property formerly owned by a 57-year-old woman with early onset dementia, who had "sold" her £375,000 property to Mr Doherty for £49,000. In the light of these factors, the Master decided that Mr Doherty had no realistic prospect of success at trial and therefore it was appropriate to undo the transaction and restore the house to the ownership of the dead woman's estate, which meant that it would go to Mrs Moursi.

### Third Parties and Undue Influence

In *Credit Lyonnais Bank Nederland NV v Burch* [1997] 1 All ER 144, a bank was held to be compromised by a third party's undue influence over Miss Burch. The bank had written to and informed her that the charge being placed on her property in favour of the third party was unlimited in amount and time and advised her to seek independent advice. However, at no time was she told of the extent of the third-party company's borrowings, which stood at £270,000, nor did the bank satisfy themselves that she had in fact received independent advice. It was held that the bank had constructive notice of the third party's undue influence, not least because the transaction was so obviously to her disadvantage. They had then taken insufficient steps to come "off notice". As a result, the transaction could be set aside.

In the leading case on this issue in the modern era, *Royal Bank of Scotland v Etridge (No 2)* [2002] 2 AC 773, the House of Lords considered undue influence in general, and the position of non-commercial third-party guarantors in particular. As the court noted, transactions secured by the latter are a regular feature of modern commercial life; finance raised by (second) mortgages on a principal borrower's home is a significant source of start-up capital for many small businesses in the UK. As a result, it is essential that banks can lend in these situations, confident that they can enforce the security provided for such loans. Nevertheless, guarantees of this type often carry grave risks, especially for borrowers' spouses/partners who are staking their (marital) homes on the outcome.

In *Etridge*, the House of Lords considered eight conjoined appeals in which homeowners had mortgaged their (share of a) property to a bank to secure a loan that was used by a husband for his business, where the wives had not *directly* and very clearly benefited from the transactions. The businesses had subsequently failed, and the wife had then alleged that she had been under undue influence when she signed the security agreement and argued that it should be void over her share of the matrimonial home's equity as a result, so that it could not be repossessed (and she could not be rendered homeless). This does not mean, of course, that the bank writes off the debt. It can still sue the husband as an unsecured creditor, even if this might not always be very fruitful.

As Lord Nicholls noted, the first issue for the courts to consider in such cases is whether the bank has been "put on inquiry", that is, given constructive notice as to the possibility that undue influence has been used to procure the guarantor's agreement. The threshold for satisfying this requirement is quite low. If a case involves securing a loan on a domestic home, where the loan would only *directly* benefit one person while the intended charge or guarantee is not, on its face, to the advantage of the co-owner, the lender is put on inquiry. It is not just wives who are covered; any non-commercial guarantor will fall into this situation: "The position is likewise if the husband stands surety for his wife's debts. Similarly, in the case of unmarried couples, whether heterosexual or homosexual, where the bank is aware of the relationship".

A bank will not be put on inquiry where money is being advanced to husband and wife jointly, unless the bank is aware that the loan is being made for the husband's purposes, as distinct from their joint purposes: *Conoco Ltd v Khan & Khan* [1996] EWCA Civ 968. What if a guarantor has some other involvement in the business activity of the debtor? *Etridge* makes clear that the wife does not have to be an entirely passive party in her husband's business to receive protection. Where she becomes surety for the debts of a company in which she has an equal shareholding with her spouse, or where she is a director or secretary of the company, a bank can *still* be put on inquiry. Such cases cannot be equated with joint loans, if only because shareholding interests, and the identity of the directors, are not necessarily a reliable guide to real control of the company.

Once on notice or inquiry, the bank must take certain steps to avoid being tainted by possible undue influence and so "come off notice". Essentially, to have an enforceable security they must have ensured that the spouse or other non-commercial guarantor has received proper independent legal advice before entering the agreement. Although this can be provided by a private meeting between the bank's representative and the guarantor, *Etridge* recognised that banks would usually prefer that this be done by a suitably briefed solicitor, acting for the wife, who then provides the bank with written confirmation that the risks of the transaction have been properly explained. As Lord Nicholls noted, "The furthest a bank can be expected to go is to take reasonable steps to satisfy itself that the wife has had brought home to her, in a meaningful way, the practical implications of the proposed transaction. This does not wholly eliminate the risk of undue influence or misrepresentation. But it does mean that a wife enters into a transaction with her eyes open so far as the basic elements of the transaction are concerned". Provided the banks ensured that the wife had received such independent advice, they could not be held responsible if it was defective. Instead, in these situations, the possibility of a professional negligence action by the wife against the solicitor or his insurers would arise. However, this would be a personal action, and would not help her remain in the family home.

In these situations, the bank should communicate directly with the wife, informing her that for its own protection it required written confirmation from a solicitor, acting on her behalf, that the effect and practical implications of the documents that she was being asked to sign had been fully explained to her. Before advising, it was necessary that the solicitor be given full particulars concerning the borrower's account, such as the purpose of the new facility, the borrower's current level of indebtedness and the amount of their overdraft facility, and the amount and terms of any new borrowing. They must also supply a copy of the borrower's application form. If the bank fails to provide the requisite information, the solicitor should decline to provide them with any form of confirmation. The solicitor's discussion with the wife should take place at a lengthy face-to-face meeting, in the absence of the husband (or vice versa if appropriate) and be couched in non-technical language.

Lord Nicholls identified a core minimum of advice that a solicitor in such situations should convey. Thus, it would include the fact that the bank, if it became necessary, would rely on the solicitor's involvement to counter any suggestion that the client did not properly understand the implications of the transaction. It would explain the nature of the documents and the serious consequences they would have for the wife if she signed them--for example, that she could lose her home if her husband's business failed. As part of this advice, the wife should be told the purpose and size of the proposed new facility and the nature of its other major terms. She should also be told the precise amount of her liability under the guarantee. Furthermore, the solicitor should discuss the wife's financial means, including her understanding of the value of the property being charged and whether the wife or her husband had any other assets out of which repayment could be made if the husband's business failed (these matters being relevant to the seriousness of the risks involved).

The solicitor would need to state clearly to the wife that she had a choice as to whether to proceed or abandon the transaction altogether, this decision being hers alone, and should carefully check that she was content for him to write to the bank confirming that he had advised her. Alternatively, she might prefer him to negotiate with the bank on the terms of the transaction, in which case this would be done. The advice provided should be recorded in a full attendance note and confirmed in detail in a letter sent promptly after the meeting. (A suitable draft letter covering these points is now provided as a template by the Law Society).

Lord Nicholls also considered what he termed the "much-vexed question" as to whether the solicitor advising the wife must act for her alone. He felt that, in the right circumstances, the solicitor could be the same lawyer as the one acting for her husband (arranging the loan). However, the wife should be expressly asked if she would prefer a different solicitor. Vitally, to avoid the risk of a conflict of interest, the lawyer must advise the wife in private, in the absence of her husband, and remember that when doing so it is the guarantor (and not the borrower) who is the client, and to whom their professional duty is owed. In many situations, it would be easier, albeit more expensive, for a separate solicitor, uninvolved in the loan, to represent the wife.

Although the *Etridge* principles have sometimes been criticised for creating a tick-box approach to liability and legal advice, it is at least arguable that they make a reasonable attempt at balancing fairness with commercial reality.

# Chapter 11: Frustration and *Force Majeure*

## The Absolute Obligation Rule/Rule in *Paradine v Jane*

The starting point to understanding the doctrine of frustration is to consider the rule to which it provides an exception, the so-called absolute obligation rule. An influential historical illustration of this rule can be seen in *Paradine v Jane* [1647] Alleyn 26, which has also given its name (as an alternative) to the same rule. In this case, the claimant, Paradine, leased farmland to the defendant, Jane, and brought an action against him for arrears of rent. The defendant advanced as a defence for his non-payment that the land had been occupied by enemy (Royalist) troops during the English Civil War. As a result, his cattle had been driven off, and he had been forcibly expelled from the farm, making it impossible to earn any income from which to pay the rent. The court rejected this as a valid excuse. Where a party has a contractual duty, he is normally bound to perform it, notwithstanding any untoward event that might occur, not least because he could have put a clause in the contract covering such an eventuality (what is often now termed a *force majeure* clause). The defendant was in breach of contract if he failed to pay his rent on time as required under the agreement.

Nevertheless, in practice, the rule in *Paradine v Jane* was not *always* applied, even in the seventeenth and eighteenth centuries. It was accepted that certain supervening events did bring agreements to an end, even if they had not been provided for in the contract, so that the harshness of the absolute obligation rule was alleviated. For example, in contracts of personal service it was always accepted that the estates of those engaged could not be sued for their apparent breach of contract in dying before fulfilling their obligations, as can be seen from the facts of *Cutter v Powell* [1795] 101 ER 573.

More generally, in *Hartley v Ponsonby* [1857] 7 EB 872, after almost half of a ship's crew deserted on a voyage, and only six of the remaining men were able seamen, it was held that the crew were entitled to negotiate new contracts because the voyage had become so dangerous that it had discharged the original agreement. Similarly, in *Avery v Bowden* (1856) 5 E & B 714, a ship was contracted to pick up cargo at Odessa. With the outbreak of the Crimean War in 1853, the Government made it illegal to load cargo at an enemy port (Russia in this context), so the ship could not perform its contract without breaking the law. As a result, the contract was deemed to have been brought to an automatic end. These cases might be seen as tacit examples of frustration, even if the word was not used, and other explanations, such as recourse to implied terms, may have been advanced.

### *Taylor v Caldwell*

However, although there were several specific situations in which a supervening event was held to have discharged a contract, it was not until the case of *Taylor v Caldwell* [1863] 3 B&S 826 that there was a judicial attempt at producing an overarching legal doctrine that would govern all such cases and decide when a contract was "frustrated". In this case, the claimant contracted to hire a music hall and its surrounding grounds from the defendant for four days to hold a series of concerts and outdoor entertainments. However, before these could take place, the music hall was destroyed by fire, neither party being held to be at fault for this.

The claimant sued for breach of contract, the breach being the unavailability of the hall. Under the doctrine of absolute obligations, the defendants would still be liable. Even so, Mr Justice Blackburn noted the potential harshness of this rule and held that the defendant was released from their obligations by the doctrine of "frustration". The court further noted that a contract might be frustrated where its "performance depends on the continued existence of a given person or thing [in which case] a condition is implied that the impossibility of performance arising from the perishing of the person or thing shall excuse the performance". However, and importantly, the judge also noted that an express contractual term, providing that, even in the light of such an event, the parties' obligations were to continue, would take precedence over frustration.

The onus is on the party seeking to rely on a frustrating event to establish that it has occurred. In practice, the courts usually consider the issue when one party to a contract (the defendant) claims that there has been such an event, one that excuses their non-performance of obligations under the agreement, but the other party (the claimant) does not accept this and sues for breach of contract.

It should be stressed immediately that frustration has been narrowly construed and applied, so that it is only rarely successful when advanced in court. As Lord Roskill observed in *The Nema* [1982] AC 724, the doctrine is "not lightly to be invoked to relieve contracting parties of the normal consequences of imprudent bargains". In its absence, the "normal" position remains that parties are strictly liable for the performance of their contractual obligations.

## Rationale and Test

As the quotation from Blackburn J suggests, the justification adopted in *Taylor v Caldwell* for the expanded notion of frustration was to say that the parties had, themselves, intended that there be an "implied" condition that the contract should terminate if their adventure was frustrated by such an extrinsic event.[1] During the twentieth century, this was increasingly viewed as a fiction, and doubted as a sensible rationale for the doctrine, with the open acknowledgement of judicial intervention occurring in certain situations to prevent unjust results as a better explanation for its presence: *Davis Contractors Ltd v Fareham UDC* [1956] AC 696. Thus, in *The Eugenia* [1964] 2 QB 226 Lord Denning MR thought that the position was reasonably clear: "...if it should happen, in the course of carrying out a contract, that a fundamentally different situation arises for which the parties made no provision--so much so that

1 SJ Stoljar, *History of Contract at Common Law* (Canberra: Australian National University Press, 1975), p. 195.

it would not be just in the new situation to hold them bound to its terms--then the contract is at an end".

What then should the test be for a frustrating event? In *Canary Wharf v European Medicines Agency* [2019] EWHC 335 (Ch), Marcus Smith J identified two earlier attempts at framing a general test for frustration which, he felt, had stood the test of time. In *Davis Contractors Ltd v Fareham UDC* [1956] AC 696, Lord Radcliffe had suggested that "frustration occurs whenever the law recognises that without default of either party a contractual obligation has become incapable of being performed because the circumstances in which performance is called for would render it a thing radically different from that which was undertaken by the contract".

Another formulation that received Smith J's approval, and one that was enunciated in rather fuller terms, was set out by Lord Simon in *National Carriers Ltd v Panalpina (Northern) Ltd* [1981] AC 675: "Frustration of a contract takes place where there supervenes an event (without default of either party and for which the contract makes no sufficient provision) which so significantly changes the nature (not merely the expense or onerousness) of the outstanding contractual rights and/or obligations from what the parties could reasonably have contemplated at the time of its execution that it would be unjust to hold them to the literal sense of its stipulations in the new circumstances: in such case, the law declares both parties to be discharged from further performance".

The strictness of the test for frustration helps explain why it is only rarely encountered in practice. Another reason is that the doctrine will not apply where the parties themselves have provided for the relevant event. As Lord Denning MR observed in *The Eugenia*, in these situations, the "contract must govern. There is no frustration". This is usually done by including what are termed *force majeure* (literally superior force) clauses in the contract. These are ubiquitous in modern commercial agreements and so worthy of detailed consideration.

### *Force Majeure* Clauses

*Force majeure* clauses alter the parties' obligations under a contract when an unusual event, beyond their reasonable control, prevents or severely hinders one or (less commonly) both from fulfilling their contractual duties. Where operative, such a clause will excuse non-performance or, alternatively, regulate performance, in situations that might otherwise lead to the non-performing party being liable for a breach of contract (unless the doctrine of frustration could be invoked). Frequently, the effect of a *force majeure* clause will be to excuse a party from further performance of a contract, either in full or in part, for the time that *force majeure* is operative--unlike frustration which automatically ends a contract--or allow them to bring the agreement to an end without being in breach of contract for doing so.

At common law, and unlike some Roman law systems (it originated as a civil law concept), there is no single definition of *force majeure*. Ideally, such clauses would always be carefully and individually negotiated and tailored to suit the particular contract. In practice, they are often contained in so-called boilerplate clauses and sometimes receive only a modest degree of consideration before being added to an agreement. As a result, they can fail for uncertainty and vagueness, as was the situation in *British Electrical and Associated Industries (Cardiff) Ltd v Patley Pressings Ltd* [1953] 1 WLR 280, although this is rare.

Occasionally, such a clause might simply refer to "*force majeure*" without any further elaboration as to what this means. Although it is not a term of art in English law, in which the words carry a precise legal meaning, there is an exposition of what such a phrase might entail in *Lebeaupin v Richard Crispin & Co* [1920] 2 KB 714, where the court held that it went beyond a simple natural disaster or "Act of God", so that an epidemic might fall within its ambit. In this case, McCardie J also observed that a *force majeure* clause should be construed "with a close attention to the words which precede or follow it, and with a due regard to the nature and general terms of the contract".

Nevertheless, the words *force majeure* (if employed) are rarely unqualified, and many such clauses are very specific, containing a long list of events that will come within its ambit, such as war, public disorder, insurrection, pandemics (like Covid-19), epidemics, industrial action, flood, fire, and, of course, "Acts of God". So, for example, and to consider this last stipulation, where present, if an earthquake shuts down a port, someone contracted to ship goods through that facility might not be liable for their late delivery because of the natural disaster. Conversely, even very specific *force majeure* clauses often follow a list of events with a general clause, such as "or any other causes beyond our control", so that the list is not treated as exhaustive.

Furthermore, such clauses do not have to use the words "*force majeure*" to be effective. For example, they might merely provide that neither party will be in breach by reason of any failure or delay in the performance of any obligation under the contract where, for example, this "arises out of any cause beyond the reasonable control and without the fault or negligence of such party". As this suggests, such clauses will also usually specify that the designated event must hinder, prevent, or delay a party's ability to perform their contractual obligations. Sometimes, a specific time is given for this to be operative. For example, in *European Professional Club Rugby v RDA Television LLP* [2022] EWHC 50 (Comm), the High Court held that a broadcaster could terminate a media rights agreement relating to rugby union competitions in Europe as a result of the postponement of the final stages of the 2019-20 season due to Covid-19. The *force majeure* clause had expressly referred to this occurring where the effects of an "epidemic" hindered or delayed performance for a period of more than 60 days. (The court also noted that a party's motive in relying on such a clause, if it could be established, was irrelevant.)

Occasionally, a *force majeure* event might even be defined as one that "cannot be overcome by reasonable endeavours", as was the situation in *MUR Shipping BV v RTI Ltd* [2022] EWCA Civ 1406. This case involved a contract for the shipment of bauxite from Guinea to Ukraine. The Court of Appeal held (Arnold LJ dissenting) that MUR should accept payment in Euros, instead of the contractually agreed American Dollars, after the USA imposed sanctions on RTI's Russian parent company that prevented it from accepting payment in the latter currency. Males LJ held that a problem might be deemed to have been overcome if its adverse consequences were avoided and the contract's purpose was achieved. This was the situation in the instant case, especially as RTI was willing to bear any losses occasioned by converting Euros to Dollars. As a result, MUR could not rely on the *force majeure* clause to avoid or suspend the contract.

As with exemption clauses, it is for the party seeking to rely on a *force majeure* clause to show that the relevant event falls within its terms, and such clauses are usually interpreted narrowly by the courts. Thus, in *Classic Maritime Inc v Limbungan Makmur SDN BHD* [2019] EWCA Civ 1102, a *force majeure* clause provided that a charterer would not be liable for any failure to deliver a cargo "resulting from" an event that "directly affected" its performance of its contractual obligations. It was held that the charterer would be able to rely on the clause only if it could prove that, but for the relevant event, it would have fulfilled those obligations.

For another example of strict interpretation can be considered *2 Entertain Video Ltd & Ors v Sony DADC Europe Ltd* [2020] EWHC 972 (TCC), which involved a contractual dispute relating to the 2011 riots in London, during which a warehouse, owned by the defendant, in which the claimant had stored CDs and DVDs, had been looted and burned down and its contents destroyed or stolen. The agreement contained a clause stating that, "Neither party shall be liable for its failure or delay in performing any of its obligations hereunder if such failure or delay is caused by circumstances beyond the reasonable control of the party affected including but not limited to industrial action (at either party), fire, flood, wars, armed conflict, terrorist act, riot, civil commotion, malicious damage, explosion, unavailability of fuel, pandemic or governmental or other regulatory action".

Sony, the defendant, argued that the damage to their warehouse was a *force majeure* event under this clause (fire, riot, or civil commotion), so that they were not liable. However, the High Court found that they had failed to use reasonable skill and care to protect the contents of the warehouse, and so could not rely on the clause. The Court found that, had it acted reasonably, it could have prevented the conflagration. Although the riots were unforeseen and unprecedented, the risk of intruders was foreseeable, because there had been previous break-ins to the warehouse, while the danger of arson should also have been anticipated. If Sony had taken adequate security and fire-safety measures, the attack on the warehouse would probably have been deterred or at least delayed, and any damage significantly reduced.

If they fail to establish that a *force majeure* clause extends to the specific circumstances that have arisen, parties will have to rely on frustration (which might be difficult if *force majeure* does not apply) if they are to avoid liability for breach of contract, the prerequisites for which common law doctrine will be considered next.

## The Prerequisites for Frustration

Strict prerequisites must be met before a contract is deemed to be discharged by frustration, something that explains why it is so rarely advanced successfully as a defence in court. In particular, the risk of the frustrating event must be unallocated and unforeseen, cannot be self-induced, and must do more than make performance of the contract more onerous. These will be dealt with in turn.

## Unallocated and Unforeseen

Frustration can arise only where the contract cannot be said to have expressly or impliedly allocated the risk of the frustrating event to one of the parties to the agreement: *The Sea Angel* [2007] EWCA Civ 547. For example, in *Wilmington Trust SP Services (Dublin) Ltd v SpiceJet Ltd* [2021] EWHC 1117 (Comm), the claimant sought unpaid rent that was due under the leases on three Boeing aircraft that had been taken out by Spice Jet Ltd. The defendant argued that the restrictions on its use of the aircraft occasioned by the Covid pandemic and the mandatory grounding of Boeing 737 Max aircraft following fatal crashes resulted in their contract with Wilmington being frustrated. In principle, in the right circumstances, the High Court agreed that these circumstances *might* have given rise to frustration. However, in the instant case, the leases included a clause which expressly provided that the defendant's obligation to pay rent would be absolute and unconditional, irrespective of, amongst other things, the unavailability of the aircraft. As a result, SpiceJet had assumed the "entire commercial risk of operating the aircraft" including that of the aircraft being grounded.

Irrespective of such express provisions, the more likely a supervening extrinsic event is to occur at the time the contract is made, that is, the more it has been foreseen, the less likely it is to be viewed as frustrating, and the more likely it is that the courts will conclude that the risk has been impliedly allocated between the parties. However, as Rix LJ noted in *The Sea Angel*, foreseeability is a matter of degree, while even foreseeable events can occur to an unforeseeable degree. Nevertheless, the "less that an event, in its type and its impact, is foreseeable, the more likely it is to be a factor which, depending on other factors in the case, may lead on to frustration". This issue had earlier been considered by Lord Denning MR in *The Eugenia* [1964] 2 QB 226. He noted that although it was frequently said that the doctrine of frustration only applied when the new situation was "unforeseen" or "uncontemplated", what was vital was that the parties had made no provision for it. If the parties did not foresee anything of that kind happening, "you can readily infer that they have made no provision for it. Whereas, if they foresaw it, one would expect them to make provision for it". It should be noted that such provision might be express or implied.

For example, if someone contracts with an architect (purely) to design an extension for his house, and then fails in his application to secure planning permission, the courts are likely to say that there was always a strong possibility of this occurring, as gaining such permission is known not to be a formality. The person employing the architect assumed the risk that this might happen, and so cannot claim that his contract with the architect is frustrated by the refusal of such permission. Similarly, contracts entered *after* the arrival of the coronavirus began to be widely publicised (but before it declined in effect) are unlikely to have been frustrated by Covid because the courts are likely to conclude that the inability to perform by reason of the disease was foreseeable and the risk (impliedly) allocated.

More specifically, in *The Flying Music Company v Theatre Entertainment* [2017] EWHC 3192 (QB), the High Court had to consider whether a contract to stage Michael Jackson's "Thriller Live" in Greece had been frustrated by civil unrest. The contract had been negotiated in April and May 2010, and signed in the latter month, with performances to take place in June that same year. The months of May and June 2010 had been a period of acute civil unrest in Greece due to the financial crisis. Ticket sales for performances were very poor as a result, and the end of the run was cancelled. Theater Entertainment claimed that the contract had been frustrated by the unrest, so that TFMC should lose their right to claim for the outstanding payments under their agreement. However, the evidence showed that the situation in Greece was already bad when the contract was signed. According to Greek police reports, the civil unrest was no worse in June than it had been in May, meaning that the frustrating event had not occurred *after* the contract had been formed. Although the situation did not improve, the prolongation of the existing bad state of affairs did not amount to the "radically different" circumstances required for a frustrating event. As the judge observed, Thessaloniki and Athens had already erupted while, "The parties both knew enough about the risks that this posed to the success of the production for it to be wrong, now, with the benefit of hindsight, to re-allocate those risks by releasing the Theater Entertainment from its Contract obligations. ... To say that things did not improve is not to say that they got worse, or even changed. If a bad situation becomes protracted, the consequences may be increased by the passage of time. But that does not mean that there has been a frustrating event".

Similarly, in *Armchair Answercall Limited v People in Mind Limited* [2016] EWCA Civ 1039, the Court of Appeal refused to find that a contract had been frustrated. In part, this was because the alleged frustrating event (refusal of franchisees to agree to a defendant's changes in their relationship with the latter) and the effect that this had on a contract between the defendant and claimant should have been foreseen by the parties. It had always been recognised that the franchisees might object to the changes and could not be forced to accept them. In like manner, one of the reasons (there were several others) that Brexit did not constitute a frustrating event in *Canary Wharf v European Medicines Agency* [2019] EWHC 335 (Ch) was that the issue of the UK's continued membership of the European Union was on the political agenda at the time that they entered the lease.

## The Frustrating Event Cannot Be Self-Induced

The allegedly frustrating event must be the fault of neither party. More pertinently, it cannot have been brought about, whether deliberately or negligently, by the party who seeks to rely on it. The rules on this issue are strict. Thus, any element of choice or "election" in the events that are advanced as constituting frustration will very likely preclude the doctrine's operation: *Maritime National Fish Ltd. v Ocean Trawlers Ltd.* [1935] AC 524. In this Privy Council case, Maritime National Fish contracted to hire the *St. Cuthbert* steam trawler, which was fitted with an 'otter trawl' (a large net used for cod), from Ocean Trawlers Ltd. for a year, to add to its fleet of such vessels. The use of such a trawler and net without a special licence was illegal. Subsequently, Maritime National Fish applied for five licences from the Canadian government for the five trawlers they were using or planning to use. However, only three were granted. Maritime National Fish did not name the *St. Cuthbert* as one of the licensed vessels, preferring to grant the three licences to vessels it owned, and then refused to go through with the hire, on the grounds that the contract to do so was frustrated by their failure to secure the two extra licences. This was rejected by the Privy Council. Maritime National Fish had not been bound to grant the licences to the other trawlers in preference to the *St. Cuthbert.* The latter vessel could have been amongst the three trawlers licensed, noting that: "The essence of 'frustration' is that it should not be due to the act or election of the party".

More recently, and even more harshly, in *Lauritzen A.S. v Wijsmuller B.V. (The Super Servant Two)* [1990] 1 Lloyd's Rep 1, the Court of Appeal held that a contract was not frustrated where there had been another forced election. In this case, the claimants were the owners of a drilling rig that the defendants agreed to transport from Japan to Rotterdam using either one of two specialist carrying ships, *The Super Servant One* or the *Super Servant Two*. The defendants decided to use the second vessel, as the first ship was being used for other contracts. However, in July 1981 the *Super Servant Two* was sunk, through no fault of the defendants, while transporting another rig. The defendants argued that the contract had been frustrated as they could not transport the drilling rig without breaking another contract, for which the surviving *Super Servant* was being used. Even so, the Court of Appeal ruled that the defendants could not rely on frustration as the element of election meant that it was self-induced. Of course, had the contract expressly stipulated that the *Super Servant Two* be used, its (non-negligent) sinking would have frustrated the agreement, as was the case with a named vessel, the *Orlando*, that was damaged prior to carrying a cargo of cotton seed from Egypt to England in *Nicholl and Knight v Ashton, Eldridge & Co* [1901] 2 KB 126.

Negligence can have the same effect when it comes to preventing frustration from operating. In *Taylor v Caldwell* Blackburn J stressed that the evidence at trial indicated that the fire that frustrated the relevant contract had occurred "without the fault of either party". By contrast, in *The Eugenia* [1964] 2 QB 226, an example of self-inducement occasioned by negligence was rejected as a frustrating event.

In this case, the Suez Canal became a "dangerous zone" during the Suez Crisis of 1956, even as the vessel, carrying a cargo of steel from Odessa to India, sailed towards it. Despite this, the charterers, in breach of a clause in the contract saying that dangerous zones should be avoided, sailed to Port Said, thinking that they could still make it through the canal. The ship was impounded when the canal was closed. The owners of the steel claimed that the charterers' failure to deliver the cargo was a breach of contract, while the latter alleged, *inter alia*, that the contract was frustrated by the impoundment. The Court of Appeal, Lord Denning presiding, held that there was no frustration on this issue. The seizure of the vessel was self-induced, as it had unnecessarily sailed into an area of conflict rather than choosing the safer option of sailing round the Cape of Good Hope, and "that was their own fault".

It should be noted that although the defendant has the onus of establishing that he has experienced what is, *prima facie*, a frustrating event, once he has done so, it is for the claimant to establish that it was occasioned by their negligence or default and so is not operative. This is necessary, as Lord Simon LC observed, to avoid the defendant having to prove a negative (that he had not been negligent), something that is inherently very difficult: *Joseph Constantine Steamships Line v Imperial Smelting Corporation* [1942] AC 154. In this case an explosion at sea rendered a vessel inoperable. The explosion may, or may not, have been occasioned by negligence, but this could not be proved one way or the other, so that the burden of proof became vital. It was held by the House of Lords that, since the claimant could not prove that it had been caused by negligence, while the defendant could establish that an explosion (a *prima facie* frustrating event) had occurred, the contract was discharged for frustration.

## Onerousness

A contract will not be frustrated simply because it has become much more costly or onerous to perform (within reasonable bounds). Thus, in *Davis Contractors Ltd v Fareham Urban District Council* [1956] AC 696, Davis contracted with Fareham Council to build 78 houses for £92,425. The expected cost to the builder was around £86,000. However, their construction took many months longer than anticipated, through no fault of either party and cost far more, some £115,000. This was due to a national shortage, and an attendant increase in the price of, both skilled labour and building materials. Davis had made a bad bargain but sought to extricate themselves from it by arguing that this drastic increase in cost rendered the contract frustrated, so that they were entitled to a *quantum meruit* award (as much as it deserved) for the value of the work that they had completed, rather than the sum they had agreed to. The House of Lords rejected this argument. Although the performance of the building contract had become more onerous, it was not impossible or pointless, and so was not frustrated. In Lord Radcliffe's words, "it is not hardship or inconvenience or material loss itself which calls the principle of frustration into play. There must be as well such a change in the significance of the obligation that the thing undertaken would, if performed, be a different thing from that contracted for".

It was for the same reason that most of the shipping contracts affected by the closure of the Suez Canal during the 1956 crisis were not frustrated. For example, in *Tsakiroglou & Co Ltd v Noblee Thorl GmbH* [1962] AC 93, a carrier planned to use the Suez Canal to fulfil his contract to ship Sudanese ground nuts to Europe, but this was not expressly stipulated in the agreement. The canal was closed after the contract was signed. Nevertheless, an alternative route existed, around the Cape of Good Hope, albeit one that took over twice as long to complete, in potentially rougher seas, and so was very much more expensive. The carrier failed in his argument that the closure of the canal meant that the contract was frustrated. Of course, if the contract had expressly stipulated that the Suez Canal be used or had involved the shipment of a commodity that would necessarily perish over a longer journey than that through the canal, even if it did not, the situation would have been different. In one of the other cases where it was held that a vessel could have gone round the Cape of Good Hope, *The Eugenia* [1964] 2 QB 226, the goods being carried were iron and steel bars and so not perishable.

Similarly, in *United International Pictures v Cine Bes Filmcheck VE Yapimcilik AS* [2003] EWHC 798 (Comm), the defendant had agreed to pay licence fees to the claimant in US dollars backed by a letter of credit. It was argued that the contract had been frustrated when the Turkish government withdrew from the Crawling Peg Exchange Rate Mechanism (CPERM), which had tied the Turkish lira to a basket of currencies, causing a huge fall in the value of the lira and making it very much harder for Turkish companies to obtain letters of credit for US dollars. This was rejected, in part because the effect of withdrawal from CPERM was simply to make the cost to the defendant more onerous. More recently, in *Tandrin Aviation Holdings Ltd v Aero Toy Store LLC* [2010] EWHC 40 (Comm), Hamblen J reiterated, in passing, that a severe downturn in economic or market circumstances, affecting the profitability of a contract, or the ease with which the parties' obligations can be performed, was not to be regarded as a frustrating event.

A selection of cases in which frustration has been held to be operative or, alternatively, has been rejected, provide illustrations of the doctrine's reach and limitations.

### Impossible or Pointless to Perform

Unsurprisingly, something that renders a contract impossible of performance is likely to constitute a frustrating event. In *Taylor v Caldwell* [1863] 3 B&S 826, it was impossible to use the music hall, as it had burned down (although the gardens might still have been employed). Nevertheless, subsequent cases have made it clear that frustration extends to events that make performance of the contract pointless, albeit not physically impossible.

For example, in *Krell v Henry* [1903] 2 KB 740 the defendant contracted to use the claimant's flat overlooking Pall Mall for the purpose of viewing King Edward VII's magnificent coronation procession as it passed by, at a price of £75 for two days. (He paid £25 in advance). Due to the King's sudden illness, the coronation and its attendant procession were cancelled, so that the defendant did not use the flat. The claimant then sought to claim the outstanding £50. He failed, as it was held that the contract was frustrated, because cancellation of the procession had deprived it of its commercial purpose. It was not impossible to carry out the agreement: the defendant could still have spent two days in the flat watching London buses go by.

However, pointlessness is a matter of degree. Thus, a different decision was reached in *Herne Bay Steam Boat Co v Hutton* [1903] 2 KB 683, in which the defendant had engaged the steamboat Cynthia from the claimant to take passengers from Herne Bay on June 28 and 29 1902 "for the purpose of viewing the naval review at Spithead and for a day's cruise round the fleet". On June 25 the review was cancelled due to the King's illness. Although the Cynthia was ready to start on the due date, the defendant repudiated the contract. The claimants sought to recover the money less the profit they made using the ship for other purposes during the relevant two days (they had "mitigated" their loss). The contract was not held to have been frustrated. In part this was because the naval review before the King was not the sole basis of the agreement; the fleet was still anchored at Spithead, and it was still possible to cruise around it, as well as spending time at sea, so that the contract had not become entirely pointless of performance. The fact that Mr Hutton was an entrepreneur acting in a business capacity, unlike Mr Henry, may also have influenced the decision.

More recently, frustration was considered in *Canary Wharf v European Medicines Agency* [2019] EWHC 335 (Ch). In this case, the EU's European Medicines Agency (EMA), which then had its headquarters in London, had taken a 25-year lease for their new HQ on a building in Canary Wharf in London. However, in 2016 the UK voted to leave the European Union (EU). In August 2017 the EMA wrote to its landlords stating that it would treat Brexit as a frustration of the lease, as their HQ would have to be transferred to a country that would remain within the EU. Nevertheless, the EMA's claim to frustration was rejected by the High Court. The court noted that, in a lease of that length, they would be expected to have considered that some change might occur over its course. Furthermore, the EU *could* (quite legally) maintain the headquarters of its agencies in third countries, albeit that there may have been many non-legal reasons why it would not wish to do so. Additionally, the EMA's subsequent subletting of the space (as permitted under their lease) showed the contract was merely more difficult rather than impossible or illegal to perform. The EMA's obligations--to pay rent and maintain the building--would not change merely because of Brexit.

Arguably, the decision in *Canary Wharf* was anticipated in *London and Northern Estates Company v Schlesinger* [1916] 1 KB 20, in which an Austrian who was an enemy alien during the First World War was prohibited by a wartime Order in Council from residing in an area where he had already leased premises. His claim that the tenancy was frustrated as a result was unsuccessful. Although he could not personally occupy it, he could sublet the premises so that the performance of the contract was not impossible. More generally, it is well established that a long lease of this type will rarely be frustrated (see below).

## Supervening Illegality and the Effect of Government Action

Government action can make performance of a contract illegal or (effectively) impossible, and this will normally constitute a frustrating event. For example, in *Fibrosa Spolka v Fairbairn* [1943] AC 32, an English company that manufactured machinery contracted in July 1939 to supply some of its products to a Polish company, for delivery towards the end of the same year. In September, Germany invaded Poland, and Britain went to war with the former country. Poland was overrun and on 23 September, Orders in Council made Poland an enemy territory so that it became illegal for British companies to trade with it. Unsurprisingly, it was held that the contract was frustrated.

To consider a less obvious situation, in 1914 the Metropolitan Water Board entered a contract for the construction of a reservoir, which was to be completed within six years. In early 1916, during the First World War, the contractors were required to cease work as a result of the Defence of the Realm Act, so that the men and materials employed in the venture could be used for the war effort. The House of Lords agreed with the contractors that the contract was frustrated on the grounds of supervening impossibility; the government order might last until the end of the conflict, and this was indeterminate: *Metropolitan Water Board v Dick, Kerr & Co. Ltd* [1918] AC 119.

Of course, government action, like sickness (see below), can also result in the unavailability of a particular person, so frustrating an employment contract. For example, in 1938 a music-hall artist entered a ten-year exclusive management contract with the claimant, agreeing to pay the latter a certain percentage of his earnings. He was subsequently conscripted into the army in 1940, following the outbreak of the Second World War, serving until the start of 1946. Towards the end of this period, he entered performing contracts without the claimant's involvement. It was held that his conscription for the wartime years had frustrated the 1938 agreement so that he was at liberty to do so: *Morgan v Manser* [1948] 1 KB 184.

## Unavailability through Illness

Where a party becomes unable to perform personal obligations under a contract due to physical/mental illness or incapacity, the court will look at how long this is likely to be and whether, given the length and terms of the agreement, it will make the contract impossible or pointless. Relatively short periods of incapacity will not necessarily frustrate a contract; lengthy periods may do so. In *Condor v Baron Knights* [1966] 1 WLR 87, the 16-year-old claimant contracted to play the drums for the defendant band for seven nights a week for five years. He subsequently suffered a mental breakdown and received medical advice that he should not perform more than four nights each week. When the band dispensed with his services, he brought a claim for wrongful dismissal, but failed as his medical condition made it impossible for him to carry out his contractual obligations properly, rendering the contract frustrated.

Similarly, in *Notcutt v Universal Equipment Co (London) Ltd* [1986] ICR 414, Mr Notcutt had a very serious heart attack that made it unlikely that he would work again. This, too, frustrated his contract of employment, being "an unexpected occurrence which made his performance of his contractual obligation--to work--impossible and brought about such a change in the significance of the mutual obligations that the contract, if performed, would be a different thing from that contracted for".

**Frustration of Leases**

Following the Court of Appeal decision in *Leighton's Investment Trust Ltd v Cricklewood Property and Investment Trust Ltd* [1943] KB 49, it had been thought that the doctrine of frustration did not apply to leases, not least because they constituted an estate in land. However, the House of Lords rejected this notion (by a majority) in *National Carriers Ltd v Panalpina (Northern) Ltd* [1981] AC 675. This case involved the ten-year lease of a warehouse, where the local authority closed the only access road for 20 months, making it of no use to the tenants for that period. They claimed that this had frustrated the lease. The House of Lords decided that the doctrine was, in principle, as applicable to leases as to any other contract, albeit not to be invoked lightly. However, the tenant failed in the instant case, as the loss of 20 months out of a ten-year term was not serious enough to bring the case within the doctrine of frustration.

This comparison between the length of the lease and the period for which the property cannot be used can also be seen in *Li Ching Wing v Xuan Yi Xiong* [2004] 1 HKLRD 754. In this Hong Kong case, the court rejected a tenant's claim that their tenancy agreement had been frustrated because the premises were a ected by an isolation order issued by the Department of Health as the result of an outbreak of SARS. This meant that it could not be lived in for ten days. The court held, *inter alia*, that the ten-day period was insignificant when compared to the two-year duration of the lease. Similarly, in *Bank of New York Mellon (International) Ltd v Cine-UK Ltd* [2021] EWHC 1013 (QB) the (English) High Court granted summary judgment to the landlords of commercial properties who sought rent from their tenants, despite extensive government restrictions imposed on the use of these premises in response to the Covid-19 pandemic. Although a forced closure of premises, as a result of a supervening event, could result in frustration, this was not the situation in the instant case. A closure of 18 months still left the tenants with most of the benefit of the leases.

## The Consequences of a Frustrating Event

Once a frustrating event occurs, a contract automatically, immediately, and permanently comes to an end, without any action having to be taken by the parties to the agreement: *Hirji Mldji* v *Cheong Yue Steamship Co.* [1926] AC 477. This remains the case, even if those parties do not learn about the frustrating event for some time afterwards, as was the case with the nocturnal fire in *Taylor v Caldwell.* In this respect, frustration differs from termination for repudiatory breach, which must be actively accepted by an injured party, after he has become aware of the breach, to bring a contract to an end. In the case of *Bank of New York Mellon (International) Ltd v Cine-UK Ltd* [2021] EWHC 1013 (QB), the High Court reiterated that there is no notion of "temporary frustration" in English law. Furthermore, once a contract is frustrated, the parties cannot elect to keep it alive: *GF Sharp and Co Ltd v McMillan* (1998) IRLR 632. This does not, of course, prevent them from entering a new contract with each other, on the same or similar terms to the previous one, after the frustrating event.

All future obligations under the contract are "discharged" on the occurrence of a frustrating event. However, a frustrated contract is not rescinded. At common law, all obligations accrued prior to frustration remained valid and enforceable. Money that had been paid was not recoverable, while money that was due to be paid before the frustrating event occurred remained payable, even if it had not yet been handed over. As a result, in *Krell v Henry* (1903) 2 KB 740, a deposit of £25 of a total payment of £75, paid in advance of the frustrating event, as required by the original contract, could not be recovered by the defendant, although the requirement to pay the balance of £50, due to be paid *after* that event, was discharged. This had more draconian consequences in *Chandler v Webster* [1904] 1 KB 493, where all the money for hire of a room for the King's coronation was payable in advance. Although not all had been paid when the coronation was postponed, the hirer was still liable to pay the balance that was outstanding.

The common law position was slightly modified by the decision in *Fibrosa Spolka v Fairbairn* [1943] AC 32. In this case, an English company contracted to supply some of its machines to a Polish company, very shortly before the outbreak of the Second World War. Under the contract, £1,600 was payable in advance, and £3,200 on delivery. The Polish company paid £1,000 in July 1939 towards the initial advance payment. War broke out in early September, frustrating the contract (see above). However, the House of Lords held that where there was a *total* failure of consideration, as in the instant case, any money paid prior to the frustrating event could be recovered. Nevertheless, such relief can only be granted when the other party fails to perform *anything* pursuant to the contract. Had even a few nuts and bolts been supplied by the English company in advance of the frustrating event, this would not have been the case, and the £1,000 would not have been recoverable. As a result, even with this refinement, the common law position remained unsatisfactory, as it could occasion considerable injustice. Because of the large number of contracts that had been frustrated by the advent of the Second World War, Parliament intervened by enacting the Law Reform (Frustrated Contracts) Act 1943.

## The Law Reform (Frustrated Contracts) Act 1943

Two things should be noted immediately about the Law Reform (Frustrated Contracts) Act 1943. First, contracts are not frustrated *under* the statute. Whether a contract is frustrated or not is still governed purely by common law--that is, by case law. The 1943 Act deals solely with the *results* of a frustrating event. Second, although the Act now applies to most frustrated contracts, there are a handful of exceptions, where the consequences are still governed by the common law rules, as set out in *Fibrosa Spolka v Fairbairn*. Most important, the 1943 Act does not apply to insurance contracts, contracts for certain perishable goods, and some shipping contracts. As a result, the 1943 Act operates as a huge exception to the common law position, rather than abolishing it, so that the latter cannot be entirely ignored.

In summary, and rather crudely, the 1943 Act provides both parties to a frustrated contract with a degree of protection, at the court's discretion. More specifically, under s.1(2) of the Act, all sums paid or payable in pursuance of the contract before it was frustrated are recoverable (and will be refunded) or cease to be payable. However, this is subject to the proviso that, if the party to whom the sums were paid or payable incurred expenses before the time of discharge, pursuant to performance of the contract, the court may, if it considers it just to do so, allow him to retain or recover the whole or part of those sums, provided the amount does not exceed the expenses so incurred. As a result, this provision is of no assistance if no monies were paid or payable in advance of the frustrating event.

The ambit of s.1(2) was considered in *Gamerco SA v ICM/Fair Warning (Agency) Ltd* [1995] 1 WLR 1226. Strangely, as Garland J noted, this was the first reported case specifically on this provision, as opposed to s.1(3), although the statute had been in force for more than 50 years. In this case, the claimant was promoting a concert at a large stadium at which the defendant's band would play. When the venue was declared unsafe (deemed to be neither party's fault), the contract was frustrated, and they both lost money as a result. The promoters subsequently sued to reclaim the considerable sum paid in advance to the band, and the court had to consider how much of it, if any, should be retained by the latter for the expenses they had incurred. Garland J said that the burden was on the payee (the band) to persuade the court to exercise its discretion under s.1(2) in their favour to reduce the amount returned (to cover their expenses). There were three possible approaches: all expenses could be deducted from the amount to be reclaimed; there could be "equal apportionment", so that the payee offset half his expenses against the amount paid to him; or the court could exercise its "broad discretion" to do justice in any given situation as it thought fit. The last found favour and was followed in the instant case. As a result, it was held that the claimants (the promoters), who had had much greater financial exposure than the defendants, were entitled to recover the full pre-payment, and the group was not entitled to retain anything under the proviso to s1(2).

Under s.1(3) of the 1943 Act, where a party to a contract has obtained a valuable benefit before the time of its discharge by a frustrating event, the other party to the agreement can recover whatever sum the court considers just, having regard to all the circumstances of the case, *provided* it does not exceed the value of the benefit. For example, and to consider (very loosely) the situation in *Taylor v Caldwell*, suppose that the contract had been due to last two weeks, that no money was payable to the owners of the music hall until after that period had expired, and that the frustrating event (the fire) had not occurred until a week into the hire, while during the previous six days the impresario had put on a series of highly profitable concerts. Section 1(3) would allow the owners of the music hall to recover some or (much less likely) all of this money, at the court's discretion.

However, the benefit under s.1(3) must survive the frustrating event: *BP Exploration Co (Libya) v Hunt (No 2)* [1983] 2 AC 352. This means, for example, that if a building was burnt down by fire (through nobody's fault), after considerable refurbishing work had been done on it by contractors, the latter would not be able to recover for the (now destroyed) work under s.1(3). Of course, they might still claim expenses under s.1(2) for at least some of this work, but these could not exceed monies paid or payable *before* the frustrating event.

In *BP Exploration v Hunt*, Hunt had obtained a potential oil concession in Libya. In 1960 he contracted with BP to develop it, transferring half the concession in exchange for contributions in cash and oil. BP would search for oil, and provide all funds required until it was found; the profits would then be shared, but with a major part of Hunt's initial share also going to BP, until half of the latter's costs had been covered. A large oil reserve was discovered in 1967. However, in 1971 the Libyan government nationalised BP's half share. By then BP had covered half its costs. Two years later the Libyan government also seized Hunt's share. BP claimed the contract was frustrated and sought a just sum under s.1(3).

In the High Court, Goff J (as he then was) held that the contract was frustrated in 1971 and awarded BP 35.4m plus interest. In his decision, Goff J suggested a two-stage process for decisions under s.1(3). First, a trial judge should identify the value of any benefit obtained, deducting any expenses that the beneficiary had been put to when obtaining it, and making allowance for any payment made under s.1(2) of the 1943 Act. Second, the judge should decide the amount, the 'just sum', that should be allowed from this to the party that had provided it, this not to exceed the value of the benefit. When doing this, a judge might have regard to the consideration provided in the agreement to provide an indication of values and so what the just sum might be. The Court of Appeal subsequently upheld this first-instance decision, Lawton LJ noting, more generally, that judges had complete discretion to award what they think is fair when deciding on a just sum.

# Chapter 12: Contractual Terms

## Introduction

Contracts consist of a set of individual promises that are called terms. If these are broken, the injured party can sue for "breach of contract", which is an abbreviation for "breach of contractual term". Even the simplest contracts will usually have several terms. Terms can be classified both by the way that they enter a contract and by their importance or rank within the agreement after they have done so. In this chapter, these issues will be dealt with in turn.

There are two ways by which a term enters a contract, expressly or by implication.

## Express Terms

Express terms are those terms that are specifically identified and agreed upon by the parties before they enter the contract, whether orally or in writing. The latter can either be set out in a formal written document or in an exchange of other writings, whether by letter or email. The distinction between pre-contractual statements that are deemed to be mere representations and those that are express terms, albeit not contained in a formal written contract, turns on the intention of the parties, objectively determined. (This issue is discussed in detail in Chapter 7). It should be noted that, where a written contract has been produced, purporting to contain the express terms of an agreement, the courts will be reluctant (but not unwilling) to allow the parties to adduce evidence to add to or vary those terms, especially if it has been signed. This is a result of the so-called parol evidence rule (briefly alluded to in Chapter 7), which warrants detailed consideration here.

## The Parol Evidence Rule

The parol evidence rule (sometimes called the extrinsic evidence rule) was aimed at preserving the integrity of written contracts. It provides that extrinsic evidence, whether oral (hence, "parol", from the French *parole*, word of mouth) or contained in non-contractual writings, such as exchanges of letters and emails, cannot be received to contradict, vary, add to, or subtract from the terms of a formal written contract. The rule was first expressly identified in England in 1833, and concisely reiterated in the Australian case of *Mercantile Bank of Sydney v Taylor* (1891) 12 LR (NSW) 252, when Innes J noted, "Where a contract is reduced into writing, where the contract appears in the writing to be entire, it is presumed that the writing contains all the terms of it and evidence will not be admitted of any previous or contemporaneous oral agreement which would have the effect of adding to or varying it in any way". For example, in *Hutton v Watling* [1948] Ch 398 an agreement was drawn up for the sale of a business and signed by the vendor. A dispute subsequently arose concerning a clause in the agreement, which the vendor claimed did not reflect the entire contract. However, it was held that the vendor was not entitled to introduce parol evidence on this point, because the written document provided the true record of the agreement.

Even so, as has often been noted, not least by the Law Commission in its 1986 report on the subject ('The Parol Evidence Rule', No. 154, Cmnd. 9700), it is not a proper rule, as there are numerous exceptions to the general principle, one of which can almost invariably be alleged by a party seeking to avoid it. Most important, as Chief Baron Pollock observed in *Harris v Rickett* (1859) 157 Eng. Rep. 734, it does not apply where the written agreement was not intended to be the whole contract. In this case, the (civil) trial jury had not found that the writing was intended to contain the whole agreement, and the judge and his colleagues were "of opinion that the rule relied on by the claimants only applies where the parties to an agreement reduce it to writing, and agree or intend that that writing shall be their agreement". Some contracts are partly written and partly oral: *Couchman v Hill* [1947] 1 KB 554.

As a result, a party wishing to adduce parol evidence can simply claim that the contractual document belonged to such a class of agreements. In the words of Lord Russell CJ in *Gillespie Brothers v Cheney Eggar* [1896] 2 QB 59: "[I]t is open to either of the parties to allege that there was, in addition to what appears in the written agreement, an antecedent express stipulation not intended by the parties to be excluded, but intended to continue in force with the express written agreement". Because, by definition, a party seeking to rely on an extrinsic term will be arguing that the written document was not intended to be the whole agreement, the rule becomes a circular argument, as the Law Commission also noted in its report.

In practice, the courts consider a variety of factors when deciding whether a written document was intended to be the entire agreement; most important, they will ask whether it appears, on its face, to be a complete statement of the parties' agreement. Where it does, it must be asked why the parties would sign it without amendment if it did not contain the whole agreement. This means that, effectively, the rule creates a powerful but rebuttable presumption. As was noted in *Gillespie Brothers v Cheney Eggar*, "[A]lthough when the parties arrive at a definite written contract the implication or presumption is very strong that such contract is intended to contain all the terms of their bargain, it is a presumption only". Even so, the courts will not lightly be persuaded that a seemingly complete written contract is not the whole agreement. As the Law Commission observed, "The apparent completeness of many commercial documents has the practical effect of deterring unwarranted efforts to vary or contradict their contents by extrinsic evidence".

There are a variety of other situations in which the rule does not apply, or where it can be circumvented, which, for the sake of convenience, can also be briefly considered here. For example, as was noted in *Hutton v Watling* [1948] Ch. 398, parol evidence may be admitted to establish that a collateral contract, separate from that set out in the written document, but which was the reason the main contract was entered into, was made and broken. In these situations, entering the main contract is usually the consideration for the collateral contract. Thus, in *De Lassalle v Guildford* [1901] All ER 495, the parties had negotiated the lease of a house. The landlord gave a verbal assurance that the drains were in good order. Subsequently, the tenant sued the landlord because this was not the case. In response, the landlord argued that the oral assurance was not written in the contract. The tenant succeeded, on the basis that the assurance constituted a separate contract; it was the consideration for which the tenant had entered the main (written) contract.

Similarly, in *City and Westminster Properties Ltd v Mudd* [1959] Ch 129, the defendant rented a shop for six years. The premises included a small room in which he slept at night, something that was known by the landlords. When the lease was up for renewal the landlords inserted a clause restricting use of the premises to "showrooms, workrooms and offices only". This would have prevented the defendant from continuing to sleep there. However, he was given a parol assurance that he would still be able to do this, on which basis he signed the new lease. Almost a decade later, the landlord sued the tenant for breaching the non-residential clause. Harman J held that there was a collateral contract that allowed him to live there, even if it contradicted the written agreement's express terms. Although the defendant had broken the written agreement, the collateral contract meant that the landlord was unable to enforce its terms against him.

Furthermore, the parol evidence rule does not apply where a party seeks to incorporate an implied term into an agreement by recourse to trade or local custom (see below). As was noted in *Hutton v Warren* [1836] 1 M&W 466, "Parol evidence is admissible to introduce the custom as part of the contract between the parties, in all cases except where, either in express terms, or by necessary implication, the covenants in the lease exclude the custom". Additionally, the rule will not apply where the operation of an agreement was subject to an extrinsic event. Thus, in *Pym v Campbell* (1856) 6 E&B 370, a signed written contract for the sale of part of the profits from a new patent was drawn up. Extrinsic evidence was admitted of an oral stipulation that the agreement should not become operative until a third party, one of Campbell's engineers, had approved the invention.

## Entire Agreement Clauses

Quite commonly, the parties to a written contract will add an express clause to the agreement that is aimed at producing the same result as the parol evidence rule (were the latter a true rule) by providing that there are no terms in the agreement *other* than those set out in the contractual document, which contains the totality of their bargain. (Such clauses are often found in the boilerplate provisions in the latter part of commercial agreements). These are known as 'entire' or 'whole' contract or agreement clauses. They have a very strong persuasive effect but can be rebutted if it is proved that, despite their presence, the parties *still* intended an additional term to be part of the agreement, although this is often difficult to do. Furthermore, they must also comply with various statutory controls, so that, for example, in commercial agreements entire agreement clauses must be deemed to be reasonable under the Unfair Contract Terms Act 1977 because they can operate as a form of exemption clause by denying a party a potential remedy. It should also be noted that entire agreement clauses will not normally exclude implied terms, which are dealt with next.

## Implied Terms

Implied terms enter a contract automatically, without being discussed by the parties to the agreement, and play a vital role in the modern law of contract. There are, broadly speaking, three ways in which terms are implied into contracts: by law, by custom, and by fact, although terminology on this issue sometimes differs.

Terms that are implied by law enter a contract via two mechanisms, by statute and by case law precedent. The former is the most common source for such terms in the modern era, although some of these statutes, such as the Sale of Goods Act 1893 (replaced in 1979), were themselves largely codifications of earlier precedents.

## Terms Implied By Statute

Numerous statutes, far too many to consider all of them, imply terms into contracts. Amongst the most important are the Unfair Contract Terms Act 1977 (UCTA), the Sale of Goods Act 1979 (SOGA), the Supply of Goods and Services Act 1982 (SGSA), and the Consumer Rights Act 2015 (CRA). The last of these is a late arrival, coming into force on 1 October 2015, and displacing the first three statutes when it comes to implying terms between traders and consumers, although many of its provisions are very similar to those found in the earlier statutes, and many of the pre-2015 decisions on those Acts involve consumer cases. The CRA is a complex statute and warrants further consideration.

## Advent of the Consumer Rights Act

The law governing consumer rights prior to the implementation of the CRA was complex and highly fragmented, being found in various pieces of primary and secondary legislation, such as, inter alia, the Supply of Goods (Implied Terms) Act 1973, UCTA 1977, SOGA 1979, SGSA 1982, and the (now abolished) Sale and Supply of Goods to Consumers Regulations 2002. The CRA 2015 was, in part, aimed at consolidating and (where necessary) clarifying and improving this legislation when it came to consumer contracts. It was also intended to update consumer rights in the light of rapid developments in the digital economy.

The CRA deals with contracts between traders and consumers. A "trader" is broadly defined as a person who acts in pursuance of his trade, business, craft, or profession. Individuals, partnerships, companies, charities, government departments, and local and public authorities can all be traders. The CRA defines a "consumer" as an individual (that is, a natural not an artificial legal person) who is acting "for purposes that are wholly or mainly outside that individual's trade, business, craft, or profession". This means that the rights set out in the CRA will not apply to legally incorporated organisations, even if they are acting entirely outside their normal business role. A small limited-liability company buying coffee mugs for its staff common room, or even flowers for its non-executive directors, does not fall within the reach of the CRA.

A selection of important provisions from some of the above statutes (there are many others) can be considered.

### Sections 12-14 Sale of Goods Act 1979

The SOGA 1979 includes provisions that imply various terms into non-consumer contracts for the sale of goods. It replaced a broadly similar predecessor from 1893. (Many of the decisions made under the latter statute are still relevant and will be cited below). For example, under s.12(1) there is an implied term that the seller has a right to sell the goods. Unusually for the statute, this provision also applies to purely private, not just business-to-business, sales. A simple illustration of the operation of s.12(1) (under the 1893 iteration of the statute) can be seen in *Rowland v Divall* [1923] 2 KB 500. In this case, the claimant, a car dealer, purchased a second-hand vehicle from the defendant for £334. He repainted it and then sold it on to a customer for £400. Two months later, the car was seized by the police, as it transpired that it had been stolen, albeit that the defendant, who had acquired it from the thief, was not aware of its provenance. It was then returned to the original owner. The claimant returned the £400 to the customer and successfully brought an action against the defendant under s.12(1) SOGA. As the defendant did not obtain good title from the thief, he could not pass title in the vehicle. Had the claimant not returned the £400, the customer could, in his turn, have sued him for a breach of s.12(1).

Under s.12(2)(b) there is an implied term that the buyer will enjoy quiet possession of the goods. This is a warranty (see below), so that the injured party can only claim damages if it is breached. This provision was considered (again under the 1893 Act) in *Microbeads v Vinhurst Road Markings* [1975] 1 WLR 218. In this case, the claimant purchased some road-marking machines from the defendant. After the purchase, a third party was granted a patent right in the machines. This meant the claimant could not use them unless they were granted a licence to do so by this third party. There was no breach of s.12(1) as, at the time of the sale, the seller had a right to sell the goods. However, there was a breach of s.12(2), as it then was, in that the buyer could not enjoy quiet possession of them.

Section 13(1) Sale of Goods Act 1979 provides that in a contract for the sale of goods by description, there is an implied term that the goods will correspond to that description. However, and slightly controversially, *Harlington & Leinster v Christopher Hull Fine Art* [1991] 1 QB 564 suggests that, for this to be operative, the purchaser must rely on the description. This will almost invariably be the case if he has never seen the goods. Thus, in *Varley v Whipp* [1900] 1 QB 513, the defendant purchased a reaping machine, unseen, from the claimant, who had described it as being new the previous year and having been very little used since then. The defendant discovered that it did not match the claimant's description, being old and worn, and sought to return it, refusing to pay the agreed price. He argued that the contract was for a sale by description, so that there was a breach of s.13 SOGA 1893. The High Court agreed, Channel J holding that "[t]he term 'sale of goods by description' must apply to all cases where the purchaser has not seen the goods, but is relying on the description alone".

Section 13 will also be operative where the purchaser has seen the goods but still reasonably relies on what he was told. Thus, in *Beale v Taylor* [1967] 1 WLR 1193, there was a breach of s.13 SOGA 1893 when a vendor sold a car, seen by the purchaser, after describing it as being a 1961 Triumph Herald. In reality, the car was a combination of two damaged Triumph Heralds, which had been welded together, only one of which was of this vintage. As a result, it was alleged that only half of the car corresponded to description. The Court of Appeal found there was a sale by description and the claimant was entitled to damages for breach of the implied condition.

By contrast, in *Harlington & Leinster*, the defendant sold a painting to the claimant for £6,000 after describing it as being by the noted German expressionist painter Gabrielle Munter. Although both parties were art dealers, the buyer, unlike the vendor, specialised in German paintings and sent his expert to inspect the painting before agreeing to buy it. By contrast, the defendant's representative told the expert that he knew little about the paintings and nothing about Gabriele Munter. Nevertheless, the claimant bought the painting for £6,000 without making any further inquiries. After the sale the buyer discovered that the painting was a forgery and worth less than £100. He brought an action based on s.13 Sale of Goods Act 1979 because the painting was not as described ("by Munter"). The Court of Appeal ruled, by a majority, that there had not been a sale by description. The claimant sending their expert to inspect the painting and relying on his conclusions precluded this. The description of the painting, as being by Gabriele Munter, did not have sufficient influence on the sale. (It should be noted that the identity of the artist was not an express term of the contract.)

Section 14 SOGA 1979 implies two terms as to quality in the sale of goods, these being the only exceptions contained in the Act to the wider contractual principle of *caveat emptor* (buyer beware). Liability is strict, and not dependent on proof of any fault on the part of the seller. Under s.14(2) there is an implied term that goods sold in the course of a business to another business (so called "B2B" contracts) are of "satisfactory quality". (This wording replaced "merchantable quality" in 1995). Thus, in *Britvic Soft Drinks Ltd v Messer UK Ltd* [2002] 2 Lloyd's Rep 368, it was breached by Messer UK Ltd when they supplied Britvic with contaminated (with benzene) carbon dioxide for use in its sparkling drinks, as a result of which Britvic had to recall many of its products. However, in less obvious cases, it should be noted that a trial judge's factual decision on this issue, for example that a new car did not have a steering defect when sold, will not lightly be overturned on appeal: *Egan v Motor Services (Bath) Ltd* [2008] 1 All ER 1156.

Furthermore, by dint of s.14(2C)(a), this implied term does not extend to any defect making the quality of goods unsatisfactory that is specifically drawn to the buyer's attention before the contract is made. For example, in the Court of Appeal case of *Bartlett v Sidney Marcus ltd* [1965] 1 WLR 1013 (decided under SOGA 1893), the claimant purchased a second-hand Jaguar from the defendant car dealer. Before the sale, the latter told the claimant that the clutch was defective and that this would require a small repair costing a few pounds. He then gave the buyer the choice of either taking the car as it was, but reducing the advertised price by £25, or his repairing it and charging the claimant the full price. The buyer chose to take it with the fault and get the (apparently much larger) discount. It subsequently transpired that the fault would cost £84 to repair. The buyer sought to bring a claim under s.14 of the 1893 Act. It was held that the seller had brought the defect to the buyer's attention, and so it could not be treated as a breach of s.14, even if the latter had been misled to some degree.

Under s.14(3) SOGA 1979 there is another implied term that, when a seller sells goods in the course of a business (to a business), and the purchaser, expressly or by implication, makes known to the seller a particular purpose for which they are being bought, the goods will be reasonably fit for that purpose. If goods have only one main use, this will be impliedly made known to the vendor, without having to be spelt out in negotiations. Thus, a football that cannot be kicked is not fit for purpose.

However, s.14(3) will not apply where the circumstances show that the purchaser has not relied, or it is unreasonable for him to rely, on the skill and judgment of the seller. For example, it would not be reasonable to rely on an 18-year-old shop assistant's assurance that a hiking boot sold in a high-street shoe shop was fit for Antarctic winter mountaineering.

Furthermore, case-law makes clear that something unusual about the purchaser, of which the vendor is unaware, which makes the goods unfit for purpose, will also preclude an action under s.14(3). For example, in *Griffiths v Peter Conway Ltd* [1939] 1 All ER 685, the claimant bought a Harris tweed coat from the defendants. Due to her abnormally sensitive skin, she contracted dermatitis from the (typically) slightly hairy coat but failed in her claim that it was unfit for purpose under SOGA 1893. The defendants did not know of her sensitive skin and could not be expected to anticipate it, so there was no breach of s.14(3). This was reiterated in broader terms with regard to SOGA 1979 in *Slater and Slater et al. v Finning Ltd.* (1996) 199 N.R. 203, in which the House of Lords noted that there is no breach of the implied condition of fitness where the failure of the goods to meet the intended purpose "arises from an abnormal feature or idiosyncrasy, not made known to the seller, in the buyer or in the circumstances of the use of the goods by the buyer. That is the case whether or not the buyer is himself aware of the abnormal feature or idiosyncrasy".

Section 14(3) often overlaps with s.14(2). For example, roof tiles that leak will not be of satisfactory quality and, given that keeping out water is their main purpose, not fit for purpose. Nevertheless, in other situations there can be a breach of s.14(3) without there being any breach of s.14(2). For example, in the Court of Appeal case of *Aswan Engineering v Lupadine* [1987] 1 All ER 135, the claimant purchased liquid waterproofing contained in plastic pails from the defendant. The pails were described as suitable for outside storage. The claimant stored them outside in the Middle East in extreme temperatures of up to 70 degrees centigrade. The pails melted, and the liquid waterproofing was ruined. It was held that there was no breach of s.14(2), as a normal user in, for example, Britain or most of the rest of the world, could have stored the goods outside without any problems. However, if the purchaser had stipulated that the pails must be suitable for extreme heat and very harsh sunlight, and been assured that they were, there might have been a breach of s.14(3).

More recently, in *BSS Group Plc v Makers (UK) Ltd (t/a Allied Services)* [2011] EWCA Civ 809, BSS had supplied a particular type of valve to Makers for use with a Uponor adaptor in renovation works being carried out in a public house. The adaptor and valve proved to be incompatible, and the valve quickly blew off, causing a flood to the ground floor of the premises. Makers claimed that BSS were in breach of the implied term as to fitness for purpose under s.14(3) SOGA. The judge, at first instance, found that Makers had expressly specified to BSS, in a fax enquiry and written order, that the valves were being bought for use with the specific type of adaptor for which, it transpired, they were unsuitable. The judge also found that Makers had (reasonably) relied on BSS's skill and judgment as to the compatibility of the valve and adaptor. The Court of Appeal dismissed BSS's appeal. Makers had made known to BSS the particular purpose for which the valves were intended, if only by implication, and they were not reasonably fit for that purpose (because incompatible).

The case of *Jewson Ltd v Leanne Teresa Boylan* [2003] EWCA Civ 1030 was much more complicated and concerned alleged breaches of both satisfactory quality under s.14(2) and fitness for purpose under s.14(3). In this case, a Mr Kelly had acquired a former convent-school with a view to converting it into 13 self-contained flats. He decided to install an individual heating system in each flat and purchased 12 electric boilers from Jewson Ltd (there was already a gas supply to the thirteenth flat). He failed to pay for all of them, arguing that the boilers had not satisfied the implied terms as to quality because they reduced the Standard Assessment Procedure energy ratings on the flats, being very costly to run. The judge at first instance ruled in Mr

Kelly's favour but this was reversed by the Court of Appeal. (By then, Mr Kelly had died, so that the respondent to the appeal was the personal representative of his estate). The boilers worked well, albeit that they were expensive to run, so that Mr Kelly received what he had bargained for. There was no breach of either s.14(2) or s.14(3).

**Sections 13 and 4 Supply of Goods and Services Act (SGSA) 1982**

The SGSA applies to non-consumer contracts for the supply of services, or a combination of goods and services, and implies a variety of terms. Very important, under s.13(1) SGSA, where a service is conducted in the course of a business (for a business), there is an implied term that it will be carried out with reasonable care and skill. For example, if a roofer contracts with a restaurant to repair their roof there will be a breach of s.13(1) if the tiles are not properly fixed. To consider a more unusual case, in *Abramova v Oxford Institute of Legal Practice* [2011] EWHC 613 the claimant enrolled on the defendant's Legal Practice Course intending to qualify as a solicitor. She failed to pass the course and brought a claim for breach of contract. She relied on s.13, which at that time still covered consumer contracts (now the province of the CRA 2015), arguing that the college had not exercised "reasonable care and skill" in her tuition, especially when it came to giving suitable feedback on her work. The court rejected this argument, feeling that failings which amounted to negligence had not been proved, and liability under s.13 SGSA arises only if the service provided has been carried out negligently.

Section 4(2) SGSA implies a condition that goods supplied along with a service will be of satisfactory quality (like s.14(2) SOGA 1979 for contracts for the sale of goods), while s.4(6) implies a condition that they will be fit for their purpose (like s.14(3) SOGA). As with s.14 SOGA, these terms can be broken even if the seller is not at fault. Thus, if the tiles provided and used by a builder contracted to repair a roof turned out to be porous, and so let water through, there would be breaches of both terms implied under s.4, even if he had purchased them from a reputable wholesaler and had no way of knowing that they were defective.

**Sections 9-11 and 49-51 Consumer Rights Act 2015**

The provisions in Chapter 2 of Part 1 of the CRA 2015 deal with the supply of goods and services in consumer contracts, and to a significant extent restate or mirror the previous law contained in, *inter alia*, ss.12-15 of SOGA and ss.4-13 of SGSA, by imposing certain implied terms on any goods sold, or services provided, by a business to consumers. Thus, under s.9(1) of the CRA, there is an implied term that goods supplied under a consumer contract will be of satisfactory quality, this being defined by s.9(2) with further guidance provided in s.9(3). Under s.10 there is an implied term that the goods are fit for their purpose, while s.11 provides that they will be as described. When it comes to the provision of services, s.49 provides that any work done must be carried out with "reasonable care and skill".

## Terms Implied by Case-Law Precedent

Certain terms are implied by law in all contracts of a certain type, such as those governing landlord and tenant or regulating employment, by reason of previously decided precedent (rather than statute). A classic example of such a term was identified (or created) in *Liverpool City Council v Irwin* [1976] 2 WLR 562, in which it was held that tenancies involving the lease of flats usually required implying a term that the landlord should take reasonable steps to keep the common parts of the blocks, such as stairwells and corridors, in order, even though no statute expressly sets this out.

This case involved a block of council flats in Everton. Mr and Mrs Irwin were tenants who complained, *inter alia*, that the common parts were often vandalised, the lifts did not work properly, while the stair lights were frequently out of order. The tenancy agreement only imposed obligations on the tenant, not on the (council) landlord. The House of Lords held that in these situations there was necessarily an implied term that the landlord should take reasonable care of the common parts of a building. (Nevertheless, on the facts of the instant case, this had not been breached, as the council did take steps to address the problems in these parts, if not as effectively or quickly as the tenants might have wished).

Lord Wilberforce noted that, in this situation, neither the business efficacy or the officious bystander tests (see below) would result in such a term being implied in the agreement by fact, but concluded, "In my opinion such obligation should be read into the contract as the nature of the contract itself implicitly requires, no more, no less: a test in other words of necessity". Lord Cross observed that in these situations, the courts were "sometimes laying down a general rule that in all contracts of a certain type--sale of goods, master and servant, landlord and tenant and so on--some provision is to be implied unless the parties have expressly excluded it". In deciding whether or not to lay down such a *prima facie* rule a court would ask itself whether, in the general run of such cases, it would be reasonable to insert such a term.

## Terms Implied by Custom

In certain situations, terms might be implied into a contract by the custom of a locality or of a particular trade, *provided* they are not inconsistent with the express terms of the agreement, especially where both parties to the agreement are from the locality or engaged in the same trade. For an example of the former can be considered *Hutton v Warren* [1836] 1 M&W 466, in which Parke B noted that it had long been settled that, in commercial transactions, "extrinsic evidence of custom and usage is admissible to annex incidents to written contracts, in matters with respect to which they are silent". In this case, the claimant became the tenant of a farm in Lincolnshire in March 1833. A year later, the tenancy was determined by the defendant landlord giving him notice to quit, as was allowed under the lease. By then, the claimant had worked the land, sowing wheat, barley, and clover, which would now be to the benefit of the landlord when harvested. According to the custom of the country (that part of Lincolnshire), the claimant, as an out-going tenant, was entitled to certain reasonable allowances in respect of his work and the provision of seed, even though it had not been written into the lease. The defendant refused to pay these. It was held that extrinsic evidence of such a customary term could be adduced by implication "except where, either in express terms, or by necessary implication, the covenants in the lease exclude the custom". (This was not the situation in the instant case).

When it comes to trade customs, *British Crane Hire v Ipswich Plant Hire* [1974] QB 303 can be considered. Both parties were engaged in the hire of earth-moving equipment. The claimants supplied a dragline crane to the defendants, who urgently needed it, as the result of a contract made speedily over the telephone, which did not mention any conditions of hire. The claimants later sent a copy of their conditions, but before the defendants could sign them, the crane sank in marshy ground. This was not the fault of either party, but it would cost a great deal of money to extract the machine, for whoever had that responsibility. The claimant's conditions, which were very similar to those used by almost all firms engaged in the plant-hire business, as both parties knew, said that in these situations the hirer should indemnify the owner for all expenses in connection with use. The court held that the terms would be incorporated into the contract, not by a course of dealing, but because there was a common understanding between the parties, who were in the same line of business, that any contract would be on these standard terms. As a result, the defendants were liable for the expense involved in recovering the crane.

**Terms Implied In Fact**

A court will sometimes imply terms in contracts to reflect what it considers, on the facts of the case before it, must have been the parties' unexpressed intentions. Because such terms are specific to the contract before the court, they are not of general applicability to other agreements, unlike terms implied by law. However, in the Supreme Court case of *Marks and Spencer plc v BNP Paribas Securities Services Trust Company (Jersey) Limited and anor* [2015] UKSC 72, Lord Neuberger noted that, in these situations, there is no need to show actual intention on the part of the particular parties in any given case. Instead, the court is concerned with the notional intention of reasonable people in the position of the parties at the time they were contracting.

It should be stressed immediately that the standard for implication in fact is very high; it is *not* sufficient that the proposed term would make the contract more sensible or fair. As Lord Hoffman observed in *Attorney General of Belize and others v Belize Telecom Ltd and Another* [2009] 1 WLR 1988, "[I]t is not enough for the court to find that such a term would have been adopted by the parties as reasonable men if it had been suggested to them: it must have been a term that went without saying, a term necessary to give business efficacy to the contract". As this comment suggests, traditionally, two tests have been identified for implying terms into a contract as a matter of fact.

## Business Efficacy Test

In *The Moorcock* (1889) 14 PD 64, the defendant owner of a wharf on the (tidal) River Thames contracted with the claimant to provide mooring facilities, so that the latter's vessel could unload her cargo after she entered the Port of London. The wharf owner knew the draft of the ship and the range of the tide, something that meant he also knew (or ought to have known) that it would necessarily settle on the riverbed at low tide. The vessel's hull was damaged when this occurred, and part of it was found to have settled over a ridge of stone, rather than the normal soft Thames' mud, producing a pressure point and so serious damage. There was no express term relating to this, but the owner of the *Moorcock* sued, arguing that there was a contractual obligation on the wharfinger to ensure that his vessel would remain safe while docked.

The Court of Appeal found for the claimant, ruling that there was an implied term that the wharfinger had, at the least, taken reasonable steps to ascertain the state of the riverbed adjacent to his jetty (albeit not an implied term that it would be a safe place to moor). Had he done so, he would have quickly discovered the stone ridge and been required to warn the shipowners of the danger. Bowen LJ observed that implying this limited term was necessary "to give such business efficacy to the transaction as must have been intended at all events by both parties who are businessmen". The contract would not work without it. (He also stressed that terms would not be implied simply because they appeared "desirable and reasonable", a point that has regularly been reiterated since that time.)

## Officious Bystander Test

An alternative to the "business efficacy" test for implying terms established in the *Moorcock* was identified in *Southern Foundries (1926) Ltd v Shirlaw* [1940] AC 701. In this case, Shirlaw had been contracted in 1933 to serve as the managing director of Southern Foundries Ltd for a ten-year period. Another company took a controlling interest in the business. The new owners altered Southern Foundries Ltd's articles of association, empowering two directors and the secretary to remove any other director. They then dismissed Shirlaw as director. If he was not a director, he was not able to be managing director. The claimant sued the company for wrongful dismissal and asked the court to imply a term in his employment contract that the defendant would not act in such a way as to make it impossible for him to perform his contract. The Court of Appeal held that there was an implied term in the 1933 agreement that the company would not alter its articles to create a right of removal without cause. MacKinnon LJ observed that, while the finding of an implied term was not to be done on vague or uncertain grounds, it included "something so obvious that it goes without saying; so that, if, while the parties were making their bargain, an officious bystander were to suggest some express provision for it in their agreement, they would testily suppress him with a common 'Oh, of course!'" In the instant case, he felt that the term being implied would have attracted such a response. This became known as the "officious bystander" test and operated as an alternative to the "business efficacy" test established in the *Moorcock*.

In *Marks and Spencer plc v BNP Paribas Securities Services Trust Company (Jersey) Limited and anor* [2015] UKSC 72 Lord Neuberger argued that the principles espoused in the two classic tests for implying a term into a contract represent a clear and consistent approach which it would be dangerous to reformulate. They will often overlap, but only one of them needs to be present. However, the term implied in fact must not contradict any express terms in the contract, so that the latter should be construed before any question of implication can be considered: *Duval v Randolph Crescent Ltd* [2020] 2 WLR 1167. In this Supreme Court case, Lord Kitchin also reiterated that it was necessary that the term to be implied was capable of clear expression.

Two recent illustrations of the strictness of these principles in practice can be considered. In *Al Jaber v Al Ibrahim* [2018] EWCA Civ 1690 the Court of Appeal held that the payment of interest should not be implied in an oral loan agreement made in 2001, in which the claimant had lent 30 million to the defendants to finance an Arabic news channel. The parties did not mention interest in the original agreement, which was not documented. Some 15 years later, the claimant brought proceedings in England seeking not only repayment of the original loan, but also 32m in interest on the relevant sum. It was argued that it was a matter of commercial common sense that such a large loan would bear interest, and so such a term should be implied into the agreement. However, the court concluded that the interest claim had no reasonable prospect of success, not least because it would be very difficult to show that an obligation to pay interest was necessary to give the agreement business efficacy or that it went "without saying".

In *Yoo Design Services Ltd v Iliv Realty PTE Ltd* [2021] EWCA Civ 560, the parties entered into an agreement regarding a luxury property development, under which Yoo Design would receive one-third of the fee for its work upfront, with the remaining two-thirds becoming payable on the sale of any flats within the development. No flats were sold, and Yoo Design claimed for breach of terms (allegedly) implied in fact requiring that Iliv Realty market the flats with due diligence and sell them within a reasonable time. In considering business efficacy, the Court of Appeal found that the agreement had "practical and commercial coherence" without the implied term. When it came to the obviousness test, the court found that asking an "officious bystander" whether the parties had agreed that Iliv Reality would sell the flats within a reasonable time would not produce an unequivocal yes, but numerous alternative opinions. Yoo Design's appeal was dismissed.

## Contractual Terms And Their Importance: Repudiatory Breaches

All those who suffer the breach of a contractual term, however trivial, are entitled to sue for breach of contract. However, not all terms are of equal significance. Most importantly, repudiatory breaches of contract must be distinguished from their non-repudiatory siblings. The victim of a non-repudiatory breach can sue for damages but is unable to terminate the agreement. By contrast, the victim of a repudiatory breach can sue for damages but also has a choice as to whether or not to terminate the contract.

To consider a simple example, suppose that a pie-manufacturer contracts with a shop, situated by the entrance to a major premier league football ground, to deliver 100 pies one hour before the start of each home game, during an eight-month season. The shop agrees to pay £1 for each pie but plans to sell them for £2. For two months, from the start of the season, the agreement works well, and the pies are delivered on time and always sell out. However, on an occasion early in the third month, the pie-manufacturer is four hours late in delivering his wares, and no pies are sold.

Breach of the term specifying time of delivery will entitle the shop, the injured party, to seek damages to compensate for their loss of profit on the pies that day, that is £100 (assuming they did not pay for them in advance). However, suppose that the shop also wishes to avoid the remainder of the contract, that is a further six months of pie deliveries, and take their custom elsewhere. They will only be able to do this if the time of delivery is of the essence so that the pie-manufacturer's breach is deemed to be repudiatory.

It should be stressed that it is always the injured party that elects to bring a contract to an end after a repudiatory breach, not the defaulting party, however egregious their breach. Although, as Lord Steyn observed in *Vitol SA v Norelf Ltd, The Santa Clara* [1996] AC 800, acceptance of a repudiatory breach does not have to be in a particular form and can be done either by express communication or by conduct, it must clearly and unequivocally convey to the contract breaker that the injured party is treating the agreement as at an end. The latter does not have to make their decision on this issue immediately that they become aware of the repudiatory breach but should do so quickly (see below).

Accepting a repudiatory breach will discharge both parties from further performance under the agreement. The injured party can then also sue for damages for any loss occasioned by the breach and attendant termination: *Howard-Jones v Tate* [2011] EWCA Civ 1330. Of course, there is no legal requirement to seek damages in such situations. If their losses are modest, the innocent party may feel that avoiding the contract is enough. However, once repudiation occurs, he also comes under an "obligation" to mitigate his loss. (See Chapter 15).

The victim of a repudiatory breach does not *have* to terminate a contract for the breach. If he wishes, he can waive the breach and "affirm" the contract by electing to treat it as ongoing, indicating his intention to continue with the agreement, and then seeking to hold the other party to it, perhaps hoping to persuade them to change their mind, or simply accepting the departure from what was agreed. For example, many authors who contract to finish a book by a set date do so in agreements that make clear that a failure to do so will be repudiatory (time "being of the essence"), but this is often not enforced if the publisher is satisfied that any overrun will be modest. If a contract is specifically enforceable, the injured party can, sometimes, also seek an order to force the counterparty to carry out their primary obligations, rather than repudiating the agreement. To affirm a contract, the injured party must know of the breach and their right to terminate the agreement. However, once they are aware of it, they should decide quickly, as inaction can, in the right circumstances, constitute implied affirmation (a similarity shared with rescission for misrepresentation).

If a party does affirm the contract, the agreement and its attendant obligations and duties (for both parties) continues, and the injured party cannot subsequently terminate it for the same breach, unless the breach is ongoing or recurs (which might provide a further right to bring the contract to an end). However, if the innocent party decides to terminate the agreement, all future contractual obligations under the agreement are discharged.

It is important not to confuse termination for breach of contract with rescission for contractual misrepresentation, duress, and undue influence, although the terminology pertaining to the two is sometimes used loosely and interchangeably, especially in old cases. In the latter situation, the contract is rescinded "from the beginning", so that it is unpicked, and the parties are (as far as possible) placed in the position in which they would have been if the contract had never existed. By contrast, although acceptance of a repudiatory breach means that both parties are absolved from future performance under the contract, the agreement is not rescinded *ab initio*, and there is no effect on any obligations that have already been performed. As Lord Wilberforce observed: "In the case of an accepted repudiatory breach, the contract has come into existence but has been put an end to or discharged. Whatever contrary indications may be disinterred from old authorities, it is now quite clear, under the general law of contract, that acceptance of a repudiatory beach does not bring about 'rescission ab initio'": *Johnson v Agnew* [1980] AC 367.

Once a repudiatory breach is accepted, any outstanding unperformed obligations of the party in breach are normally replaced by an obligation to compensate the injured counterparty for any loss caused by that non-performance; "secondary" replace "primary" obligations under the agreement: *Howard-Jones v Tate* [2011] EWCA Civ 1330.

A repudiatory breach of contract can, sometimes, be difficult to distinguish from its non-repudiatory sibling, and this can occasion problems. If a party mistakenly claims there has been a repudiatory breach and, as a result, terminates an agreement or ceases to perform their obligations under the contract, they run the risk that they will be the ones committing a repudiatory breach, which can then be accepted by the other party. This was the situation with a claimant's purportedly terminating letter in *Imperial Chemical Industries Ltd v Merit Merrell Technology Ltd* [2017] EWHC 1763 (TCC). The High Court found that the letter itself amounted to a repudiation of the contract. In the words of Mr Justice Fraser, "The inevitable conclusion to my findings that these allegations of breach all fail, and that the letter of 17 February 2015 was not the exercise of a contractual right to terminate, is that the letter was itself a repudiation of the contract by ICI". The same thing occurred in *Soteria Insurance Ltd (formerly CIS General Insurance Limited) v IBM United Kingdom Ltd* [2022] EWCA Civ 440. Nevertheless, it seems that, provided there is justification for terminating a contract, that another, non-repudiatory, breach was initially identified as the reason for doing so will be irrelevant. In *The Mihalis Angelos* [1970] 3 WLR 601, Lord Denning stated, "The fact that a contracting party gives a bad reason for determining it does not prevent him from afterwards relying on a good reason when he discovers it".

## Identifying Repudiatory Breaches

Some repudiatory breaches are obvious. If a party shows an unequivocal intention to abandon any further performance of the contract, or not to perform some obviously essential aspect of the agreement, sometimes termed "renunciation" of the contract, the innocent party is entitled to be discharged from further performance. As was noted in *Gibbs v Leeds United Football Club* [2016] EWHC 960 (QB), "Where, objectively viewed, one party to a contract shows by their conduct that they no longer intend to be bound by it in its essential terms, that is repudiatory". Such renunciation will often be effected by an express refusal to perform, but it can also be inferred from conduct, *provided* it would lead a reasonable observer to conclude that they have no intention of fulfilling their essential obligations under the agreement.

However, ordinary breaches of contractual terms will not necessarily have this effect. In these situations, everything will turn on which of three ranks is accorded to the term that has been broken and, in the case of one of them, the gravity of the consequences of that breach. As will be seen, a repudiatory breach is normally a breach of condition or, alternatively, breach of an innominate term where the consequences of the breach go to the root of the agreement. A non-repudiatory breach is breach of a warranty or of an innominate term where the breach does not go to the root of the contract.

## Conditions and Warranties

For much of the twentieth century, English law formally recognised only two classes of contractual term, just as it had in the Victorian era, these being conditions and warranties. This analysis was encouraged by the enactment of the Sale of Goods Act 1893, which was premised on such a binary distinction. It was thought that terms should be classifiable as one or the other as soon as a contract was made. Breach of the former was always repudiatory. Thus, in *Wallis v Pratt* (1910) 2 KB 1003, Lord Justice Fletcher Moulton defined a condition as an "obligation which goes so directly to the substance of the contract, or in other words, is so essential to its very nature, that its non-performance will fairly be considered by the other party as a substantial failure to perform the contract at all". However, breach of a condition remained repudiatory even if its consequences were trivial, as was (and is) sometimes the case. By contrast, breach of a warranty was never repudiatory, even if (unusually) the consequences were quite severe.

## Identifying Conditions

Sometimes, express terms are given the status of "conditions" because they have been specifically identified as such by the parties, or at least described in words that made their status clear, for example, by saying that "any breach of this term will allow the injured party to terminate the contract". Both factors were present in *Lombard North Central v Butterworth* [1987] QB 527, in which the defendant, an accountant, leased a computer from the claimant on what was, essentially, a hire-purchase basis. The former was to pay 20 instalments of £584 every three months. A term of the agreement provided that punctual payment was a "condition", and expressly stated that any breach of this term would entitle the lessor to terminate the contract. The defendant got into arrears with the instalments, and the claimant terminated the contract, recovered possession of the computer, and sold it on for the very modest sum of £175 (all they could obtain for it). The claimant then sued the defendant claiming arrears and all future payments amounting to £6,869 in total. It was held that the term relating to prompt payment was a condition. The parties had made this clear in their agreement and the consequences of any breach were also expressly and clearly set out. As a result, even one late payment would entitle the lessor to terminate, irrespective of its effect.

In *Bunge Corporation v Tradax* [1981] 1 WLR 711, the House of Lords noted that where a term was expressly stated to be a condition, it should normally be treated as such, even if the consequences of breach were relatively minor. Nevertheless, quite exceptionally, the courts might ignore the use of the word condition in a contract, without more, as indicative of a term in which any breach will be repudiatory. This is especially likely if the document has not been produced by a lawyer, and they conclude that "condition" has been employed as a synonym for "term", rather than being used in a technical sense. In *Schuler v Wickman Tools* [1974] AC 235 Schuler manufactured machine tools in Germany. Wickman was a sales company that was granted the sole right to sell these tools in the UK. A term of the contract between the two parties that was described in the agreements as a "condition" provided that Wickman would send a salesperson to each of six named companies once a week to solicit sales. This imposed an obligation to make well over 1,400 visits in total.

Wickman failed to make a few of the relevant visits and Schuler terminated the contract for breach of a condition. Although the contract had expressly stated that the term was a condition, the only clause so described in the agreement, a majority of the House of Lords held that it was merely a warranty. They held that the use of the word "condition" was a strong indication of intention, but not (quite) conclusive. It would have been unreasonable for Schuler to be entitled to terminate the agreement for Wickman's failure to make even one visit and, in light of this, and the rest of the contract, it would not be given that status. It should be noted that, in this case, Lord Wilberforce gave a very strong dissenting judgment, apparently viewing the commercial standards adopted by his colleagues as excessively relaxed.

One conclusion to be drawn from *Schuler* is that if a party wishes to make any violation of a term, especially where it involves a potentially minor matter, a repudiatory breach of contract, they should spell this out very clearly, going beyond use of the word "condition". This might be done by expressly stating than *any* breach, however small, would allow the injured party to terminate the contract, as was done in *Lombard North Central*. However, it should also be stressed that *Schuler* was an exceptional decision. In most cases, terms described as "conditions" will be treated as such.[1] Even so, in *Dominion Corporate Trustees Ltd v Debenhams Properties Ltd* [2010] EWHC 1193 (Ch), Kitchin J noted that the courts were sometimes reluctant to interpret what *might*, on its face, have appeared to be a condition where it was contained in a complex contract with many innominate terms (see below), and where the remedy of termination might seem too drastic for a minor breach.

Where there was no express evidence of an intention to make an express term either a condition or warranty, late-Victorian courts would often base their decision as to its status on their own view of the commercial importance of the term in relation to the wider contract, and whether it went to the root of that agreement. If it did, it would be treated as a condition; if not, it was a warranty. In this context, it was traditional to cite two, factually quite similar, cases which produced different results, and which can be found in the same set of Law Reports.

In *Bettini v Gye* (1876) 1 QBD 183 Mr Bettini contracted to perform as an opera singer for three months. He undertook to be in London at least six days before the first concert for the purpose of rehearsals. He arrived three days late because of illness. By then, his employer had replaced him with another singer. This would only have been possible if his absence for this period was deemed to be a breach of condition. However, it was held that Bettini was merely in breach of warranty, and therefore the employer was not entitled to end the contract, although he could

1 In the Court of Appeal, in *BS & N Ltd v Micado Shipping Ltd (The Seaflower)* [2001] 1 Lloyd's Rep 341, Waller LJ usefully set out four situations in which a term is likely to be seen as a condition.

claim damages. Missing early rehearsals could not be viewed as going to the root of the contract.

By contrast, in *Poussard v Spiers* (1876) 1 QBD 410, Madame Poussard entered a contract to perform as an operetta singer for a production's entire three-month run. She became ill five days before the opening night and was not able to perform for its first four nights. Significantly, Poussard missed both the crucial dress rehearsal and the opening night, the latter being the production's most important performance, as newspaper critics' assessments and the publicity they generated, would be based on it. Spiers replaced her with another opera singer. Shortly afterwards, Poussard recovered and unavailingly sought to return to the production. It was held that the obligation to perform from the first night was a condition, and she was in breach of it, so that Spiers was entitled to end her contract.

### The Rise of the Innominate Term

In theory, prior to the 1960s, the courts were not supposed to look at the consequences of a breach when deciding whether it was repudiatory or not. Every term was supposed to be classifiable at the time the contract was made. In practice, this was never fully the reality, even in *Poussard* and *Bettini* (see above). Lord Justice Fletcher Moulton, in his dissenting judgment in *Wallis v Pratt* (1910) 2 KB 1003 (subsequently adopted by the House of Lords), frankly conceded, "There are many terms of many contracts which cannot be fitted into either category. In such cases the Courts, for nigh on 200 years, have not asked themselves. Was the term a condition or warranty? But rather: Was the breach such as to go to the root of the contract? If it was, then the other party is entitled, at his election, to treat himself as discharged from any further performance".

For example, in *Aerial Advertising Co v Batchelors Peas Ltd (Manchester)* [1938] 2 All ER 788, Aerial Advertising Co contracted with Batchelors Peas Ltd to advertise their vegetables by flying over certain towns and cities trailing a banner reading "Eat Batchelors Peas". The pilot would have to telephone Batchelors Peas every morning to get his proposed route for that day approved by the company. On Armistice Day, 1937, the pilot failed to do this, and then flew over the main square in Salford as a crowd observed the two-minute silence for those killed in the First World War. This caused great offence, and damage to Batchelors' reputation. They terminated the contract on the basis that there had been a repudiatory breach of condition (the failure to get approval). This was upheld by the court, although had the breach occurred on any other day, it would probably have been viewed as non-repudiatory, at least on a one-off basis. As Lord Hoffman has observed, judges in these cases "did what judges usually do when the law requires them to apply a rule based upon an inadequate analysis of the issues: they cheated. If the breach was sufficiently serious, they declared the term to have been a condition and if not, they said it had been a warranty".[2]

---

2 Foreword, by Lord Hoffman, to Adam Kramer, *The Law of Contract Damages*, 2nd edn. (Oxford: Hart, 2017), p. vi.

The reality, that the courts looked at the consequences of many breaches when determining how they should be treated was finally formally recognised by Diplock LJ in *Hong Kong Fir Shipping Co Ltd v Kawasaki Kisen Kaisha Ltd* [1962] 2 QB 26, which case is credited with the creation of the "innominate" category of terms, although it did not employ the word, which was first used some years later. In *Hong Kong Fir*, Diplock LJ made it clear that the traditional division into conditions and warranties had to be supplemented by a third, intermediate, class of terms, where it was necessary to look at the gravity of the consequences of the breach before it could be decided whether it was repudiatory or not. In these situations, the issue as to whether a particular breach allows an agreement to be ended is normally determined at the time the injured party purports to terminate the contract, in the light of what has happened or is likely to happen: *Telford Homes (Creekside) Ltd v Ampurius NU Homes Holdings Ltd* [2013] EWCA Civ 577.

In *Hong Kong Fir*, a shipowner chartered out one of his vessels for 24 months. On an early voyage the ship had to spend five weeks being repaired, as its engines were old and the crew (who were provided with the vessel) were inefficient and, in the case of the chief engineer, alcoholic. On another occasion, a further 15 weeks was required to make the ship ready for sea. The charterer sought to terminate the contract on the basis that the shipowner had failed to deliver a seaworthy vessel--that is, a ship "fitted in every way for normal cargo service", as required by the contract.

However, this term could be breached in a vast range of different degrees of gravity. For example, if the vessel's medical box was found to be lacking in bandages and iodine, it would be in breach, albeit that this would be very readily remedied by a quick visit to a local chemist's shop or pharmacy. By contrast, it would also be in breach if its funnels or propellers had fallen off, which would require a huge amount of remedial work. Diplock LJ concluded that, with this term, as with many others, the factual consequences of the breach determined its legal consequences. If they were grave it was repudiatory; if not, it could be treated as a breach of warranty. A key question was whether the breach would deprive the injured party of "substantially the whole benefit of the contract". It should be noted that this phrase has been interpreted slightly more liberally in ensuing years than its wording might suggest, and in the same case Sellers LJ talked of a breach of an innominate term that "went to the root of the contract" being repudiatory.

If so, it should be treated like a condition, breach of which would allow the injured party to terminate the agreement. In the instant case, the charterers were not entitled to terminate the agreement. Although the shipowner had been in breach of contract in failing to provide a seaworthy vessel, it had (eventually) arrived at its destination, albeit somewhat delayed, and even the subsequent delay left much of the charter's term still to run, while the cost of the repairs could be compensated by an award of damages. As a result, the breach did not go to the root of the contract.

Hong Kong Fir was quickly followed in other cases. For example, in *Cehave N.V. v Bremer Handelgesellschaft m.b.H. (The Hansa Nord)* [1976] QB 44, German vendors agreed to sell 12,000 tons of US citrus pulp pellets to Dutch buyers for £100,000 for use as animal feed. A clause in the agreement stated that they had to be "shipped in good condition". The buyer sought to reject the goods on the ground that most but "not all of the goods" had been in good condition. However, all were usable for their intended purpose as feed. (Perhaps significantly, the market price of citrus pulp had fallen significantly in the meantime). The Court of Appeal held that, in the instant case, the requirement that they were in good condition was not, in fact, a condition, but an innominate term. Since the actual breach did not go to the root of the contract--it was not "serious and substantial"--it could not lead to termination of the contract. The buyers would be limited to claiming for the difference in value between the shipment ordered (in which all the pellets were in good condition) and those delivered (in which some were merely adequate), which was about £14,000.

It should, perhaps, be noted that Court of Appeal judges have disagreed with those at first instance on whether any given breach of an innominate term is repudiatory in a (perhaps) surprising number of cases, given the higher court's normal reluctance to intervene with findings on factual matters made at first instance.[3] Thus, in Telford Homes (Creekside) Ltd v Ampurius NU Homes Holdings Ltd [2013] EWCA Civ 577, the Court of Appeal, unlike the trial judge, decided that a property company did not have the right to terminate a contract with a company that was building and developing four commercial units, which it would then lease to them on 999 year leases, but which had failed to meet target dates for completion (an innominate term) by a year, as this did not deprive them of "substantially the whole benefit" of those very long leases.

After *Hong Kong Fir* it appeared possible that almost all terms that could be breached in a wide range of degrees of gravity would be defined as innominate, unless the parties to the agreement had made it clear that they were to be treated as either conditions or warranties (by expressly or impliedly stating this) or (in the case of implied terms) statute so provided. However, in *The Mihalis Angelos* [1970] 3 WLR 601, it was accepted that the benefits of commercial certainty meant that certain time-honoured terms, which were found in particular industries or types of contract, should continue to be accorded the status of conditions, as had always been the case, even if the word was not used, and the consequences of a particular breach were very small, unless the agreement expressly provided otherwise.

In *The Mihalis Angelos*, the owners of a cargo vessel chartered her to the defendant. A clause in the agreement stated that the ship was "expected ready to load" at Haiphong in what was then North Vietnam on 1 July. In fact, the owners had no grounds for believing that this would be the case, as it was in Hong Kong at the

3 Chinyere Ezeoke (2007), "Assessing seriousness in repudiatory breach of innominate terms", *Journal of Business Law*, pp.198-199.

time and would not be ready for several weeks. The defendant terminated the contract on 17 July when the vessel had still not arrived. However, at this point, the cargo that they had expected to ship in her had itself not arrived at Haiphong due to the bombing of a railway (part of the ongoing war in Vietnam), so that the shipowners' delay had not occasioned them any loss. The owners brought an action against the defendant for breach. The defendant argued that it was the claimant who was in breach of condition, by not being ready to load on 1 July, entitling them to terminate the agreement, and the fact that they did not then have a cargo to load was irrelevant. The trial judge held that there was a breach of this term, but it was not a condition, and the breach was not so fundamental as to give the right to terminate the contract; it was the non-repudiatory breach of an innominate term.

However, on appeal, it was held that the "expected ready to load" clause *was* a condition, not least because of the need for commercial certainty in shipping contracts. Any breach of such a term, whatever the consequences, entitled the injured party to terminate. Megaw LJ, discussing its significance, stated that such a term, when used in a charter party, "ought to be regarded as being a condition of the contract, in the old sense of the word 'condition'; that is, that when it has been broken, the other party can, if he wishes, by intimation to the party in breach, elect to be released from performance of his further obligations under the contract; and he can validly do so without having to establish that, on the facts of the particular case, the breach has produced serious consequences which can be treated as 'going to the root of the contract'".

Similarly, if much more obviously, by *very* long recognition, and like "expected ready to load", if the time of performance of a contractual obligation, such as delivery of goods, is stipulated to be "of the essence", any delay, however short, and even if it is not damaging, will constitute a repudiatory breach and mean that the injured party can (but does not have to) terminate the agreement and (where appropriate) claim damages. It is a term of art that designates any delay as automatically repudiatory. This was applied in the Privy Council case of *Union Eagle Ltd v Golden Achievement Ltd* [1997] AC 514. Even though the delay in paying for a property in Hong Kong was just ten minutes after the specified time, a 10 per cent deposit was forfeit by the tardy would-be purchaser.[4][41]

Occasionally, a term might still be identified as a condition in the broader context of the contract, even if the word itself is not used. For example, in *Bunge Corporation v Tradax* [1981] 1 WLR 71 Bunge sued Tradax for the latter's repudiation of an agreement to supply soya bean meal. The purported termination had been made on the basis that Bunge had given notice four days late for loading a nominated ship

4 Even if time is not of the essence, a continuing failure to perform an important obligation under an agreement will eventually become repudiatory, allowing the injured party to terminate the contract. Unfortunately, it is not always easy to know how long such a delay must be before it achieves this status. Nevertheless, it can be speeded up by the injured party giving notice that performance must occur within a reasonable time, after which he will treat any continued delay as repudiatory.

with the meal (they were required to give fifteen days' notice). Bunge argued that the delay was short enough that it did not go to the root of the contract. However, the House of Lords held that on a proper construction of the agreement the clause was a condition, so Tradax had been entitled to terminate the contract. Similarly, that time is of the essence might, occasionally, be inferred from the nature of the contract, without being set out expressly, such as an agreement for the sale of perishables, such as very ripe bananas.

Nevertheless, despite such cases, in the present day it appears that terms that have not previously been recognised as being conditions in a decided case, as was the situation in *The Mihalis Angelos*, and which can be broken in a large range of degrees of gravity, will normally be treated as innominate. Thus, in *Bunge v Tradax* [1981] 1 WLR 711 Lord Scarman observed that usually, unless a contract makes it clear "either by express provision or by necessary implication arising from its nature, purpose, and circumstances ... that a particular stipulation is a condition or only a warranty, it is an innominate term". More recently, in the Court of Appeal case of *Grand China Logistics Holding (Group) Co Ltd v Spar Shipping AS* [2016] EWCA Civ 982, Hamblen LJ observed that, where a breach could result in trivial, minor, or very grave consequences, the "modern English law approach to the classification of contractual terms is that a term is innominate unless it is clear that it is intended to be a condition or a warranty".

For an illustrative example of this approach, can be considered *Valilas v Januzaj* [2014] EWCA Civ 436, in which two dentists entered an oral contract whereby the former practised from the latter's premises, using his equipment and support staff, in exchange for half of his income, which was to be paid each month. Mr Valilas did not make payment to Mr Januzaj in August 2010, and the following month he wrote to him stating that he was stopping the monthly payments as he believed that he had been overpaid by the NHS (for routine administrative reasons) and thought it likely he would have to make them a refund. He argued that, given the strained relationship that then existed between the two dentists, he was not confident that Mr Januzaj would refund him the portion of any overpayment that he, in his turn, had received. There followed ineffective negotiations as to how the situation might be resolved, and in November Mr Januzaj gave notice that he was terminating the contract and excluding Mr Valilas from the premises for withholding the payments. Mr Valilas brought a claim for damages for wrongful termination of the agreement. On the facts of the instant case, the Court of Appeal rejected Mr Januzaj's argument that the requirement to make monthly payments on time was a condition. It was held to be an innominate term. The court said that the effect of the past and threatened future breaches could not be said to deprive Mr Januzaj of substantially the whole benefit of the contract so that they were non-repudiatory.

By contrast, in *Grand China Logistics Holding (Group) Co Ltd v Spar Shipping AS* [2016] EWCA Civ 982, the Court of Appeal had to consider whether a charterer's failure to pay an instalment of the cost of hire, as required by clause 11 in a time charter party, was a breach of condition which would automatically allow the shipowner to terminate the charter, or an innominate term. The claimant (Spar) was the registered owner of three bulk carriers chartered by the defendant's subsidiary GCS (for which GCL was responsible). GCS defaulted on payment in April 2011 and remained heavily in arrears throughout the summer of 2011. In September Spar terminated the charter party. At first instance, Popplewell J held that punctual payment of hire by GCS under clause 11 was an innominate term. The Court of Appeal agreed. The terms of the agreement had not made clear that it should be regarded as a condition. However, on the facts of the case, GCS's conduct *had* been repudiatory, as it had evinced an intention not to pay hire timeously, which constituted a renunciation of the charters. Nevertheless, because it was an innominate term, any breach would not automatically and invariably have this effect. A short, inadvertent delay might merely be treated as a breach of warranty.

More recently, in *Ark Shipping Co LLC v Silverburn Shipping (IoM) Ltd (M/V 'Arctic')* [2019] EWCA Civ 1161, the Court of Appeal had to consider whether a term in a bareboat (uncrewed) charterparty (lease) of the Arctic, a merchant vessel, on a standard form of contract, was a condition or an innominate term. The term provided that Ark would maintain the Arctic in a good state of repair, with all "required certificates in force at all times". Ark allowed the vessel's classification to lapse before she entered dry dock for maintenance. As a result, Silverburn sent notice to Ark purporting to terminate the charter party, and demanding delivery up of the vessel. In response, Ark argued that the charterparty continued in force. The Court of Appeal provided further guidance on the factors that would be considered when classifying terms, reiterating those identified in *Grand China Logistics Holding (Group) Co Ltd v Spar Shipping AS* [2016] EWCA Civ 982 and, again, noting that the court's approach should be that a term is innominate, unless it is clear it is intended to be a condition or a warranty. On the facts of the instant case, the requirement to keep the vessel with unexpired classification was an innominate clause, the breach had resulted in no significant adverse consequences to Silverburn, and so was not repudiatory.

## Statute and Innominate Terms

As already noted, the SOGA 1893 was premised on a neat distinction between conditions and warranties. This can still be seen in its successor, SOGA 1979. Thus s.14(6) notes that the "terms implied by subsections (2) and (3) [of s.14] above are conditions". The same applies to sections 13 and 15. However, and slightly confusingly, these provisions must now be seen in the light of s.15A of the Act, whereby a buyer of goods in a non-consumer sale who would normally have the right to reject them by reason of a breach of sections 13, 14 or 15 (as would be the case where there has been a breach of condition) will not be able to do so if the breach is deemed "so slight that it would be unreasonable for him to reject them". In these situations, the breach will be treated as a breach of warranty unless a contrary intention is manifest from the contract. The onus is on the seller to establish that the breach is so slight that it should not justify rejection. Arguably, s.15A has created a form of special innominate term, albeit one in which it is not enough to show that the breach does not go to the root of the agreement, but it must be also established that the consequences of the breach are positively minor.

More clearly, s.13(1) SGSA 1982 provides that in non-consumer contracts, where a service is supplied in the course of a business, there is an implied term that it will be carried out with reasonable care and skill. However, this is not defined as being a condition or a warranty, so that it is (unusually for such statutes) deemed to be an innominate term, which means that the remedy to which the injured party is entitled depends on the seriousness of the breach.

## Anticipatory Breach

An anticipatory breach occurs when, before performance is due, a party either does something that physically prevents themselves from performing it in future, or, alternatively, provides an unequivocal indication that they will not perform when performance is due, something that might be termed renunciation. It should be noted that an anticipatory breach is *always* repudiatory, there cannot be an anticipatory breach of warranty.

The first form of repudiatory breach, what might be termed self-disablement, would entail doing something that renders it impossible to perform important obligations under an agreement, such as disposing of the subject matter of the contract to a third party. For historical example there can be considered *Lovelock v Franklyn* (1846) 8 QB 371, in which the defendant promised to assign to the claimant, within seven years from the date of his promise, all his interest in a lease for the sum of £140. However, before the end of seven years, he assigned his interest to another person. It was held that this was an anticipatory breach of contract, even though seven years had yet to pass. The defendant had physically incapacitated himself from performing the contract, having disposed of the property.

The second form of repudiatory breach involves express conduct that clearly indicates that the contracting party is, and will be, unwilling to perform his obligations under the agreement. This will often (but not necessarily) be by making a statement to that effect. Thus, in *Hochster v De la Tour* (1853) 2 E & B 678, the claimant agreed to act as a courier for the defendant for three months from 1 June 1852. However, on 11 May that year, the defendant wrote to him stating that he no longer wanted his services and refusing to pay compensatory damages. This was a clear renunciation of the contract. The claimant brought an action on 22 May for breach of contract. The defendant unavailingly argued that there was no breach of contract at that time as the contract would only begin on 1 June. It was held that, where a party to a contract communicates their intention not to perform their obligations under it, the innocent party need not wait until the breach has occurred before terminating the agreement and bringing an action for damages. They may sue immediately.

Similarly, in *Frost v Knight* (1872) LR 7 Ex 111, the defendant had promised to marry the claimant when his father died (as previously noted, an engagement was a contract in those days). However, during the father's lifetime, the defendant broke off his engagement to the claimant. She sued immediately and successfully for breach of promise of marriage, without waiting for the father to die, when the breach of promise would have become operative. Moving on to the following century, in *Omnium D'Enterprises v Sutherland* [1919] 1 KB 618, the defendant chartered a ship to the claimant but, before the hire period was due to start, sold the vessel to a third party. The Court of Appeal held that this amounted to an anticipatory breach, so that the claimant could bring an action for breach of contract from the date of the ship's sale, even though it preceded the start of the charterparty.

### Election and Anticipatory Breach

However, if the victim of an anticipatory breach prefers, they can elect to keep the contract alive, by continuing to press for performance, and wait for the actual breach to occur, on the day that performance is due. If they do this, the so-called duty to mitigate does not apply until the breach occurs and is accepted. Affirmation after a repudiatory breach, but before the date of performance, will not prevent the injured party from terminating the contract when the actual breach occurs. This occurred in *Shindler v Northern Raincoat Co* [1960] 1 WLR 1038, in which the claimant entered a contract of employment as a managing director with the defendants in April 1958. This was to last for ten years, but at the start of September 1958 the latter informed him that they were going to terminate his contract at the end of the following month. They offered him other employment at the same annual salary. However, the claimant declined this and continued working. Diplock J. held that, as he had not accepted the defendants' repudiation, there was no breach of their contract until the claimant was actually dismissed, and so no need to mitigate his loss by, for example, at least considering whether to accept their offer of alternative employment. The defendant might have changed their mind at any point during the intervening period, between early September and November, and continued to employ him in his existing capacity.

Nevertheless, there are dangers entailed in failing to accept an anticipatory breach. These can be seen in *Avery v Bowden* (1856) 5 E & B 714. In this case, the claimant contracted to carry cargo for the defendant. The claimant arrived early to collect it, but the defendant told them to sail on as they did not have any cargo for the claimant to carry and, very much more important, would not have any by the agreed date. This last was a repudiatory breach. However, the claimant decided to wait in the hope that the defendant would be able to supply some cargo on the due date. Unfortunately, before then the Crimean War broke out, which meant the contract became (effectively) frustrated. As a result, the claimant lost their right to sue for breach. Had they brought their action immediately, they would have had a valid claim.

In *SK Shipping (S) Pte Ltd v Petroexport Ltd* [2009] EWHC 2974 (Comm), Flaux J, sitting in the Commercial Court, provided a more recent consideration of the law governing anticipatory breach. He reiterated that it could be committed in two ways: by a party renouncing their obligations under the contract, or by rendering it impossible for them to perform those obligations by their own actions. He went on to note that the impact of their words or conduct had to be clear and unequivocal to a reasonable person, in the light of all the circumstances pertaining at the time. In addition, the innocent party must also have formed a subjective belief that the other party would breach the contract. Only when these conditions were satisfied could the latter terminate the contract and mitigate its losses.

In *SK Shipping* a shipowner (SK) sought damages for the defendant charterer's (P's) anticipatory breach by renunciation. SK identified several facts that gave them the impression that the charter party would not be performed. These included: slowing the vessel down while en route to its loading port; failing to carry out the relevant steps for loading cargo; and attempting to renegotiate the charter party, because no buyer for the cargo could be found. In response, P argued that none of its actions or words made it clear that it would not perform as agreed. Flaux J held that the words and conduct of D *had* evinced a clear intention not to perform the charter party. The judge also concluded that SK had subjectively believed that P would not perform the charter party. As a result, the company was entitled to treat the contract as repudiated.

Flaux J also noted that, since Hochster, renunciation had become the preferred means of establishing anticipatory breach, not least because it is comparatively rare for circumstances to make it genuinely impossible for a party to perform its obligations, so making it less likely that they will be seen as renunciatory. For example, if a party contracts to sell goods to one party but sells them to a third party, he might, in theory, still purchase the goods back, and honour the contract or, more realistically, if the goods are fungible, purchase a fresh supply from elsewhere to honour the agreement.

# Chapter 13: Exemption Clauses

## Introduction

Although there is considerable variation in terminology, the phrase "exemption clause" can usefully be treated as a generic term covering both exclusion and limitation-of-liability clauses. The former are contractual terms totally excluding the liability of one of the contracting parties for breach of another term in the same agreement, at least in certain circumstances. The latter are terms limiting the maximum amount of damages that can be paid for such a breach, but not excluding liability altogether.

Exemption clauses can take a variety of forms. However, and very important, they are not confined to clauses that announce their function by using words such as "excludes" or "limits" when restricting liability. Exemption clauses may operate indirectly by, for example, restricting the remedies normally available in the event of a breach of contract. This breadth of definition is formally set out for the purposes of the Unfair Contract Terms Act (UCTA) 1977 by s.13(1) of that statute, which provides that such clauses include provisions that: make the liability or its enforcement subject to restrictive or onerous conditions; exclude or restrict any right or remedy in respect of the liability; or subject a person to any prejudice in consequence of his pursuing any such right or remedy, excluding or restricting rules of evidence or procedure.

For example, in *Stewart Gill Limited v Horatio Meyer & Company Limited* [1992] QB 600, Gill argued that a particular clause in their company's terms and conditions was applicable to a contract. It provided that "[t]he customer shall not be entitled to withhold payment of any amount due to the company under the contract by reason of any payment credit set off counterclaim allegation of incorrect or defective goods or for any other reason whatsoever which the customer may allege excuses him from performing his obligations hereunder". One issue at trial (there were others) was whether the clause fell into the definition of exclusion clauses set out under s.13 of UCTA 1977. The Court of Appeal held that it did. Indeed, the very purpose of s.13 was to control this form of exemption clause; the "no set off" provision purported to preclude a remedy for breach of contract and so was caught by s.13(1)(b).

More recently, in *Saint Gobain Building Distribution Limited (t/a International Decorative Services) v Hillmead Joinery (Swindon) Limited* [2015] BLR 555, an obligation placed on the customer to inspect delivered goods in a careful fashion and immediately notify International Decorative Services (IDS) of any visible defects, failing which IDS would have no liability for such defects, was also held to be an exemption clause. It limited a normal remedy. Another provision, by which IDS would be under no liability unless a written complaint was delivered to them within three working days, was treated in the same way.

Similarly, in *Nobahar-Cookson & Ors v The Hut Group Ltd* [2016] EWCA Civ 128, the Court of Appeal noted that it was well settled that contractual limitation periods for the notification or bringing of claims, that would otherwise be open to the injured party, are forms of exclusion clause. More generally, a clause limiting a buyer to a right of repair or replacement in respect of defective products, rather than the normal right to reject such goods, would be treated as an exemption clause.

## History and Role

Historically, the courts have shown a certain degree of ambivalence, if not outright hostility, towards exemption clauses, feeling that they are open to abuse, especially when used against consumers. It is certainly true that they can work injustice. They are often found in standard-form contracts; these are written agreements in which the terms of the contract are set by one of the parties, and the other (often, but not always, a consumer) has no ability to negotiate any changes in them. For this reason, they are sometimes called "contracts of adhesion". One of the parties is placed in a "take it or leave it" situation, his only choice being whether to enter the contract or not. For example, when a consumer books a package holiday, he normally must agree to all of the extensive list of contractual terms advanced by the travel company. He cannot say, "I don't like clause 7(b). Can we leave it out?"

Nevertheless, it should also be noted that exemption clauses can serve very valuable functions. They allow the parties to apportion risk and so increase contractual efficiency, saving costs. As Lewison LJ noted in *Interactive E-Solutions v O3B* [2018] EWCA Civ 62, in the context of commercial contracts, exemption clauses are often an "integral part of pricing and risk allocation". It is not just in commercial contracts that they produce benefits. Their use helps to explain why, for example, package holidays sold to consumers in the UK are often much cheaper than equivalent vacations sold in some parts of Continental Europe.

As a result, such terms are not illegal per se, but an awareness that they could be abused meant that several common law rules were used or developed to limit potential unfairness. This process was caught by Lord Denning at the Court of Appeal stage (it went on to the House of Lords) in *George Mitchell (Chesterhall) Ltd v Finney Lock Seeds Ltd* [1983] 2 AC 803, when he noted that, "Faced with this abuse of power--by the strong against the weak--by the use of the small print of the conditions--the judges did what they could to put a curb upon it". When deciding whether an exemption clause applies, it must be asked whether, at common law, it has been "incorporated" into the contract's terms and then whether, on its true construction or interpretation, it covers the breach that has arisen. Subsequently, and very important, statutory controls on such clauses, such as those contained in the Unfair Contract Terms Act (UCTA) 1977 and Consumer Rights Act (CRA) 2015 were introduced, adding a third tier of control.

Occasionally, an exemption clause violates all three layers of protection, although just one is sufficient to render it inoperative. For example, in *Green v Petfre (Gibraltar) Ltd (t/a Betfred)* [2021] EWHC 842 (QB) Foster J concluded that the defendant's tendered exclusion clause had failed on all three grounds: it was not adequately brought to Mr Green's attention and so had not been incorporated into the contract; its wording was insufficiently clear to cover the circumstances that had arisen; and it was not "fair" and so was caught by the CRA 2015. These three tiers of protection will be discussed in turn.

## Incorporation of Exclusion (and other) Clauses

A key question is whether the exemption clause became part of the contract, that is, was it incorporated into the agreement? In *Olley v Marlborough Court Hotel* [1949] 1 KB 532, Denning LJ noted that, when seeking to establish incorporation of an exclusion clause (or any other term), the "best way of proving it is by a written document signed by the party to be bound. Another way is by handing him before or at the time of the contract a written notice specifying its terms and making it clear to him that the contract is on those terms. A prominent public notice which is plain for him to see when he makes the contract or an express oral stipulation would, no doubt, have the same effect. But nothing short of one of these three ways will suffice". Essentially, the distinguished judge was referring to incorporation by the signing of a written contract and (alternatively) incorporation by notice that has been provided orally, by an unsigned contractual document, or by a prominent sign. However, notice can also be provided by a previous course of dealing, although this was not mentioned by Denning LJ. These methods of incorporation will be considered *seriatim*. Nevertheless, it should also be stressed that they apply to *all* contractual terms, not just exemption clauses, although many of the cases in this area do involve exclusion or limitation of liability clauses. Some non-exemption clauses will also be cited.

### 1. Incorporation by Signature

In *L'Estrange v F Graucob Ltd* [1934] 2 KB 394 it was held that a person is bound by his or her signature when it is appended to a contractual document, even if they have not read it. Miss L'Estrange ran a cafe in Llandudno and purchased a cigarette vending machine from Graucob for use in her business. She signed, without reading, a sales agreement which stated in "regrettably small", but still clearly legible, print, set out on brown paper, "This agreement contains all the terms and conditions under which I agree to purchase the machine specified above, and any express or implied condition, statement, or warranty, statutory or otherwise not stated herein is hereby excluded." Subsequently, the machine proved defective, and Miss L'Estrange claimed that it was neither of merchantable (now "satisfactory") quality nor fit for purpose, terms that would normally have been implied by s.14 of the Sales of Goods Act 1893 (now SOGA 1979).

Graucob contended that such statutory terms were expressly excluded by the contractual agreement (this would now also be governed by UCTA 1977). Although L'Estrange won at first instance, she lost on appeal, albeit with some expressions of regret from the judges at the higher forum. The exclusion clause *had* been successfully incorporated into the contract. It was irrelevant that Miss L'Estrange had not read it; she was bound by her signature. Scrutton LJ observed, "When a document containing contractual terms is signed, then, in the absence of fraud or, I will add, misrepresentation, the party signing it is bound, and it is wholly immaterial whether he has read the document or not." For a more recent example of the terms of a signed but unread document being binding can be considered: *Peekay Intermark Ltd v Australia & New Zealand Banking Group Ltd.* [2006] 2 Lloyd's Rep 51. It should be noted that, under s.7 of the Electronic Communications Act 2000, an electronic signature can be legally binding.

However, as Scrutton's comment suggests, misrepresentation, whether fraudulent or not, will preclude the signature rule applying, while in the same case Maugham LJ also noted that the rule would not apply if the party signing had done so in circumstances where the *non est factum* doctrine of mistake applied. (The latter is considered in Chapter 9). An example of the former occurred in *Curtis v Chemical Cleaning and Dyeing Co* [1951] 1 KB 805. In this case, the claimant took her wedding dress to professional cleaners. The defendants asked her to sign a form, prompting Mrs Curtis to ask what the implications of this would be. She was told that the form included a clause excluding liability for damage caused to any sequins on the garments. In fact, it excluded liability for damage of any type to the garment. When Mrs Curtis returned to pick up her dress, she found that the fabric (not just the sequins) had been badly stained by the defendants. She sued for breach of contract, and the company sought to rely on the exclusion clause. The Court of Appeal found for Mrs Curtis, holding that the clause was not enforceable because the defendant (or their agent) had misrepresented its effect prior to the claimant signing the document.

It should be noted that although the "bound by signature" rule applies where the signed document contains the relevant clause, it does not operate if the claimant signs a document that refers to *another* document in which the clause can be found. For example, in *Blu-Sky Solutions Ltd v Be Caring Ltd* [2021] EWHC 2619, Blu-Sky sent Be Caring an electronic order form for mobile phones, for a minimum period of 48 months, for a monthly rental of £9,600. The order form stated that all contracts were subject to and incorporated their standard terms and conditions and that "by signing this document I agree I have logged on to the Blu Sky website at www.bluskysolutions.co.uk, have read agree and fully understand all terms and conditions regarding the contract and the policy protection scheme & free trial (*where applicable) and am bound by the same". Be Caring did not log on to Blu Sky's website as indicated to read the conditions, but still returned a signed order form the following day. The terms and conditions included a harsh cancellation clause. Unaware of this, Be Caring subsequently emailed Blu Sky to cancel the agreement. Blu Sky then drew their attention to the relevant clause and demanded a cancellation fee of £180,000. HHJ Stephen Davies concluded that the defendant's signature did not automatically incorporate the referred clause under which Blu Sky purported to be entitled to its cancellation fee. This was still subject to the test of reasonable notice (see below). Given its draconian nature and the obscure way it was set out, he concluded that it had not been incorporated.

## 2. Incorporation by Reasonable Notice

As *Blu-Sky Solutions* suggests (see above), a written term in an unsigned contractual document or set out in a publicly displayed notice can be incorporated into a contract if the court deems that reasonable steps were taken to bring it to the other party's attention, before they entered the agreement, even if they have not, in fact, read it. In the historic case of *Parker v South Eastern Railway* [1877] 2 CPD 416, Mr. Parker left a bag in a railway left-luggage office run by the South Eastern Railway. When depositing his bag and paying the 2d fee he received a ticket. On the front, it said, "See back". On its back, the ticket stated that the railway excluded liability for items worth £10 or more. Mr. Parker failed to read the clause, as he thought the ticket was only a receipt for his payment. However, he admitted that he knew that there was writing on it. Mr. Parker's bag, which was worth more than £24, was lost and he sued the railway company. At trial the jury (following the judge's direction) found for Mr. Parker, feeling that, as he had not read the ticket, the exemption clause did not apply to him. Nevertheless, the Court of Appeal held (by majority) that there should be a retrial. Unsurprisingly, they said that if Mr Parker had read the conditions, he would be bound by them (although this might be hard to prove). More pertinently, they held that he would *still* be bound if "reasonable" steps were taken to bring the term to his notice, this being a question of fact, even if he had not, in fact, read it.

As *Blu-Sky Solutions Ltd* also suggests, exemption clauses can, in the right circumstances, be incorporated by reasonable notice, where writing refers to another written document. In the historic case on this issue, *Thompson v London, Midland and Scottish Railway Co Ltd* [1930] 1 KB 41, Mrs Thompson fell on a slippery ramp while disembarking from a train operated by the defendant. A special jury found the railway to have been negligent in allowing such a situation. However, Mrs Thompson had an excursion ticket, which said on its front, "For conditions see back," which in turn referred to the railway's timetables. These could be bought for sixpence and stated that the tickets were issued on condition that holders would have no rights of action against the company in respect of personal injury "however caused". Mrs Thompson could not read (although the railway did not know this). Even so, the Court of Appeal held that, on the facts of the case, reasonable steps had been taken to bring the conditions to her notice. The indication of further conditions in the ticket was sufficient. (Such clauses would be unenforceable today by dint of statute.)

*O'Brien v MGN Ltd* [2002] CLC 33 provides an example of a clause, *other* than one exempting liability, being incorporated by reference. The claimant, Mr O'Brien, took part in a newspaper scratch-card game and, on one occasion, satisfied the criteria to win a £50,000 prize. However, an administrative mistake meant that almost 1,500 other entrants met the criteria to win the prize at the same time as Mr O'Brien. To escape this potentially enormous liability, the newspaper relied on its competition rules, whereby if there was more than one winner, a draw would be held to decide who received the prize. This raised the question as to whether the rules had been incorporated by notice into Mr O'Brien's unilateral contract with the newspaper. The full rules were not published in the newspaper every day and had not been published on the day he entered the competition. In consequence, he argued the newspaper had not done enough to bring them to the attention of entrants. The newspaper contended that publishing the words "Normal Mirror Group Rules Apply" on the day in question was sufficient to incorporate the terms by reference. The rules were published in the paper from time to time, and they were available at their offices, so that, they claimed, Mr O'Brien had sufficient notice of them. This was accepted by the court, which concluded that the paper had taken sufficient steps to bring them to the attention of the competition's participants, especially as they were not particularly unusual. However, every case will turn on its facts. How readily to hand the referred-to terms are will always be an important factor.

When it comes to determining whether reasonable notice has been provided by an unsigned contractual document or public notice, several factors are important. Amongst them are timing, the nature of any unsigned document containing the clause, prominence, and how draconian the clause is to the party against whom it is being employed.

### i. Timing

Reasonable notice of the exemption clause must be provided *before* the formation of the contract. As a result, in *Transformers & Rectifiers Ltd v Needs Ltd* [2015] EWHC 269 (TCC), Edwards-Stuart J observed that an "invoice following a concluded contract effected by a clear offer on standard terms which are accepted, even if only by delivery, will or may be too late". This had been the case in *J Spurling Ltd v Bradshaw* [1956] 2 All ER 121 where one of the issues was whether an exclusion clause contained in unsigned documentation had been incorporated into a contract for the warehousing of barrels of orange juice. Ultimately, this had to be by notice provided by course of dealing (see below), as the relevant documentation, a landing account and invoice were issued *after* the goods had been received and could not therefore be part of the contract if it was considered as a one-off transaction. In like manner, in *British Crane Hire v Ipswich Plant Hire* [1975] QB 303, a contract between the parties for hire of a crane had been concluded orally over the phone. A copy of the terms and conditions of hire was handed to the defendant on its delivery. These stipulated that the risk of hire remained with the hirer. However, it was held that the term relating to risk was not incorporated into the contract as the defendant was unaware of it at the time the contract was made. (Nevertheless, the court implied the same term into the contract by trade custom because both parties were in the business of plant hire, and the use of such terms was prevalent in that trade, see Chapter 12).

More specifically, in *Olley v Marlborough Court Hotel* [1949] 1 KB 532, Mrs Olley was staying at a hotel in London on a long-term basis. While she was resident, her fur coat and jewellery were stolen from her room, due to the hotel's failure to properly secure residents' keys left behind reception (the porter was temporarily absent from his post). Mrs Olley asked the hotel to pay the cost of the stolen items. The hotel refused and referred to an exclusion clause contained in a notice in her room, which said that it would not be responsible for lost or stolen articles, unless they had been handed to the manageress for safe keeping. The Court of Appeal held that this notice was ineffective. The contract had already been made by the time the claimant saw it (in her room), so that it did not become part of the agreement, while the hotel was in breach for failing to secure the keys. Had the notice been placed behind the reception desk, where the contract was made, or had she been shown the room before contracting, the situation might have been different.

Timing was also a supplementary issue in *Chapelton v Barry Urban District Council* [1940] 1 KB 532 (discussed below). In this case, the wording of a publicly displayed notice suggested that a person could collect and use a beach deck chair and get a ticket for it later, which would be too late to introduce new terms via the ticket.

### ii. Nature of the Document

Some documents are inherently more likely to contain contractual terms, and so to incorporate those terms by providing reasonable notice, than others. In *Chapelton v Barry Urban District Council*, the claimant hired a deck chair for 2d from Barry UDC for use on a local beach and was given a ticket in the form of a receipt which showed the attendants that he had the right to sit in the chair that day. The claimant put it straight into his pocket without reading it. However, a notice printed on the ticket excluded the council's liability for personal injury caused when using the deckchair (this would not be legal nowadays). The claimant was injured when he sat down, and the (defective) chair broke under him. He sued the council and they sought to rely on the exclusion clause. However, it was held that it had not been incorporated into the contract. A reasonable person would regard the ticket as nothing more than a receipt to prove payment, and would not expect it to contain contractual terms, one judge observing: "I cannot imagine that anybody paying 2d under those circumstances for the privilege of sitting in a chair on the beach would think for one moment that some conditions were being imposed upon him which would limit his ordinary rights, or that the document he received when paying his 2d was a contractual document in any shape or form."

### iii. Prominence

Unsurprisingly, the more obvious the exemption clause or other term, the more likely it is to be incorporated by reasonable notice. A small handwritten notice is less likely to incorporate a clause than a large, printed, notice in red block capitals. How prominent the notice must be is a question of fact for the trial judge to determine. For example, in *Transformers & Rectifiers Ltd v Needs Ltd* [2015] EWHC 269 (TCC), a seller had responded to orders for gaskets by sending the purchaser an acknowledgement of order which stated, "The quoted prices and deliveries are subject to our normal Terms and Conditions of Sale (copies available on request)". However, according to Edwards-Stuart J, a seller who wishes to incorporate his terms and conditions by referring to them in his acknowledgement of order--making it a counter-offer in the process--must, at the very least, refer to those conditions on the face of the acknowledgement in terms that make it plain that they are to govern the contract. If the conditions are not of a type that is commonly found in the relevant industry (as was the situation in the instant case), he must go further. In these situations, the seller must give the buyer reasonable notice of the conditions by, for example, printing them on the reverse of the acknowledgement of order, along with a statement on the face of that order indicating that it is subject to the conditions set out on the back. In the instant case, the defendant neither printed its terms and conditions on the reverse of the acknowledgement of order nor provided the claimant with a copy of these terms. As a result, it did not do enough to bring them to the attention of the claimant and thereby turn the acknowledgement of order into a counter-offer.

### iv. Draconian Terms

It is well established that a term that is particularly draconian, onerous, or unusual will require that greater steps be taken to bring it to the other party's attention than one which is more modest or commonly encountered, before it is deemed to have been incorporated. As Denning LJ observed in *J Spurling Ltd v Bradshaw* [1956] 2 All ER 121, "the more unreasonable a clause is, the greater the notice which must be given of it. Some clauses which I have seen would need to be printed in red ink on the face of the document with a red hand pointing to it before the notice could be held to be sufficient".

The recent decision in *Blu-Sky Solutions Ltd v Be Caring Ltd* [2021] EWHC 2619 (discussed above) reiterates this point. The relevant term was on a website. A key question was whether it was sufficiently brought to Be Caring's attention to be incorporated into the contract. HHJ Stephen Davies found that the ordinary terms on the website referred to had (just) been incorporated, "albeit only by a small margin". However, and vitally, the key cancellation clause in the contract was considered highly onerous, and as a result, and unlike the other terms, not reasonably drawn to the purchaser's attention to be incorporated by reference. Blu Sky had made no attempt to highlight the relevant clause in what was a lengthy contract; instead, it was "cunningly concealed in the middle of a dense thicket which none but the most dedicated could have been expected to discover". The contract's terms were set out in closely spaced small type with no separate clause headings, in a manner that was not in any way user-friendly to a reader.

By contrast, in *Goodlife Foods Ltd v Hall Fire Protection Ltd* [2018] EWCA Civ 1371 the Court of Appeal had to decide, *inter alia*, whether the defendant company Hall Fire's exclusion clause, contained in their (unsigned) standard Terms and Conditions, had been incorporated into the contract. Hall Fire had supplied and installed a fire-suppression system at Goodlife's factory in Warrington some ten years earlier. After their factory burnt down, the latter claimed that they had done so negligently. The clause stated, "We exclude all liability, loss, damages or expense consequential or otherwise caused to your property, goods, persons or the like, directly or indirectly resulting from our negligence or delay or failure or malfunction of the systems or components provided".

On appeal, Goodlife argued that the clause was especially onerous, citing the High Court judge's finding at first instance that it was at the "far-reaching end of the spectrum" in terms of excluding liability. As a result, its (allegedly) unusual nature meant that the notice given to the counterparty had to be "over and above the norm", which, the appellant argued, had not been the situation. The Court of Appeal decided that the clause was not particularly unusual or onerous in the circumstances; it involved a one-off supply contract carried out, for a modest sum, in 2002, while Hall Fire had no maintenance obligations or any other connection with the premises after they had installed the system. Potential liability, if unrestricted, was enormous. The contract did allow recovery up to the contract price while the exemption clause was widely used in such situations around the country. Nevertheless, the court felt that, even if it had been unusually onerous, it was *still* fairly and reasonably brought to the claimant's attention before they entered the contract. Hall Fire's written quotation expressly included the reference "standard HFS terms and conditions apply" beneath the quotation price, and Hall Fire sent a copy of its terms to Goodlife with the quotation. The court noted that it was not buried away in the middle of a raft of small print but was set out in clear type in a prominent part of this document.

Again, this consideration applies to all contractual terms, not just those, like *Spurling*, involving exemption clauses. Thus, in *Interfoto Picture Library Ltd v Stiletto Visual Programmes Ltd* [1989] 1 QB 433, Bingham LJ noted that the "more outlandish the clause, the greater the notice which the other party, if he is to be bound, must in all fairness be given". In this case, Stiletto ordered 47 photographic transparencies of life in England in the 1950s from Interfoto, for possible use in a documentary on that decade. On the delivery note was a clause stating that they should be returned within 14 days of delivery. If they were not so returned, a holding fee of £5 per transparency per day would be charged. The defendant did not read this document. He then forgot about the transparencies and failed to return them for six weeks. The claimants brought an action claiming a fee of £23,783 as specified in the note. The defendants refused to pay and Interfoto was awarded judgment at first instance. Nevertheless, Stiletto won on appeal. The late-payment fees were ten times higher than the industry norm, and so required exceptional steps to be taken before sufficient notice was deemed to have been provided, and the clause on the delivery notice had not satisfied this requirement in the instant case.

Inevitably, and as *Goodlife* suggests, sometimes judges will not agree on whether a clause should be deemed to be onerous, not least because it must be seen in relation to the contract as a whole, rather than in isolation. For example, in *AEG (UK) Ltd v Logic Resource Ltd* [1996] CLC 265 Hobhouse LJ disagreed with his fellow judges on the issue of incorporation, because he thought that the relevant clause was not unusual, dealing with an issue that was "commonly, and indeed normally, dealt with in the standard conditions of sellers of goods".

### 3. Incorporation by Previous Course of Dealing

Sometimes a problem with timing or simple forgetfulness means that, had a contract been unique--that is, a one-off transaction--there would not have been reasonable notice of an exemption clause. However, because there had been a previous course of dealing, in which the same exemption clause was used, the party must or ought to have been aware of its existence, so it is deemed to have been incorporated in the current transaction. For example, in *Circle Freight International Ltd v Medeast Gulf Exports Ltd* [1988] 2 Lloyd's Rep 427, the previous course of dealing consisted of 11 contracts made over the previous six months. On each occasion, the contract had been made orally by telephone, but the invoice that was sent afterwards stated that all business was transacted under the current conditions of the Institute of Freight Forwarders (IFF), a copy of which was available on request. (A copy was never requested.) Because the invoice followed the oral contract, it would have arrived too late to incorporate a term in a one-off transaction. However, the Court of Appeal held that the IFF conditions, which were not particularly onerous, were incorporated into the contract by the previous course of dealing.

Three factors appear to determine whether there has been a successful incorporation by notice provided by a previous course of dealing: frequency, consistency, and the nature of the contract.

#### i. Frequency

A course of dealing must be regular--that is, there must be sufficient previous dealings over a suitable length of time to incorporate the term. This is a question of fact, dependent on the circumstances of each case. For example, in *J Spurling Ltd v Bradshaw* [1956] 2 All ER 121, the claimant received a receipt, containing an exclusion clause, from the defendant. Although this was sent after the contract (for storage) was made, and so too late, on a one-off basis, to incorporate the term, the claimant had entered many contracts with the defendant on previous occasions and always received similar receipts when he did so. As a result, he was bound by the exclusion clause. Denning LJ noted, "Mr. Bradshaw admitted that he had received many landing accounts before. True he had not troubled to read them. On receiving this account, he took no objection to it, left the goods there, and went on paying the warehouse rent for months afterwards. It seems to me that by the course of business and conduct of the parties, these conditions were part of the contract".

There does not always have to be very many instances of previous dealing for this to occur, especially in commercial contracts. In *Transformers & Rectifiers Ltd v Needs Ltd* [2015] EWHC 269 (TCC), Edwards-Stuart J reiterated that, in the right circumstances: "Where there is reliance on a previous course of dealing it does not have to be extensive. Three or four occasions over a relatively short period may suffice". By contrast, consumer contracts might require more previous dealings. In *Hollier v Rambler Motors* [1972] 2 WLR 401 the claimant, a private individual, employed the services of the defendant garage on a maximum of four occasions, over a five-year-period. Each time he was asked to sign a document excluding liability for damage occasioned by repair work. However, on the fifth occasion, the contract was made over the telephone and no reference was made to the exclusion clause. The garage damaged his car during the repair work and sought to invoke the clause, on the basis that it had been incorporated through the previous course of dealing. The Court of Appeal held that there had neither been a sufficient number or regularity of transactions for this to occur. In the circumstances, it was not reasonable to expect the claimant to be aware of it, given the modest incidence of dealing and the considerable length of time involved.

### ii. Consistency

The previous course of dealings must be consistent. This was considered in the Scottish case of *McCutcheon v David MacBrayne Ltd* [1964] 1 WLR 125 which went to the House of Lords (the same principle applies in England). In late 1960 the defendant's ferry sank, taking Mr McCutcheon's car with it. He had shipped the vehicle on numerous earlier occasions. Sometimes the defendant required its customers to sign a risk note absolving them from any responsibility for the loss of their cars before they embarked. This had occurred on four previous occasions with Mr McCutcheon. However, at other times, there had been a purely oral contract, which did not contain such a provision. Mr McCutcheon had not signed such a risk note on the instant occasion. The defendant argued that the term had been incorporated into the contract through a previous course of dealing. The House of Lords concluded that as there was no regular course of dealing the term had not been incorporated on the day the ferry sank, so that the claimant was not bound by it. As Lord Reed observed, there had been "no consistent course of dealing; sometimes he was asked to sign and sometimes not".

By contrast, in *Hardwick Game Farm v SSAPA* [1969] 2 AC 31, a lengthy series of oral contracts had been made between SSAPA and its bird-meal supplier. However, they were followed by a contract note from the sellers which contained "conditions of sale" on its back. The buyer's agent knew about these, although he had never read them. Vitally, every one of the earlier contracts had been followed by the dispatch of the contract note, with the same standard terms on the reverse. The House of Lords held that the conduct of SSAPA in accepting these contract notes and their conditions of sale, without challenge, would lead the seller to believe that SSAPA intended to enter the contracts on those terms.

More recently, in *Transformers & Rectifiers Ltd v Needs Ltd* [2015] EWHC 269 (TCC), Edwards-Stuart J reiterated that a course of dealing "has to be consistent and unequivocal". In the instant case, the claimant had not bothered to add its terms and conditions to orders sent by fax or email, which made up a considerable majority of the orders made on a weekly basis over many years, although those sent by post did have the terms on the letter's reverse. As a result, an exemption clause contained within its standard terms and conditions was not held to be incorporated by previous course of dealing. As the purchaser did not follow a consistent practice of enclosing its terms with each order, the supplier was entitled to assume he was not relying on them for the contested transaction, despite being aware of their general existence.

### iii. The Nature of the Contract

In *Transformers & Rectifiers Ltd v Needs Ltd* [2015] EWHC 269 (TCC), Edwards-Stuart J also noted that, where there were trade or industry standard terms for the type of transaction in question, and the parties were in that industry, it would usually be easier (take fewer previous transactions) for a party contending for those conditions to persuade the court that they should be incorporated in their contract by previous course of dealing.

## Construction/Interpretation of Exemption Clauses

To cover a breach, exemption clauses must be clear and unambiguous. Traditionally, the courts went further, and the primary principle of construction for such clauses was the so-called *contra proferentem* rule, whereby any ambiguity in the meaning or reach of such a clause would be resolved against the party seeking to rely on it. In the past, ambiguity was sometimes found quite readily, if only to avoid an extremely draconian clause being applied. This was especially common before the advent of statutory control of such clauses. A selection of illustrations can be considered.

In *Andrews Bros ltd v Singer Cars* [1934] 1 KB 17, the claimant contracted to buy some "new" Singer cars from the defendant. The contract contained a clause excluding "all conditions, warranties and liabilities implied by statute, common law or otherwise". One of the cars they received had previously been driven on public roads. The claimant sought to reject it on the basis that it was not new, but the defendant argued that the exemption clause prevented him from being able to do so, since the implied term under s.13 of the Sale of Goods Act 1893, requiring that goods correspond to description, was excluded. However, the court found in favour of the claimant because the wording of the exclusion clause, interpreted *contra proferentum*, was held not to cover the *express* (rather than implied) term that the cars be "new".

Similarly, in *Baldry v Marshall* [1925] 1 KB 260, the claimant asked the defendant motor dealers to supply a suitable car for touring. The defendants recommended a Bugatti, which the claimant purchased. The written contract excluded the defendant's liability for any "guarantee or warranty, statutory or otherwise". The car turned out to be unsuitable, so the claimant rejected it and sued to recover his money. The Court of Appeal held that the requirement that the car be suitable for touring was a condition. Since, on its narrowest construction, the clause did not exclude liability for breach of a condition (rather than a warranty), the claimant was not bound by it, although warranty had very probably been intended in its looser sense (at that time) as referring to any (not just a minor) term.

In like manner, in *Houghton v Trafalgar Insurance Co. Ltd* [1954] 1 QB 247 the defendant insured the claimant's car. The insurer's contract included a clause that excluded liability where the vehicle had an accident while carrying a "load" exceeding its recommended maximum. The claimant attempted to claim on his insurance policy after having an accident while there were six people in the vehicle, although it was only intended for a maximum of five. It was held that giving the narrowest meaning to "load", that is, interpreting the word *contra proferentem*, it would only apply to freight, not human passengers. Somervell LJ opined, "If there is any ambiguity, it is the company's clause and the ambiguity would be resolved in favour of the assured".

This rule of interpretation has occasionally been alluded to in recent years, especially, but not solely, when it comes to consumer contracts. In *Association of British Travel Agents Limited v British Airways Plc* [2000] 2 Lloyd's Rep. 209, Clarke LJ, discussing an exclusion clause noted: "In my opinion, in all these circumstances, where there is doubt as to the true meaning of the expression 'other charges', it should be construed against the airlines contra proferentes both for the reasons already given and because it appears in an exclusion clause".

Nevertheless, in the modern era, the courts have become much more cautious about over-straining the interpretation of exemption clauses, and are not so eager to find ambiguity, especially where they involve limitation (rather than exclusion) of liability or an exemption clause that has been agreed between large commercial bodies. As Lewison LJ noted in *Interactive E-Solutions v O3B* [2018] EWCA Civ 62, although the courts were traditionally hostile to such clauses, since the advent of statutory regulation under the Unfair Contract Terms Act 1977 they have interpreted them less narrowly.

An early sign of this approach can be seen in the House of Lords case of *Ailsa Craig Fishing v Malvern Fishing* [1983] 1 WLR 964. In this case, Securicor contracted with the Aberdeen Fishing Vessel Owners Association to provide security in the harbour where the latter's vessels were moored. As a result of Securicor's negligence, and consequent breach of contract, some of these vessels were sunk, at huge cost. The contract contained a clause which provided that, in this event, Securicor would not be liable for any amount exceeding £1,000 in any one claim or for more than £10,000 in any twelve-month period. The House of Lords found in favour of Securicor. Lord Wilberforce observed, "One must not strive to create ambiguities by strained construction, as I think the appellants have striven to do. The relevant words must be given, if possible, their natural, plain meaning. Clauses of limitation are not regarded by the courts with the same hostility as clauses of exclusion". Why limitation clauses should be treated more favourably is not entirely clear. Presumably, it is because they are more likely to reflect a conscious negotiation and apportionment of risk.

Over the past few decades, this approach has been adopted more widely, especially in high-level business-to-business contracts between sophisticated parties. For example, in *Persimmon Homes v Ove Arup* [2017] EWCA Civ 373, the Court of Appeal declined to apply the *contra proferentem* rule in such a way as to prevent an exclusion clause from operating. Persimmon Homes had developed a large site near Cardiff. Arup were engaged by them as engineers on the project. Asbestos was discovered on the site, and Persimmon decided that Arup had been negligent in failing to identify its presence much earlier; they sought damages for breach of contract and negligence. The contract between the two parties contained a clause stating that Arup's, "Liability for any claim in relation to asbestos is excluded". Persimmon argued that the exclusion clause should be interpreted narrowly, in accordance with the contra proferentem principle, so that "liability for" meant "liability for causing" asbestos pollution, preventing Arup from relying on it. The judge at first instance found against Persimmon and referred to recent case law limiting the effect of the contra proferentem rule. The Court of Appeal agreed with his conclusion, stating, "The contra proferentem rule now has a very limited role in relation to commercial contracts negotiated between parties of equal bargaining strength". Jackson LJ noted that it would only be in circumstances where the wording is truly ambiguous that the courts would be prepared to consider its application.

Nevertheless, even if the *contra proferentem* rule is not always expressly identified, its influence lives on, even in commercial agreements. In *Nobahar-Cookson & Ors v The Hut Group Ltd* [2016] EWCA Civ 128, the Court of Appeal noted that exclusion clauses should still be narrowly interpreted if it was necessary to resolve ambiguity. In *Burnett or Grant (Respondent) v International Insurance Company of Hanover Ltd (Appellant)* (Scotland) [2021] UKSC 12, an insurer's exclusion clause covered deliberately occasioned injury. The insurer sought to rely on this when faced by a claim based on death caused by a bouncer's bungled attempt to eject an inebriated customer using an improper headlock. Although this resulted in an assault conviction, the criminal court where this occurred said that there had been no intention on the bouncer's part to cause injury. The Supreme Court held that the insurer's exemption clause did not cover such a situation. Had the bouncer intended to cause some form of injury, even if it was not death, the situation would have been different. Although this was a Scottish case, the court noted that the decision would have been the same if it had originated South of the Border.

Arguably, the Consumer Rights Act 2015 has put the *contra proferentum* rule into statutory form for consumer contracts, albeit without using the phrase, and although (and very important) the provision applies to all contract terms, not just exemption clauses. Section 69 of the statute notes, "If a term in a consumer contract, or a consumer notice, could have different meanings, the meaning that is most favourable to the consumer is to prevail". Furthermore, the courts still expect draconian exclusion clauses to be particularly clear, if only because, in practice, what was once termed the doctrine of fundamental breach has had a residual survival as a rule of construction.

## Fundamental Breach and Interpretation

At a time when statutory controls on exemption clauses were almost non-existent, the Court of Appeal developed the doctrine of "fundamental breach" to help restrict abuse of such terms. This viewed some breaches as so fundamental to the agreement that they automatically discharged the entire contract, and so could not be excluded or limited. This notion was rejected by the House of Lords in *Suisse Atlantique Société d'Armement Maritime S.A. v N.V. Rotterdamsche Koken Centrale* [1967] 1 AC 361. Although it was partially revived by Lord Denning in *Harbutt's "Plasticine" Ltd. v Wayne Tank and Pump Co. Ltd* [1970] 1 QB 447, it was finally, and very firmly, ended by the House of Lords in *Photo Production v Securicor Ltd* [1980] AC 827. In this case, a clause in Securicor's standard terms excluded liability when one of its guards, of hitherto irreproachable character, lit a fire inside the Chatham factory he was supposed to be protecting. The factory burnt down. Rejecting the doctrine of fundamental breach, the House of Lords held that Securicor was entitled to rely on the exclusion clause because it covered what had occurred, irrespective of the gravity of the act.

Nevertheless, it is apparent that exemption clauses that cover what might be viewed as a fundamental breach must be expressed in particularly clear terms. As Lord Diplock observed in *Photo Production v Securicor*, "the degree of strictness appropriate to be applied to their construction may properly depend upon the extent to which they involve departure from the implied obligations". The more extreme the exclusion clause, the stricter the court must be before construing it in such a way as to allow the party in breach to avoid liability: *Kudos Catering (UK) v Manchester Central Convention Complex Ltd* [2013] EWCA Civ 38.

For example, in *Soteria Insurance Ltd (formerly CIS General Insurance Limited) v IBM United Kingdom Ltd* [2022] EWCA Civ 440 the Court of Appeal decided that, as a matter of linguistic construction, a clause excluding liability for "consequential losses, or loss of profits, revenue or savings" did not preclude a claimant recovering damages for "wasted expenditure" that had been incurred in anticipation of receiving a new IT system that was not, ultimately, delivered; that is, reliance rather than expectation loss. (These are discussed in Chapter 15). The court felt that its conclusion on this issue was reinforced by general principles governing the construction of exclusion clauses. Most important, the more valuable the right that the clause seeks to exclude, the more draconian the clause, the clearer it will need to be; in the instant case, excluding liability for what might be a catastrophic failure of performance required a very clearly worded clause.

## Excluding Negligence

At common law it is possible to exclude liability for both contractual and tortious negligence in a contract, albeit that this is now subject to very important statutory controls, such as s.2 UCTA 1977 (see below). Nevertheless, historically, the courts were nervous about allowing this to occur, irrespective of such legislation, and developed stringent controls that such a clause had to satisfy before it was deemed to be operative. There were sound reasons for such caution. As Salmon LJ observed, contracting parties are often a "little shy" about expressly referring to negligent performance in their exemption clauses, if only because it is damaging to customer confidence to publicly anticipate such a possibility and then restrict liability for it: *Hollier v Rambler Motors* [1972] 2 WLR 401.

The issue was considered in *Alderslade* v *Hendon Laundry Ltd* [1945] KB 189. in which Lord Greene MR noted that, where the basis of liability can *only* rest on negligence, and nothing else, a properly worded clause will cover it, even if it does not expressly mention negligence, because it would otherwise lack subject matter. Essentially, in this situation, general words such as "howsoever caused", might be effective in excluding liability for negligence. However, where a claim can, simultaneously, be based on some other ground, as well as on negligence, the operation of a generally worded clause must be confined to that other cause of action, without exempting the liability arising from negligence. In these cases, if a contracting party wishes to restrict his liability for negligence, he must do so expressly, in very clear terms.

The same point was reiterated in the Privy Council case of *Canada Steamship Lines Ltd v The King* [1952] UKPC 1 where Lord Morton noted that if a clause contains language which expressly exempts the *proferens* from negligence, effect must be given to that provision, but if there is no such reference, and the head of damage can be based on some other ground than negligence, it will be "fatal to the *proferens* even if the [general] words used are prima facie wide enough to cover negligence."

A classic illustration is provided by *White v John Warwick* [1953] 1 WLR 1285. In this case, the claimant hired a tradesman's tricycle from the defendants from which to sell goods and advertise his business. The written agreement stated, "Nothing in this agreement shall render the owners liable for any personal injury". (Such a clause would now be rendered void by statute.) While the claimant was riding the tricycle, the saddle, which was damaged when hired, tilted forward, and he was injured. The defendants were potentially liable in tort as well as in contract (supplying a defective tricycle). The Court of Appeal held that the wording of the exclusion clause would protect them from their strict contractual liability, but it would not exempt them from liability for common law negligence. Arguably, this approach is justified, because it is inherently improbable that one party would intend to absolve the other from the consequences of the latter's own negligence.[1]

As a result, those wishing to exclude liability for negligence in these situations must do so expressly and clearly. For example, in *Goodlife Foods Ltd v Hall Fire Protection Ltd* [2018] EWCA Civ 1371, the defendant's words achieved this effect, by stating, "We exclude all liability, loss, damages or expense consequential or otherwise caused to your property, goods, persons or the like, directly or indirectly resulting from our negligence or delay or failure or malfunction of the systems or components provided". Nevertheless, a very clear synonym for negligence can have the same effect as the word itself. In *Monarch Airlines Ltd v London Luton Airport Ltd* [1997] CLC 698 the clause excluded liability for any damage to aircraft resulting from an "omission, neglect or default" by the defendant (in this case, debris left on the runway). It was held that the wording of the clause, in particular use of synonyms such as "neglect" and "omission", was sufficiently clear for the exclusion clause to cover negligence.

## Statutory Control of Exemption Clauses: The Unfair Contract Terms Act 1977

The misleadingly named Unfair Contract Terms Act 1977 (UCTA) regulates exemption clauses (the only unfair terms considered by the statute) that exclude or restrict liability for breach of express and implied contractual (and some tortious) obligations in business-to-business contracts (and a tiny number of private-to-private agreements where liability for breach of s.12(1) SOGA 1979 is excluded). Since 2015 the Consumer Rights Act (CRA), rather than UCTA, has fulfilled the same function for consumer contracts, although older consumer cases were dealt with under the 1977 statute and are still relevant to decisions under the newer Act. The CRA will be dealt with briefly after UCTA has been considered.

It should be noted that, under Schedule 1 of the statute, UCTA does not normally cover: insurance contracts; contracts relating to the formation, dissolution, or constitution of a company or to the rights or obligations of its members; contracts relating to the creation or transfer of securities or rights in securities; contracts

1 Jane Swanton, "Exclusion of Liability for Negligence", *University of Queensland Law Journal*, v. 15, no. 2 (1988), p.159.

relating to the creation, transfer or termination of an interest in land; employment contracts; certain marine/shipping contracts, and contracts relating to the creation, transfer, or termination of intellectual property rights. Furthermore, UCTA does not extend to "international supply contracts", under which possession or ownership of goods that will be carried between different states changes hands. (However, contracts for the international supply of services remain within the remit of UCTA, assuming English law is the applicable law to the agreement). A selection of the statute's most important provisions will be considered.

**Section 2 UCTA**

Section 2 of UCTA covers attempts to exclude liability for negligence, including negligently occasioned breach of contract (as well as tortious negligence). This would include breach of the implied term under s.13 SGSA 1982 that a contract of service should be carried out with reasonable skill and care. Section 2(1) prevents a party to a business contract from excluding or restricting liability for death or personal injury resulting from negligence. Such clauses are automatically rendered null and void. Under s.2(2) liability for other forms of loss occasioned by negligence, such as financial loss and property damage, *can* be restricted, but only in so far as the party relying on the clause can persuade the court (on the balance of probabilities) that it satisfies the test of reasonableness set out in s.11(1) of UCTA (see below).

**Section 3 UCTA**

Section 3 UCTA covers contracting parties where one of them deals on the other's written standard terms of business. In these situations, the party who produced the written agreement cannot use any of its terms to exclude or restrict liability for a breach of contract or, alternatively, claim to be entitled to render no contractual performance, or one that is substantially different from that "reasonably expected" of him, except in so far as the term satisfies the requirement of reasonableness under s.11. For example, if a hotel chain contracts with a major company to provide four-star accommodation in Central London for its executives while they do a course, a clause on the hotel's standard form allowing them to substitute a two-star hotel in Maidstone would be subject to (and might well not pass) the reasonableness test.

However, it should be noted that, for the purposes of s.3 of UCTA, the meaning of dealing "on the other's written standard terms of business" is interpreted quite strictly; any negotiated variation of the standard terms is likely to preclude its operation. For example, in *African Export-Import Bank v Shebah Exploration & Production Company Ltd* [2017] EWCA Civ 845, a syndicate of banks entered into a facility agreement with a Nigerian oil company, basing their negotiations on a form recommended by the Loan Market Association. A dispute arose, and the judge at first instance stated that s.3 would apply only if any negotiation and amendment of the draft contract had left the terms "effectively untouched". Upholding this decision, if not (quite) the strictness of the judge's interpretation, the Court of Appeal concluded that s.3 required proof that these terms were habitually used by the other party to the contract, that the deal had been done on them, and that they had not been subject to significant alteration. If there had been major, rather than "insubstantial", variations, it was unlikely that the party seeking to rely on s.3 would have discharged the burden of showing that the contract had been made on the other's written standard terms of business. As the variations in the instant case were found to be substantial, and had been specifically negotiated, the court held that s.3 of UCTA did not apply.

## Sections 6 and 7 UCTA

As already noted, the Sale of Goods Act 1979 (as amended by the Sale and Supply of Goods Act 1994) implies important terms into non-consumer contracts for the sale of goods. For example, s.12 implies terms as to title and quiet possession; s.13 that goods correspond to description; s.14(2) and (3) that they are of satisfactory quality and fit for purpose; and s.15 that they conform to sample. Similar terms are implied into hire-purchase contracts by the Supply of Goods (Implied Terms) Act 1973. Attempts to exclude these terms are regulated by s.6 UCTA. Under s.6(1), liability for breach of the terms implied by s.12 SOGA cannot be excluded or restricted under any circumstances (this is a rare provision that also applies to private-to-private contracts), just like attempts to exclude negligently occasioned personal injury under s.2 UCTA. Such a clause would be rendered null and void, even if successfully incorporated.

However, under s.6(2) of UCTA, liability for breach of the terms implied under, for example, ss.13-15 *can* be excluded or restricted, but *only* in so far as the *proferens* can persuade the court that the clause in question satisfies the requirement of reasonableness set out in s.11 of the statute (see below). Similarly, s.7 UCTA 1977 deals with attempts to exempt liability for breach of the terms implied by s.3 and s.4 of the Supply of Goods and Services Act (SGSA) 1982. Thus, attempts to exclude liability in contracts where, for example, the ownership of goods passes under a contract not governed by the law pertaining to the sale of goods or hire purchase, in respect of their correspondence with description or sample, or their quality or fitness for any particular purpose, cannot be excluded or restricted except in so far as the term satisfies the requirement of reasonableness in s.11.

## Section 11 UCTA and the Reasonableness Test

The requirement of reasonableness is fundamental to the operation of UCTA 1977. Many of the provisions in the statute that exclude exemption clauses become operative only if those clauses are not deemed to be "reasonable". This key term is defined at s.11 of the statute, which provides that the clause must have been a "fair and reasonable one to be included having regard to circumstances which were, or ought reasonably to have been, known to or in the contemplation of the parties when the contract was made". Although a somewhat circular definition, it makes clear that it is the time that the contract was made, not when it was breached, that is vital when determining reasonableness. Furthermore, under s.11(5), the burden of establishing that an exemption clause is reasonable lies on the party seeking to rely on it: "It is for those claiming that a contract term or notice satisfies the requirement of reasonableness to show that it does". This will, of course, normally be the defendant, and must be established on a balance of probabilities (the normal civil standard of proof).

Frequently decisions on reasonableness will require a balancing act. As Lord Bridge observed in *George Mitchell (Chesterhall) Ltd v Finney Lock Seeds Ltd* [1983] 2 AC 803, the courts must often entertain a range of considerations, both for and against a clause being reasonable, put them in the scales, and decide on which side the balance comes down. Sometimes there will be room for a legitimate difference of judicial opinion as to what the answer should be. As a result, appellate courts will not readily second-guess a trial judge but treat the original decision with the: "...utmost respect and refrain from interference with it unless satisfied that it proceeded upon some erroneous principle or was plainly and obviously wrong". Lord Justice Lewison reiterated this point in *First Tower Trustees Limited v CDS (Superstores International) Limited* [2018] EWCA Civ 1396, noting that the issue of reasonableness was an evaluative judgment for the judge at first instance, and the Court of Appeal will not lightly interfere with his or her decision.

*George Mitchell (Chesterhall) Ltd v Finney Lock Seeds Ltd* [1983] 2 AC 803 provides an illustration of factors going both ways on the issue of reasonableness. Mitchell, a farmer, had purchased 30 pounds of cabbage seed from the defendants for £192 and then sown 63 acres of his land with it. He subsequently spent many hours and much money tending the growing vegetables. Unfortunately, the cabbage seed was defective (it was for the wrong planting season) and did not produce a harvestable crop. The claimant lost over £60,000 as a result. However, the contract contained a limitation clause that restricted their liability to the price paid for the seeds (the £192).

In favour of the clause being reasonable was that a relatively low value contract could lead to enormous liability for the seed-seller, while it was also a limitation not a total exclusion clause. Against this, it was normal practice for Finney Lock Seeds not to rely on the clause where a settlement could be negotiated, and this had been attempted in the instant case, suggesting that even they accepted that it was rather harsh. Very important, the seed company was best placed to insure against the risk of defective seeds. It could take out a general policy to cover such situations and add the relatively modest cost to its seed sales. The House of Lords held that the clause was unreasonable.

When determining reasonableness for the purposes of sections 6 and 7 of the Act, attention is expressly drawn to the matters specified in Schedule 2 of the statute. However, case law since the advent of UCTA suggests that many of these factors are also highly relevant to decisions on reasonableness under other sections of the statute: *Stewart Gill Limited v Horatio Meyer & Company Limited* [1992] QB 600. Amongst the factors set out in Schedule 2 are the relative strength of the bargaining positions of the parties; the alternative means by which a customer's requirements might have been met; whether the customer received an inducement to agree to the term; whether the goods were manufactured, processed, or adapted to their special order; and whether the customer knew or should have known that the term was included.

For example, if a claimant company was given a significant discount to agree to an exemption clause in a contract with another company of equal size, but could just as easily have entered a contract without it, albeit at a higher price, both with the counterparty and other local suppliers, who were readily available, and was fully aware of this, there is a much greater chance that it will be deemed "reasonable" than if all these factors were absent. However, all decided cases on reasonableness turn on their particular facts, and so are merely of persuasive authority to future decisions. Nevertheless, with this caveat, a mass of case law has put flesh on the statutory bones of UCTA and provided guidance on the issue of reasonableness, some of which identify factors that are not contained in Schedule 2. (Some of these cases are also relevant to decisions made under the CRA 2015.)

Very important, and as *George Mitchell v Finney Lock Seeds* suggests, the ready availability and affordability of insurance against the contingency that has arisen often appears to be a vital factor in the modern era. Thus, in *Smith v Eric Bush* [1990] 1 AC 831, a surveyor was employed by a building society to inspect and value a terraced house for a mortgage survey (primarily conducted to reassure the lender) on an £88,000 house in Norwich. He excluded any liability for negligence that led to damage to the property of the purchaser, Mrs Smith, although he knew she would have sight of his report, for which she paid about £37. The valuation mistakenly said that no essential repairs were needed to the property. The chimney subsequently collapsed, its bricks falling through the roof, because the surveyor had not noticed that an important support had (fairly obviously) been removed without replacement by an RSJ. Mrs Smith argued that the clause excluding liability for negligence in their agreement was unreasonable under s.2(2) of UCTA. The House of Lords agreed. In reaching this decision the court stated that it was appropriate that a professional surveyor bear the risk of liability, not least because he could conveniently arrange affordable insurance which would merely lead to a small increase in the average price of such surveys. (The court also noted that spotting such an obvious structural defect was not a difficult task, with a high risk of failure).

Similarly, in *Phillips Products v Hyland* [1987] 1 WLR 659 the claimant hired a manned excavator from the defendants on the latter's standard terms which provided that the driver should be regarded as employed by the claimant, who would thereby remain liable for any loss arising from the machine's use (a veiled exclusion clause). The driver negligently damaged the claimant's factory whilst carrying out work at his request. It was held that several factors meant that the clause failed the s.11 reasonableness test. Among them was the brevity of the hire period, which meant that the claimant had little opportunity to arrange insurance cover. (Others included the claimant having nothing to do with the selection of the driver.)

## Recent Cases on Reasonableness

In the modern era the courts have been especially reluctant to intervene in negotiated commercial contracts made between parties of roughly comparable bargaining power, particularly if they were advised by lawyers, often preferring to leave them free to apportion the risks of their agreement as they see fit and readily deciding that exemption clauses satisfy the reasonableness test: *Watford Electronics Ltd v Sanderson CFL Limited* [2001] 1 All ER (Comm) 696. In this case, the Court of Appeal, when deciding that a limitation clause was reasonable, noted that not only were both parties experienced commercial negotiators, but that the claimant appeared to have made a conscious decision to accept the limitation clause in return for other concessions from the defendant. In *Granville Oil & Chemicals Ltd v Davis Turner & Co Ltd* [2003] EWCA Civ 570, Tuckey LJ reiterated that, when it came to UCTA, he was not "enthusiastic about its intrusion into contracts between commercial parties of equal bargaining strength, who should generally by considered capable of being able to make contracts of their choosing and expect to be bound by their terms". More recently, in *Goodlife Foods Ltd v Hall Fire Protection Ltd* [2018] EWCA Civ 1371, Coulson LJ observed that the trend in UCTA cases that had been decided in recent years had been "towards upholding terms freely agreed, particularly if the other party could have contracted elsewhere and has, or was warned to obtain, effective insurance cover".

In *Goodlife*, Hall Fire had designed and installed a fire-protection system in Goodlife's factory premises at Warrington in 2002 (see above). In 2012 the factory caught fire, occasioning losses worth about £6.6 million, which Goodlife claimed was caused by a failure in the protection system. Goodlife sued Hall Fire for negligently installing the system (a contract action would probably have been time-barred). The original agreement had excluded such liability. One of the issues in the High Court was whether the exclusion clause breached the reasonableness requirement in UCTA. The trial judge concluded that the clause was reasonable and so enforceable. The Court of Appeal upheld his conclusion and reviewed authorities that emphasised, inter alia, the significance of terms having been freely agreed by commercial parties of roughly equal size. It was also noted that the claimant could have gone elsewhere for the service, and that it was best placed to insure against the loss that had occurred, while their attention had been specifically drawn to the availability of insurance to cover the relevant risk. Additionally, Hall Fire had been prepared to accept wider liability if requested by Goodlife, in exchange for an increase in the contract price. Furthermore, Hall Fire's terms and conditions were not out of kilter with those of other fire-suppression contractors.

By contrast, in *Saint Gobain Building Distribution Ltd (t/a International Decorative Surfaces) v Hillmead Joinery (Swindon) Ltd* [2015] BLR 555, the High Court concluded that various exemption clauses contained in IDS's standard terms in a contract to supply Hillmead with laminate sheets were unreasonable. Amongst them was a term excluding liability for breach of both the implied terms contained in s.14 SOGA 1979 (satisfactory quality and fitness for purpose). The High Court's decision was partly based on the parties' unequal bargaining power. Hillmead was tiny in comparison to IDS. Furthermore, the exclusion of the statutory implied terms had not been replaced by an express term governing quality in any form.

Similarly, in *Phoenix Interior Design Ltd v Henley Homes plc* [2021] EWHC 1573 (QB), the High Court found that although an exclusion clause in a supplier's standard terms and conditions had been successfully incorporated by reference, it did not satisfy the requirement of reasonableness under s.11 UCTA. Interestingly, one reason for the judge's decision in this case was that a degree of notice that was sufficient to incorporate an exemption clause (as had been the case) could *still* be deemed inadequate for the purposes of reasonableness under s.11. In the instant case, an unusual clause was "tucked away in the undergrowth" of the defendant's standard terms without any highlighting of its consequences. Even though the claimant had had various opportunities to consider it during a course of dealing, its obscurity was still relevant in the context of Schedule 2, and whether the customer ought reasonably to have known of the existence and extent of the term. Furthermore, the judge noted that, even if there had been detailed consideration of the term, its consequences were not obvious.

**Clauses Falling Foul of UCTA**

If an exemption clause is rendered invalid by UCTA, whether because it purports to exclude a type of liability which cannot be avoided under any circumstances, or because the clause is not deemed to be "reasonable" for the purposes of s.11, it will have no effect, being rendered null and void. The court will not rewrite the clause to substitute an acceptable alternative. In the years immediately after 1977, the courts went further, and were reluctant merely to exclude the offending part (rather than the whole) of an exemption clause, even if doing so would still have left a coherent provision. However, in recent years a more liberal approach to this issue has been evident, so that, because part of an exclusion clause is invalid under the statute, it does not mean that this will necessarily apply to the remainder.

Thus, in *Goodlife Foods v Hall Fire Protection* [2018] EWCA Civ 1371, the defendant sought to rely on a widely drafted contractual provision which excluded all liability for loss caused by negligence to "property, goods, persons or the like". Goodlife argued that the reference to "persons" was an attempt to exclude liability for death or personal injury, something that is forbidden by s.2(1) UCTA 1977. The High Court agreed but found that this part of the exemption clause *could* be severed, and the remainder then upheld as enforceable. This analysis was not challenged on appeal.

Nevertheless, it is still probably prudent for those drafting exemption clauses to reduce the theoretical risk of an entire clause being unenforceable by drafting it as a series of readily distinguishable terms or parts. It also should be noted that no other sanctions, such as a fine or other penalty, apply to a party who has employed an invalid clause in their contracts.

**Statutory Control of Exemption Clauses: The Consumer Rights Act 2015**

Under s.65(1) CRA, and like s.2(1) UCTA, a trader cannot use a term set out in a consumer contract or a public notice to exclude or restrict liability for death or personal injury resulting from negligence. Similarly, under s.31(1) CRA a term in a contract to supply goods is not binding on a consumer in so far as it excludes or restricts the trader's liability under ss.9-17 and s.28 of the same statute. Thus, and *inter alia*, if it purports to exempt the trader from supplying goods that are of satisfactory quality, fit for a particular purpose, as described, matching a sample, or in which he does not have title, they will be null and void.

More generally, a clause that purports to exclude or restrict a trader's liability may be deemed to be "unfair" under the CRA and so void, as s.62(1-2) of the Act provides that an unfair term or notice is not binding on the consumer in an agreement. Section 62(4) provides that a term or notice will be unfair if, "contrary to the requirement of good faith", it causes a significant imbalance in the parties' rights and obligations under the contract, to the detriment of the consumer. Schedule 2 Part 1 CRA provides an indicative and non-exhaustive list of 20 terms which may be regarded as unfair. These terms are not automatically unfair, but the "grey list" can be used to assist the court when considering the application of the general fairness test in section 62 to a particular case. Thus, a term that has the object or effect of inappropriately excluding or limiting the legal rights of the consumer in relation to the trader in the event of non-performance or inadequate performance of any of the latter's contractual obligations may be regarded as unfair.

For an example, *Green v Betfred* [2021] EWHC 842 (QB) can be considered. In this case, Mr Green played blackjack on Betfred's gaming website. After several hours of playing, an undetectable "glitch" in the game's software led to Mr Green's being dealt numerous winning cards and so making over £1.7 million. However, Betfred subsequently refused to let him cash in his (electronic) chips, relying on exclusion clauses, including one stating that "a malfunction voids all pays and plays". However, in an application by Mr Green for summary judgment, Foster J held that the clauses were not effective in excluding liability. In part, this was because they were poorly drafted and did not clearly cover what had occurred, and they had not, in any event, been incorporated into the contract as they were buried in electronic documentation that was inadequately signposted, being set out in unnumbered and closely typed paragraphs. (See above). However, the judge also held that, irrespective of these problems, the exclusion clauses would have been ineffective under the Consumer Rights Act 2015. Section 62(1-2) CRA requires terms to be "fair", and under s.64(4) they must be transparent, prominent, and their meaning clear to an average and informed consumer. The terms in the instant case did not meet these requirements, and for these (and other) reasons the exclusion clauses were not effective.

# Chapter 14: Discharge of Contracts by Performance

## Introduction

A contract becomes discharged through performance after both parties have fully carried out their obligations under the agreement. However, parties to a mutually uncompleted contract can discharge any or all outstanding obligations under it by entering a separate agreement to do so. This will require the presence of the three formalities required by all legally binding agreements: offer and acceptance, consideration, and intention to create legal relations, these establishing what is traditionally termed, in such situations, "Accord [agreement] and Satisfaction". Provided both parties have executory consideration still to perform, it can be traded to provide the requisite element of bargain or "satisfaction", each party giving up outstanding entitlements in exchange for being released from their own outstanding obligations, so bringing the contract to an end (if that is sought). Thus, if a builder contracts with another to build a six-foot wall for £3,000, they can subsequently agree to change this to five feet for £2,000. The loss of a foot of wall in exchange for a reduction of £1,000 will be binding. However, if only one party has outstanding obligations, release via a deed (Sometimes called a "deed of release") or the provision of fresh consideration (even if nominal) will normally be required to make the agreement binding. (See also acceptance of part-performance in otherwise 'entire' contracts, below).

## The Entire Contract Rule

In a contract where the price is payable on completion, full performance by one party is sometimes a condition precedent to any liability arising on the part of the other, performance triggering the requirement for payment. This is termed the entire contract rule. The question of whether a contract is entire depends on the intention of the parties, objectively determined. However, a contract where one party's obligation is to pay a lump sum in exchange for the other's goods or services is particularly likely be held to be entire, so that in the absence of full performance there is often no right to payment. As was observed in *Re Hall and Barker* (1878) 9 ChD 538, "If a man engages to carry a box of cigars from London to Birmingham, it is an entire contract, and he cannot throw the cigars out of the carriage half-way there, and ask for half the money; or if a shoemaker agrees to make a pair of shoes, he cannot offer you one shoe and ask you to pay one half the price". Many types of contract have been deemed to fall into this category, in the right circumstances, including those pertaining to employment, solicitors' retainers, and consultancy agreements. Nevertheless, many modern cases on this topic involve construction or building work.

The facts of the historic case of *Cutter v Powell* [1795] 101 ER 573 provide an illustration of the rule. The claimant's husband contracted to serve as a second mate on a vessel that was making a two-month return voyage from Jamaica to England. A term in the contract stated that he would be paid 30 guineas (£30.75 in modern sterling) provided he "proceeds, continues and does his duty as second mate in the said ship from hence to the port of Liverpool". Six weeks into the voyage, and two weeks before arrival at Liverpool, the second mate died suddenly. His wife sought payment on a *quantum meruit* basis for the six weeks of the voyage he had successfully completed. Her action failed, as this was held to be an entire contract, and the money became payable only on completion of the full journey to Liverpool. It should be noted that he had been offered over the normal rate of pay for making the voyage, and his wages were due to be paid ten days after arrival in England, both of which factors may have influenced the court's decision in this regard.

More gruesomely, in *Vigers v Cook* [1919] 2 KB 475 the Court of Appeal concluded that providing a funeral was an entire contract to dispose of the body (for want of a better phrase) in a proper and dignified manner, in the absence of which no payment need be made. In this case, a failure to leave a sealed coffin's vent open led to bodily emissions or gas accumulating and the coffin bursting at church, which meant that it could not be brought into the building, and there was a distressing (and smelly) scene. Nevertheless, the body had (eventually) been buried, something that led the county court to allow a reduced payment at first instance. Even so, on appeal, Bankes LJ concluded that "it being one entire contract, in my opinion he [the claimant] fails in proving that he is entitled to any portion of the one entire price which was payable for the entire contract". More recently, in *Buxton v Mills-Owens* [2010] EWCA Civ 122 the Court of Appeal affirmed that a solicitor's retainer constitutes an "entire contract", so that *prima facie* solicitors are entitled to payment only on completion of the task for which they have been retained, although this can easily be circumvented by the lawyer's own express terms of business.

There has been periodic judicial and academic criticism of this potentially harsh rule since the nineteenth century. Some have suggested that the non-completing party should still be able to claim a reasonable sum for his work. By contrast, others argue that it plays a valuable role in securing performance. For example, some small firms of builders have a reputation for starting jobs simultaneously, and the rule does discourage them from abandoning such work when a better opportunity presents itself, as they know that they will often not be paid for what they have already done if they do so. Nevertheless, even if harsh, the rule is greatly ameliorated by, *inter alia*, the doctrines of substantial performance, voluntary acceptance of part performance, and divisibility of contracts.

### Substantial Performance

Substantial performance allows parties to be paid pursuant to what is an entire contract even if they have (technically) failed to comply with the precise terms of the agreement. Essentially, while substantial performance may not be full and complete performance, it is deemed by the courts to be close enough to such an outcome, because the deviation does not amount to a major breach of the agreement. In these situations, the courts may award the contractually agreed price but then deduct sums to reflect the defective performance, such as the cost of repair. This makes sense, not least because, in the case of large and complex contracts, such as major building projects, it is often very difficult to render a performance that is completely defect-free. However, if the performance is not held to amount to substantial performance, the entire-contract rule still applies, and the claimant is entitled to nothing.

Inevitably, difficulty sometimes arises as to what amounts to substantial performance. This is determined on the facts of each case. Nevertheless, two factors appear to influence the courts on this issue. First, has the contract been, at least ostensibly, fully carried out? Is it a case of defective performance or incomplete performance? The latter is somewhat less likely to see the doctrine being invoked. In *Dakin v Lee* [1916] 1 KB 566, the defendants promised to rebuild a house according to certain specifications but failed to meet some of them. Thus, the concrete underpinning was not four feet deep as specified, the concrete employed not always properly mixed, the joining of certain steel joists had been done poorly, and the window supports were less sturdy than specified. At first instance, the Official Referee found that the builders had not completed the contract and so were not entitled to any payment. However, the Court of Appeal distinguished between failing to complete a contract, as in *Sumpter v Hedges* (1898) 1 QB 673 (see below) and completing the work poorly, as in the instant case. It was held that the builders were entitled to recover the contract price, less so much as ought to be allowed in respect of the items found to be defective.

The second factor relates to the extent of any defects and the cost of putting them right, especially as a proportion of the whole contract. Even if a contract has been (ostensibly) fully carried out, there will come a point when the defects in performance are so severe that the contract is deemed not to have been substantially performed. This is always a matter of degree, something that is often captured by comparing two contrasting cases.

In the Court of Appeal case of *Hoenig v Isaacs* [1952] 2 All ER 176, the claimant, an interior decorator and furniture designer, agreed to decorate and furnish the defendant's one-room flat for £750, payable by two instalments, with the balance to be paid on completion. When the work was done, there were problems with some of the decoration and, more especially, a fitted bookcase and a wardrobe, which would cost £56 to rectify. Mr Hoenig refused to pay the £350 outstanding second and final instalment. It was held that, although very close to the borderline, the claimant *had* substantially performed the contract and so was entitled to the contractually agreed price less the cost of remedying the defects (just over a seventh of the instalment). Denning LJ observed that when a contract provided for a specific sum to be paid on completion of specified work, the courts lean against a construction of the agreement that would deprive the contractor of any payment at all, simply because there are some defects or omissions: "Unless the breach does go to the root of the matter, the employer cannot resist payment of the price. He must pay it and bring a cross-claim for the defects and omissions, or alternatively set them up in diminution of the price. The measure is the amount which the work is worth less by reason of the defects and omissions, and is usually calculated by the cost of making them good".

By contrast, in another Court of Appeal case, that of *Bolton v Mahadeva* [1972] 1 WLR 1009, the claimant installed central heating in the defendant's home, the agreed contract price being £560. The defendant was not satisfied with the work, as the overall temperatures produced were rather low, making the house colder than was desirable, the heat came unevenly, and the system gave off fumes. Bolton refused to correct it, which would have cost £174 (almost a third of the total cost). Mahadeva refused to pay any money at all and Bolton sued. The County Court judge, Sir Graeme Finlay, held that the contract price needed to be paid, minus a sum for the cost of putting the heating system right. However, the Court of Appeal held that Bolton was entitled to nothing because there had been no substantial performance. Sachs LJ observed, "It is not merely that so very much of the work was shoddy, but it is the general ineffectiveness of it for its primary purpose that leads me to that conclusion". For a more recent illustration of substantial performance, can be considered *Williams v Roffey Bros & Nicolls* [1991] 1 QB 1, where the need to make "some small deduction for defective and incomplete items" from the value of £4,600 due for a divisible part of a contract to refurbish flats, did not preclude payment for the work done.

### Acceptance of Part Performance

It is open to a contracting party to voluntarily accept part-performance of what would otherwise be an entire contract for a lesser sum. Essentially, this means forming a new contract with the counterparty, if only by conduct. Thus, in *Christy v Row* (1808) 1 Taunt 300 consignees accepted delivery of a cargo at another port to that originally specified in the agreement (rendered difficult for political reasons) and were required to pay for freight at the contract rate for the proportion of the voyage completed.

However, such acceptance must be truly voluntary, so that rejection of the part performance is a realistic alternative option. This issue was considered in the Court of Appeal case of *Sumpter v Hedges* (1898) 1 QB 673, in which the claimant contracted to build two houses and stables for the defendant for a lump sum of £565, this being payable on completion (an entire contract). The claimant started the building work but ran out of money, and for this and other reasons was unable to complete the project, although by then he had performed just over half the work. The trial judge found that he had abandoned the contract. The defendant then completed the buildings himself, albeit using some of the building materials (bricks, etc.) left behind by the claimant. The latter sought to recover £333, representing the value of the work he had completed. He argued that the defendant, in completing the work himself, had accepted partial performance.

The Court of Appeal rejected this argument and held that the defendant had no choice but to act as he did, as he would otherwise have been left with an unsightly and unusable half-completed house. Collins LJ observed, "He is not bound to keep unfinished a building which in an incomplete state would be a nuisance on his land. I am therefore of opinion that the claimant was not entitled to recover for the work which he had done". However, the claimant *could* recover money for the building materials he had left behind that the defendant had employed, as the latter had a real choice as to whether to use them or not. More generally, Smith LJ reiterated the entire-contract rule, noting that where there is a contract to do work for a lump sum this could not be recovered until the work was completed: "It is suggested however that the claimant was entitled to recover for the work he did on a quantum meruit. But, so that may be, there must be evidence of a fresh contract to pay for the work already done".

## Divisibility/Severability

The rule relating to discharge through full performance applies where the agreement is deemed to be an entire contract. Where it is possible to divide a contract into separate parts, which are independent from each other, and that can be carried out on their own, the courts can award a sum for those parts that have been completed, even if the rest of the contract is not performed. Indeed, they can even apply the doctrine of substantial performance in relation to such individual parts, which can also be subject to their own liquidated damages clauses for late completion, as was the case in the building contract in *Vinci Construction UK Ltd v Beumer Group UK Ltd* [2017] EWHC 2196 [TCC].

Whether a particular obligation is entire or severable is a matter of construction for the courts. Most obviously, divisibility or severability might occur where the parties have expressly provided for this in the contract. For a common example of the former can be considered a house-building contract which expressly specifies separate sums and completion dates for the laying of foundations, building of walls, completion of joinery, and finishing the roof. Alternatively, a contract can be severable by implication. This last is important, as the courts are often very reluctant to construe complex or lengthy contracts as requiring complete performance before any payment is due. Implied severability might occur where, for example, it is agreed that a sum will be payable per day, week, or month worked, or per unit of measurement (whatever that might be).

Thus, an example of implied divisibility was identified in *Ritchie v Atkinson* (1808) 10 East 295. In this case, the claimant contracted to transport a specified quantity of hemp and iron for £5 per ton for the former, and 5 shillings per ton for the latter (which was much more compact and so easier to carry). The claimant carried only part of the agreed quantity. The defendant argued that the contract had not been fully performed and therefore no payment at all was due. However, it was held that the contract could be divided into separate parts, as the parties had agreed a price per ton. The claimant was thus entitled to payment for the amount already carried, although the defendant was entitled to damages for non-performance in relation to the remainder (the amount not carried).

Similarly, in *Taylor v Laird* (1856) 1 H&N 266, a captain employed to command a steam-vessel going up the River Niger in Africa, for payment of £50 a month, refused to go further than Dagbo, a riverine trading post below its intended destination, giving up his position as a result. Even so, and unlike *Cutter v Powell*, he succeeded in claiming payment for his earlier work on the basis that his wages were payable each month, so that the agreement was severable (for each completed month). More recently, and subtly, in *Williams v Roffey Bros & Nicolls* [1991] 1 QB 1 (discussed elsewhere in relation to consideration), Mr Williams contracted to refurbish 27 flats in a mansion block for a payment of £20,000. It was held that although there was no express term providing for payment to be made by stages, the contract was "subject to an implied term that the defendants would make interim payments to the claimant, related to the amount of work done, at reasonable intervals".

## Wrongful Prevention of Performance

Sometimes a party to a contract will be prevented from completing his obligations under the agreement by the counterparty, making the performance of the entire obligation impossible. In these circumstances, the injured party has a choice. He can terminate the agreement and sue for breach of contract, seeking to recover damages for his lost profit. Normally, this will be the contract price less any expense he would have been put to (for example, the materials and casual labour he would have employed in a building contract). He will, of course, also come under an obligation to mitigate his loss. Thus, a builder would have to seek other (suitable) work for the time he would otherwise have given over to the agreement. Alternatively, the injured party might seek a *quantum meruit*, seeking a reasonable amount for the work that he has already done; this is, essentially, a restitutionary claim. For example, in *Planche v Colburn and Another* (1831) 8 Bing 14, the defendants engaged the claimant to write a monograph on ancient armour for a periodical publication for payment of £100. The claimant started the work, but, before he had completed it, the defendants abandoned the project. The Court of Appeal held the claimant might sue for compensation for the work he had completed, without having to deliver the entire monograph. He was entitled to £50 for this work.

## Rejection of Tender of Performance

Where a party tenders performance of their obligations under an agreement, but the counterparty refuses to accept it, he will often be discharged further obligations under the contract, and the non-accepting party becomes liable in damages. Such cases frequently involve contracts for the sale of goods, and the measure of damages will normally be assessed by selling the rejected goods in the market and seeking the difference (if any) from the non-accepting party.

Of course, there can sometimes be a question as to whether performance has been satisfactorily tendered. This will be a question of fact for the court to determine. Thus, in *Startup v Macdonald* (1843) 6 Mann & G 593, 10 tuns of linseed oil were to be delivered to the defendant within the last 14 days of March and "paid for at the expiration of that time in cash". The claimant tendered the oil at the defendant's warehouse at 8.30 pm on the last day of the month (a Saturday), but the defendant refused to accept delivery because of the late hour, although he was present and so had a reasonable opportunity to ascertain both the quantity and quality of the oil delivered. It was held that the claimant had tendered performance within the agreed contractual period and was entitled to damages for non-acceptance. Aspects of the decision in *Startup v Macdonald* are now reflected in s.34 Sale of Goods Act 1979, which provides that: "Unless otherwise agreed, when the seller tenders delivery of goods to the buyer, he is bound on request to afford the buyer a reasonable opportunity of examining the goods for the purpose of ascertaining whether they are in conformity with the contract and, in the case of a contract for sale by sample, of comparing the bulk with the sample."

# Chapter 15: Damages and Action for an Agreed Sum

## Introduction

Once a breach of contract has been established, the injured party will usually seek a remedy, although termination for a 'repudiatory breach', allowing them to avoid the agreement and further obligations under it, might (sometimes) be enough, given the potential cost and stress of litigation. The primary (common law) remedy for breach of contract is an award of money, termed damages, that is payable by the party in breach, and which is intended to compensate the injured party for the loss that they have suffered because of that breach. Such damages are claimed as of right, not given at the court's discretion, and will be considered below. However, in certain situations, the courts will award an agreed sum of money (rather than damages) in an action like that for a debt, which remedy is also dealt with in this chapter. Occasionally, the courts will have recourse to alternative, equitable, remedies such as the power to order specific performance of a contract or to grant an injunction restraining a (potential) breach of contract. Unlike damages, equitable remedies are discretionary awards. They are considered in the next chapter.

## Damages

Normally, any breach of contract entitles the injured party to an award of damages. However, to receive "substantial" damages, the injured party must establish that he has suffered identifiable loss of a type and in circumstances that produce an entitlement to compensation. A breach of contract where there is no recoverable loss will only produce an entitlement to "nominal" damages. These are a purely token amount, usually between £1 and £10, awarded to acknowledge that there has been a breach of contract. Thus, in *Marathon Asset Management LLP and Anor v Seddon and Ors* [2017] EWHC 300 (Comm), nominal damages of £1 were awarded against two former workers who breached a duty of confidence to their erstwhile employer, an asset-management firm, but made no use of the information they had secured, so that the employer did not suffer loss.

Suing for a breach of contract where only nominal damages are likely to result can have serious consequences when it comes to an award of costs at the end of the trial, even if the claimant "wins", if only to discourage people from pointless and time-consuming litigation. In these situations, the general rule that the unsuccessful party in proceedings pays the costs of the successful party might be ignored by exercising the discretion (now contained) in Rule 44.2(2)(b) of the Civil Procedure Rules (CPR). For example, in *Obagi v Stanborough (Developments) Ltd* (1993) TLR Dec 15, the claimants were awarded nominal damages of £5 but were required to pay the defendant's costs.

## Limitations on the Award of Damages for Breach of Contract

It is generally recognised that compensating a claimant for all the losses that might, in some sense, be said to flow from any given contractual breach could lead to rather unsatisfactory, if not positively harmful, results. Consequently, the recovery of such damages is limited by four legal rules. Most important, a claimant cannot recover damages for loss where: there is no (legally recognised) causal connection between the breach and that loss; the breach was not reasonably foreseeable when they entered the contract and so is deemed too "remote"; the breach could have been avoided by the claimant's taking reasonable steps in mitigation; the breach falls under heads which are deemed irrecoverable such as, normally and most importantly, injury to feelings. These will be considered *seriatim*.

### 1. Causation

There must be a causal connection between the defendant's breach of contract and the claimant's loss. (Strictly speaking, causation is required to found a claim, rather than being a limit to recoverability.) Although the defendant's breach does not have to be the only cause of the loss, it must be an effective one. Traditionally, English courts have been reluctant to lay down formal tests for causation, which is rarely an issue in practice. As has been observed, "No clear test or set of principles has emerged from the contract cases to determine whether the chain of causation has been broken or not".[1] Instead, the courts have usually relied on common sense to guide decisions as to whether a breach of contract was a sufficiently substantial cause of the claimant's loss. As Gross LJ observed in *Borealis AB v Geogas Trading SA* [2011] 1 Lloyd's Rep. 482, this question is very fact sensitive, so that it is almost impossible to generalise.

Nevertheless, in *Galoo v Bright Graham Murray* [1994] 1 WLR 1360, the Court of Appeal considered this issue in slightly more conceptual terms when deciding whether a firm of chartered accountants were liable for the losses incurred by a company that had continued to trade after they (the accountants) conducted an (allegedly) negligent audit, one that failed to identify potential insolvency. In the instant case, the Court of Appeal held that this was not enough to establish causation between the breach of contract (the conduct of the audit) and the loss; the former was not the "effective" or "dominant" cause of the latter. Importantly, the court noted that it was necessary to distinguish between a breach of contract that causes loss to the claimant and one that merely provides an opportunity for him to incur such loss (as it decided was the situation in the instant case). *Galoo Ltd v Bright Grahame Murray* also makes it clear that causation in tort (the "but for" test) is very different to that for contract, with its stress on effective/dominant cause.

In practice, a key issue will usually be whether there was an unforeseeable act by a third party or the claimant himself, or the intervention a natural phenomenon (this last being rare), which broke the chain of causation between the breach and the loss. For example, in the historic case of *Monarch Steamship Co Ltd v Karlshamns Oljefabriker* (1949) AC 196, the defendant's ship was chartered to carry a cargo from Manchuria to Sweden. The vessel should have reached Sweden in July 1939, but its

1 Burrows, *Restatement*, p. 137.

boilers were defective, which constituted a breach of the defendant's duty to provide a seaworthy vessel. As a result, it did not leave Port Said until late September I939. By then, the Second World War had broken out. The British Admiralty prevented the (British-registered) ship from sailing to Sweden, with its attendant risk of enemy attack, and ordered her to proceed to Glasgow. There, her cargo was eventually transferred to neutral vessels, which delivered them to Sweden, at considerable extra cost. The purchasers of the cargo sued the ship owners for breach of contract, seeking this extra cost. In their defence, the ship owners claimed that the additional expense was occasioned by the order from the Admiralty, rather than their own breach of the agreement.

The House of Lords rejected this argument, and held that damages were recoverable, while also considering what should be the general test in such situations. Lord Porter suggested that it had to be determined whether the breach of contract was the "effective cause" of the loss. Lord Wright noted that the common law was not concerned with philosophical speculation but (effectively) employed common sense to determine this issue. In the circumstances, he would not hesitate to say that, because of the delay it occasioned, unseaworthiness caused the Admiralty order diverting the vessel, and so was the "dominant cause". As a result, the carriers were held liable for the cost of trans-shipment, even though it was caused by a combination of unseaworthiness and the acts of the British authorities. Neither factor was the sole cause of the loss, and both could be said to have operated with "equal efficacy".

Similarly, in *Smith, Hogg & Co v Black Sea and Baltic General Insurance Co Ltd* [1940] 3 All ER 405 the owners of the steamship *Lilburn* were held liable to a charterer for the loss of a cargo being carried by the vessel. Although this had been caused by a combination of perils of the sea (which could not reasonably be guarded against) and the unseaworthiness of the ship itself (a clear breach of contract), the latter was deemed sufficient to establish the claim for damages.

In contrast, can be considered *Quinn v Burch Bros* [1966] 2 QB 370. In this case, the defendants were the main contractors on a building project. The claimant was an independent sub-contractor engaged in carrying out plastering. Under the contract between them, the defendants were required to supply any equipment necessary for the claimant's work. On the day in question, the latter needed a stepladder to work on ceilings at a height of about 10 feet, but despite several requests the defendants failed to supply one. The claimant eventually found a folded trestle, which he propped against the wall, and then used as an improvised ladder. It slipped and he fell and broke his heel and injured his hand. He claimed that his injuries were the result of the defendants' breach of contract. Paull J held that the defendants were in breach of contract in failing to supply a stepladder, but that this breach did not cause the claimant's accident. The Court of Appeal agreed. Salmon LJ observed that it was "quite impossible to say that in reality the Claimant's injury was caused by the breach of contract. The breach of contract merely gave the plaintiff the opportunity to injure himself". The primary cause of the claimant's injuries was his decision to use unsuitable equipment to reach the ceiling; his negligence broke the chain of causation.

More recently, in *County Ltd v Girozentrale Securities* [1996] 3 All ER 834, the claimant underwrote the issue of shares in an oil-exploration company and engaged the defendant stockbrokers to find investors to buy them. Due to the latter's breach of contract, many shares went unsold, and the claimant sought £7 million in damages. The defendant argued that the loss had been occasioned by several events (including the claimant's own conduct), of which their breach was just one. Nevertheless, the court held that the defendant's breach remained the *effective* cause of the claimant's loss, so that they were liable for damages.

### Contributory Negligence and Contract

It should be noted that, if the claimant's negligence is not enough to break the chain of causation, but has, nevertheless, contributed to his loss, in certain, albeit limited, circumstances, his damages might be reduced under s.1(1) the Law Reform (Contributory Negligence) Act 1945. For a hypothetical example can be considered a car owner who takes his vehicle to a mechanic for a service. The mechanic fails to exercise reasonable skill and care when doing this and does not rectify an obvious defect in the car's steering. Later, while driving it, the owner exceeds the speed limit by a very large margin. The combination of excessive speed and, to a lesser extent, the steering fault causes the car to crash, occasioning serious damage to the vehicle.

In these situations, it seems that the claimant's damages can be reduced for his contributory negligence, *provided* the defendant is co-extensively liable in tort and contract, but not where he is liable solely in contract: *Vesta v Butcher* [1988] 2 All ER 43. Thus, and for illustrative example, the trial judge in *Trebor Bassett Holdings Ltd and The Cadbury UK Partnership v ADT Fire and Security plc* [2012] EWCA Civ 1158 found that one of the claimants, Cadbury, was seriously negligent in failing to segregate a potentially dangerous production area from the rest of the manufacturing building that had burned down, due (it was alleged) to the defendant's defective fire suppression system. Since the contractual duty owed by the defendant company was co-extensive with its tortious duty (not to be negligent) to the claimant, he applied s.1 of the 1945 Act to reduce their damages by 75% which, he felt, reflected this claimant's considerable degree of responsibility for the loss.

## 2. Remoteness of Damage

Many losses can flow from a breach of contract. For example, to draw on the facts of an old proverb, suppose that a blacksmith did not exercise reasonable skill and care when shoeing a horse, and his negligence resulted in the loss of a shoe, and so a battle, and thus a kingdom. Ignoring the issue of causation (see above) and the fact that he would be a man of straw for the purposes of paying damages, could the blacksmith be sued for the entire cost of the lost realm or is this too remote?

In *Attorney General of the Virgin Islands v Global Water Associates Ltd* [2020] UKPC 18, the Privy Council noted that the "historic" starting point for discussions on this issue remained *Hadley v Baxendale* [1854] EWHC Exch J70. In this historic case, the claimant operated a flourmill in Gloucestershire. Its iron crankshaft broke. He contracted with the defendant to deliver it to a repair yard in Greenwich, and then to return with a new crankshaft, after the broken original had been used as a template for the replacement. Due to the defendant's breach of contract, the crankshaft was returned a week late. The claimant was unable to use the mill during this period and claimed his loss of profit for those seven days. The defendant stated that he was unaware that the mill would have to be closed during the week's delay, so that the loss of profit was too remote to be claimed.

Alderson B gave the judgment of the court, providing a two-limb test, stating that, where two parties have made a contract which one of them has broken, the damages that the other party ought to receive should be such as "may fairly and reasonably be considered either arising naturally, according to the usual course of things, from such breach of contract itself, or such as may reasonably be supposed to have been in the contemplation of both parties, at the time they made the contract, as the probable result of the breach of it". Everyone is deemed to know the "natural" consequences of a breach of contract, in which the loss occurs according to the usual course of events (the first limb). Anything beyond that requires that the party in breach has been given information that makes the loss foreseeable (the second limb). Arguably, and as subsequent cases have noted, the two limbs can be subsumed under a general principle of foreseeability, although they should be considered individually.

In *Hadley v Baxendale*, the claim for loss of profits was too remote, because the information that the mill could not operate until the new shaft was delivered had not been communicated to the carriers, and most mills (unlike the claimant's) had a spare crankshaft to cover such eventualities, as would have been widely known. It should be stressed that the time for an examination of the parties' knowledge is the date on which the contract is made, not the date of breach, something that was reiterated in *Jackson v Royal Bank of Scotland* [2005] 1 WLR 377. The decision in *Hadley v Baxendale* is reasonable; had the defendant known about the risk he was running, he may not have accepted the contract or, alternatively, might have sought an enhanced payment for doing so.

Remoteness was also considered in the Court of Appeal case of *Victoria Laundry (Windsor) Ltd v Newman Industries Ltd* [1949] 2 KB 52. Newman Industries contracted to deliver a boiler for Victoria Laundry but was five months late in doing so, due to accidental damage. As a result of this delay, and the attendant shortage of capacity that it produced, Victoria Laundry not only lost some of the profit that it normally made from its routine cleaning business but was also unable to take advantage of an unusual, and potentially very lucrative, military dyeing contract with the Ministry of Supply.

The Court of Appeal held that Newman Industries only had to compensate the defendant for its ordinary, not its extraordinary, loss of profits. Profits from the lucrative dyeing contracts were distinguished from those for routine cleaning. As such, they would only be recoverable if the defendant had been given sufficient knowledge of them to make it reasonable to attribute to him acceptance of liability for such losses (not the case). Lord Justice Asquith reiterated that everyone (and every contract breaker), as a reasonable person, is assumed to know the "ordinary course of things" (whether or not he does know it) and consequently what loss is liable to result from a breach of contract in that ordinary course, this being the "first rule" in *Hadley v Baxendale*. However, to this knowledge, "...there may have to be added in a particular case knowledge which he actually possesses, of special circumstances outside the 'ordinary course of things', of such a kind that a breach in those special circumstances would be liable to cause more loss. Such a case attracts the operation of the "second rule" so as to make additional loss also recoverable".

Knowledge of such special circumstances is normally provided by the counterparty to the contract. The amount of information, and the circumstances in which it is conveyed, that are necessary to make the defendant liable for substantial damages is always a question of fact. Thus, in *Kemp v Intasun* (1987) BTLC 353, the Court of Appeal held that a casual conversation between a travel agent and Mrs Kemp, in which she mentioned, in passing, that her husband was not with her because he had asthma, was not enough to make Intasun liable for Mr Kemp's serious asthma attack when, on the first day of their holiday in Mallorca, the couple were (in clear breach of contract) accommodated in the staff-wing of an inferior hotel with sub-standard and dusty rooms, something that triggered his medical condition. This was especially the case, as the couple had not taken advantage of a space in the booking form to alert the Tour Operator to their special circumstances.

By contrast, in *Simpson v London and North Western Railway Co* (1876) 1 QBD 274, the defendant's representative contracted to carry the claimant's samples of cattle feed from an agricultural show at Bedford to another such show at Newcastle. The samples were clearly marked "must be at Newcastle by Monday certain", although there was no express reference in the agreement to the Newcastle show. Even so, the defendant was liable for the claimant's loss of profits at this show when the samples were delivered late, after it had finished. Sufficient information had been given to their agent for them to appreciate that a delay in delivery could result in such a loss; the claimant's intended use for the samples might be inferred from the surrounding circumstances.

## Type or Extent of Loss?

It should be noted that, unless dyeing is seen as distinct from cleaning, or physical harm is distinguished from a pure loss of profit, *Victoria Laundry* raises some conceptual difficulties when seen in the light of *Parsons (Livestock) Ltd v Uttley Ingham & Co Ltd* [1978] QB 791, in which the Court of Appeal held that losses occasioned by a breach of contract are recoverable if the *type* of loss experienced, rather than its extent, is a likely result of the breach of contract. Parsons, who operated a commercial pig farm, bought a bulk-food storage hopper to dispense pignuts from Uttley Ingham, who also installed it on their farm. Unfortunately, and carelessly, the ventilator was not unsealed during installation. As a result, the pignuts became mouldy so that 254 pigs died from a rare but very powerful form of E. coli. Parsons sued Uttley Ingham for the losses this occasioned.

The Court of Appeal held that the loss was not too remote. The majority held that it was the *type* of loss, rather than its extent, that was relevant. Uttley Ingham ought to have foreseen that, if the animals ate mouldy pignuts, there was a strong possibility that they might become ill in some way. Although the actual illness in the instant case was much worse than might have been foreseen, the type of damage (gastric food poisoning) was not. In *Brown v KMR Services Ltd* [1995] 4 All ER 598, the Court of Appeal reiterated that the scale of losses occasioned by a breach of contract (negligent advice in the instant case) did not, on its own, make damages too remote if the type of loss was foreseeable.

More recently, in *Wellesley Partners LLP v Withers LLP* [2015] EWCA Civ 1146 the claimant, Wellesley, was a headhunting firm, specialising in finding high-level investment-bank executives. In 2008 Wellesley retained Withers to draft a limited-liability partnership agreement after a Bahraini bank agreed to invest £5 million in exchange for a 25 per cent stake in their business. Although Wellesley's instructions to the solicitor's firm were that an option to withdraw their money should be exercisable only 42 months after the date of LLP agreement, the agreement did not reflect this, and provided that the option was exercisable at any time. The Bahraini bank exercised its option 12 months into the agreement. Wellesley argued that the capital that this denied the business had prevented it from expanding its operations in New York. As a result, it lost a particularly lucrative contract with Nomura, which had £6 million to spend on recruitment. In the Court of Appeal, Floyd LJ held that the Nomura loss was not too remote, being in the "reasonable contemplation" of the parties. Although the Nomura contract was particularly lucrative, unlike several other agreements that had also been lost, the distinction was one of degree. It was the sort of business Withers would have expected Wellesley to engage in.

More typically of most cases on contractual remoteness, in the Commercial Court case of *Transfield Shipping Inc of Panama v Mercator Shipping Inc of Monrovia* [2007] 1 All ER (Comm) 379, the owners of a vessel suffered substantial losses after charterers failed to return their ship on time, as required by the contract. It was held that such losses were not too remote. The charterers knew that late redelivery could mean that the vessel would miss her cancellation date for the next contract, while variations in market rates and the need, on account of delay in redelivery, to adjust the dates for the subsequent employment of the vessel with a reduction in any previously agreed rate of hire, was within the contemplation of the parties as a not unlikely result of the breach.

In *Attorney General of the Virgin Islands v Global Water Associates Ltd* [2020] UKPC 18, the Privy Council took the opportunity to review the law on contractual remoteness since the mid-nineteenth century, and to restate the appropriate test for such remoteness, although it did not say anything that was particularly novel. In this case, the BVI Government breached a contract with the defendants by failing to provide a prepared site to enable them to install a water-reclamation plant. As well as recovering damages under this contract, the Privy Council held that the contractor was entitled to claim damages for the loss of profits it would have earned under a separate 12-year contract to operate the plant on behalf of the BVI government, after it had been built. The breach of the construction contract had resulted in the plant not being built, so that the contractor was unable to earn these profits. That loss was within the reasonable contemplation of the parties when they entered the construction contract, so falling within the second limb of the *Hadley v Baxendale* test for recoverability of damages; that is, it was based on special circumstances known to the parties, rather than losses arising naturally from the breach. As a result, a loss of profits under one contract was recoverable for breach of another.

More generally, the court reiterated that the test was an objective one, being what the defendant should be taken to have had in his or her contemplation, rather than what he actually contemplated. It required an assumption that the defendant had thought about the consequences of their breach at the time the contract was made.

### Probability

How likely must it be that a loss will occur for it to be foreseeable? This issue was considered in *Zarnikow Ltd v Koufos (The Heron II)* [1969] 1 AC 350, in which a carrier agreed to take a cargo of sugar to Basra, in Iraq. Although there was a major sugar market in the city, the carrier/defendant had not been expressly told that *Zarnikow Ltd* intended to sell the cargo there promptly on arrival. The vessel's arrival at the port was delayed by nine days because the defendant departed from the agreed route, something that was a breach of contract. In the meantime, another cargo of sugar had arrived at Basra, so that the spot market price for the commodity had dropped significantly. Had the vessel arrived on time, the claimant would have enjoyed a higher price for his sugar, and he sought to recover the difference between the two prices—what he got and what he would have got—as his measure of damages.

The carrier argued that these damages were too remote since it was just as likely that the market price would have increased during the extra nine days as that it would fall, while not (quite) all sugar sent to Basra went to the market there. However, it was held that, under the second limb in *Hadley v Baxendale*, it was only necessary that the losses were in the reasonable contemplation of the parties. The defendant knew that there was a sugar market in Basra, that it was probable that the sugar would be sold on arrival, that market prices fluctuate, and that the loss sustained would have been a possible result of their breach. The principal focus of the debate in the House of Lords concerned the requisite likelihood of this result occurring. Lord Reid settled on "not unlikely", which, he felt, denoted a degree of probability that was "considerably less than an even chance but nevertheless not very unusual and easily foreseeable". Lord Upjohn adopted the test of a "real danger" or a "serious possibility" when considering the necessary probability.

Lord Reid's approach was reiterated by Floyd LJ in *Wellesley Partners LLP v Withers LLP* [2015] EWCA Civ 1146. The judge stated that someone who breaks a contract is liable for damages flowing from that breach if, at the time of making the agreement, a reasonable person in his situation would have thought (had they addressed their mind to the issue) that damage of that kind was "not unlikely" to result from such a breach.

Pulling these decisions together, in the first edition of his *Restatement of the English Law of Contract* (2016), Professor (now Lord) Burrows appears to have been particularly influenced by Lord Upjohn in this regard when he described the general rule on remoteness of damage in contract: "[L]oss is too remote if that type of loss could not reasonably have been contemplated by the defendant as a serious possibility at the time the contract was made assuming that, at that time, the defendant had thought about the breach". This definition received express support as an accurate summary of the common law position from the Privy Council in *Attorney General of the Virgin Islands v Global Water Associates Ltd* [2020] UKPC 18.

## 3. The "Duty" to Mitigate

A claimant's damages will be reduced for any failure to mitigate the loss flowing from a breach of contract. This is sometimes described as their "duty to mitigate". This is slightly misleading. As was noted in *Thai Airways International Public Company Limited v KI Holdings Co Limited* [2015] EWHC 1250, there is no legal *duty* to mitigate loss; a claimant is free to act as he wishes in response to a breach of contract. However, damages will be limited by an assumption that he has taken reasonable steps to reduce his loss, whether he has taken those steps or not. The courts will not allow the recovery of damages that could reasonably have been avoided, although the onus is on the defendant to raise this issue and prove the failure to mitigate, on the balance of probabilities, something that is not always easy to do. The relevant time for mitigating occurs when the claimant becomes aware of the breach and repudiates the contract, although a reasonable time is allowed for him to decide what steps should be taken to reduce his loss.

For example, if a buyer refuses to accept delivery and pay for goods he has ordered, the seller will generally be expected to attempt to sell those goods to an alternative buyer for the best price he can get, the difference becoming the measure of damages. Similarly, where there has been an unfair dismissal from work, the employee is expected to actively seek new employment of an appropriate type. In like manner, if a breach of contract occasions damage to the claimant's car that puts it out of use, it will normally be reasonable for him to hire a substitute vehicle while it is repaired. However, he must spend no more than is necessary when procuring such a vehicle. If, for example, a larger or more luxurious car than that damaged was hired, although vehicles equivalent to the damaged car were readily available at less cost (and the defendant can prove this), there is likely to be a reduction in the damages awarded, which will then be assessed as if the claimant had acted reasonably. Thus, it will not usually be "reasonable" to hire a Rolls-Royce while a Mini is out of service. So, if a Rolls-Royce was hired at £4,000, but a hatchback was readily available at £500, the defendant might successfully argue that damages be limited to the latter sum. (It is usually prudent for a potential claimant to obtain several quotations for hire vehicles to strengthen their position in this regard.) Similarly, a claimant who had his damaged (but very ordinary) car repaired, rather than replacing it with a similar second-hand vehicle, where the cost of repair was (for example) more than twice the market value of his car before the accident, might be deemed to have failed to mitigate his loss.

More specifically, in *Payzu v Saunders* [1919] 2 KB 581, the claimant agreed to buy certain goods from the defendant over a period of nine months, with payment being made within one month of the delivery of each monthly consignment. The claimant failed to make prompt payment for the first instalment, and the defendant, in breach of contract, as the claimant had broken a warranty, not a condition (see Chapter 12), refused to deliver any more instalments under the contract. Instead, he offered to deliver the goods at the same (discounted) price if the claimant paid cash on delivery for each order. The claimant refused to do this and claimed damages, these being based on the difference between the contract price and the market price of the goods when purchased elsewhere. It was held that the claimant had failed to mitigate his losses when rejecting the defendant's offer. He had sufficient cash readily available to meet the defendant's demands and could have mitigated his loss by purchasing from the defendant at the contract price, as the latter had offered, instead of going into the market to purchase at a higher price. He was, therefore, not entitled to substantive damages.

Similarly, in *Brace v Calder* [1895] 2 KB 581, the court decided that the employee of a four-man partnership that dissolved when two of the partners retired, five months into his two-year contract, who then sought compensation for the remaining 19 months of his agreement, could properly have accepted similar employment that was offered by the new two-man partnership that was immediately established by the still-working pair of men who continued the business.

However, mitigation does not require that the injured party go to unreasonable expense, risk, humiliation, or inconvenience to save a contract-breaker from the consequences of his breach: *Banco de Portugal v Waterlow* [1932] AC 452. In this case, Waterlow contracted to produce Portuguese banknotes for the Bank of Portugal. In breach of contract, Waterlow was tricked into printing 580,000 bank notes for criminals, who subsequently put them into circulation. The public became aware of this, prompting a run on the bank and prompting the latter to withdraw all notes (including legitimate specie) of the relevant denomination. However, Waterlow argued that the bank's response was excessive, and that it might have taken less drastic, more targeted, measures to eliminate the unauthorised notes, which would have been cheaper, and led to a lower level of loss. In the House of Lords, Lord McMillan acknowledged that, while a claimant should take reasonable steps to mitigate their loss, the appropriateness of their behaviour should not be weighed "in nice scales at the insistence of the party whose breach of contract had occasioned that difficulty". The bank had acted reasonably in the circumstances in withdrawing all banknotes of that denomination and so could recover the full cost of doing so.

Similarly, in *Pilkington v Wood* [1953] 2 All ER 810, a solicitor, in breach of his contract with his client, failed to notice that the house he was buying on behalf of the latter had a defective title. The client sued the solicitor, who argued that he could have mitigated his loss by suing the vendor of the property under the Law of Property Act 1925. Harman J noted, "The so-called duty to mitigate does not go so far as to oblige the injured party, even under an indemnity, to embark on a complicated and difficult piece of litigation against a third party…to protect his solicitor from the consequences of his own carelessness."

More recently, one of the issues in *Gibbs v Leeds United Football Club* [2016] EWHC 960 (QB) was whether the claimant had acted unreasonably after his constructive dismissal as assistant manager by subsequently rejecting an offer from the chairman to take over as a very well-paid head coach at the same club. Although, as *Payzu v Saunders* suggests, accepting a suitable offer from a defendant might be appropriate mitigation in the right circumstances, in the instant case the trial judge concluded that there was nothing unreasonable about the claimant refusing the offer; his humiliating treatment meant that his position had been made untenable by the club.

A claimant can claim ancillary expenses as part of his mitigation. For example, in *Holden Ltd v Bostock & Co. Ltd* (1902) 18 TLR 317, the claimant had been sold sugar by the defendant, for use in his brewing business, which had been contaminated with arsenic. He was allowed to recover the cost of advertisements placed to reassure customers that the problem had been dealt with, and that they faced no danger from his beer. Indeed, provided the steps taken by the claimant to mitigate his loss are reasonable, their cost will be recoverable, even where (as occasionally happens) they have increased the claimant's loss: *Lagden v O'Connor* [2004] 1 AC 1067. Thus, and for example, in *Hoffberger v Ascot International Bloodstock Bureau Ltd* [1976] 120 SJ 130, the claimant sold a horse to the defendant, who then failed to take delivery and pay for the animal. The claimant hoped to make another private sale of the horse, for a similar sum, and incurred considerable costs in keeping it for several months (feed, vets' bills, and livery etc.). At the end of this period, the animal had still not been sold so that they put it into a general auction, where it secured only a modest price. The Court of Appeal approved as damages both the loss of profit on the sale (the difference between the price agreed with the defendant and that achieved at auction) and the wasted costs sustained in keeping the horse for a several months while looking for a more lucrative private sale that came closer to matching the defendant's offer, as the claimant had acted reasonably in the circumstances.

### Mitigating the Loss Away

In some situations, mitigation will eliminate the whole loss, so that the injured party will only be entitled to nominal damages if they sue the contract-breaker. This occurred in the historic case of *British Westinghouse Electric Co Ltd v Underground Electric Railways Co of London Ltd* [1912] AC 673. Underground Electric (UE) purchased turbines from British Westinghouse (BW). These were defective. UE used them for a time, and then purchased new turbines. These were to a new and radically different design, and far more efficient than the defective ones would have been, even if they had not been faulty. When UE brought an action for breach of contract, claiming the cost of the replacement turbines, BW argued that, even if the original turbines had not been defective, the new, and far more efficient, turbines would have been swiftly purchased in their place, so that UE had not suffered any loss from their breach of contract. The court agreed and held that UE could not claim substantial damages for the cost of the new turbines. Any additional profits made because of acts done in mitigation should be considered when quantifying damages, and the savings made by using the new turbines exceeded the cost of the old ones. More recently, in *Omak Maritime v Mamola Challenger Shipping* [2010] EWHC 2026 (Comm), a (reliance) loss claim in a charter party was fully mitigated out of existence because the defendant was able to rehire the vessel at a far higher rate.

This aspect of mitigation was also considered by the High Court in *Thai Airways International Public Company Limited v KI Holdings Co Limited* [2015] EWHC 1250, which involved a breach of contract occasioned to supply new economy-class seats for the claimant airline's planes. The defendant, a Japanese company, was late in supplying the seats, and in some cases failed to supply them at all, putting several new aircraft, to which they were to be fitted, out of service for up to 18 months. To mitigate its losses, Thai Airways leased three aircraft and purchased alternative seats. Although more expensive, these new seats were lighter than those originally contracted for, significantly reducing the aircrafts' fuel consumption when fitted. When Thai Airways sought to recover the costs incurred in mitigating its losses, the defendant argued that an allowance should be made, *inter alia*, for any fuel savings that would be occasioned over the life of the lighter seats. Thai Airways resisted this claim, as they had been forced to such action, but the defendant supported their case by citing *British Westinghouse*. Leggatt J, sitting in the Commercial Court, held that Thai Airways was liable to account for such savings, but noted that the (difficult) burden of proving any such benefit would fall on the defendant.

In *Thai Airways* the High Court also reiterated basic principles when it comes to mitigation, which bear restating. Thus, the court noted that the law gives a fair degree of latitude to the innocent party and provided their response to a breach of contract was reasonable, that there may have been better options open to them will not *per se* be a reason to reduce their damages. Furthermore, less will be expected of a claimant mitigating in the heat of a crisis, while their resources will also be considered when deciding what is reasonable. The defendant always has the burden of proving that there was a reasonable alternative course of action open to the defendant that he did not adopt. The need for proportionate cost when mitigating loss, preferably established by reference to the open market, will always be important in deciding whether the mitigation was reasonable. A claimant need not risk their reputation to mitigate a breach. Any benefits that are gained by a claimant when mitigating must be considered when assessing damages.

## 4. Damages for Emotional Distress

In general, if only for policy reasons, a contract-breaker is not liable for any distress, upset, or anxiety that his breach occasions, that is for non-pecuniary loss. As Mr. Justice Mellor observed in *Hobbs v London & South Western Railway* (1875) LR 10 QB 111, it is a long-established rule in English law that a claimant in such situations cannot recover damages for mere "annoyance and loss of temper, or vexation, or for being disappointed in a particular thing which you have set your mind upon, without real physical inconvenience resulting".

This principle was reiterated in *Addis v Gramophone Co Ltd* [1909] AC 488. In this important case, the claimant was employed as an overseas manager by the defendant, who dismissed and replaced him with a new manager before his notice period had expired, forbidding him to act in an official capacity in the meantime. The claimant brought an action for breach of contract claiming that the level of damages should reflect not just his financial loss, but also what Lord Atkinson termed the "harsh and humiliating" circumstances in which he had been fired. This was reflected at first instance in his award of damages. However, the House of Lords held that English contract law seeks to put the parties into the position they would have been in *financially* had the contract been properly performed. He could recover any lost wages and commission flowing from the breach of contract, but not damages for injury to his feelings. As a result, his damages were reduced. As Lord Atkinson observed, the claimant was to be "paid adequate compensation in money for the loss of that which he would have received had his contract been kept, and no more".

This remains the underlying rule in English contract law, being reiterated by the House of Lords in *Farley v Skinner* [2001] UKHL 49, where it was noted that it is "clearly established" that damages cannot normally be awarded for the annoyance occasioned by a breach of contract. It was also stated in a specifically business context by the House of Lords in *Johnson v Gore Wood & Co* [2001] 2 WLR 72, where Lord Cooke observed, "Contract-breaking is treated as an incident of commercial life which players in the game are expected to meet with mental fortitude". Thus, in *Hayes v Dodd* [1990] 2 All ER 815 the Court of Appeal held that damages for what it acknowledged was "great anxiety and distress" could not be recovered from a solicitor whose negligent breach of contract occasioned the closing of his clients' business. Similarly, in *Alexander v Rolls Royce Motor Cars Ltd* [1996] RTR 95, after the claimant's Rolls-Royce motorcar was not repaired in a timely fashion by the defendant's garage following an accident (this being a breach of contract), the Court of Appeal was not prepared to award damages for the claimant's distress at being unable to use his highly prized vehicle whilst it was off the road. However, this general rule has been limited and qualified over the years.[2]

**Distress Occasioned by Physical Inconvenience**

One such qualification was already in existence when *Addis* was decided. As the comment by Mellor J (above) suggests, and as Bingham LJ observed in *Watts v Morrow* [1991] 1 WLR 1421, damages have long been recoverable for physical inconvenience and discomfort caused by a breach of contract and for the mental suffering that was directly related to this inconvenience, even where there is no financial loss. There is a (legal) distinction between annoyance at the failure of the other party to carry out his contractual obligation and vexation at the physical discomfort occasioned by it. As Cockburn LCJ noted in *Hobbs v London and South Western Railway* (1875) LR 10 QB 111 there is "no authority that personal inconvenience, where it is sufficiently serious, should not be the subject of damages". In *Hobbs*, a railway's failure to stop at a designated station (a breach of contract) required the claimant and his family to walk five miles home, on a cold, wet, night, for which damages of £8 were recoverable.

Similarly, in *Bailey v Bullock* [1950] 2 All ER 1167, a solicitor failed to take action to recover the claimant's house, in breach of his contract with the claimant. As a result, the claimant and his wife had to move into his in-laws' house for two years. At

2 See generally Z. Zlatev, "Quantification of damages for non-pecuniary losses deriving from breach of contract", *Legal Studies*, v. 40, no. 4 (2020), pp. 548-564.

trial, Barry J reiterated the distinction between mere annoyance and actual physical inconvenience occasioned by a breach of contract and held that the claimant was entitled to recover damages to reflect the inconvenience of having to live in very cramped and overcrowded circumstances for this time.

## Giving Pleasure or Avoiding Distress

However, as Bingham LJ observed in *Watts v Morrow* [1991] 1 WLR 1421, during the course of the twentieth century another special category developed in which the general rule did not apply: "Where the very object of a contract is to provide pleasure, relaxation, peace of mind or freedom from molestation, damages will be awarded if the fruit of the contract is not provided or if the contrary result is procured instead". This category was founded on the Court of Appeal decision in *Jarvis v Swan Tours* [1972] 3 WLR 954.

Mr Jarvis, a busy local-authority solicitor with a limited holiday allowance, booked a two-week Christmas skiing vacation in Switzerland with Swan Tours, at a price of £63.90, after reading the company's holiday brochure. This made attractive claims about what the holiday would entail, promising a house party, an English-speaking hotel owner, a variety of skis and ski runs, afternoon tea with special alpine cakes, and an evening of entertainment from a local yodeller. Many of these either did not take place, for some or all the time, or were not as described. For example, there were hardly any other guests staying in the hotel, the cakes were small and dry, the skis were short and unsuitable, and the yodeller came in his ordinary working clothes and sang a selection of standard pop songs. As a result, during the first week Mr Jarvis received a holiday that was somewhat inferior to that promised, and in the second week one that was very largely inferior. He sued for breach of contract. At trial, the county court judge awarded him £31.72 in damages, on the basis that he had received half of what he had paid for. He had, after all, been flown to Switzerland and back, fed, and housed during the two weeks. However, the judge held that no damages could be recovered for Mr Jarvis's disappointment.

On appeal, it was held that, where a contract is entered for the specific purpose of providing enjoyment or entertainment, damages *can* be awarded for the distress occasioned by a breach of contract. As a result, Mr Jarvis was awarded £125 in damages, almost twice what he had paid for the entire vacation. (It should, perhaps, be noted that such generosity has only rarely been matched in the decades since this decision.) Lord Denning observed that, "It is true that he [Jarvis] was conveyed to Switzerland and back and had meals and bed in the hotel. But that is not what he went for. He went to enjoy himself with all the facilities which the defendants said he would have. He is entitled to damages for the lack of those facilities, and for his loss of enjoyment". In the same case, Lord Justice Edmund Davies provided another illustration of the sort of contract that might attract such damages, when he suggested that, if a man purchased a ticket for the Glyndbourne opera, on the only night that he was free to go, and hired a car to take him there, which then failed to turn up, his damages would not be limited to the cost of the opera ticket. He would be entitled to general damages for the disappointment and loss of the entertainment he had suffered.

*Jarvis* was followed in *Jackson v Horizon Holidays Ltd* [1975] 1 WLR 1468, another luxury package holiday case, in which Sri Lanka was the destination. More recently, this principle lay behind the award of *some* of the damages in *Milner v Carnival Plc (Trading As Cunard)* [2010] EWCA Civ 389. In this case, the Court of Appeal also took the opportunity to provide some further guidance on the appropriate measure of damages in "holiday" cases, when reducing the £7,500 given to each claimant (a husband and wife) at first instance for their disappointment when a luxury cruise did not match their expectations, to awards of £4,000 and £4,500 respectively.

Holiday and entertainment cases involve contracts that are designed to give pleasure. The principle quickly extended to those that are specifically aimed at preventing distress. For example, in the case of *Heywood v Wellers* [1976] 2 WLR 101, the claimant instructed solicitors to secure an injunction to prevent a man with whom she had earlier had an acrimonious relationship from molesting or harassing her. The solicitors put the matter into the hands of a very junior and unqualified clerk, and it was conducted negligently. As a result, the claimant was late securing the injunction and suffered further harassment, occasioning considerable (avoidable) distress. The claimant won her case against the firm of solicitors in the county court but appealed against the very limited damages that had been awarded at first instance, repayment of the legal costs she had paid to her solicitors, which did not compensate her for her emotional distress. The Court of Appeal held that she was entitled to a sum for the additional anxiety occasioned by the lack of an injunction and her former boyfriend's continued harassment.

### A Facet of the Contract

What of contracts in which giving pleasure or avoiding distress is an important facet, but not the whole, sole, or primary purpose of the wider agreement? This does not appear to have been enough in *Knott v Bolton* (1995) 11 Const LJ 375, where the defendant architect failed to carry out instructions to include an impressive staircase and entrance hall in his design for a new house. The claimant's attempt to recover general damages for the disappointment and distress they suffered by reason of this failure was rejected by both the trial judge and the Court of Appeal.

However, the situation was reconsidered by the House of Lords in *Farley v Skinner* [2001] UKHL 49. In this case, the claimant, Mr Farley, wanted to purchase an imposing property in the country as a retirement retreat, and settled on Riverside House in Sussex. The property was only 15 miles from Gatwick Airport, and he was anxious that his peace should not be disturbed. He instructed the defendant, a chartered surveyor, to inspect the property. Obviously, and as with any survey, the latter would report on the building's structural condition and inherent value. Farley also expressly asked that Skinner report on whether the property would be adversely affected by aircraft noise. Skinner subsequently provided Farley with a detailed report, which noted, inter alia, that it was "unlikely that the property will suffer greatly from such noise." Unfortunately, Skinner's inquiries had failed to notice that the skies near the house were sometimes used to hold circling (around a navigation beacon) aircraft waiting to land at Gatwick. This failure on the part of Skinner amounted to a breach of contract.

If Mr Farley had received the information about aircraft noise, to which he was contractually entitled, he would not have purchased the house. Having purchased the property, he put in hand extensive renovations. It was only after these had been completed that he moved into the property and discovered that it was affected by aircraft noise. This interfered with his enjoyment of the house, especially its extensive garden, where he liked to take an evening drink. Nevertheless, having had the house renovated and become attached to it, Mr Farley decided not to sell, but sued for damages. At trial, the judge concluded that the aircraft noise did not result in any diminution in the value of the property. However, he held that Mr Farley was entitled to damages for impairment of use and enjoyment of the house, for which he awarded him £10,000, rather than confining him to nominal damages.

In the Court of Appeal, two judges held that he was entitled to such compensation, but three (the majority) decided that he was not, and so was limited to nominal damages. The matter then went to the House of Lords. There, the original award at first instance was reinstated. Damages for distress *can* be recovered where a major or important object of the contract (as opposed to its primary purpose) was to give pleasure, relaxation, or peace of mind. However, the judges also noted that the first-instance judge's award was generous.

*Farley v Skinner* was followed in *Herrmann v Withers LLP* [2012] EWHC 1492 (Ch), where damages of £2,000 were awarded against the defendant solicitors specifically for their clients' distress and disappointment (in addition to their pecuniary loss due to a diminution in value), after receiving negligent advice concerning the purchase of a very high value house in Kensington and its right of access to a communal garden. In this case, the court noted that it was apparent from *Farley v Skinner* that such awards should be relatively modest, explaining the small sum awarded.

How far this process can go is a matter of debate. In *Shaw v Leigh Day* [2017] EWHC 825 (QB), Andrews J allowed a claimant's appeal against a district judge's striking out of her claim for damages for distress occasioned by the negligence of the defendant firm of solicitors. The latter had represented her at the inquest into her father's death following an allegedly negligent surgical procedure to fit a trans-aortic valve. The judge allowed the claimant's appeal because, she felt, inquests have an "emotional element that is unique, and absent from other forms of legal process. If the solicitor retained to put the necessary materials before the coroner and jury does not carry out his or her job with sufficient diligence, the client will never receive that comfort". In her view, there was a realistic, rather than merely fanciful, prospect of persuading a trial judge that, when Mrs Shaw engaged the defendant to represent her at the inquest, an important object of that contract was to obtain peace of mind or 'closure'. As a result, the judge thought that it was clear that the point was sufficiently arguable to get over the threshold to avoid summary judgment or strike-out. Indeed, the judge went "so far as to suggest that the Claimant may well have the better of the argument". Subsequently, the matter does not appear to have gone for a full trial, presumably being settled out of court, so what the decision would have been on this issue is unknown, although such an extension would constitute a major development to the principle.

### Time of Assessment of Damages

Damages in contract law are usually assessed as at the time that the breach of contract occurs. Thus, and as put into statutory form in s.50(3) SOGA 1979, where there is an available market for goods that have not been accepted, the measure of damages is ascertained by the difference between the contract price and the market price "at the time or times when the goods ought to have been accepted". Nevertheless, there are exceptions to this general rule. For example, and somewhat controversially, in *Golden Strait Corporation v Nippon Yusen Kubishika Kaisha* [2007] 2 AC 353, a majority of the House of Lords were prepared to reduce damages in light of (very significant) subsequent events, that were known at the date of the trial but not when the contract was broken.

In *Golden Strait Corporation* a ship was returned four years early in breach of a charterparty. However, just over a year later, the First Gulf War broke out, which would have allowed the charterer to quite legally terminate the contract pursuant to a "war clause" in the agreement. Lord Scott, with the majority, observed that the rule requiring damages to be assessed at the date of breach is not inflexible, and limited the claimant to 14 months' worth of damages (the period prior to the outbreak of hostilities), rather than four years, since the latter would put him in a better position than would have been the case had the contract been properly performed. Lord Bingham gave an important dissenting judgment, focussing on the importance of deterring potential breaches of contract and being able to assess with a degree of certainty the consequences of such breaches. Under the position reached by the majority, a backlog in cases that delayed a matter coming for trial might actively benefit a defendant.

### The Quantum of Damages for Breach of Contract

The aim of damages is purely compensatory rather than punitive. As Lord Hoffman observed in *Co-op Insurance Society v Argyll Stores* [1997] 2 WLR 898, "The purpose of the law of contract is not to punish wrongdoing". However, this then raises the question as to what the measure of contractual damages should be. This is usually based on the claimant's 'expectation loss'.

## Expectation Loss

The fundamental principle governing the assessment of quantum of damages for breach of contract was enunciated in *Robinson v Harman* (1848) 1 Exch 850. In this case, Mr Harman agreed to grant Mr Robinson a lease on a house in Croydon, at a rental of £110 a year. Mr Robinson had made a very good deal, as the house was worth much more than the agreed annual payment. Subsequently, Mr Harman changed his mind and refused to complete the agreement. He argued that Mr Robinson was merely entitled to the £20 in legal expenses he had lost due to his (admitted) breach of contract. However, Robinson was awarded £200 at *nisi prius* (civil side) at the Surrey Assizes, to cover the loss he had sustained. Mr Harman then appealed unsuccessfully to the Court of Exchequer Chamber, where Parke B famously declared that "where a party sustains loss by reason of a breach of contract, he is, so far as money can do it to be placed in the same situation, with respect to damages, as if the contract had been performed". In the instant case, £200 was needed to allow Mr Robinson to find an equivalent property at the then market rate. The judge's analysis was reiterated in *Livingstone v Rawyards Coal Co.* (1880) 5 App. Cas. 25, when Lord Blackburn noted that compensatory damages should, as nearly as possible, place the injured party "in the same position as he would have been in if he had not sustained the wrong".

This means that attempts to compensate the injured party will normally look forward to what would have happened if the contract had been properly performed, not backwards to the financial position he was in before contracting, unlike the situation with tortious damages.[3] In *Co-op Insurance Society v Argyll Stores* [1997] 2 WLR 898 Lord Hoffman noted that this meant that the aim of damages was to satisfy the "expectations" of the party entitled to performance. This is sometimes termed the injured party's "expectation interest". Depending on context and type of contract, such expectation damages can be measured by the difference in value between the actual and expected performance, the cost of rectification or cure if there has been defective performance, or the value of the loss of amenity required to put the injured party into the position they would have been in if the contract had been properly carried out. These will be dealt with *seriatim*.

### 1. Difference in Value

For the first of these can be considered the sale of a hypothetical antique bureau (discussed elsewhere in connection with misrepresentation). If it was an express term that it was an authentic Louis Quinze desk which, if true, would mean that it would be worth £20,000, it was sold for £10,000, but was (in reality) a Victorian copy worth just £5,000, the measure of damages would be £15,000 if the purchaser retained the bureau. This would be the amount of money required to put them in the same financial position they would have been in had the contract been fulfilled and the purchaser had acquired an authentic Louis Quinze desk, not the £5,000 that would put them back into the financial position they were in before they entered the contract.

3 Burrows, *Restatement*, p. 18.

To consider an actual and more complicated case, in *Thompson (W.L.) Ltd v Robinson (Gunmakers) Ltd* [1955] 1 Ch 177, Robinson, the defendant, ordered a new Vanguard car from the claimant dealer but refused to accept delivery. Thompson returned the vehicle to the distributor, then claimed its £61 loss of profit on the transaction, this being the difference between what would have been paid to the distributor and what they would have sold it for to Robinson. The defendant argued that the claimant had suffered only a nominal loss because it could have sold the vehicle to another customer. However, Upjohn J noted that, unlike the situation in the then recent past, in which there had been long waiting-lists for new cars of this type, so that a dealer would suffer only a nominal loss if a purchaser withdrew because the latter could immediately be replaced, there were as many Vanguards as customers could be found for them. If the claimant had been able to find another customer for the vehicle, he would have been able to make two sales and profits. As a result, he had irrecoverably lost the £61 profit on the sale to the defendant, and so was entitled to that sum in damages to put him in the situation he would have been in had the contract been performed.

By contrast, in *Charter v Sullivan* (1957) 2 WLR 528, the defendant purchased a Hillman Minx motorcar from the claimant, but then refused to take delivery of the vehicle. However, as Jenkins LJ noted in the Court of Appeal, the evidence was that the claimant could sell every car of this type that he could obtain from the manufacturers, which number was strictly limited at the time, unlike the situation in *Thompson v Robinson*. As a result, the claimant did not receive the profit of just over £97 that he would have made on the sale, but merely nominal damages, as he could (and did) mitigate his loss out of existence by selling the same car to another customer. (See below for mitigation).

More recently, in *Barry v Davies* [2000] 1 WLR 1962, a failure to knock down new engine analysers at auction for bids of £200 each led to the claimant being awarded the difference between their list price of about £14,000 each and what he had offered, producing damages of well over £27,000. However, although the Court of Appeal held that the judge was entitled to decide that the manufacturer's list price of £14,000 was the relevant market price for each machine, the court also noted that this was unusual, and the claimant rather fortunate. In most cases involving the sale of second-hand equipment, even when unused, there will be evidence of second-hand prices which would preclude the judge from adopting a figure from the manufacturer's list. In the instant case, the defendant had objected to such evidence being given in the (unavailing) hope that the judge would assess damages on the basis of the £750 for which each of the machines was eventually sold after the auction.

Unsurprisingly, when assessing expectation damages in a contract that gives the defendant a choice between different means of discharging their obligation, the court will assume that he would choose the least onerous option, and so normally the one which provides the lowest quantum of damages for the claimant: *Durham Tees Valley Airport Ltd v Bmibaby Ltd* [2010] EWCA Civ 485. For example, if the defendant contracted to deliver 100 tons of potatoes, "plus or minus 10 per cent", for £100 a ton, and then failed to provide them, the claimant being forced to source them at £150 a ton, the prima facie measure of damages would be £4,500 (90 x £50) as he could have performed the contract by providing 90 tons of the root vegetables.

## 2. The Cost of Rectification

In some situations, the cost of rectification, repair, reinstatement, or cure (terminology varies)--that is, of putting physically right what is wrong so that the claimant gets what he bargained for--is used as the prospective measure of damages. This is usually assessed as at the time the defect was discovered: *East Ham Corporation v Bernard Sunley* [1966] AC 406. In this case, Bernard Sunley contracted to build a school for East Ham Council. The exterior walls were to be covered in Portland stone. Two years after completion (by which time the school was in use), some of the stone panels fell off. Investigation revealed that they had not been properly secured to its walls. West Ham spent £21,301 refixing the panels securely. They successfully sought to recover this sum as damages from Bernard Sunley. Lord Upjohn observed that in a case of defective building work reinstatement was the normal measure of damages. Of course, incidental expenses, such as paying for alternative accommodation during the rebuilding, where necessary, might also be claimed.

For another illustration can be considered *Linklaters Business Services v McAlpine Ltd & Ors* [2010] EWHC 2931 (TCC). In this case, Linklaters Business Services (LBS) sued building contractor McAlpine (several other parties were joined later). In 1995 McAlpine had carried out major refurbishment of LBS's City of London headquarters and (as permitted) had subcontracted the work to instal an air-conditioning system. In 2006 a leak was identified in the system, and it was discovered that the pipes were subject to extensive rust and corrosion, due to a failure to apply suitable thermal insulation and a vapour barrier. LBS's building consultants advised that the pipework be stripped out and fully replaced. At trial in the High Court, McAlpine argued that some lesser scheme involving a combination of replacement and repair would have been more appropriate and cheaper. Nevertheless, the court held that the decision to fully replace the pipework was reasonable, particularly as the firm had taken appropriate and independent expert professional advice before seeking that remedy. The cost of a comprehensive replacement of the pipework was the suitable measure for damages.

## 3. Loss of Amenity

"Loss of amenity" is a more recent, and rarely used, measure when it comes to expectation damages. Exceptionally, the court might conclude that it would be unreasonable for the wronged party to insist on damages to allow the contract to be fulfilled as intended and, instead, limit them to an award for their loss of amenity in not getting what they contracted for, rather than the cost of reinstatement or repair. This measure was identified (in this context) in *Ruxley Electronics and Construction Ltd v Forsyth* [1996] AC 344, in which a contractor agreed to build a swimming pool in the claimant's garden. The contract expressly specified that it should have a maximum depth of 7 feet, 6 inches (deeper than normal for such pools), Mr Forsyth being a rather tall man. When it was finished, and in breach of contract, it transpired that the maximum depth was only 6 feet. The pool was safe to dive into from the side (there were no plans to instal a diving board), and the shortfall in depth had not affected its value in any way, so that substantial damages could not be given for diminution in that value (the financial difference between the pool as it was and as it should be). Adopting this approach would have limited the claimant to an award of nominal damages, even though he had not received what he had expressly contracted for.

By contrast, the cost of reinstatement--that is, the expense of tearing up and rebuilding the pool to the appropriate depth, so putting the claimant into the position he would have been in had the contract been properly performed--would have been £21,560. Of course, once he had secured such damages, there would have been nothing to prevent him keeping the existing pool as it was and enjoying a £21,560 windfall, something that was likely to occur. (It is entirely up to a claimant what he does with his damages.)

Both options were seen as unsatisfactory: the former would, effectively, condone a breach of contract, and make a mockery of agreements; the latter would grant the claimant a potentially huge bonus. Instead, the judge at first instance held that the claimant was entitled to damages of £2,500 for loss of amenity, but rejected his claim for the cost of reinstatement, on the ground that it was unreasonable in the circumstances. The Court of Appeal rejected this analysis and held that the claimant *was* entitled to recover the full £21,560 cost of reinstatement. On further appeal, the House of Lords held that reinstatement would be unreasonable, and the cost out of all proportion to the benefit to be obtained. The House of Lords upheld the original first-instance award of £2,500 for loss of amenity.

This decision reflects a common-sense *via media*, although it raises problems of its own. Nevertheless, it does mean that, as Lord Mustill noted, "There is no need to remedy the injustice of awarding too little, by unjustly awarding far too much". Lord Lloyd observed that, although what the claimant intended to do with the money was irrelevant once the extent of his loss had been established, it was relevant in determining the measure of that loss. The theoretical basis on which such a loss-of-amenity award is given is subject to some debate. However, Lord Lloyd felt that it was granted under the established principle of compensating for loss of pleasure under an agreement, or the distress occasioned by its breach, as previously identified in cases such as *Watts v Morrow* [1991] 1 WLR 1421.

Of course, if there was a very good reason for insisting on a pool that was 7 foot, 6 inches deep or, even if there was not, if the claimant had made it clear when contracting that (for some eccentric reason) these dimensions were paramount to their decision to order a pool, the situation may have been different, and the cost of full reinstatement ordered.

## The Reliance or Wasted Expenditure Measure

Occasionally, it is very difficult or impossible to assess what profit, if any, would have been made by a contractual venture--that is, to quantify the loss of bargain that it entailed. For example, some films make a huge profit, others break even, and some make a very substantial loss. A claimant would naturally argue that a broken contract that had led to the making of a film being abandoned would have been in the first category, while the defendant in such an action would equally naturally claim that it would be in the third. In these circumstances, a claimant might necessarily have recourse to the reliance measure of damages. These seek to establish the value of the expenditure that has been wasted in anticipation of, or in reliance on, a contract, due to a breach of that contract, and reimburse it.

For a widely cited illustrative example of the use of the reliance measure can be considered *Anglia Television v Reed* [1971] 3 All ER 690. In this case, Anglia Television, the claimant, contracted with the actor Robert Reed to play the leading role in a film. Subsequently, and in breach of contract, Mr Reed withdrew from the agreement. Anglia was unable to find a suitable replacement in the time available, so it abandoned the project. By then, it had incurred expenses amounting to £2,750, some of it spent before entering the contract with Mr Reed and some of it afterwards. It was impossible to estimate the loss of profit (expectation loss) because the reception given to films (even those made for television) is notoriously unpredictable, and advertisers would not be attracted to a "turkey". As Lord Denning MR noted, Anglia "cannot say what their profit would have been on this contract if Mr Reed had come here and performed it". It was held that, in these circumstances, the claimant might, instead, elect to claim his reliance loss, and recover wasted expenditure incurred in pursuant to a broken contract. As a result, Anglia was able to recover expenses--director's fees, props, etc.--from the defendant. It was also held that these extended to expenditure that had been incurred *before* he entered the agreement (about £1,900 in the instant case), and would, nevertheless, "reasonably be in the contemplation of the parties as likely to be wasted if the contract was broken".

Similarly, a salvage expedition to recover a wrecked vessel in a remote location might be a great success or a costly failure. It was for this reason that that the claimants in the Australian case of *McRae v Commonwealth Disposals Commission* (1951) 84 CLR 377 sought damages on the reliance measure.

It might be argued that the reliance measure is a quasi-tortious assessment of damages, as, at first sight, it appears to put the parties back into the financial position they were in before they entered the contract, as if it had never been made, rather than the position they would have been in if the contract had been performed properly (the normal situation with the expectation measure of contractual damages). As such, it is ostensibly a retrospective, not a prospective, measure of damages, akin to that found in misrepresentation. However, whatever may have been the case in the past, recent cases make it clear that reliance damages can still be seen as a species of expectation damages, as their award remains subject to the compensatory principle; it cannot be used to put the claimant in a better position than he would have been in if the contract had been properly performed: *Omak Maritime Ltd v Mamola Challenger Shipping Co* [2010] EWHC 2026 (Comm).

In *Omak Maritime*, the owner of a ship was required to instal a crane and make other modifications to the vessel pursuant to a charter party. The charterers then repudiated the contract, before even taking control of the ship. The owner then obtained an arbitral award for the wasted expenditure incurred making the modifications. Nevertheless, despite this expenditure, the owner had suffered no net loss because he had been able to find a replacement charterer, who, because charter rates had soared in the meantime, was willing to pay far more than the original defaulting charterer. On appeal to the High Court, the original charterers argued that the owner should not recover more than nominal damages because the wasted expenditure would be more than offset by this increased amount. Teare J agreed and held that where a defendant charterer had repudiated a charter party, and the owner sued for wasted expenditure on the "reliance" basis, the court was entitled to look at what the owner would have earned had the contract been performed, and so (in the instant case) consider benefits received on alternative, more profitable, charter parties. The claimant was unable to claim for its wasted expenditure as it had suffered no net loss.

Of course, expectation loss of the *Robinson v Harman* type and reliance loss are mutually exclusive; both cannot be claimed together, as this would lead to what is termed 'double recovery'. As Lord Denning put it in *Anglia Television v Reed*, "It seems to me that a claimant in such a case as this has an election: he can either claim for loss of profits; or for his wasted expenditure. But he must elect between them. He cannot claim both". Subsequent cases have suggested that all that was meant by an "election" was that a claimant may choose to frame his claim for damages on the reliance rather than an expectancy basis. In the case of *Filobake Limited v Rindo Limited* [2005] EWCA Civ 56, the Court of Appeal observed, in *obiter* comments, that it was wrong to advance alternative claims for loss of profits and wasted expenditure until late in a contract action, not least because the burden of proof might lie on different parties in each situation (see below).

## Limitations on Reliance Claims

In *C&P Haulage v Middleton* [1983] 1 WLR 1461, the Court of Appeal placed a limitation on reliance claims, holding that a claimant could not claim wasted expenditure when it was apparent that the agreement he had entered, even though broken by the defendant, would not have occasioned him loss in any event. A claim for reliance loss could not be used to circumvent what was always a bad bargain. In this case, C&P Haulage granted Middleton a contractual license to occupy premises from which to conduct his business. The agreement stipulated that this was renewable every six months, and that any fixtures introduced to the premises were not to be removed at the end of the licence. Middleton incurred significant expenses installing fixtures when making the premises suitable for his work. Ten weeks prior to the expiry of a term, Middleton was unlawfully evicted, not having been given the requisite notice period. However, he was able to conduct his business from home. Subsequently, he sought damages from C&P for the unlawful eviction and claimed compensation for the improvements he had made to the premises. In reply, C&P argued that Middleton could not have legally removed the fixtures. As a result, he had not sustained any loss by their breach of contract. This was accepted by the court, and he was merely awarded nominal damages for the wrongful eviction. As Ackner LJ noted, citing Canadian authority, awarding him the cost of the improvements would place him in a better position than he would have been had the contract been fulfilled, and this was not the function of the courts.

This issue was considered again, at first instance, by Hutchison J in *CCC Films (London) Ltd v Impact Quadrant Films Ltd* [1985] 1 QB 16. In this case, the judge permitted the claimant to abandon their claim for loss of profits at a very late stage of the proceedings, and to substitute a claim for wasted expenditure. He also noted that, in these situations, it was for the defendant who was in breach to prove (on the balance of probabilities) that all or part of the expenditure would have been wasted in any event, because it was an inherently bad bargain, and so was not recoverable. In *Filobake Limited v Rindo Limited* [2005] EWCA Civ 56, the Court of Appeal accepted, in *obiter* comments, this analysis of the shifting burden of proof in such situations.

## Difficult Assessments and Contractual Damages

The courts will attempt to provide financial compensation for a breach of contract, even where it is very difficult to calculate, or requires a degree of ingenuity to do so. For example, where a defendant prevents the claimant from adducing evidence on the issue of damages, the court can make presumptions in favour of the latter when assessing their level. To consider an old case, in *Armory v Delamirie* (1722) 1 Strange 505, a chimney-sweep's assistant found a jewelled ring and took it to a jeweller for valuation. The latter alleged that the gem was glass so that it was worth less than 2d. However, he returned the ring with an empty socket, without the jewel. Experts gave evidence about the potential value of the gem which a socket of that size might have accommodated, and Pratt CJ directed the jury that, unless the defendant produced it, and established that it was not of the finest quality, they should "presume the strongest against him, and make the value of the best jewels [that could be accommodated by the setting] the measure of their damages". Much more pertinently, the courts will also compensate "loss of a chance"--that is, a lost opportunity--even though such an award must necessarily be highly speculative.

## Loss of an Opportunity

In the Court of Appeal case of *Chaplin v Hicks* [1911] 2 KB 786, the claimant was an actress who entered a beauty contest organised by Hicks and advertised in a newspaper. Its readers were to vote on the contestants' published photographs, and the top 50 selected by them would be invited to an interview, where 12 would be engaged for theatrical work over the following three years. The claimant got through to the final 50 (from 6,000 applicants) but, in breach of contract, did not receive her invitation for interview in time to attend, so losing her chance of gaining employment. There was, of course, no guarantee that she would have been one of the fewer than a quarter of the short-listed women who got through. Even so, she was awarded £100 in damages by the trial jury (still used at this time in such civil cases). Hicks appealed, contending that the damages were speculative in nature and incapable of assessment, and that, even if there had been a breach of contract, damages should be nominal. However, his appeal was dismissed. The claimant was entitled to damages for her loss of a chance, difficult though this would be to assess. She did not have to prove that she would have been successful at interview. Vaughan Williams LJ noted that the "fact that damages cannot be assessed with certainty does not relieve the wrongdoer of the necessity of paying damages for his breach of contract".

Perhaps more typically, in the Court of Appeal case of *Dunk v George Waller and Son* [1970] 2 All ER 630, the defendant engaged the claimant under a four-year apprenticeship to train as an engineer. Subsequently, he terminated the contract, without justification, before the completion of the contractually agreed time. The claimant successfully bought an action for wrongful dismissal. It was held that he was entitled not only to the wages he would have received during the remainder of the contractually agreed period, but also a sum of money to reflect his loss of training. As Widgery LJ observed, contracts of apprenticeship provided valuable skills that would "provide employment opportunities in the labour market following the successful completion of the training". Similarly, the trial judge in *Sadler v George Reynolds* [2005] EWHC 309 (QB) added £1,000 to the claimant's estimated loss of £35,000 in profits for the defendant's breach of a contract to ghost-write the latter's autobiography, this being deemed to be a "reasonable estimate" to compensate him for the loss of an opportunity to enhance his reputation as a writer by producing such a book. As even the claimant's counsel in this case conceded, this was a difficult sum to quantify.

In a different context, in *Jackson v Royal Bank of Scotland* [2005] 1 WLR 377, Mr Jackson and his partner, trading as Samson Lancastrian, imported specialist pet food from Thailand, which it then sold on to other distributors. Its principal customer was another business called Economy Bag who supplied dog chews. Unknown to Economy Bag, Jackson made a substantial mark-up of 19 per cent on these trades (a lot by the standards of the dog-food industry). Economy Bag did business with Samson by means of transferable letters of credit, which meant that Samson could conceal the high mark-up it applied to purchases from its Thai supplier. Business between the parties ran smoothly from 1990 to 1993. By chance, both parties banked with the Royal Bank of Scotland (RBS). In March 1993, RBS mistakenly sent documents, including an invoice from the Thai company, disclosing the heavy mark-up, to Economy Bag, instead of to Samson. This was a breach of confidence and so of contract with their client.

The management of Economy Bag was surprised at the size of the mark-up and annoyed by what they viewed as the claimant's attempts to conceal it. They decided to import the goods direct from the Thai company themselves. Samson, which was heavily dependent on this contract, went into liquidation as a result, and sued RBS for breach of contract (their banking agreement), and the loss of the opportunity to make further profits on the dog-chew trades. A key issue at trial, *inter alia*, was the measure of damages. Economy Bag might have discovered the high mark-up at any time, even without the bank's error, as it was not difficult to find out. In theory, this might have been as early as April 1993. Conversely, they might have remained in ignorance, and the relationship could have lasted for a decade or more. At first instance, the trial judge decided that the relationship would have continued for four more years on a decreasing scale of probability, after which further dealings would be too speculative. However, the Court of Appeal held that damages should be limited to within one year of the breach, and that all other losses were too remote. Nevertheless, on further appeal, the House of Lords held that the trial judge's assessment was a good one, allowing for the fact that it was increasingly likely, as time passed, that Economy Bag would want to squeeze Jackson's profit margins or would find out about the size of the mark-up. To avoid further litigation costs, the initial award (four years, but at a reducing rate) would be restored.

Nevertheless, there is a threshold below which loss of a chance will not be compensated. In *Allied Maples Group Ltd v Simmons & Simmons* [1995] 1 WLR 1602, the Court of Appeal observed that there had to be a real and substantial chance, and not merely a speculative possibility, for substantial damages to be awarded. This was repeated by the same forum in *Wellesley Partners LLP v Withers LLP* [2015] EWCA Civ 1146. More recently, in *Moda International Brands Ltd v Gateley LLP & Anor* [2019] EWHC 1326 (QB), the High Court reiterated that when considering loss of a chance the claimant was not obliged to prove his case was more probable than not, only that the lost chance was a "real or substantial" one. This means that a *de minimis* rule will apply in such situations. An example of what might fall within such a rule can be seen in *Obagi v Stanborough (Developments) Ltd* (1993) TLR Dec 15. In this case the defendants were in breach of contract in failing to apply for planning permission, but the High Court held that the prospects of such permission being granted were minimal, and a mere theoretical possibility. In these circumstances, they could be ignored, without requiring an assessment of prospects, unlike the situation in *Chaplin v Hicks*. As a result, only nominal damages of £5 were awarded.

Conversely, in *Bugsby Property LLC v LGIM Commercial Lending Ltd & Anor* [2022] EWHC 2001 (Comm), the Commercial Court awarded the claimant huge "loss of a chance" damages. The claim was brought by Bugsby, a Delaware company, against the Legal & General Group (L&G). Bugsby had approached L&G, unavailingly seeking finance from them to acquire the Olympia Exhibition Hall in London. Over a year later, and in inadvertent breach of an exclusivity agreement (and so a contract) with Bugsby, L&G financed the acquisition of Olympia by another consortium. L&G argued that Bugsby had not suffered loss as a result of this breach, because their Olympia bid would have failed in any event and, even if Bugsby *had* succeeded in acquiring Olympia, it would not have made a profit. The Court assessed Bugsby's damages on a loss-of-a-chance basis. This required the judge to consider a very complex series of related possibilities as to what might have happened if L&G had not financed the successful rival Olympia bid. Knowles J concluded that there was a 35 per cent chance that Bugsby would have acquired Olympia if L&G had not done so (a real chance), and quantified Bugsby's damages at £14.98 million; this sum consisted of a percentage of the return that Bugsby would, in the court's opinion, have obtained on its investment in Olympia.

### Wrotham Park/Negotiating Damages

As already noted, the purpose of contract damages is to compensate the victim of a breach, not to penalize the wrongdoer for any gain that he has made. In Lord Atkinson's words in *Addis v Gramophone Co Ltd* [1909] AC 488, "I have always understood that damages for breach of contract were in the nature of compensation, not punishment". As a result, they cannot normally be awarded so as to deprive a defendant of the profits that he has made from his breach. This has given rise to the notion of "efficient breach", whereby a contract breaker makes a conscious decision to break contract A so that he can enter a more lucrative contract B, knowing that paying damages for the former will be outweighed by the profit made from the latter.

For example, in the Court of Appeal decision in *Surrey County Council v Bredero Homes Ltd.* [1993] 1 WLR 1361, a local authority had sold land to a developer, having first obtained a covenant that the latter would develop the land in accordance with an existing grant of planning permission, which limited the number of houses to be built on the plot. In breach of the covenant (and so contract), the developer obtained planning permission for, and built, extra homes on the plot of land. The local authority brought a claim for the amount they might have received for agreeing to modifications to the original covenant. However, the erection of the larger number of houses had not caused them any financial loss. The judge at first instance awarded nominal damages of £2, and the Court of Appeal dismissed the local authority's appeal.

Nevertheless, even then, there was an alternative, if little followed, approach to such issues, one that had been identified in *Wrotham Park Estate Co. Ltd. v Parkside Homes Ltd.* [1974] 1 WLR 798. In this case, the claimant owned land which had the benefit of a restrictive covenant preventing it being built on. In breach of that covenant, houses were constructed on the land. As a result, the claimant asked the court for a mandatory injunction ordering the demolition of the newly built houses (See Chapter 16). At the time, there was an acute housing shortage, and the court refused to order this, something that would also have been unfair to the homes' new occupants. However, the presence of the new houses did not reduce the value of the benefited land. As there was no loss, it might have been argued that the claimant would be limited to an award of nominal damages. Nevertheless, the judge considered that this would be manifestly unjust. Instead, he assessed the damages at five per cent of the developer's anticipated profit, this being the amount of money which could reasonably have been demanded for a relaxation of the covenant. It was a hypothetical negotiated release fee. In this situation, the claimant would not have to prove actual loss.

Similarly, in *Jaggard v Sawyer* [1995] 1 WLR 258, a trial judge refused to grant an injunction with regard to a new building that violated a covenant (because of the claimant's delay in seeking such an order) and, instead, made an award of damages based on the sum the defendants might reasonably have paid for being released from that covenant. The Court of Appeal upheld the judge's decision, agreeing that the value of the right should be what a reasonable seller would ask for it. In these situations, the claimant should not be treated as eager to sell but, on the other hand, the court should not value the right at the extortionate price a very reluctant seller might place on it.

In *Pell Frischmann Engineering Ltd v Bow Valley Iran Limited & Others* [2009] UKPC 45, the Privy Council gave further guidance on how and when "Wrotham Park damages" can be awarded in lieu of a mandatory injunction for breach of contract. The court noted that the decision to deprive a party of his strict legal rights should not be taken lightly and only occur in exceptional circumstances. These would include situations where the claimant himself indicated that a money payment would compensate for the breach of his rights, or where other factors might make it oppressive to grant an injunction. Such damages would represent such an amount as would hypothetically have been agreed between the parties, acting *reasonably*, at the time the breach occurred, as the price for releasing the defendant from its obligations to the claimant. It was irrelevant that the parties concerned might never have reached such a deal.

The use of "negotiating" damages (as they are often called) as a basis of assessment for breach of contract claims increased during the early years of the twenty-first century, with the courts sometimes making such awards where they considered it "just" to do so in the circumstances of a particular case, rather than in the circumstances originally envisaged in *Wrotham Park*. This created uncertainty, especially for lawyers advising clients who entered restrictive covenants, such as non-compete, non-solicit, and non-disclosure agreements.

For example, in *Marathon Asset Management LLP & Anor v Seddon & Ors* [2017] EWHC 300 two employees of Marathon Asset Management LLP copied numerous files containing confidential information belonging to their employer onto USB drives in the months before they left the company to set up a competing investment management business. This was a breach of the employees' contractual duties to Marathon. However, very few if any of the confidential files were accessed, and none were used, after they left the company, so that Marathon did not allege that they had suffered any financial loss as a result. Nevertheless, Marathon claimed that they were entitled to "*Wrotham Park* damages" of £15 million, this being what, they felt, the employees would have had to pay for being released from their contractual duty of confidentiality if they had negotiated the matter. The Court rejected their claim and merely awarded nominal damages. The principal reason was that the two former employees had not used the confidential files to obtain any benefit. The Court reiterated that its role was not to punish, but to compensate loss.

The whole issue was reviewed by the Supreme Court in *Morris-Garner and another (Appellants) v One Step (Support) Ltd (Respondent)* [2018] UKSC 20, which case has had the effect of narrowing, and so restricting, the scope of this category of damages, while providing guidance on the limited circumstances in which they should be awarded. One Step had purchased from the appellants a business providing support for young people leaving care. As part of that transaction, the latter agreed to be bound for three years by restrictive covenants prohibiting them from competing with One Step or from soliciting its clients. One Step later brought proceedings alleging breach of this agreement. At first instance, the trial judge held that the appellants had breached the restrictive covenants, and that One Step was entitled to damages to be assessed either in the usual way (ordinary compensatory damages) or on the Wrotham Park basis (for such amount as would notionally have been agreed between the parties, acting reasonably, as the price for releasing the defendants from their obligations). One Step elected to claim damages using the latter method of assessment. The first-instance decision was upheld by the Court of Appeal.

However, the Supreme Court concluded that the lower courts had erred in believing that "negotiating damages" (the term preferred by the majority) should be available whenever the court considers it to be a just response. Judicial discretion has no part to play in deciding the basis on which such damages are awarded. Negotiating damages should be granted only where it is appropriate to measure the claimant's loss by reference to the economic value of the right that has been breached, with that right being treated as an asset for which the claimant could require payment. Breaches of non-compete or non-solicitation clauses did not fall within this category, so that the claimant had to prove financial loss in the usual way. In Lord Reed's words, the Court of Appeal had been mistaken in treating the deliberate nature of the breach and the difficulty of establishing the consequent financial loss, "or the claimant's interest in preventing the defendants' profit-making activities, as justifying the award of a monetary remedy which was not compensatory".

Taking the conventional approach to assessing contractual damages in the case, the Supreme Court held that the respondent had suffered financial loss because of the appellants' breach of contract, the effect of which was to expose the former's business to competition that would otherwise have been avoided. Although this was very difficult to quantify, damages would still have to be assessed on that basis. The Supreme Court also noted that, although economic value can be given to contractual rights to control the use of land via a restrictive covenant, to an intellectual-property agreement, or to a confidential-information agreement, it was hard to envisage other situations where "negotiating damages" might be appropriate, exceptional circumstances apart.

## An Account of Profits

In *Attorney General v Blake* [2001] 1 AC 268, it was held that, in quite exceptional situations, restitutionary damages or an "account of profits" might be awarded for breach of contract. George Blake had been a member of MI6 during and after the Second World War, signing the Official Secrets Act 1911. He became a Soviet double agent, committed repeated breaches of his undertaking not to divulge official information obtained from his work, and was eventually caught and imprisoned. He escaped before defecting to the Soviet Union. He later wrote a book about his experiences and received a publishing contract for its release in 1989, for which he was given advance payments. He was entitled to more. However, the government then brought an action to secure all the outstanding profits he had made on the book, arguing that a restitutionary principle should apply. (Although *Wrotham Park* was discussed in *Attorney General v Blake*, negotiating damages were not sought.)

The House of Lords held (Lord Hobhouse dissenting) that, in very rare cases, when the normal remedy is inadequate to compensate for breach of contract, and a "just response" so requires, the court can order a defendant to account for all his profits to the claimant. Blake was a traitor who had caused immense damage to the public interest by his revelations, even if they were no longer classified by the time he released his book. An absolute rule against disclosure in such cases was vitally necessary, so that it was in the Crown's legitimate interest to ensure that he did not benefit from his activity. As a result, the normal contractual remedies (damages, specific performance, or injunction) were not adequate, and the publishers were required to pay any money owing to Blake to the Crown. More generally, the court noted that, although fixed rules could not be prescribed as to when these unusual situations would arise, they would normally involve a claimant who had a legitimate interest in preventing the defendant's profit-making activity, as was the situation in the instant case.

*Blake* has very rarely been followed since it was decided, suggesting that the circumstances in which an account of profits will be awarded are quite extreme (as was the case with *Blake*), and that Lord Hobhouse's reservations have, perhaps, been influential. Nevertheless, shortly after that decision, in *Esso Petroleum Co Ltd v Niad Ltd* [2001] EWHC 458 (Ch), the High Court ordered an account of profits as a remedy for breach of a contractual scheme termed Pricewatch operated by the claimant with its dealers, one of whom was the defendant. Under this scheme, dealers in Esso petrol agreed to report local competitors' prices and to abide by prices set daily by Esso to match those prices. They received financial support from Esso for doing this. The defendant, who was a dealer in Yorkshire, failed to keep to these prices, despite giving assurances that he would do so, and receiving the relevant financial support. Conventional damages were inadequate since Esso could not attribute lost sales to breach by any one dealer. However, the defendant's failure had, potentially, damaged Esso's advertising campaign. As a result, Esso had a legitimate interest in preventing the defendant from profiting from his breach. In these circumstances, an account of profits (the difference between agreed and actual prices) was appropriate, although the claimant was also offered the (alternative) choice of claiming the financial support that had been granted on a restitutionary basis.

## Penalty and Liquidated Damages Clauses

Penalty and liquidated/specified/agreed damages clauses (terminology varies for the latter, but "liquidated" will normally be used in this text) are pre-determined quantifications of the damages that will be deemed to flow from given breaches, that are stipulated in the contract itself. However, and vitally, a "penalty clause" is unenforceable because it is thought to be an exorbitant or excessive alternative to common law damages. (It should be noted that laymen often use this term indiscriminately for any liquidated-damages clause). By contrast, if such a pre-determined payment is considered a genuine attempt to estimate likely loss *or* to be present for another legitimate reason, it will be enforceable as a liquidated-damages clause, even if it transpires, in retrospect, to be mistaken in its estimation (as most such clauses are to some extent).

The main benefit of introducing such a clause to the contract is that it allows the breaching party to know their liability in advance, and the injured party to obtain compensation for the specified amount, once the breach has been proven, without the trouble, uncertainty, and potential legal expense of establishing common law damages. As Lady Arden observed in the Supreme Court decision in *Triple Point*

*Technology Inc v PTT Public Company Ltd* [2021] UKSC 29, parties agree a liquidated damages clause to provide a remedy that is predictable and certain on the occurrence of a particular event, so that the claimant does not then have to quantify its loss, "which may be difficult and time-consuming for it to do." Furthermore, in these situations, the injured party is not under any obligation to mitigate their loss, as it would be in an ordinary claim. Additionally, questions of remoteness do not arise. Nevertheless, if a pre-estimate *is* deemed to be a penalty and so unenforceable, or it fails for some other reason, it is ignored, and the normal common law rules on determining damages for breach of contract will apply instead.

Normally it is the breaching party who argues that a pre-estimate of damages is a penalty clause, on the basis that common law damages will be more favourable to them. An interesting question is whether the party who is entitled to receive liquidated damages can also claim that the relevant clause is a penalty. They might wish to do this if it transpires that (unexpectedly) the loss they sustained exceeds that provided for by the liquidated-damages clause, even though this might require them to say that, at the time it was set, it was clearly exorbitant. The law on this issue is uncertain, if only because of the rarity with which the situation occurs. Although *Wall v Rederiaktiebolaget Luggude* [1915] 3 KB 66 suggests that such a course of action might be permissible, it has been the subject of academic criticism, and the issue was left open in *Cellulose Acetate Silk Co Ltd v Widnes Foundry Ltd* [1933] AC 20 and regarded as unclear by at least one member of the Court of Appeal in *Robophone Facilities Ltd v Blank* [1966] 1 WLR 1428. Arguably, the rules on penalty clauses are designed to protect defendants, not claimants, and the latter should not be allowed to rely on them.

Liquidated-damages clauses are particularly common in certain types of agreement. Foremost amongst these are construction contracts. These might provide that, if completion of a building contract is delayed, the builder or contractor will be liable to pay (or will be entitled to a reduced payment of) a specified sum for each day, week, or month the delay lasts. However, they are also found in many other situations. For example, in *Triple Point Technology Inc v PTT Public Company Ltd* [2021] UKSC 29, a clause provided for the payment of liquidated damages "per day of delay" in installing new software. Many other liquidated-damages clauses are unrelated to any form of delay.

Historically, the leading case on the distinction between penalty and liquidated-damages clauses was the long-lived House of Lords decision in *Dunlop Pneumatic Tyre Company v New Garage & Motor* co [1915] AC 79. In this case, Dunlop, the claimant, manufactured tyres and sold them to retailers for resale. The contract between Dunlop and New Garage (a retailer) contained a clause preventing the latter from selling the tyres below a specific list price (as was then allowed) and provided that any failure to observe this would be a breach of contract for which £5 per tyre would be payable.

The defendants in *Dunlop* sold some tyres below the list price, and the claimant sued for damages in accordance with the amount specified in the contract. The defendant argued that the relevant provision was a penalty clause and thus unenforceable. At first instance, the trial judge rejected this argument and held that it was an enforceable liquidated-damages clause; as a result, he awarded the £5 per tyre. The Court of Appeal reversed this decision, holding that it was a penalty clause, and awarded the claimant £2 per tyre, which they thought represented the actual loss suffered. The claimant then appealed to the House of Lords which decided that the clause was, indeed, a legitimate liquidated damages clause and restored the trial judge's decision and the £5 payment.

In this case, Lord Dunedin also took the opportunity to make several important observations about the distinction between liquidated-damages and penalty clauses. He noted that the essence of a penalty clause is a payment of money that acts *in terrorem* of the offending party, being an attempt to frighten them into performing their obligations, while the essence of a liquidated-damages clause is that it is a genuine attempt to pre-estimate likely loss having regard to the circumstances at the time the contract was made (not when it was breached). However, the judge observed that various indicia can be considered when making this distinction. Thus, he noted that the wording employed in a clause is not conclusive; even if the parties to a contract describe a clause as a "penalty" it could be a liquidated-damages clause and vice versa. If the stipulated sum was extravagant and unconscionable when compared to the greatest loss that could conceivably have followed from the breach, it is likely to be a penalty. There is a presumption (but no more) that any clause that stipulates the payment of a single sum on the occurrence of several different events, some of which may occasion serious and others only trivial loss, is a penalty.[4] A provision will normally be presumed to be penal if the breach consists solely of the non-payment of money and the contract stipulates a larger sum in damages. The judge also observed that simply because the consequences of a breach are such as to make a precise pre-estimation almost impossible, it does not stop the sum stipulated being a genuine pre-estimate of loss, even though it will probably be seriously inaccurate. Indeed, it is often in such situations that a liquidated-damages clause is most valuable, and the pre-estimated damage likely to be deemed a genuine attempt to assess potential loss.

*Dunlop v New Garage* was the leading case in the field until 2015, although subsequent decisions refined, elucidated, and illustrated it. For example, in *Philips Hong Kong v The Attorney General of Hong Kong* [1993] UKPC 3, the Privy Council noted that it was almost inevitable that an ingenious argument could be made for saying that in some, very specific, situation, a substantially higher sum might be recovered than would be recoverable if the claimant was required to prove his

4 In *GPP Big Field LLP v Solar EPC Solutions SL* [2018] EWHC 2866 (Comm) the High Court considered whether the fact that the liquidated damages clauses for delay in commissioning five solar power stations was the same for each plant, even though they were of significantly (but not enormously) different generating power, meant that they were penalties, and decided that they were not.

actual loss under common law principles. Even so, it was very important that parties to commercial contracts were able to rely on the damages clauses that they had agreed, and to know with a reasonable degree of certainty the risks they ran by entering an agreement. As a result, such clauses should, if possible, be upheld.

More specifically, in *Murray v Leisureplay Plc* [2005] EWCA Civ 963, the Court of Appeal decided that a liquidated-damages clause in an executive's contract of employment, providing for the payment of one year's gross salary, pension, and various other benefits in the event of wrongful termination, was not a penalty clause. The sum was generous but not unconscionably so and may have been set to allow for the difficulty involved in obtaining suitable alternative work. Similarly, a valid liquidated damages clause was also found to be present in *Azimut-Benetti Spa v Healey* [2010] EWHC 2234 (Comm), in which a luxury-yacht builder agreed to sell a boat, with payment in instalments. The parties agreed that, if the buyer abandoned the agreement before any payment had been made, the seller would be entitled to 20 per cent of the total price. The buyer failed to pay the first instalment; the seller terminated the agreement, and duly claimed the 20 per cent. The High Court rejected the buyer's argument that this was excessive and so a penalty clause, holding that it was an agreement between commercial parties of equal standing, and that the clause was not designed to deter the other party from defaulting, but was a genuine pre-estimate of the damages likely to be incurred on breach.

### *Cavendish Square*

In 2015 the Supreme Court carefully reviewed and reconsidered the entire law on penalty clauses in the joint appeals in *Cavendish Square Holding BV v Talal El Makdessi (El Makdessi) and ParkingEye Ltd v Beavis* [2015] UKSC 67. The *ParkingEye* case related to a parking fine of £85 imposed after a driver overstayed the two-hour limit in a privately run car park. The driver, Mr Beavis, argued that this was a penalty, as the owner of the car park had not suffered any clear loss and (more pertinently) it could not have been anticipated that he was likely to suffer such loss. The *Cavendish Square* case related to the sale of a Middle Eastern media business and the provisions of a share purchase and shareholders' agreement. The latter provided that if the seller was in breach of certain non-compete restrictions, he would lose his entitlement to deferred consideration that would otherwise have been payable and could be required to sell his remaining shares at a price that excluded goodwill. The Court of Appeal, applying *Dunlop v New Garage*, held that both these provisions were penal, as their purpose was to deter an act rather than to compensate the innocent party's loss.

However, the Supreme Court noted that the test established in *Dunlop v New Garage* had aged badly, acquiring the status of a quasi-statutory rule, which, the court opined, was never the House of Lords' intention. In the words of Lord Sumption, it had become "an ancient, haphazardly constructed edifice which [had] not weathered well". More particularly, it had been applied too rigidly in cases where there may have been interests beyond the purely compensatory that warranted protecting, and which justified the imposition of an additional financial burden on the party in breach.

In the consolidated appeals, the Supreme Court introduced a more flexible test. The court held (by a majority) that the provisions in the two cases were not unlawful penalties. Lords Sumption and Neuberger, who were with the majority, felt that the correct test for identifying a penalty clause turned on whether it imposed a detriment on the contract breaker that was: "...out of all proportion to any legitimate interest of the innocent party in the enforcement of the primary obligation". In the case of a straightforward damages clause, such an interest would rarely extend beyond compensation for the breach that had occurred, and Lord Dunedin's four tests would "usually be perfectly adequate to determine its validity". As a result, the decision in *New Garage* is still of considerable practical significance when it comes to guidance, albeit no longer the test itself. Thus, and for example, in *GPP Big Field LLP v Solar EPC Solutions SL* [2018] EWHC 2866 (Comm), Richard Salter QC decided that references to "penalty" in a liquidated damages clause did not make it a penalty clause.

Nevertheless, as *Cavendish Square* noted, financial compensation was not necessarily the *only* legitimate interest that an innocent party might have in the performance of the defaulter's primary obligations. For example, the £85 asked of Mr Beavis after he overstayed a two-hour limit on free parking was deemed to be reasonable. The term was prominently advertised, such penalties are a normal feature of parking contracts, and play an important role in the efficient management of space as they deter over-stayers. As a result, they were beneficial not just to the landowner (ParkingEye) and the adjacent retail outlets, but to motorists themselves, because they ensured that parking space was available that might otherwise be clogged up with long-stay users. Furthermore, the amount of the charge in the instant case was not exorbitant in comparison to the general level of such penalties found elsewhere, and there was no reason to think that it was higher than necessary to ensure considerate use by motorists. A lesser or more finely graduated charge would probably be ineffective. Consequently, the charge was not "out of all proportion" to the innocent party's legitimate interest in enforcing the contract and so was binding. In *Talal El Makdessi* the provisions were also held not to be a penalty clause because they were there for a legitimate reason.

The decision in *Cavendish Square* prompted a mixed response from lawyers. Some argued that where the parties to an agreement had negotiated on a level playing field, with legal advice, it would make it harder to claim that a clause was a penalty. Others felt that in focussing on the legitimate interests of the parties the new test was significantly more flexible than its predecessor. However, several have argued that, in abandoning the categorisation of penalty clauses seen in *Dunlop*, the Supreme Court has created uncertainty.

The new test has shaped all recent decisions on the issue. For example, Thus, in *ZCCM Investments Holdings plc v Konkola Copper Mines plc* [2017] EWHC 3288 (Comm) the High Court held that there was nothing "extravagant, exorbitant or unconscionable" in requiring a Zambian company to pay the full amount of a loan immediately, under an acceleration clause that was activated by non-compliance with the terms of the agreement. Similarly, in *GPP Big Field LLP v Solar EPC Solutions SL* [2018] EWHC 2866 (Comm) Richard Slater QC, sitting as a Deputy High Court Judge, noted that the sum specified in a liquidated damages clause for delayed completion of a construction contract was not "extravagant or unconscionable" in comparison with GPP's legitimate interest in ensuring timely performance.

By contrast, in *Blu-Sky Solutions Ltd v Be Caring Ltd* [2021] EWHC 2619, the High Court held, in *obiter* comments, that even if a cancellation clause described as an "administration charge" had been incorporated by reference (not the case), it was out of all proportion to any legitimate interest of the supplier in the performance of the primary obligation, making it penal and so void as a penalty clause. Similarly, in *Ahuja v Victorygame* [2021] EWHC 2382 (Ch), the High Court concluded that default interest for a breach of contract was an unlawful penalty. Ahuja had borrowed a sum of money from Victorygame to buy one of the latter's properties and had subsequently defaulted on a scheduled payment. Victorygame sought to enforce a provision in the loan agreement by which interest at the rate of 12 per cent, compounded each month, was then payable on the amount that remained outstanding. This was a fourfold increase from the 3 per cent per month previously paid. The court had to consider whether the clause was "out of all proportion" to any legitimate interest or otherwise "exorbitant, extravagant or unconscionable". The court acknowledged that there *were* valid reasons for imposing a higher interest rate in such situations. For example, a borrower who has defaulted is a higher credit risk. Nevertheless, there was no satisfactory evidence to justify such a drastic increase. Had it had been lower, limited to 6 per cent or less, the court *might* have been prepared to accept the provision as non-penal, but in the instant case it was an unlawful penalty clause.

## Award of an Agreed Sum/The Price

Most contracts involve an exchange of goods and/or services for money. An action for an "agreed sum" (the price) allows a party to claim the specific amount of money owed under a contract from the party in breach, this being the latter's *primary* obligation under that agreement. It is a very common contractual remedy where someone has failed to pay for goods or services that have been provided to them. It should be stressed that an agreed sum is different to an award of damages, although both involve the payment of money, because paying damages (including liquidated damages) involves fulfilling *secondary* obligations under a contract, those that arise on breach. With damages the measure is calculated by reference to the loss sustained by the claimant, whereas the award of an agreed sum is the recovery of money due under the contract. This makes it (effectively) the same as a claim for the payment of a debt.

An action for the price is normally brought where the party supplying goods or services has *fully* fulfilled their side of the bargain so that the duty to pay has arisen, and then seeks the fulfilment by the counterparty of their primary obligation under the agreement, namely, to pay the agreed sum. Thus, and for example, if A contracts with B to deliver a ton of potatoes following which B will pay him £1,000, and A delivers the root vegetables, in satisfactory condition, property in them passing to the buyer, but B fails to pay the money, A can bring an action for the £1,000 as an agreed sum. This principle has been put into statutory form for the sale of goods by s.49(1) SOGA 1979. Similarly, once a builder has finished a job of work, to an appropriate standard, he can claim the sum agreed for that work.

Such an action has several advantages. The claimant does not need to prove loss, worry about remoteness, or show that they have attempted to mitigate their loss. That there is a due sum which has not been paid is sufficient. However, there is a major area of legal difficulty in this topic, which was raised in the unusual case of *White and Carter (Councils) Ltd v McGregor* [1962] AC 413, in which a party to a contract refused to terminate the agreement after a repudiatory breach by their counterparty and continued to perform their obligations, which did not require the counterparty's cooperation to finish, before seeking an agreed sum on their completion, several years later.

In 1957 White & Carter entered a three-year contract to display advertisements for McGregor's garage on litter bins and lamp posts. Very shortly afterwards, the company sought to withdraw from the agreement, this being an anticipatory (and so repudiatory) breach. White & Carter ignored this, and displayed the advertisements, as they had originally agreed, for the three years specified, and then, having completed all their obligations under the agreement, brought an action for the price (an agreed sum), not damages. The House of Lords held by a bare majority (three to two) that, in these circumstances, the claimants were not obliged to accept the breach but could continue with the contract and then recover the agreed price. Because it was not a claim for damages, the need to mitigate did not arise. This decision was controversial, not least because the claimants had "saddled themselves with an unwanted contract causing an apparent waste of time and money". The dissenting judges submitted that White & Carter had acted unreasonably by ignoring the defendant's wishes.

Although Lord Reid was one of the three-judge majority in *White and Carter*, he placed two important qualifications on this principle. If one of these is operative, the claimant will not be able to claim the agreed sum and will be confined to damages. First, a claimant is entitled only to the agreed sum when performance has been completed, this being a precondition to payment; as a result, if the contract requires the defendant's cooperation, active or passive, to reach this point, and he prevents the claimant from performing their obligations, the claim will necessarily be restricted to one for damages: *Ministry of Sound (Ireland) Ltd v World Online Ltd*

[2003] EWHC 2178. Thus, in *Hounslow LBC v Twickenham Garden Developments Ltd* [1971] Ch 233, Megarry J noted that a builder working on somebody else's land could not ignore their repudiation of the agreement and continue with the contract so as to claim the agreed sum for the project. He required the owner's permission, and so cooperation, to finish the work.

Second, in *White & Carter v McGregor* itself, it was stated, "If it can be shown that a person has no legitimate interest, financial or otherwise, in performing the contract rather than claiming damages, he ought not be allowed to saddle the other party with an additional burden with no benefit to himself". The meaning of this is uncertain, not least because the claimant will almost always have a financial interest in making a claim for an agreed sum, but in practice a narrower interpretation is normally used by the courts.

For example, in *The Alaskan Trader* [1983] 2 Lloyds Rep 645, a ship was chartered for a term of 24 months. After one year, the vessel had a serious engine failure. The defendant then informed the claimant that they no longer wanted the vessel; even so, the latter went ahead with expensive repairs on it, which cost 800,000 and took five months. The claimant did not treat the defendant's rejection of the contract as a repudiation and kept the ship and crew ready for the defendant for another seven months after this work was completed (the remainder of the charterparty). Even if no alternative charter could have been found for the vessel during this time, it would have been much cheaper to lay her up and discharge her crew (part of the charter as it was not a 'bare-bones' agreement) during this period. At the end of the two-year term, the claimant claimed the full price of the outstanding seven months' hire. In response, the defendant successfully argued that their repudiation of the contract should have been accepted. It was held that the claimant had no legitimate interest in performing the agreement, so that it was "wholly unreasonable" for them not to terminate the contract, and they could not claim an agreed sum for the seven months. Lloyd J noted that an innocent party did not always have an unfettered right to enforce the agreement according to its strict legal terms.

# Chapter 16: Equitable Remedies

## Introduction

In the vast majority of cases, common law damages are considered adequate as a remedy for breach of contract. However, there are a few situations in which the courts might feel it necessary to have recourse to an equitable remedy, one that was originally developed in the Chancery jurisdiction prior to the unification of the courts under the Victorian Judicature Acts. Most important, these include orders for specific performance and the granting of injunctions. They are potentially drastic remedies, explaining why they are comparatively rarely used.

Unlike common law, which acts *in rem*, equity acts *in personam*. A failure to comply with an order to pay damages might, eventually, lead to High Court sheriffs or, in some situations, County Court bailiffs, seeking to levy items from the defendant for sale, placing garnishee orders on his bank accounts (also known as Third Party Debt Orders), or attachment-of-earnings orders on any income from his employer, to satisfy the debt, but nothing will happen to the defendant himself. By contrast, a failure to comply with an equitable order is a contempt of court and may be met with punitive measures, such as fines or even a sentence of imprisonment (whether immediate or suspended).

## Specific Performance

In a few situations the breaching party might be ordered to fulfil his primary obligations under the contract. This means that the defendant is required by the court to do the very thing that he has contracted to do. This is termed an order for specific performance. In England, such an order is rarely made. (It is a much more important remedy for breach of contract in civil law systems.) Most important, and as Lord Sumption noted in *Makdessi v Cavendish Square Holdings BV* [2015] UKSC 67, "specific performance of contractual obligations should ordinarily be refused where damages would be an adequate remedy". Thus, and as Vice Chancellor Kindersley observed in *Falcke v Gray* (1859) 4 Drew 651, if a contract to sell common generic goods and items, such as a consignment of coal (or, for that matter, tin spoons), was not honoured, specific performance would not be granted because the injured party could simply "go into the market and buy similar articles, and get damages for any difference in the price of the articles". This raises the question as to when damages will be deemed inadequate to compensate an innocent party. Several situations have been identified.

## Inadequacy of Damages

In cases where a breach of contract involves a failure to deliver property that is deemed to be unique, so that money (damages) will not readily provide the means of obtaining a replacement, an order of specific performance might be the appropriate remedy. Thus, in the old case of *Nutbrown v Thornton* (1805) 10 Ves 159, the claimant entered a contract to purchase some very unusual machinery from the defendant, its only manufacturer. In breach of contract, the latter subsequently refused to deliver the machines. The claimant brought an action for breach of contract, seeking specific performance of the agreement. This was granted; awarding damages for non-delivery of goods would be inadequate because he would not be able to buy the same machines elsewhere.

Unusual works of art or antiques are particularly likely to fall into this category, although the issue is always case specific and a matter of degree. For example, in *Phillips v Lamdin* [1949] 2 KB 33, an ornamental Adam-style door, which had been removed after the defendant contracted to sell his house to the claimant, was deemed to be sufficiently unique for it to be made the subject of an order for specific performance. By contrast, in *Cohen v Roche* [1927] 1 KB 169, the claimant owned a furniture shop and entered an agreement to purchase a quantity of antique Hepplewhite chairs with a view to selling them. (George Hepplewhite was a prominent English furniture-maker of the eighteenth century.) The defendant, in breach of contract, subsequently refused to deliver the chairs. The claimant sued for breach of contract and sought to enforce their delivery. However, the court refused to grant specific performance on the basis that the claimant would be adequately compensated by an award of damages. The chairs were considered "ordinary articles of commerce and of no special value or interest". The claimant could, apparently, have purchased very similar chairs elsewhere. (This might not be the situation today). Perhaps even more important, the claimant's interest in the chairs was purely financial, as he intended to sell them on, not to enjoy them himself, so that damages were an adequate remedy.

In quite exceptional circumstances, even generic goods might be subject to an order for specific performance, although this is highly unusual. Nevertheless, in *Sky Petroleum v VIP Petroleum* [1974] 1 WLR 576, Goulding J granted such an order when a party failed to honour its commitments to supply petrol and diesel to the claimant during the 1973 oil crisis. This had led to very severe national shortages, so that the claimant had no realistic prospect of finding an alternative fuel source. Normally, the courts will only grant damages for a failure to supply non-specific goods.

Real estate is special in this regard. It is always deemed to be unique, perhaps because no piece of land, house, or flat, is exactly like any other, even if a sale involves a nondescript terraced property, one of dozens in the same area. As a result, specific performance is usually available in a contract for real estate as a matter of course. As Lord Diplock observed in *Sudbrook v Eggleton* [1983] 1 AC 444, "the normal remedy is by a decree for specific performance by the vendor of his primary obligation to convey, upon the purchaser's performing or being willing to perform his own primary obligations under the contract". (Whether this should be the case is sometimes questioned.) Of course, it will often not be sought. For example, in a rapidly falling property market, the purchaser of a house will frequently be content to recover their disbursements and look for another property, knowing that they can make a better bargain elsewhere.

A more unusual situation in which damages were deemed to be inadequate occurred in *Wolverhampton Corp v Emmons* [1901] 1 KB 515. In this case, the claimant sold land to the defendant, who covenanted to demolish and replace the houses already situated on it. After the old houses had been pulled down, the defendant refused to build new ones. Specific performance was ordered, in part because damages would be inadequate, as the defendant had possession of the site, so that the claimant could not employ another contractor to do the same work with any money awarded.

The situation in *Beswick v Beswick* [1968] AC 58 raised another scenario in which specific performance *might* be considered appropriate because damages were inadequate. In this case, specific performance of an agreement was granted to Mrs Beswick in her capacity as administratrix of her husband's estate, in a situation where she *might* otherwise have been confined to nominal damages. (See Chapter 15). From this it might be inferred that such a remedy will be granted wherever it is necessary to circumvent such a risk and so produce a "just" result, to employ the word used by the House of Lords. However, this has not been borne out as a general proposition by subsequent cases, particularly those involving less sympathetic defendants than an elderly widow and should not necessarily be taken as being of general applicability.

### A Discretionary Award

Unlike the common law remedy of damages, which is given as of right, the grant of an equitable remedy, such as specific performance, is discretionary, which means that it might be withheld, even in situations where damages might otherwise be viewed as inadequate. In *Tamplin v James* (1880) 15 CH D 215, James LJ and Cotton LJ noted that in these situations, where the discretion is not exercised, and specific performance is refused, the court should award damages to the claimant in lieu of such an order, where appropriate, and this often occurs in practice. It should also be noted that damages can be granted in addition to specific performance in suitable cases. Thus, in *Grant v Dawkins* [1973] 1 WLR 1406, the vendor's title to land was subject to an encumbrance, the presence of which amounted to a breach of contract with the claimant. It was held that the latter could get specific performance of what title the defendant had and, additionally, damages based on the cost of discharging the encumbrance.

The exercise of the discretion is not unfettered. Because it is an equitable remedy, specific performance follows the maxims of equity, where relevant, as well as other general principles, which govern when it should be granted. The presence or absence of these factors can be decisive.

## Maxims and Principles

To an extent, the maxims of equity place a premium on the conduct of the person seeking a remedy. However, other factors, independent of the merits of the claimant, such as the danger of occasioning extreme hardship to a party who is likely to be subject to an order of specific performance, or the difficulty of enforcing such an order, are also considered by the courts. A selection of these maxims and principles can be considered in greater detail.

## Clean Hands

Unconscionable or inequitable behaviour by the claimant may lead to a refusal to grant specific performance, because "he who comes to equity must come with clean hands". It is not necessary to commit a legal wrong to lose clean hands; what could be termed sharp dealing might be sufficient. For example, in *Lamare v Dixon* (1873) LR 6 HL 414 the claimant induced the defendant to take a lease of some cellars by promising they would be made dry. As this was a statement of future intention, it did not constitute a misrepresentation. (See Chapter 8). Even so, when the defendant failed to proceed with the lease, the court refused to grant the claimant specific performance because the claimant had made no attempt to carry out his promise, which amounted to unconscionable behaviour.

Similarly, in *Walters v Morgan* (1861) 3 DF & J 718, the claimant wished to mine the defendant's land and produced a draft lease that he then pressured the defendant into signing before the latter appreciated the true value of the mining rights involved. Once the defendant had discovered their real value, he refused to allow the defendant to enter and work on his property. The claimant sued for breach of contract and sought specific performance of the agreement. The court refused this, as the claimant had sought to take advantage of the defendant's ignorance by rushing him into signing the disadvantageous lease.

Similarly, in *Falcke v Gray* (1859) 4 Drew 651, the parties contracted for the sale and purchase of a pair of Chinese vases for £40. The seller did not complete the agreement, after learning of their true value, which was at least £200, and the buyer sought specific performance. Although the vases were of "unusual beauty, rarity and distinction" and, as such, and as the court accepted, would normally have been the subject of specific performance (see above), in the instant case it was refused because the parties were not on an equal footing, so that, on its facts, and in its special circumstances, the contract had been obtained unfairly. The claimant was aware of the true value of the vases and had obtained the vendor's agreement unfairly, the defendant being ignorant of their worth and the price agreed woefully inadequate.

## Equity Will Not Assist A Volunteer

An order of specific performance will not be granted where consideration is lacking. As a result, this limitation is of little significance to most contractual situations.

One of its main applications occurs where someone purports to make a gift, which proves not to be effective (the donor retaining the legal title), and then changes his mind about making the gift. In these circumstances, the court will not grant specific performance to the donee to enforce the gift, even if it involves real estate: *Cannon v Hartley* [1949] Ch 213.

### Delay Defeats Equity

Those seeking the assistance of equity must act timeously because "delay defeats equity". Thus, in *Smith v Clay* (1767) 3 Bro. C.C. 639, it was noted that equity would not assist "where a party has slept upon his right and acquiesced for a great length of time". Similarly, in *Milward v Earl Thanet* (1801) 5 Ves 720, Lord Alvanley MR observed that a "party cannot call upon a Court of Equity for specific performance, unless he has shown himself ready, desirous, prompt, and eager". What is an excessive delay will be a question of fact for the court to decide in light of all the attendant circumstances in the case.

### Equity Will Not Act In Vain

Equity will not act in vain, so that the court will not make an order that cannot be enforced or intervene where it would be pointless to do so. Performance of the contract must be possible. This means that the defendant must be able (as opposed to willing) to comply with any order that is made. As a result, the court will not make an order for specific performance if, for example, a third party has acquired good title to the subject matter of the contract.

This maxim was considered in *Jones v Lipman* [1962] 1 WLR 832. In this case, the defendant contracted to sell a house in Chiswick to Mr Jones for £5,250, then changed his mind and refused to complete the sale. He knew that, in these circumstances, if Mr Jones brought an action for specific performance, it would probably be successful, as the case involved real estate. As a result, Mr Lipman sold the land to a limited company of which he was the director, which had been established for this very purpose, hoping that the court would then refuse specific performance and award damages instead, on the basis that since he would no longer (personally) own the land, he could not transfer it. In this case, he failed, because the court was prepared to "pierce the corporate veil". The defendant had total control of the sham company that now owned the property, and so an order addressed to him (and the company) could still be effective, as he could make the company complete the contract with Mr Jones. As Russell J observed, "The defendant company is the creature of the first defendant, a device and a sham, a mask which he holds before his face in an attempt to avoid recognition by the eye of equity". Nevertheless, the result would have been different if he had sold the property to a genuinely independent third party.

Whether the court order can be stated with precision, so that any violation can be clearly identified and dealt with, is also likely to be important to any decision to grant equitable relief (it is also a very important factor when it comes to injunctions): *Tito v Waddell (No 2)* [1977] Ch 106. This was significant in *Wolverhampton Corp v Emmons* [1901] 1 KB 515, where specific performance of an agreement to build houses was ordered, in part, because the defendant's obligations were precisely defined by council approved building plans. Its importance was reiterated in *Blue Manchester Ltd v North West Ground Rents Ltd* [2019] EWHC 142 (TCC), where Davies HHJ, sitting in the High Court, upheld a tenant's claim for an order of specific performance requiring its landlord to repair Manchester Beetham Tower's external glass facade by replacing defective glazing units.

**Requirement for Constant Supervision**

Linked to the above limitation, specific performance will not normally be granted where such an order would require constant supervision by the court, if only to prevent repeated applications for its assistance. In *Ryan v Mutual Tontine Westminster Chambers* [1893] 1 Ch 116, the lease (i.e. a contract) for a service flat provided that the lessors would provide a hall porter who was to be "constantly in attendance". Instead, a cook was appointed to this role who employed others to cover for him whilst he worked at a local restaurant. One of the residents found this unsatisfactory. Nevertheless, it was held that the undertaking could not be specifically enforced, as to do so would require that there be "constant superintendence by the court which the court has always in such cases declined to give".

Even so, this appears to be matter of degree. In *Posner v Scott-Lewis* [1987] 3 All ER 513, the court *did* grant an application for specific performance of a lessor's covenant to employ a resident hall porter for certain duties. The landlord argued that the remedy was inappropriate since he had in fact employed a non-resident porter. The court distinguished *Ryan v Mutual Tontine*, where supervision of the execution of the undertaking had been required. Here neither personal services, nor a continuous series of acts, were required, but merely the execution of an agreement containing provisions for such services.

By contrast, the traditional approach in such cases was followed by the House of Lords in *Co-op Insurance Society v Argyll Stores* [1997] 2 WLR 898, being one of the reasons the court refused specific performance in this case. Co-op Insurance was the landlord of Hillsborough Shopping Centre in Sheffield, which consisted of 25 retail outlets. In 1979 Argyll Stores took a 35-year lease on one of these properties, with a view to operating a Safeway supermarket. The lease contained a covenant by which Argyll agreed to use the outlet as a supermarket, which would be kept open during the usual hours of business. However, in 1995, Argyll Stores took the decision to close 27 of their supermarkets, including the one in Hillsborough, which had made a major loss the previous year. After they gave notice of their intention to do this, Co-op Insurance sought specific performance of the original covenant, fearing the impact on other retailers at the site if the supermarket closed. The House of Lords held that a covenant in a lease of retail premises to keep open for trade during the usual hours of business was not specifically enforceable, other than in exceptional circumstances, as such an order required constant supervision.

In *Co-op Insurance Society*, the court was also influenced by policy factors when reaching their decision. Lord Hoffman noted that it could not be in the public interest for the courts to require someone to carry on business at a loss if there was any plausible alternative means by which the other party could be given compensation: "It is not only a waste of resources but yokes the parties together in a continuing hostile relationship. The order for specific performance prolongs the battle. If the defendant is ordered to run a business, its conduct becomes the subject of a flow of complaints, solicitors' letters and affidavits. This is wasteful for both parties and the legal system. An award of damages, on the other hand, brings the litigation to an end".

**Mutuality**

The courts may be reluctant to order specific performance if "mutuality" between the parties cannot be achieved. Essentially, the remedy will not usually be awarded against one party where a satisfactory remedy would not be available to the other, in similar circumstances. Originally, it was sometimes suggested that this might mean that specific performance should be (potentially) available to the counterparty. Thus, and for historic example, in *Flight v Bolland* (1828) 4 Russ 296, the claimant sought an order of specific performance without indicating that he was a minor. Upon discovering this, the defendant successfully asked the court to dismiss the application. Because of his age, the claimant could avoid the contract at any time. Accordingly, it would be inequitable to allow him to demand specific performance where it could not have been demanded of him. The lack of mutuality was fatal to the application.

However, in the modern era, it seems that a claimant should not be denied equitable relief simply because it would not be available to the defendant, *provided* that the latter would have had access to an adequate remedy of some kind, if it was the claimant who had failed to perform. Thus, in *Price v Strange* [1977] 3 All ER 371, it was held that the form of "mutuality" available was merely a factor to be considered in the exercise of the court's discretion. In this case, Mr Price had been promised a new underlease on a property in exchange for carrying out repairs. When the underlease was withheld, he sought specific performance (the case involved real estate). However, as he was performing personal services as consideration this could not have been required of him. This was accepted as a bar to specific performance at first instance but overturned on appeal. The case also held that relevant time for considering the defence of want of mutuality is not the date the contract was made, but the date of trial.

## Occasioning Extreme Hardship

An order of specific performance might be refused if it would occasion extreme, and disproportionate, hardship to the defendant. Thus, in the old case of *Denne v Light* [1857] 8 DM&G 774, the claimant agreed to sell the defendant a plot of land which was surrounded by land owned by other people. The defendant subsequently refused to complete the purchase unless the claimant could establish that there was a legal right of way over this adjoining land, by which he could access the plot he had bought without seeking permission to do so. In the absence of this, the court refused to grant specific performance to the claimant, although the contract involved real estate, because of the hardship that the defendant would face in owning land he could not access as of right.

This principle applies even where there is no suggestion of misconduct or sharp practice by the claimant. For example, in *Patel v Ali* [1984] 1 All ER 978, Mr and Mrs Patel agreed to sell their (very standard) house to Mr Ali. At that time Mrs Patel was in good health. However, completion was considerably delayed, rather than taking the (then) customary month, and during this intervening period Mrs Patel fell ill with bone cancer and had to have a leg amputated. She became heavily reliant on friends and neighbours to assist her with day-to-day activities. Mr Ali sought specific performance of the contract. However, this was denied on the grounds that it would cause excessive hardship to Mrs Patel if she was required to move out, as it would isolate her from nearby friends and family who might assist her. Whilst this was not the fault of Mr Ali, Goulding J held that it would be a "hardship amounting to injustice if specific performance was ordered".

## Contracts for Personal Service

The courts will not normally order specific performance of a contract for personal service, at least when it comes to an employee. In *Giles & Co v Morris* [1972] 1 All ER 960, Megarry J suggested that this constituted a "strong reluctance" rather than a rule. If so, it is very strong indeed. The courts are often unwilling even to order an injunction to prevent someone working for a third party, in violation of an earlier contract for personal services, if it would have the effect of forcing them to honour the original agreement and constitute an indirect form of specific performance (see below).

There are several justifications for the general presumption against granting specific performance in such cases. Most important, it is thought to be contrary to public policy to force one person to work for another against their wishes, this being a violation of their personal liberty, what might be termed the "slavery" argument. However, there are other reasons for the courts' reluctance. Ordering specific performance of contracts for personal services might require continuous supervision while enforcement could be very difficult if not impossible, if only because of the difficulty of identifying infractions. As Megarry J noted in *Giles & Co v Morris*, "If a singer contracts to sing, there could no doubt be proceedings for committal if, ordered to sing, the singer remained obstinately dumb. But [if] instead, the singer sang sharp, or flat, or too fast or too slowly … the threat of committal would reveal itself as a most unsatisfactory weapon".

Although there is not quite the same antipathy when it comes to compelling an employer to continue employing an employee as compared to ordering the latter to work for the former, the courts will be very reluctant to do so where there has been a breakdown of the trust necessary between the two parties in such a relationship, as will usually be the case if a matter has come to court. As a result, such an order will only be made in exceptional circumstances. This was the case in *Powell v Brent London Borough Council* [1988] ICR 176, in which a local-authority benefits officer secured an interim injunction (indirectly a form of temporary specific performance) that required her employer to continue employing her after it emerged that her appointment may have been invalid for technical reasons that did not reflect on her personally, and where, in the words of Ralph Gibson LJ, the employer still had "sufficient confidence" in the officer to make such an order reasonable.

More typically, specific performance will be refused in these situations, as occurred in *Ashworth and others v Royal National Theatre* [2014] EWHC 1176 (QB). In this case, several musicians sought an order for specific performance of their breached employment contracts, one that would require the Royal National Theatre to continue employing them in a production of *War Horse*. In the instant case, there had been a loss of confidence in the musicians by the theatre, which no longer considered that they could "contribute positively to the play", so that such an order was considered inappropriate.

### Prohibitory Injunctions

A prohibitory injunction is a court order preventing a person from taking (or continuing with) an action that breaches the legal rights of another. These can include rights provided under a contract. Thus, they might be sought, *inter alia*, to prevent the improper use of confidential information that has been obtained during a commercial or employment relationship, the breach of intellectual property rights granted under a contract, or situations where workers leave an employer to work for themselves or others in breach of restrictive covenants in their employment contracts. Such injunctions can be awarded on both an interlocutory and final basis. The former are usually applied for at an early stage in proceedings, and will normally remain in force until trial, when a final injunction might be sought. This will last indefinitely (or to a specified date beyond which it is not deemed to be necessary). Unsurprisingly, given its smaller impact, it is easier to secure an interlocutory than a final injunction. Both are more frequently awarded than specific performance, if only because the courts are more willing to enforce a negative duty than a positive one.

As with specific performance, a person who breaches a prohibitory injunction can be held in contempt of court, which can result in a fine or imprisonment. Indeed, such sanctions are also available against a third party who has knowingly aided or abetted the breach of an injunction. As a result, an injunction will only be granted where it appears just and convenient. It is a discretionary remedy and subject to normal equitable principles (see above) so that, and for illustrative example, it can be lost by delay. Thus, in *Shaw v Applegate* [1977] 1 WLR 970, the claimant's failure to take action for three years after becoming aware of a breach of covenant not to use property as an amusement arcade precluded the award of an injunction (but not damages).

Similarly, in *Jaggard v Sawyer* [1995] 1 WLR 258, the defendants built a property in a residential development situated in a private cul-de-sac, although this was in breach of covenant. The claimant, who owned another house in the development, only began proceedings when construction of the building was at an advanced stage and did not seek an interim injunction to stop development pending a full hearing of the matter. The judge at first instance refused to award her a final injunction and awarded damages instead. The Court of Appeal upheld this decision.

As with specific performance, the party seeking an injunction must have 'clean hands'. As part of this, in *Chappell v Times Newspapers* [1975] 1 WLR 482, Megarry J (sitting in the Court of Appeal) observed that a claimant seeking an injunction to restrain a breach of contract, to which he is a party, must himself be ready to uphold that contract in all its parts: "If on the other hand he seeks the injunction but in the same breath is constrained to say that he is ready and willing himself to commit grave breaches of the contract...then it seems to me that the claimant cannot very well contend that in relation to that contract he is ready to do equity".

Furthermore, a prohibitory injunction will not normally be granted if its effect is to (indirectly) compel the defendant to do something for which the claimant could not have obtained an order for specific performance, such as forcing someone to work for others (see above). As Nourse LJ observed in *Warren v Mendy* [1989] 1 WLR 853, "It is well settled that an injunction to restrain a breach of contract for personal services ought not to be granted where its effect will be to decree performance of the contract". Indeed, in this case the court refused an injunction to prevent a rival boxing promoter (rather than the boxer himself) from inducing a professional pugilist to breach his contract with his promoter because it would have just this effect. Nevertheless, this is a question of degree, and judicial attitudes have changed considerably over the years.

In *Lumley v Wagner* (1852) 64 ER 1209, the defendant agreed to sing in the claimant's theatre twice a week for three months and, at the same time, not to sing elsewhere during this time without the latter's consent. However, a third party offered the defendant a larger sum to sing in his (nearby) theatre. Sir James Parker granted an interim injunction to restrain Ms Wagner from doing so. She appealed the order. Lord St Leonards LC, in the Court of Chancery (this being before the Judicature Acts), held that the injunction did not constitute indirect specific performance of Wagner's obligation to sing. As a result, an order could be granted that prohibited Ms Wagner from performing other than at Lumley's theatre: "It is true that I have not the means of compelling her [the claimant] to sing, but she has no cause of complaint if I compel her to abstain from the commission of an act which she has bound herself not to do, and thus possibly cause her to fulfil her engagement". Of course, in this situation, the agreement was only for three months, with just two months being left to run when the injunction was granted, so that Wagner would have been idle for just nine weeks.

More drastically, can be considered *Warner Brothers Pictures Inc. v Nelson* [1937] 1 KB 209, in which the defendant was the celebrated film actress Bette Davis. She entered a contract to provide her services exclusively to the claimant company for two years. She could not work for any other film company, without the claimant's express written consent, during this period. Nelson thought that her career was being damaged by being asked to act in poor or mediocre films by the claimant. She fled to Britain to feature in two films for another company. The claimant sought an injunction to restrain her from this course of action. The matter was ultimately considered in the English High Court, where Branson J reiterated that the court would not order specific performance of a contract of personal service. However, it was held that the defendant could be restrained by injunction from breaking the undertaking not to work for other film companies, as she could still earn a living by doing other, non-acting, work. Her description of her contract with Warner Brothers as one of "slavery" was not accepted. Ms Davis returned to Hollywood.

Whether it was reasonable to expect a film star like Bette Davis to undertake the type of work that she was otherwise qualified to perform is open to question. (She had been an actress from the age of eighteen). Certainly, in recent decades, the courts have often taken what is, perhaps, a more realistic approach towards the effect of awarding injunctions in these situations, as *Warren v Mendy* suggests. Thus, in *Page One Records v Britton* [1968] 1 WLR 157, a pop group called 'The Troggs' appointed the claimant as their manager for five years and agreed not to act themselves in such capacity nor to appoint another person to do so during that time. Unfortunately, the group subsequently fell out with him, and decided to replace the manager. He sought an injunction preventing this. It was held that this must be refused because to grant it would, effectively, compel the group to continue to employ him, as such groups necessarily required a manager. Stamp J observed, "I should, if I granted the injunction, be enforcing a contract for personal services". Clearly, it was not deemed to be reasonable to expect the four members of The Troggs to become, for example, ordinary workers as an alternative to their making music commercially.

## Mandatory Injunctions

Mandatory injunctions are an order of the court requiring someone to put right a breach of contract or tort that they have already committed. For example, to rebuild what they have pulled down in breach of a covenant not to do so, or to tear down buildings that have been put up in breach of a covenant not to develop a plot of land. Thus, it was the remedy originally sought in *Wrotham Park Estate Co. Ltd. v Parkside Homes Ltd.* [1974] 1 WLR 798, in which a claimant who had the benefit of a restrictive covenant preventing a parcel of land from being built on unavailingly sought a mandatory injunction ordering the demolition of new houses that had been constructed on it.

In the tortious case of *Redland Bricks v Morris* [1970] AC 652, the House of Lords considered a case in which a strawberry farm had suffered land slippage because excessive amounts of clay were being extracted from under neighbouring premises for use in a brick manufacturing business. At first instance, the judge granted an injunction restraining the appellants from withdrawing support from the respondents' land without leaving sufficient support (the prohibitory aspect) but also ordered (the mandatory aspect) that "[t]he [appellants] do take all necessary steps to restore the support to the [respondents'] land within a period of six months".

Such injunctions are only rarely granted, especially in contract (rather than tort), and particularly at the interlocutory stage, not least because the consequences for the defendant are often drastic, while drafting them so that the recipient knows precisely what is required of him can be very difficult. As Lord Upjohn observed in *Redland Bricks v Morris*, "[T]he court must be careful to see that the defendant knows exactly in fact what he has to do and this means not as a matter of law but as a matter of fact". In the same case, he noted that a mandatory injunction can be granted only where the claimant shows a very strong probability that, without it, he will suffer grave damage in the future. It was a "jurisdiction to be exercised sparingly and with caution". Nevertheless, and to consider a contractual example, in *Wakeham v Wood* [1982] 43 P & CR 40 the defendant built on land in breach of a restrictive covenant not to obstruct the claimant's view of the sea. Although a mandatory injunction was refused at first instance, it was granted on appeal, and he was ordered to pull the building down.

# Frequently Used Acronyms

| | |
|---|---|
| UCTA | Unfair Contracts Terms Act |
| CPR | Civil Procedure Rules |
| CRA | Consumer Rights Act |
| SGSA | Supply of Goods and Services Act |
| SOGA | Sale of Goods Act |
| BFPV | Bona Fide Purchaser for Value |
| NOM | No Oral Modification |
| MRA | Misrepresentation Act |

# Select Bibliography


Austen-Baker, Richard (2008) "A Strange Sort of Survival for Pinnel's Case: Collier v P & M J Wright (Holdings) Limited", *The Modern Law Review*, v. 71, no. 4, pp. 611–620.

Beatson, J. et al. (2020) *Anson's Law of Contract* (31st edn.) Oxford: Oxford University Press.

Beale, Hugh (2022) *Chitty on Contracts* (34th edn.). London: Sweet and Maxwell.

Burns, Fiona R. (2003) "The elderly and undue influence inter vivos". *Legal Studies*, v. 23, no. 2, pp. 251-283.

Burrows, Andrew (2020) *Restatement of the English Law of Contract* (2nd edn.). Oxford: Oxford University Press.

Cartwright, John (2002) *Misrepresentation, Mistake and Non-Disclosure*. London: Sweet & Maxwell.

Chinyere, Ezeoke (2007) "Assessing seriousness in repudiatory breach of innominate terms", *Journal of Business Law*, v.3, pp.198-217.

Fisher, James C. (2018) "Contract variation in the common law: A critical response to Rock Advertising . MWB Business Exchange", *Common Law World Review*, vol.47, no.3, pp. 196-207.

Hudson, A. (1996) "Retraction of Letters of Acceptance". *Law Quarterly Review*, v. 82, p. 169.

Kiralfy, Albert (1980) "Absolute Liability in Contract". *The Journal of Legal History*, v. 1, no.1, pp. 89-93.

Kramer, Adam (2017) *The Law of Contract Damages* (2nd edn.). Oxford: Hart.

Matthews, Paul (1989) "A Note on Cooper v. Phibbs". *Law Quarterly Review*, v. 105, p. 599.

McMeel, G.P. (2002) "Equitable Mistake Repudiated--The Demise of Solle v. Butcher? (The Great Peace)". *Lloyd's Maritime and Commercial Law Quarterly*, pp. 449-453.

O'Sullivan, J. (1996). "In Defence of Foakes v. Beer", *The Cambridge Law Journal*, v. 55, no. 2, pp.219-228.

O'Sullivan, J. (2020) *O'Sullivan & Hilliard's The Law of Contract* (9th edn.) Oxford: Oxford University Press.

Peel, Edwin (2007) *Treitel on the Law of Contract* (12th edn.). London: Sweet & Maxwell.

Peel, Edwin (2011) *Treitel on the Law of Contract* (13th edn.). London: Sweet & Maxwell.

Peel, Edwin (2020) *Treitel on the Law of Contract* (15th edn.). London: Sweet & Maxwell.

Silverstein, Joshua M. (2020) "Contract Interpretation and the Parol Evidence Rule: Toward Conceptual Clarification". *Chapman Law Review*, v. 24, no. 1, p. 91.

Spark, Gareth (2013) "Misrepresentation". In *Vitiation of Contracts: International Contractual Principles and English Law*, pp. 170-211. Cambridge: Cambridge University Press.

Stoljar, S.J. (1975) *A History of Contract at Common Law*. Canberra: Australian National University Press.

Stone, Richard (2012) "Forming Contracts without Offer and Acceptance: Lord Denning and the Harmonisation of English Contract Law", *4 Web Journal of Current Legal Issues*, http://webjcli.ncl.ac.uk/2012/issue4/stone4.html

Stone, Richard et al (2022) *The Modern Law of Contract* (14th edn.). Abingdon: Routledge.

Swain, Warren (2020) "Without the Power to Drink or Contract". *Edinburgh Law Review*, v. 24, no. 1, pp. 26-48.

Swanton, Jane (1988) "Exclusion of Liability for Negligence". *University of Queensland Law Journal*, v. 15, no. 2, pp. 157-182.

Tweeddale, Andrew and Tweeddale, Karen (2011) "*Scott v Avery* Clauses: O'er Judges' Fingers, Who Straight Dream on Fees", *Arbitration*, v. 77, pp. 423-427.

Woollcombe-Clarke, Michael (2016) "Case Note: MWB Business Exchange Centres Ltd v Rock Advertising Ltd", *Trinity College Law Review*, placed online 13 December 2016.

Zlatev, Zlatin (2020) "Quantification of damages for non-pecuniary losses deriving from breach of contract", *Legal Studies*, v. 40, no. 4, pp. 548-564.

# Index

www.ingramcontent.com/pod-product-compliance
Ingram Content Group UK Ltd.
Pitfield, Milton Keynes, MK11 3LW, UK
UKHW051449290926
15471UKWH00008B/1107

9 781845 498146